Charanis Studies

Charanis Studies
Essays in Honor of Peter Charanis

Edited by Angeliki E. Laiou-Thomadakis

Rutgers University Press
New Brunswick, New Jersey

Library of Congress Cataloging in Publication Data
Main entry under title:

Charanis studies.

   1. Byzantine Empire—History—Addresses, essays,
lectures. 2. Charanis, Peter. I. Charanis,
Peter. II. Laiou-Thomadakis, Angeliki E.
DF552.C46 949.5 79-12618
ISBN 0-8135-0875-4

Contents

Preface   vii

Abbreviations   ix

1   The Term *Neoterikoi* (Innovators) in the *Exabiblos* of Constantine Armenopoulos and Its Cultural-Linguistic Implications   1
     Demetrios J. Constantelos

2   Two Documents Concerning Mid-Sixth-Century Mopsuestia   19
     Gilbert Dagron

3   Titles of the Rulers of the Second Bulgarian Empire in the Eyes of the Byzantines   31
     Ivan Djurić

4   Some Remarks on the *Chronicle of Monemvasia*   51
     Ivan Dujčev

5   Important Recent Research in Byzantine-Western Relations: Intellectual and Artistic Aspects, 500–1500   60
     Deno J. Geanakoplos

6   Two Letters of Athanasius I, Patriarch of Constantinople: An Attempt at Reinterpretation   79
     A. P. Každan

7   Saints and Society in the Late Byzantine Empire   84
     Angeliki E. Laiou-Thomadakis

8   Monastic Stability: Some Socioeconomic Considerations   115
     Ernest W. McDonnell

9   A Contribution to the Historical Geography of the Island of Kythira during the Venetian Occupation   151
     Chryssa Maltezou

10   The Properties of the Deblitzenoi in the Fourteenth and Fifteenth Centuries   176
     Nicolas Oikonomidès

11   The Anconitan Colony in Constantinople and the Report of Its Consul, Benvenuto, on the Fall of the City   199
     Agostino Pertusi

12 The Country and Suburban Palaces of the Emperors   219
      Steven Runciman
13 The Naval Engagement at Phoenix   229
      Andreas N. Stratos
14 The Case of Bishop Guichard of Troyes   248
      Joseph R. Strayer
15 Albanian Settlements in Medieval Greece: Some
      Venetian Testimonies   261
      Peter Topping
16 The Flight of the Inhabitants of Greece to the Aegean
      Islands, Crete, and Mane, during the Turkish Invasions
      (Fourteenth and Fifteenth Centuries)   272
      Apostolos E. Vacalopoulos
17 Travelers as a Source for the Societies of the Middle
      East: 900–1600   284
      Speros Vryonis, Jr.
18 Two Historical Parallels: The Greek Nation under
      Roman and Turkish Rule   312
      D. A. Zakythinos

Preface

In June 1976, when Peter Charanis retired from Rutgers University, where he had taught for many years, some of his students and friends suggested that it would be appropriate to honor him by publishing two volumes of essays, one from his students and one from his colleagues. The first volume, edited by John Barker, is now being published as a special issue of *Byzantine Studies/Etudes byzantines*. It includes a biographical essay and a full bibliography, which it has seemed unnecessary to reprint here. The volume at hand consists of studies on various aspects of Byzantine, Near Eastern, and Western European history, dedicated to Peter Charanis by a number of his colleagues, in America and in Europe. It is, perhaps, a measure of the variety of Charanis's scholarly interests that, although the articles included here cover several different subjects, they are all subjects to which he himself has, at one time or another, made a contribution.

Peter Charanis has had a long and distinguished career, both as a scholar and as a teacher. Continuing the work of his own masters, A. A. Vasiliev and Henri Grégoire, he spent a lifetime in the service of Byzantine studies. His erudition, his humanity, his profound commitment to his field have made him a major academic figure. These qualities, along with a boundless energy, have allowed him to become one of the people most responsible for the expansion of Byzantine studies in America. In his work as a teacher, he has presented to generations of students a lively and compelling picture of the Byzantine Empire and has aroused in them an interest in things Byzantine that has often been abiding, in those who then followed a scholarly career and even in those who did not. In his work as a scholar, he has made important and lasting contributions to the social history of the Byzantine Empire. Perhaps his strongest interest and his most significant research has been on the ethnic composition of the multinational state that was the Byzantine Empire. This is a problem that at times can become very thorny, both because of source limitations and because of modern national sensibilities. Toward its solution, Charanis has worked through a close analysis of the sources and with a deep commitment to historical truth.

In this, as in the rest of his work, he has shown an unfailing ability to distinguish the important elements of a historical question and to bring his profound erudition to bear upon it. Thus, he was among the first to realize the importance of the *Short Chronicles* as a source of information; and his studies on the social structure of the Byzantine Empire have retained their significance as major contributions in a field in which much research has been done in recent years.

The importance of Peter Charanis's work has been recognized both nationally and internationally. Among the honors he particularly cherishes are the awards he has received at Rutgers University, both for his teaching and for his research, and his recent election as a corresponding member of the Academy of Athens.

Several people and institutions have helped with the publication of this volume. My colleague and friend, Herbert Rowen, applied his erudition and his great editorial skill to the translation of Professor Dujčev's article from the original German. Dumbarton Oaks, one of the most important centers for Byzantine studies in the United States and the world, is an institution with which Peter Charanis has had a long and cherished association. The editor is grateful to its director, Giles Constable, and to Dumbarton Oaks itself, for a grant generously given. Many thanks are also due to the Research Council of Rutgers University for funds that made publication possible. It is a particularly happy event that this work has been brought out by the Rutgers University Press. The association of Peter Charanis with the press and the interest of the press in the history and civilization of the Byzantine Empire are too well known to require any comment. But the editor is happier still for the interest that the principal academic officers of the university, President Edward J. Bloustein, Senior Vice-president Paul G. Pearson, and Vice-president for Academic Affairs James K. Martin, have shown in the publication of this volume. It has demonstrated that the university continues to honor its distinguished faculty members even after they have retired.

Angeliki E. Laiou-Thomadakis

Abbreviations

AASS	*Acta Sanctorum*
AN	Archives Nationales
BCH	*Bulletin de Correspondance Hellénique*
BMGS	*Byzantine and Modern Greek Studies*
BZ	*Byzantinische Zeitschrift*
CIG	*Corpus Inscriptionum Graecarum*
CJC	*Corpus Juris Canonici*
CSCO	*Corpus Scriptorum Christianorum Orientalium*
CSEL	*Corpus Scriptorum Ecclesiasticorum Latinorum*
EEBS	*Epeteris Hetaireias Byzantinōn Spoudōn*
EI	*Encyclopedia of Islam* 2d ed.
GSND	*Glasnik Skopskog naučnog društva*
HF	*Recueil des historiens des Gaules et de la France*
HL	*Histoire générale de Languedoc*
Izv. Rusk. Arheol. Inst. v Konst.	*Izvestija Ruskago Arheologičeskago Instituta v Konstantinopole*
MAMA	*Monumenta Asiae Minoris Antiquae*
Mansi	J. D. Mansi, *Sacrorum Conciliorum nova et amplissima collectio*
MGH, SS	*Monumenta Germaniae Historica, Scriptores*
PG, or PGL	Migne, *Patrologiae cursus completus, ser. Graeco-latina*
PL	Migne, *Patrologiae cursus completus, ser. latina*
PPTS	*Palestine Pilgrim's Text Society*
REB	*Revue des études byzantines*
RIS	*Rerum Italicarum Scriptores*
SC	*Sources chrétiennes*
Sem. Kond.	*Seminarium Kondakovianum*
TU	*Texte und Untersuchungen zur Geschichte der altchristlichen Literatur*
Viz. Vre.	*Vizantijskij Vremennik*
ZRVI	*Zbornik radova Vizantološkog Instituta*

Charanis Studies

Chapter 1

The Term Neoterikoi (Innovators) in the Exabiblos of Constantine Armenopoulos and Its Cultural-Linguistic Implications

Demetrios J. Constantelos, *Stockton State College*

The fourteenth-century legal expert Constantine Armeno-poulos has preserved in his manual of laws *Exabiblos* the following clause:

> The so-called *neoterikoi*, and those who cause public disturb-ances, if they persist in their ways, even though they have been admonished by the archon, should be sent into exile. If they have caused many disorders and have been apprehended and punished many times in the past and continue to cause turbulence even now, they should be shaved, receive lashes, and be sent into exile permanently. If, however, they have not been cautioned before by the archon, they should be whipped only and then be set free.[1]

The law cited by Armenopoulos was not issued for the first time in Byzantium nor was it a fourteenth-century enactment. The earliest decree concerning the *neoterikoi* was promulgated be-tween 870 and 879 as part of the *Procheiros Nomos*, published in the name of Emperor Basil I and his co-emperor sons, Leo and Constantine.[2] Nevertheless, Basil's statute retained its authority and continued to be valid and enforced in fourteenth-century Byzantium and even later.

Who were the *neoterikoi* and what were their aims? Was the term used in an empirical context or was it by then a dead letter and only of academic interest? What did it mean to *neoterizein* and what were its consequences? Did the word have a different meaning in the late Byzantine Empire than in previous centuries?

1

What follows here is a lexical study concerned with these questions and also with the historical context in which these two concepts were applied. An analysis of both, as they were employed in the course of the Greek literary tradition, and an examination of the historical milieu in which they were utilized, may add to our knowledge concerning the degree of continuity in the Greek legal and intellectual tradition.

* * *

A survey of Greek literature (historical, philosophical, religious, and legal) reveals that there was very little, if any, semasiological change in the meaning either of the verb *neoterizo* or of the epithet *neoterikos* from the fifth century before Christ to the middle of the fourteenth century of our era. In ancient Hellas, *neoterizo* meant to make innovations, usually accompanied by violence, to use seditious means in search of political changes, to raise a revolt. *Neoterizo* became synonymous with inciting to revolution or leading to public disorder and was used to describe neoterisms in the political, social, and religious life of a given community. A *neoterikos, neoteropoios,* or *neoteristes,* all synonyms, was any person who introduced neoteric measures and sought political, administrative, social, or religious changes even through violent means. Frequently *neoterikos* became homologous to a rebel who was youthful and thoughtless, an agressor, even a tyrant. Whereas there is very little change in the concept and the nature of *neoterizo* and *neoterikos* throughout the ancient and the medieval period of Greek thought, the historical contexts and the circumstances in which these two terms were applied were different. This becomes apparent through the illustrations that follow.

In the fifth century before the Christian era, *neoterizein* in the sense of change through violent means was used repeatedly by Thucydides in the *History of the Peloponnesian War.* For example, immediately after the naval battle between Athens and Corinth at Kerkyra, the Athenians took certain precautions against the Potidaeans, who were colonists of Corinth. The Potidaeans on the other hand sent envoys to Athens to persuade them not to resort to violent means (*neoterizein miden*) against themselves.[3] Elsewhere Thucydides uses the same verb to speak of violence. In the year 431 B.C. some three hundred armed Thebans entered Plataea, an ally of Athens, in order to eliminate the

opposition and bring the city on the side of Thebes and Sparta.
But the entry into Plataea was effected by intrigue and with the
cooperation of certain Plataeans; thus the Thebans did no violence against anyone (*ouden eneoterizon*).[4]

When the Athenians assumed leadership over the Delian League,
they assessed the contributions of their allies and established the
office of Hellenic treasurers (*Hellenotamiae*) to receive the tribute
and also to take measures against their own allies in case they attempted revolutions. *Neoterizein* here implied uprisings for political change.[5] When a war broke out in 440 B.C. between the Samians and the Milesians, the latter pressed charges against the
Samians. They were supported by some private citizens from
Samos itself who wanted to revolutionize the government of their
island. Thucydides writes of *neoterisai* in order to indicate that
political changes could be wrought through revolution.[6] Several
years later, circa 418 B.C., a movement in Samos conspired to over-
throw the oligarchy that had been imposed upon the Samians.
The plot of the movement for the political change was described
as *neoterismos*.[7]

Thucydides was not the only author of classical Greece who
made frequent use of the terms under discussion. Xenophon
characterizes an impending rebellion as *neoterismos*. He relates
that, to prevent a revolt of his troops stationed in Chios in the
year 406 B.C., their commander Eteonikos invited the people of
Chios to a consultation. His soldiers, he said, were without food,
poorly clad, and unshod, as a result of which they were planning
to attack and plunder the island. To avoid such a revolt (*neoterismos*) of his soldiers, Eteonikos asked the Chians to contribute
one month's salary for each soldier.[8] On the other hand, Plutarch recounts that when the Spartans invited the Athenians to
come to their assistance against the Messenians and the Helots of
Ithome, they became suspicious of the Athenians because of their
boldness and sent them off as dangerous conspirators—*neoter-
istas*.[9]

Neoterismoi as revolutionary outbreaks were considered by
Plato as unavoidable events in the life of a state. He proposed
measures to prevent their possible occurrence and recommended
that in case they do occur the state should move expeditiously
and remedy the situation as swiftly as possible.[10] But not all innovations through revolutionary movements were regarded as
evil. Antiphon, the Attic rhetorician, for example, though of
strong aristocratic inclinations and prejudices, emphasized that to

neoterizein, to innovate by revolutionary means, is to benefit the less fortunate among the population, and revolutions may effect worthy results for them.[11]

In inscriptions of the late fourth century before Christ, *neoterismos* was used in the sense of a bad innovation, such as uprising, sedition, and ruinous revolution.[12] It was in that perception that in the Hellenistic period *neoteristai* meant *stasiastai* whose acts had destructive results upon the state as a whole.[13] Thus people were admonished to avoid *neoterizein* because it brings calamities and insecurity upon society. For example, the fourth book of Maccabees relates that when "certain persons" defied the unanimous agreement of the Jews and went contrary to the policies of Seleucus Nicanor, the whole Jewish nation suffered from the rebellion of the few.[14]

In the New Testament language, *neoterismos* continued to carry a prohibitory connotation associated with rebellious youthfulness, moral rebellion, and the perils of youth, such as lack of self-control, indulgence in drinking, fornication, undirected energies, and other attributes common to youth. When Saint Paul advised his disciple Timothy to avoid youthful desires (*neoterikas epithymias*), he used the epithet *neoterikas* to mean all the above and other tendencies such as "impatience with the status quo, aversion to rule and routine, grudging obedience to authority, interest in theoretical arguments, eagerness to accept new ideas and procedures, insistence on testaments and novelties" as a contemporary exegete observes.[15]

Why such a condemnation by Saint Paul and other early Christian authors of *neoterikas epithymias* in the sense of youthful desires? Because youthful passions and deeds "proceed from a heart not yet established, from a mind not deeply grounded, but in a wavering state" in the scholia of Saint John Chrysostom.[16] Other ancient Christian commentators used the same epithet to speak of youthful folly,[17] whereas still others, such as Clement of Rome, advised against *neoterismos* because it inherently implied revolutionary or radical desires and it was equated with slander, foulness, egotistical pride, and other human passions.[18]

The continuity in the gist of *neoterizo* and *neoterikos* between ancient and medieval Greek thought (political, legal, social, and religious) is very striking. Eusebios of Caesarea describes some of the harsh policies of Licinius as revolutionary changes (*neoterismous*). Licinius was condemned not only because of his persecutions against the Christians and his inhumanity toward those in prison but also because he dared to annul ancient laws concerning marriage and those departing this life and decrees pertaining to assessments and fines, revaluations of land, and the banishment of nobles and other highly esteemed people.[19] Licinius eventually was put to death because he raised a revolt against Constantine. Following his defeat in 322, Licinius was allowed to retire in Thessalonike. While there and in cooperation with the Goths, he defied Constantine and revolted once again (*palin neoterizonta*), as a result of which Constantine ordered his execution.[20]

Some fifty years later those who joined in a revolution against the emperor were condemned as *neoteristai.* The ecclesiastical historian Philostorgios relates that the army stationed in Paeonia raised to the throne Valentinian the Younger without the knowledge and consent of the legitimate emperor, Gratian, Valentinian's own brother. Gratian suppressed the revolt and several of the *neoterisantes* were punished even though he decided not only to forgive Valentinian but also to accept him as a junior co-emperor.[21]

Whether in the political or in the religious sphere, a *neoterikos, neoteristes,* or *neoteropoios* was considered a violator of established tradition and frequently a dangerous revolutionary. To convert from Greco-Roman paganism to Christianity was an undesirable neoterism. Constantine the Great was accused of being a *neoteristes* because he gave up his ancestral religion in order to embrace Christianity.[22] To depart from traditional Christianity, too, was considered a heretical innovation. Both "orthodox" and "heretics" accused each other of making sinful changes in the creed. The Tome of Pope Leo and the decisions of the Synod of Chalcedon were condemned by the Monophysites as innovations and additions that had been imposed upon the faith. The iconoclasts in the eighth century as well as the Hesychasts in the fourteenth were condemned each from a different perspective as unorthodox neoterists.[23]

The leader of a *neoterismos* affecting either the state or the church was considered to be a leader of a revolution. For example, Caesar Gallus, after suppressing the insurrection of the Jews of Diocaesarea in Palestine, became intoxicated with his military success and aspired to become emperor. But his *neoterismos* was reported to the emperor Constantius, who masterminded Gallus's assassination in the year A.D. 354.

In the conflict between Patriarch Nicephoros and Emperor Leo V during the second phase of the iconoclastic controversy, *neoterismos* meant disturbance and revolution. When the patriarch held an all-night vigil in the Cathedral of Hagia Sophia in protest of the emperor's policy, the latter perceived the patriarch's reaction as an attempt to stir up a revolution against the imperial policy. The emperor complained that his measures were intended to secure religious peace.[24]

In addition to a political, legal, and military usage, the term was used in a religious context. The fourth-century pagan Neoplatonist Iamblichos complained that pagan sacred names and prayers lost their efficacy because they were continually changed through the innovation (*kainotomian*) and the illegality (*paranomian*) of the Greeks. He writes that the Greeks are by nature innovators (*neoteropoioi*) and are carried everywhere by their volatility; they transform everything through an unstable desire to discover something new. In order to avert the progress of Christianity and ensure the progress of Greco-Roman religion, Iamblichos appealed for conservatism in ancient religion: "It is necessary that ancient prayers, like sacred asyla, should be preserved invariably the same, neither taking anything from them, nor adding anything to them which is elsewhere derived."[25] Iamblichos's statement reminds us of the appeal of various church synods and Byzantine theologians who stressed that nothing new should be added to the faith without the deliberation of an ecumenical council and nothing should be subtracted. Not only pagans but Christians as well were accused of innovation.

John Chrysostom was accused of being a leader of a revolution of a different kind. As patriarch of Constantinople (398–404), Chrysostom introduced several measures to effect reforms in the church, including the elimination of unworthy bishops. He deposed several of them in Asia Minor and other provinces, but the deposed hierarchs and their followers complained to the emperor, condemning the patriarch "as the leader of a revolution in the Churches." On the whole, an innovation (*neoterismos*) in the established orthodoxy and accepted norms of faith and practice provoked the indignation and sometimes even the condemnation of both church and state because it was identified with rebellion and heresy.[26]

Not all condemnations of the *neoterikoi* were carried out, however. For instance, during the brief reign of Michael I (812–814), certain *neoteristae* (revolutionaries) were determined to revive the iconoclastic movement. They intended to restore the policies of Constantine V, for they had attributed his successes against the enemies of the empire to his religious views concerning the icons, whereas on the other hand, the defeats and failures of Michael Rangabe were attributed to his iconophile policies. Michael suppressed the revolt in 812, but he was lenient to the protagonists of the movement. He sent the sons of Constantine V into exile and intimidated the revolutionists with a few whippings (*tous pollous ton neoteriston di'oligon plegon kateptoesen*).[27] Theophanes, the source of this information, employed the term *neoterismos* in the sense of rebellion to record also the insurrection of the Bacaudae peasants of Gaul under the leadership of Amandus and Aelianus. In 285 Diocletian dispatched his old friend, Caesar Maximian, to quell the revolt.[28]

The lexicographers of the ninth and tenth centuries, such as Photios and the compiler of the *Souda Lexicon,* confirm that in their time *neoterizo* meant to pursue new things but also to incline to rebellion. To join in a *neoterismos* was to participate in a revolt (and in an uprising). *Neoteropoios* or neoterist became homologous not only to rebel and agressor but also to tyrant.[29]

There is no need to elaborate extensively and search for more evidence in every author of the middle Byzantine period. It is certain that the same vein runs throughout the Byzantine era. When Byzantine authors described events of Greek antiquity, they used vocabulary that was understandable in their own times. For example, writing in the thirteenth century, Nicetas Choniates describes the measures introduced in sixth-century Athens by Peisistratos as a neoterism. Peisistratos, unlike his intimate friend and more democratic colleague Solon, organized a new party that adopted radical measures to secure him the supreme power. Constitutional though it might have been, Peisistratos's political system was condemned by Choniates as a tyrannical innovation.[30]

The verb *neoterizein* was employed repeatedly by another thirteenth-century historian to denote rebellious acts. Writing about the events that followed the capture of Constantinople by the Crusaders in 1204, George Acropolites relates that the former Byzantine emperor Alexios III Angelos with his wife and daughter were expelled from Thessalonike by the Latins. Alexios was discovered to be preparing a revolution (*neoterizesthai*) against the Latins who had destroyed his empire. In Corinth a certain Byzantine general named Sgouros had revolted (*neoterisas*) against the Latin conquerors following the Fourth Crusade.[31]

Theodore Angelos of Epiros was taken captive by the Bulgarian king John Asen II in 1230 at the battle of Klokotnitza. Treated mildly at first, the Greek despot was later blinded by Asen, who suspected Theodore of plotting against him. George Acropolites, who relates this episode, uses the term *neoterismos* to indicate Theodore's suspected revolt.[32]

Acropolites uses the word *neoterismos* as a synonym for revolt when he writes of John III Doukas Vatatzes' expedition against Leo Gabalas. Soon after 1204, Leo Gabalas, who had served as imperial governor of the island of Rhodes, revolted and called himself Caesar. Vatatzes dispatched an expedition against the rebel and wrested the island away from him. Gabalas's revolt was a *neoterismos*.[33] On the other hand, an extravagant way of living, expensive hunting trips, luxurious dinners, indulgence in drinking—ways of life usually associated with youthfulness—were described by Theodore II Lascares as neoterisms (*neoterismoi*).[34]

Even change in the monastic or clerical attire was viewed by the conservative element of society as a dangerous innovation or suspiciously revolutionary. For example, when Eustathios, one of the leaders of monasticism in Asia Minor, adopted in the fourth century the *peribolaion* as a garment in order to demonstrate his contempt for worldly matters by imitating the ancient philosophers, his father, who was at the time bishop of Sebasteia, became so angered that he expelled his own son from his diocese. Later, when Eustathios became the leader of an ascetic movement, the wealthy laity and the bishops of the northeastern part of Asia Minor opposed him because they considered Eustathios's movement as a threat on account of its many innovations. Eustathios and his followers were accused of innovations in many things (*kai alla pleista neoterizontas*).[35]

*   *   *

Notwithstanding the evidence from the preceding quick excursion into ancient and medieval Greek sources, several major questions still remain before us: In what context did Constantine Armenopoulos use the epithet *neoterikoi* and who were they in fourteenth-century Byzantium? Does Armenopoulos's clause concerning the *neoterikoi* reflect contemporary empirical realities? Were the *neoterikoi* revolutionary activists whom Armenopoulos had personally encountered? Neither John Kantakouzenos and Nicholas Kabasilas nor Nicephoros Gregoras, the most important sources of the period, provide us with any answers or even with

clues. They do not use the term *neoterikoi* in describing the contemporary political and social activists who went by the name
Zealots.

Nevertheless, we may venture to suggest that Armenopoulos
did not simply copy a ninth-century manual as an academic
exercise. When he transcribed the law against the *neoterikoi* he
might have had in mind the Zealots. When Armenopoulos wrote
his *Exabiblos* in 1345, he was still chief magistrate of Thessalonike.[36] It was in the same year that the Zealots, who drew their
strength from the impoverished classes, made their third attack
on the city, capturing and putting to death over one hundred local
aristocratic families. Not only did they establish an organized
revolutionary regime for seven years, but they followed a well-
defined program to improve the lot of the poor in contrast to the
exploitation of the nobles and monasteries. Their efforts failed
and finally they succumbed to the combined forces of "monasticism and the nobles."[37] In other words, the Zealots of Thessalonike proved to be *neoterikoi,* or revolutionaries in fourteenth-
century Byzantium. Armenopoulos was taken captive, but he
was spared and was only expelled from the city.

In the beginning of the conflict between the Zealots and the
aristocracy, Armenopoulos had maintained a neutral position,
but soon after he changed and turned against the Zealots.[38] It is
logical to infer that Armenopoulos not only became critical of
the rebels but also wrote against them. Political sagacity and personal experience convinced him to use expediency and avoid a
direct confrontation with his adversaries. Thus, instead of writing
boldly against the Zealots, he attacked them by indirectly imply-
ing that they deserved the treatment of the *neoterikoi.* To be
sure, Armenopoulos was a compiler of laws and rules of previous
centuries, and only occasionally does he express personal notions
concerning justice, law, and order. Nevertheless, what he compiled was in agreement with the legal mind of his time, and his
Exabiblos is representative of that late Byzantine mind. Furthermore, behind the theoretical considerations and the philosophical
reasoning of a law lay practical implications. Although some laws
may remain a dead letter or atrophic, a law is usually accompanied
by active dispensations. Whatever the interpretation of this may
be, the fact remains that Armenopoulos has preserved a portion
of the legal and intellectual mind of both ancient and medieval
Hellenic thought.

*   *   *

Even though respect for established institutions and for tradition (*paradosis*) in general were pervasive characteristics of the Byzantine mind, tradition did not always go unchallenged. In every century there were intellectuals, laymen and clergymen alike, who pursued innovations and changes. New canon and civil law, new theological doctrines, additions to the liturgy, formulations of new religious services, litanies, and sacramentalia, new styles in art and architecture, and modes of dress, all were indeed innovations. Nevertheless, in theory at least, *neoterizein* and its synonymous *kainotomein* were frequently an anathema, whereas the *neoteropoios*, or *neoterikos* and *kainotomos*, were suspected as dangerous revolutionaries. Despite the many intellectual challenges to the authority of tradition,[39] innovation was not looked upon favorably.

Why did the Byzantines fear innovation? Did they view their own society as perfect or superior to the ancient? But the heritage of ancient Hellas was a permanent category of their civilization. Even though the Byzantines were robbed of their national name because Hellenic, Hellene, Hellenismos had become synonymous with paganism, their language and ethnic and cultural consciousness was no less Greek than that of the ancient Greeks.[40] The aesthetic achievements and the political mind of ancient Hellas were admired by the Byzantines, who regarded the heritage of ancient Hellas as pagan, but nevertheless their own, and as an integral part of their secular education. It was respect and admiration for the past that prompted their fear of innovation rather than a feeling of superiority over the ancients.[41]

Under the weight of the past, the emphasis was on preservation, commentary, study, and imitation. With a few exceptions, Byzantine *paideia* was a *paideia* through imitation rather than through search, inquiry, and discovery. Thus, admiration of the classical patrimony prevented innovation, while fear that neoterisms might disrupt their continuity with the past suppressed the human impulse to break through and contribute to the genesis and development of new things.

In addition to their attachment to the classical heritage, the Byzantines were fearful of innovations on account of Christianity's absolute claims. Christianity emphasized that it possessed the full and final revelation of the truth; thus it impeded the intellectual quest and the anxieties of the Byzantine Christian mind, which was not encouraged to search for new horizons and intellectual pursuits—save for certain areas, such as religious art and poetry.

Nevertheless, the glossological continuity between ancient and medieval Hellenism and the interest in the conservation and preservation of the past may be explained on the basis of other factors. History reveals that the nature of a people is reflected in their human values, their emotions, their attitudes, and other elements that have remained constants in human nature. Language is the most outstanding of them all. The intellectual ethos—the cultural activity and the thought activity of a people—is rooted in and condioned by their language.

Several eminent linguists and anthropologists, such as Edward Sapir and Benjamin Lee Whorf, as well as psychologists, literary critics, and sociologists, have emphasized that language is the supreme evidence not only of the survival and existence but also of the character and psyche of a people. They have theorized and also demonstrated convincingly that a people's perception of the cosmos and their ways of thinking about it are profoundly influenced by the structure of the language they speak. The structure of a language and the import of its vocabulary not only determine the manner in which one understands the environment but also reflect one's cultural milieu. A language sustains ethnic character as well as inhibits a people from seeing other cultures and other realities.[42]

The morphology of a language and the content of its vocabulary affect the mind and thereby much of the thought, the culture, and the outlook upon life of a given people. Edward Sapir, in particular, has amassed detailed evidence that supports the above observations and upholds the thesis that the language of a community or a nation directly reflects its physical, social, cultural, and ethnic physiognomy and character. In his opinion, the complete vocabulary of a language is "a complex inventory of all the ideas, interests and occupations that take up the attention of the community."[43] Whorf, on the other hand, in a discussion of Indian languages, notably Hopi, versus European languages, has argued that differences between the grammars of different languages correspond not merely to differences in modes of thought but to differences in the cultures as well.[44]

What is the relation between a vocabulary such as *neoterizo, neoterikoi,* and related terms and the experiences of a people? Vocabulary influences perception by calling attention to certain aspects of experience. Abundant direct evidence reveals the close relationship between the mechanisms of language, such as vocabulary, inflection, and sentence formation on the one hand and either

perception and organization of experience or the broad patterns
of behavior on the other. There is a strong causal relationship
between vocabulary and the interests of a society. People have
words for objects and experiences with which they are concerned,
and they lack words for objects and experiences with which they
have fewer dealings.[45]

How applicable is the thesis of the linguists cited above to the
Byzantine situation? Most native "Byzantines" were Greek speaking. How many of the minorities within the empire, especially
after the beginning of the seventh century, could converse and, in
particular, could write in languages or dialects other than Greek?
By the tenth century most minorities in Asia Minor and in the
Balkan peninsula, excluding the Bulgarians and the Slavs, who had
formed their own states, were Hellenized minorities. Is it justifi-
able then to call Heraklios and Nikephoros Phokas Armenians
when they could neither speak nor write Armenian, when they
had identified themselves with the language and culture of an empire Greek in language and Greek in secular education? Is it valid
to say that because Nikephoros was of Armenian descent he was
in a better position to understand the character and the inclinations of the Armenians?[46] The harsh law that he issued against
"the wandering and unstable nation of the Armenians"[47] reveals
neither appreciation nor understanding of the Armenian nation;
on the contrary, the legislation of the emperor indicates that he
was indifferent and even callous to the nation of his own ethnic
origins. Perhaps we can draw some analogies between the Byzantine Empire and the United States. For example, how German
was Dwight Eisenhower and to what degree was John F. Kennedy
an Irishman?

The Byzantine minorities, whether of Armenian, Bulgarian,
Jewish, or Slavic origin, spoke Greek as their native tongue, and if
they were educated, their secular education was based on the
Greek literary and intellectual heritage. Thus the only difference
between a Greek and a Jew was in religion. All subjects considered
themselves integral elements of the Byzantine state, which they
viewed as their home and their country.[48] Language and education
were decisive factors in the formation of their national identity
and their state's ethnic character. It was not incidental that the
Arabs, Armenians, Persians, Russians, the Latin peoples of the
West, and Germans called the subjects of the Byzantine Empire
simply Greeks or Romans—two terms that in the last analysis became synonymous. For example, the eleventh-century Armenian

historian Stephanos Taronites writes of the Armenian soldiers in the service of the "Greek Empire." The examples of course could be multiplied on the basis of Latin, German, Russian, Persian, and Arabic sources.[49]

As in Greek antiquity in which a Greek was identified with his city or home and was referred to as an Athenian, Spartan, Messenian, Samian, Arcadian, and so on, likewise in the Byzantine Empire the identification of a person with his city or eparchy of birth was very common. Thus the sources speak of Irene e Athenaia, Theodoros o Thebaios, Phokas o Kappadokis, Vasileios o Makedon, Loukios o Alexandreus, or Ioustinos o Thrax. Of course when a specific context warranted it, one would call himself a Roman, a subject of the Roman Empire, which for the Byzantines had not perished with the decline and fall of old Rome. In addition, as the ancient Persians, Romans, Egyptians, and others called the Athenians, Spartans, and citizens of other city-states of ancient Hellas "Greeks," likewise all the neighbors of the Byzantine Empire and other foreign nations designated its subjects as Greeks (or Romans). The difference, of course, between self-identification and the identification by others as we observe it in the history of both ancient and medieval Hellenism is neither a paradox nor a unique phenomenon, for it is common in many societies and on several levels.[50]

Social scientists for many years have emphasized that a nation or nationality is not a matter of race or blood but the product of a common language, common religion, common customs and traditions, and especially of a common consciousness of belonging together. All these elements and characteristics were present in the Byzantine Empire.

The notion that language is a fundamental element of ethnicity and of cultural identity, as contemporary linguistics has emphasized, was not a strange one to the Byzantines. In fact, several of their intellectuals echo this very "modern" theory. Nikephoros Choumnos urged his contemporary writers to imitate and remain faithful to the purity and clarity of ancient Greek as befits Greeks. Pletho Gemistos's definition of his own ethnicity and that of his compatriots on the basis of the language they spoke and their *paideia* (education, culture) is well known and requires no additional comments.[51]

The very attachment to ancient Greek, as well as the numerous admonitions of Byzantine intellectuals and writers concerning its preservation and the cultivation of its purity, is strong evidence that the Byzantines had no doubts about their links with ancient Hellas. "For them it was unthinkable to express their mind and their feelings in a language other than ancient Greek," in the words of a prominent language specialist.[52] To depart from the ancient language was a *neoterismos*, a departure from the right rules introduced by the ancestor Greeks.[53]

Furthermore, the persistence of archaic forms and the emphasis on ancient Greek, the Attic language in particular, indicate that Byzantine society was very conservative and slow in making changes. A developing and changing society is usually accompanied by changes in its language, including its lexicon, semantics, syntax, grammar, and other elements. The language of every era—its internal structure and its use—reflects both the mind of a people and its needs and changes as well.[54]

*   *   *

If the propositions of the language and anthropological experts cited earlier are valid, the conclusion to be drawn here is clearly discernible. The state of mind of a race either tends to stay the same or changes extremely slowly and very little in the course of time. We have observed that formulas and forms around the terms *neoterikoi* and *neoterizo* maintained themselves, with appropriate adjustments to historical circumstances, from the fifth century before Christ to the fourteenth century of our era. In spite of some change in emphasis, there has been an emphatic continuity in the Greek intellectual tradition.

Language, as well as religious beliefs, popular religiosity in particular,[55] and the intellectual heritage of a given nation at a given time are relative to the whole mental attitude of that time. In the language, the culture, and the philosophical outlook of a people, no abrupt or even permanent changes take place.

To be sure, the cultural continuity between ancient (archaic, classical, Hellenistic, Roman) and medieval (Byzantine) Hellenism can be demonstrated in several other ways. The linguistic exposition here has implied the close relationship between language and culture. It is well known that language shapes culture and culture shapes language. There is a constant interaction between the two.

Even though the ways of cultural, social, religious, and even of linguistic influence and continuity are unpredictable, the sense of continuity in all these areas of the Greek tradition of the Byzantine millennium is rich and satisfying. It confirms the truism that new ideas and new traditions have roots in the immediate and even in the remote past. Notwithstanding a series of invasions and even dominations by a variety of nations such as the Persians, Romans, Visigoths, Huns, Slavs, Arabs, Franks, Venetians, and primarily by Turks, the Greek cultural tradition survived because the vehicle and the organs of transmission had survived. Here we possess one more piece of evidence indicating that no language is dead that contains great ideas.

Robert Browning and Guyla Moravscik[56] have emphasized the existence of continuity and the perpetuation of Greek culture through language. Others have indicated continuity in other aspects of the Greek tradition, such as the lament (*mirologia*), epic poetry, and even the romance.[57] It is apparent that any literate culture or what is written about a literate culture can be identified not only through artifacts but also through a linguistic analysis in a historical context.

Thus the identification of the legal and intellectual traits of fourteenth-century Byzantium through language analysis and historical interpretation clearly demonstrates the unbroken continuity between the different chronological stages of the Greek mind. The Byzantine term *neoterikoi* shares with that of the Hellenistic and classical Hellenism a sufficient number of usages to establish that they belong to the same intellectual tradition.

Admittedly, the problem of the continuity of a nation on the basis of its language alone is a difficult one, and the language approach should be supplemented by cultural anthropology for more fruitful results. The analysis of even a few terms in a variety of historical circumstances illustrates, however, that the state of mind of Byzantium was akin to and in a direct continuity with that of the Hellenic past. The usage and the implications of *neoterikoi* and *neoterizo* in the Byzantine millennium reaffirm the Hellenic character and the Hellenic intellectual climate in which the so-called Byzantine mind was born and nurtured.

Notes

1. Constantine Armenopoulos *Exabiblos,* bk. 6, 7. 10, ed. Konstantinos G. Pitsakis (Athens, 1971), p. 357.

2. J. Zepos and P. Zepos, *Jus Graeco-Romanum,* vol. 2 (Athens, 1931).

3. Thucydides *History of the Peloponnesian War* 1. 58. 1.

4. Ibid., 2. 3. 1.

5. Ibid., 1. 97. 1.

6. Ibid., 1. 115. 2.

7. Ibid., 8. 73. 1.

8. Xenophon *Hellenika*, bk. 2, 1:1–5.

9. Plutarch *Cimon* 16. 17. 2.

10. Plato *Laws* 6. 758.

11. Antiphon *First Tetralogy* 4. 9. Ed. with an English trans. K. J. Maidment, in *Minor Attic Orators*, vol. 1 (Cambridge, Mass., 1968), p. 80.

12. G. Dittenberger, ed., *Sylloge Inscriptionum Graecarum*, vol. 1 (Leipzig, 1915), p. 237; vol. 2 (1917), pp. 198, 593.

13. Josephus *Antiquities of the Jews*, bk. 17, 9. 3; Dionysius of Halicarnassus *Roman Antiquities*, bk. 5, 75. 3; Aristotle *Politics* 2. 7. 5.

14. 4 Macc. 3:21.

15. 2 Tim. 2:22. Cf. Fred D. Gealy, "Exegesis to 2 Timothy," in *The Interpreter's Bible*, vol. 11 (Nashville and New York, 1955), p. 494.

16. John Chrysostom, "Homily VI—Homilies on 2 Timothy," *PG* 62. 651.

17. Origen, "Excerpta in Psalmos" 36:25, *PG* 17. 136b.

18. Clement of Rome *First Letter to Corinthians* 30. 1, trans. James A. Kleist, in *The Epistles of St. Clement of Rome and St. Ignatius of Antioch* (Westminster, Md., 1946), p. 27. The Greek text in *Library of Greek Fathers and Ecclesiastical Writers*, vol. 1, *Klemes o Romes* (Athens, 1955), p. 25.

19. Eusebios *Ecclesiastical History* 10. 8. 11–13.

20. Zosimus *Historia Nova*, bk. 2, 22–28; Gelasios of Caesarea *Epitome*, in *Theodoros Anagnostes Kirchengeschichte*, ed. G. C. Hansen (Berlin, 1971), p. 159; cf. Sozomenos *Ecclesiastical History*, bk. 1, 7.

21. Philostorgios *Ecclesiastical History*, in *Philostorgius Kirchengeschichte*, ed. J. Bidez (Leipzig, 1913), bk. 9, 16, p. 122. Cf. Socrates *Ecclesiastical History* 4. 31.

22. Philostorgios *Ecclesiastical History*, bk. 14. 4b, pp. 24, 34; Hansen, *Theodoros Anagnostes*, p. 7.

23. Zachariah of Mytilene *The Syriac Chronicle*, bk. 4, 11 (London, 1899), pp. 80–81; *Life of Nikephoros*, *PG* 100. 136ab; Nikephoros Gregoras *Historiae Byzantinae* (Bonn, 1830), p. 875.

24. Charles de Boor, ed., *Nicephori . . . opuscula historica* (Leipzig, 1880), p. 167. Cf. Paul J. Alexander, "Religious Persecution and Resistance in the Byzantine Empire of the Eighth and Ninth Centuries: Methods and Justifications," *Speculum* 52 (1977): 257, n. 79.

25. Iamblichos *Mysteries* 7. 5, in *Jamblichi de mysteriis liber*, ed. Gustavus Parthey (Berlin, 1857; Amsterdam, 1965).

26. Sozomenos *Ecclesiastical History*, bk. 8, 6; bk. 1, 17; bk. 1, 18; bk. 2, 18; bk. 4, 6; bk. 4, 9; bk. 7, 13.

27. Theophanes *Chronographia*, ed. Charles de Boor, vol. 1 (Leipzig, 1883), pp. 496–497; Theophanes Continuatus *Chronographia* (Bonn, 1838), pp. 496–497. Cf. J. B. Bury, *A History of the Eastern Roman Empire* (London, 1912; repr. New York, 1965), pp. 40–41.

28. Theophanes *Chronographia*, 1:7.

29. S. A. Saber, ed., *Photii patriarchae lexicon*, vol. 1 (Leiden, 1864), p. 445; Ada Adler, ed., *Suidae Lexicon*, pt. 3 (Stuttgart, 1967), p. 454; Leo Diakonos *Historiae*, bk. 7, 1–2.

30. Nicetas Choniates *Historia*, ed. I. Bekker (Bonn, 1835), pp. 770–771; for Peisistratos and his policies, see J. B. Bury, *A History of Greece*, 4th ed., rev. R. Meiggs (New York, 1975), pp. 127–132.

31. George Acropolites *Annales*, chap. 8, ed. I. Bekker (Bonn, 1836), p. 15. Cf. D. Nicol, "Refugees, Mixed Population and Local Patriotism in Epiros and Western Macedonia after the Fourth Crusade," to be published in the *Proceedings of the 15th International Congress of Byzantine Studies* (Athens, 1976).

32. George Acropolites *Annales*, chap. 26, p. 47.

33. Ibid., chap. 27, p. 49.

34. Nicolaus Festa, ed., *Theodori Ducae Lascaris Epistolae CCXVII* (Firenze, 1898), p. 58.

35. Sozomenos *Ecclesiastical History*, bk. 3, 14.

36. K. D. Triantaphyllopoulos, *E Exabiblos tou Armenopoulou kai e Nomike Skepsis en Thessalonike kata ton Dekaton Tetarton Aeona* (Thessalonica, 1960), p. 10; Pitsakis, *Exabiblos*, pp. ka–kd.

37. O. Tafrali, *Thessalonique au quatorzième siècle* (Paris, 1913), pp. 225–272, esp. 239–254; John Kantakouzenos, *Historia* 3. 569.

38. B. Laourdas, "Engomia eis ton Agion Demetrion kata ton 14on Aiona," *EEBS* 24 (1954): p. 283; cf. Triantaphyllopoulos, *Exabiblos*, p. 33.

39. See D. J. Constantelos, "Intellectual Challenges to the Authority of Tradition in the Medieval Greek Church," *The Greek Orthodox Theological Review* 15, no. 1 (1970): 56–84.

40. Cf. Norman H. Baynes, *Byzantine Studies and Other Essays* (London, 1960), p. 22.

41. Cf. Glanville Downey, "The Byzantine Church and the Presentness of the Past," *Theology Today* 15, no. 1 (1958): 93; see also pp. 85, 94.

42. Cf. John B. Carroll, ed., *Language, Thought and Reality: Selected Writings of Benjamin Lee Whorf* (Cambridge, Mass., 1956), p. 23.

43. Edward Sapir, "Language and Environment," in *Selected Writings of Edward Sapir*, ed. D. Mandelbaum (Berkeley, 1949), pp. 90–91; Paul Henle, ed., *Language, Thought, and Culture* (Ann Arbor, 1966), pp. 1–6.

44. Henle, *Language, Thought, and Culture*, p. 20.

45. Ibid., pp. 4–8.

46. H. Bartikian, *E Metanasteusis ton Armenion ton IA' Aiona: Aitiai kai Synepeiai* (Athens, 1976), p. 23.

47. Nov. 18, in Zepos and Zepos, *Jus Graeco-Romanum* 1:247.

48. See Andrew Sharf, *Byzantine Jewry* (New York, 1971), esp. pp. 74, 116.

49. H. Bartikian, *Metanasteusis*, p. 28; for other sources see my article, "Canon 62 of the Synod in Trullo and the Slavic Problem," *Byzantina* 2 (1970): 34–35; also n. 26.

50. Cf. M. I. Finley, *The Use and Abuse of History* (New York, 1975), p. 133.

51. J. F. Boissonade, *Anecdota Graeca*, vol. 3 (Paris, 1833), p. 359; S. Lambros, *Palaiologia Kai Peloponnesiaka*, vol. 3 (Athens, 1926), p. 247.

52. E. Kriaras, "E Diglossia Sta Ysterobyzantina Grammata . . . ," *Byzantina* 8 (1976): 221.

53. Ioannis Glykis, *Opus de vera syntaxeos ratione*, ed. A. Johnius (Bern, 1848), p. 58. Cf. p. 35.

54. Cf. Brian Silver, "Bilingualism and Maintenance of the Mother Tongue in Soviet Central Asia," *Slavic Review* 35, no. 3 (September 1976): 406–407.

55. For the problem of continuity versus discontinuity in ancient Greek and Byzantine Greek religiosity, see my article "Ancient Greek Religiosity and Byzantine Religiosity" in *The Past in Medieval and Modern Greek Culture*, ed. Speros Vryonis, Jr. (Los Angeles, 1978).

56. R. Browning, "Byzantine Scholarship," *Past and Present* 28 (1964): 3–20; idem, *Greece—Ancient and Medieval*, an Inaugural Lecture Delivered at Birkbeck College (London, 1966); Gyula Moravcsik, "Byzantinologie et Hellenologie," *Byzantion* 35 (1965): 291–301, esp. 297–300.

57. Margaret Alexiou, *The Ritual Lament in Greek Tradition* (Cambridge, 1974), in particular pp. 187–189, 195–197; idem, "The Lament of the Virgin in Byzantine Literature and Modern Greek Folk Song," *BMGS* 1 (1975): p. 121; idem, "A Critical Reappraisal of Eustathios Makrembolites' Hysmine and Hysminias," *BMGS* 3 (1977), esp. pp. 33–38; Albert B. Lord, "Parallel Culture Traits in Ancient and Modern Greece," *BMGS* 3 (1977): 71–80.

Chapter 2

Two Documents Concerning Mid-Sixth-Century Mopsuestia

Gilbert Dagron, *Collège de France*

The Latin version of the acts of a minor council held at Mopsuestia in 550 to ascertain whether the name of Theodore was then or at any previous time inscribed in the diptychs of the church of that city is not unknown;[1] this cannot be said for the inscription dated 560, also from Mopsuestia, which is discussed in this article. These documents share a common origin, and a similar date in the same reign, and they contain the name of an enigmatic personality, Marthanius/Marthanes/Malthanes, whose authority is known from other sources to have weighed heavily upon Cilicia at this time. This discussion looks at these documents mainly for a cross-section of contemporary provincial society, and it displays two harmonizing illustrations of a new balance of power.

* * *

The council dossier opens with two letters from the emperor Justinian I, dated 22 and 23 May 550, and addressed to Bishop Cosmas of Mopsuestia and to the metropolitan, John of Justinianopolis/Anazarbus. John was instructed to assemble at Mopsuestia the eight bishops of the province of Cilicia Secunda, in other words, his suffragans (all of whom responded to his summons), there to inquire of the aged persons of the city, both clerical and lay, and to prove (the result was laid down in advance) that Theodore, as he was no longer considered to be an orthodox bishop at the time of his death, had not been entered in the diptychs of the church formerly committed to his care. The dossier concludes with two covering letters, one addressed to the emperor (Justianian), the other to Pope Vigilius, sent together with the account of an uneventful session that had heard the witnesses and that was held in the *secretum* of the cathedral church of Mopsuestia on 13 June in the thirteenth year of the indiction.

The metropolitan John had presided, assisted by (*considentibus*) the other bishops, an imperial representative named Marthanius, and by all the priests belonging to the clergy of the city, in the presence (*praesentibus*) of the deacons, subdeacons, and readers from the same clergy and of those laymen who had been chosen as witnesses. The inquiry was conducted in several stages.

1. Julianus, a deacon and a notary, acting as secretary of the session, summarized the measures taken in conformity with the emperor's orders and enumerated the persons present, by categories: the holy bishops of the province; Marthanius *vir magnificus*; the clergy of Mopsuestia; the *defensor civitatis*, who was qualified as an *honestus vir*; the *clarissimi possessores* and *laudabiles habitatores*, among them the *seniores* chosen as witnesses by the *defensor civitatis*. The Holy Scriptures were then brought into the assembly and the imperial letters were read.

2. Next appeared the sixteen clerical witnesses selected by the *defensor* of the Church of Mopsuestia; the deacon, Eugenius; followed by the seventeen lay witnesses chosen by the *defensor* of the city, Paulus; each stated his name (in the case of two of the laymen, followed by a *cognomen*), the office he held or his occupation, his place of birth, or the fact of his belonging to the clergy of the Church of Mopsuestia (*Martyrius dicor, presbyter sum istius sanctae ecclesiae. . . . Eumolpius dicor, comes sum, in hac civitate natus*). Here, as elsewhere, the translation of the acts of the council into their original language, that is, Greek, is an easy matter.

3. The *custos sacrorum vasorum* ($\kappa\epsilon\iota\mu\eta\lambda\iota\acute{\alpha}\rho\chi\eta\varsigma$) of the church, the priest John brought the diptychs. These were read aloud and the nonappearance of Theodore's name was ascertained; each bishop then had the opportunity of satisfying himself to this effect by reading the diptychs in a low voice. After this the priest John declared that he possessed no earlier versions.

4. The sixteen clerical and the seventeen lay witnesses next approached, swore an oath upon the Scriptures, stated their age (since their birth for the laymen, since their entrance in the clergy for the ecclesiastics), and gave the evidence expected of them in almost identical terms: the name of Theodore of Mopsuestia, as far as men could remember, had never been inscribed in the diptychs; instead there figured most unexpectedly that of Cyril of Alexandria; there was indeed a Theodore, but he was a recent bishop of the city, a native of Galatia, who had died some three year earlier.

5. The metropolitan John together with all the bishops, de-

clared that no trace of heresy was to be discovered lurking in any text, or in the memory or conscience of any person, and this redundant affirmation terminated in a prayer for the emperor: *Salvum fac, Domine, imperatorem. . . .*

6. In the text the official subscription or signatures follow, and the document concludes with the translation of the letters sent to the emperor and, for appearance's sake, to the pope.

There is hardly any need to insist on the way in which the hearing of witnesses is transformed into ceremony and the inquiry into a demonstration of loyalty. Should we see this as a Stalinist parody? It is clear that the testimonies have been worked upon, even gilded, but above all disposed and given in an order, and in accordance with a hierarchy, that would give to any discordant voice the appearance of a faux pas. One cannot speak of falsehood when it is not at all a matter of truth. Justinian's message sets in motion the performance of a ceremony, as formal as it is necessary, the purpose of which is to make the emperor's wishes plain for all to see and thus to convey to the emperor an amplified resonance and the most perfect image possible, namely that of a consensus disguised as the straightforward finding of an inquiry. Absolute power thus results in a form of narcissism in which the "people" fulfil the function of a mirror and of a sound box. The people, or a representation of the people, of a city, namely Mopsuestia, in the mid-sixth century—this is what the document presents and this we shall endeavor to circumscribe.

* * *

Ecclesia and *civitas* are closely paralleled: Marthanius appears as the counterpart to the metropolitan of Anazarbus; the *defensor civitatis* (ἔκδικος τῆς πόλεως) to the *defensor ecclesiae* (ἔκδικος τῆς ἐκκλησίας); the lay witnesses to the clerical witnesses, with a difference consisting of one person, a difference of which it cannot be said whether it is intentional, accidental, or derived from a flaw in the manuscript tradition; the membership of the clergy to the *origo*; and so forth. We are here in the presence of a concerted design, as it were, of the play of a ceremony, a twofold organization recalling that of the people at the hippodrome. This division does not indicate a separation but rather goes to prove the homogeneity of provincial society at this time. Laymen are attentive to decisions concerning orthodoxy just as the bishop and his clergy care for the administration of the city and the appointment of its magistrates. Bishop, clergy, κτήτορες καὶ οἰκήτορες: here we see the coherent social group upon which all responsibility in the *polis* is conferred by law.[2]

As the choice of witnesses was in theory based on considerations of age (*seniores, aetate priores*), the information given in this respect is of an unusual accuracy and for this very reason interesting. We find that eight of the sixteen ecclesiastics and also eight of the seventeen laymen can only give their age approximately (*plus minusve*); these are neither the oldest nor in social terms the most humble. In fact the oldest witness is eighty years old and the youngest, fifty, if we except Comitas, the *pater civitatis*, who is forty years old, and the *clarissimus comes* Theodore, both undoubtedly participating by virtue of their offices. Clearly the selection is governed by considerations not only of age but also of respectability (the list of witnesses is drawn up in terms of a hierarchy and, for the clergy at least, according to their age within each order of the ministry) and perhaps too for representative reasons: the laymen indeed constitute a cross-section of officeholders and dignitaries, although not a faithful image of the community. As for the members of the clergy, we are fortunate in being able to calculate the age at which each entered into the clergy of the church at Mopsuestia (see Table 1).

It is possible that one or two figures were distorted or confused in the manuscript tradition,[3] but the general picture cannot be contested. Particularly this shows a considerable disparity in the ecclesiastical career of the priests or deacons. Some appear to have entered the clergy at the age of five, six, seven, or ten years, which recalls the saints whom the hagiographers portray as adopted by a church or a monastery when still at "an age to play," either because they were orphans, or because the vocation or the situation of their families suggested such a choice. But what do we really mean by entering into the clergy? It usually means receiving the first ordination, which is that of "reader" (ἀναγνώστης). If this is so, we can consider the extreme example of the Mopsuestia clergy in 550 as a good illustration of abuses that Justinian tried in vain, in 546, to do away with by imposing eighteen as a minimum age limit for the ordination of readers (Novel 123). There is another interpretation, however, which I think is preferable: the *Life of Saint Peter of Atroa*, the Fourteenth Canon of the Second Council of Nicaea (787), and in particular the long commentary that Balsamon added, inform us that ecclesiastical tonsure was sometimes made without any other ordination on very young

Table 1. **Participating Clergy—Ages upon Entering**

Name of witness	Position	Age in years	Length of service in years	Age in years upon entering the clergy
Martyrius	priest	± 80	+ 60	± 20
Paulinus	priest	79	49	30
Stephanus	priest	± 69	3	± 66
Olympius	priest	65	55	10
Johannes	priest	± 65	28	± 37
Thomas	priest	60	55	5
Theodorus	priest	± 62	55	± 7
Thomas	priest	± 60	50	± 10
Eudoxius	priest	63	42	21
Paulus	priest	58	28	30
Theodorus		± 52	28	± 24
Paregorius	archdeacon	66	28	38
Johannes	deacon	58	48	10
Thomas	deacon	55	49	6
Johannes	deacon	± 65	50	± 15
Paulus	deacon	± 56	23	± 33

children who were then dressed in black and considered as "amongst those consecrated to divine service" (*Life of Saint Peter of Atroa*). Balsamon writes even more clearly that they were considered "amongst the clergy." This tonsure "taking the form of a clerical crown" was administered to Peter of Atroa at the age of twelve according to V. Laurent's commentary, perhaps even earlier according to the text: the canon of the second Nicene council uses the expression νηπιόθεν, which suggests that many children received it in their earliest childhood.[4] Other witnesses of Mopsuestia take orders at the age of thirty-seven or thirty-eight, in other words, after a professional or family life as laymen, sometimes prolonged after ordination; the evidence of inscriptions and papyruses provides several telling examples.[5] It is also to be noticed that all those who began their ecclesiastical career at the age of twenty-four (with perhaps one or two exceptions[6]) use in their evidence a different formula from that used by the others: *nescio, nec cum laïcus essem, nec postquam factus sum clericus. . . .* The impression is given that, even if lay and clerical society are most carefully distinguished, they are interrelated in very many ways.

For the laymen, a criterion (in addition to that of age) that is unquestioningly used is the *origo*: *in hac civitate natus* is a formula uttered by all the witnesses, except for one who declares, "*civis sum*," which probably comes to the same thing, and the *pater civitatis*, who does not specify his *origo*, doubtless to avoid redundancy. But above all to be noticed are the order of presentation and the designation of the title, offices, and trades of the witnesses. When the information provided by the text is combined, the following picture emerges:

Present Not as Witnesses

Marthanius, *vir magnificus, comes domesticorum*, and imperial representative [μεγαλοπρεπ (έστατος) κόμης (τῶν καθοσιωμ-ένων) δομεστικῶν]
Hypatius and Paulus, *clarissimi tribuni* (λαμπρότατοι τριβοῦνοι)
Paulus, *vir honestus, defensor civitatis* (ἔκδικος τῆς πόλεως)

Witnesses

Clarissimi possessores istius civitatis (λαμπρότατοι κτήτορες)

Eumolpius et Theodorus, *clarissimi comites* (λαμπρότατοι κόμη-τες)
Eusebonas, *clarissimus palatinus* (λαμπρότατος πριβατάριος or παλατῖνος)

Laudabiles habitatores istius civitatis (οἰκήτορες)

Stephanus, *vir laudabilis, praefectianus* (ἐπαρχικός)
Paulus, *cognomina Neonis*
Anatolius, *principalis* (πρωτεύων)
Marinus, *praefectianus* (ἐπαρχικός)
Eustachius, *cognomine Rhoda*
Anatolius
Rufinus, *architectus*
Comitas, *agens in rebus et pater istius civitatis* (μαγιστριανὸς καὶ πατὴρ τῆς πόλεως)
Theodorus, *agens in rebus* (μαγιστριανός)
Johannes, *tabularius* (ταβουλάριος)
Addaeus
Marcus, *praefectianus* (ἐπαρχικός)
Johannes, *lecticarius* (δεκανός, λεκτικάριος)
Nicetas, *tabularius* (ταβουλάριος)

The sole lay representative to play an active part in the conduct of the council is the *defensor* (ἔκδικος). His place in the administration would seem to be higher than that of the *pater,* who is here a mere witness. It is to be noted that these posts coexist and, however uncertain their attributions may be, they should not be confused.[7] One witness describes himself as a *principalis,* that is, a member of the assembly or, more precisely, of the small group of primates (πρωτεύοντες) that is in the process of replacing the curia;[8] other witnesses undoubtedly are members of the curial class or even, though without saying so, πρωτεύοντες, unless the high proportion of officials is to be explained by a desertion of the curia for the public service.[9]

Among the officials or former officials, a precise career cannot be established for the two *clarissimi comites* (one of whom adds to his testimony *"militabam ministrans divinis et maximis jussionibus"* to indicate that he spent part of his service "on assignment" away from Mopsuestia), whereas the others are found distributed throughout the main branches of the administration. They depend upon the praetorian prefect (*praefectiani* or ἐπαρχικοί), the *magister officiorum* (*agentes in rebus* or μαγιστριανοί), the *res privata* and the *sacrae largitiones (palatini* or πριβατάριοι). To these may be added the palace administration and army (*comes domesticorum*) and the imperial chancery (*tribuni*), if it is a question, as it would appear to be, not of soldiers but of *tribuni (et) notarii* (τριβοῦνοι (καὶ) νοτάριοι).[10] The city is an administrative microcosm; the terms employed in this document reveal the same cleavages as funerary epigraphy from the same period and region.[11] There is, however, one passage that suggests a new interpretation: by clearly balancing the *clarissimi possessores* (λαμπρότατοι κτήτορες) and the *laudabiles habitatores* (οἰκήτορες), the document seems to indicate, more clearly than the legislation of this period, some kind of equivalence between the senatorial rank (at its lowest degree) and a qualification one might hesitate to define strictly as "owner of land."[12] Κτήτορες/οἰκήτορες would thus correspond to the antithesis senator/nonsenator. A transition has taken place from the traditional conception of an order, to that of a class defined in fiscal terms, and, finally, to that of a local aristocracy. Trades are relatively underrepresented: one architect, two notaries, one undertaker—far less than in the funerary inscriptions of Corycus, where shopkeepers and tradesmen form the overwhelming majority.

Two leading figures dominate the scene and it is they who stage the performance: Marthanius and John of Anazarbus, the pro-

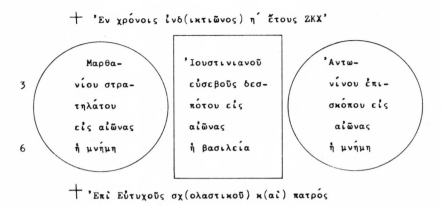

✝ 'Εν χρόνοις ἰνδ(ικτιῶνος) η΄ ἔτους ΖΚΧ'

	'Ιουστινιανοῦ	
Μαρθα-	εὐσεβοῦς δεσ-	'Αντω-
νίου στρα-	πότου εἰς	νίνου ἐπι-
τηλάτου	αἰῶνας	σκόπου εἰς
εἰς αἰῶνας	ἡ βασιλεία	αἰῶνας
ἡ μνήμη		ἡ μνήμη

✝ 'Επὶ Εὐτυχοῦς σχ(ολαστικοῦ) κ(αὶ) πατρός

Figure 1. Plaque in honor of Emperor Justinian, Bishop Antoninus, and Marthanius.

fessional soldier and the metropolitan, between them representing church and state, or in short, the empire.

* * *

This balance of power is even more forcibly represented in the arrangement of a hitherto unpublished inscription, preserved in the former Museum of Adana, that although it is to be published elsewhere,[13] deserves a brief mention here as a pendant to the conciliar text.

On a plaque, which must originally have been embedded in the wall of a church, are engraved, in a cartouche, an acclamation in honor of the emperor and, in two strictly symmetrical medallions, acclamations—to the right, in honor of Bishop Antoninus—to the left, in honor of the military commander (στρατηλάτης) Marthanius. A line at the top of the inscription supplies the date according to the indiction and the year; a line below confirms this with a reference to the *pater civitatis* (Figure 1). The provenance of the stone is unknown but may be inferred from the date: that found on the inscription—627—can only be reconciled with an eighth year of an indiction falling within Justinian's reign by recourse to the era of Mopsuestia. The year in question is A.D. 559–560, toward the close of Justinian's reign.

Bishop Antoninus is not otherwise known, but he fits without difficulty into the far-from-complete episcopal list of Mopsuestia as an immediate or indirect successor of the Cosmas, who appears in the acts of the council of A.D. 550. Eutyches, *pater civitatis,* has also succeeded to the relatively unimportant office held by Comitas at that time: they both possess a real administrative capacity, surely a positive recommendation, in as much as Comitas was previously *agens in rebus* and Eutyches, like so many *pateres,* is a *scholasticus,* that is, a jurist, an advocate or legal adviser to the provincial government.[14] As for Marthanius, described as *vir magnificus et comes domesticorum* in 550, he now appears in 560 as a στρατηλάτης or military commander (usually *magister militum*) as on a very similar inscription, discovered at Beirut among the debris of a monument, that reads also as an acclamation but without any precise indication of date: Μαρθανίου στρατηλάτου πολλὰ τὰ ἔτη.[15]

His is thus an effective military career that the person in question followed first in Cilicia and thereafter throughout the *pars Orientis.* These are military commands, but in exercising them, Marthanius appears to have superceded, first, as *comes domesticorum,* the governors of both Cilicia, then, as *magister militum (per Orientem?),* the *comes Orientis.*[16] Procopius in his *Anecdota*[17] furnishes details supplementing the official information supplied in the documents: Malthanes (Procopius's version of his name) was a Cilician, son-in-law to the *referendarius* Leo who taught Justinian venality in affairs of justice. Charged by the emperor to repress agitation in Cilicia, he seized the occasion to pillage the province, sending part of the proceeds to Justinian and keeping the rest for himself (despite Procopius's insinuations, this sounds very much like tax gathering). The inhabitants suffered these exactions in silence, all except the Blues of Tarsus who, counting upon the emperor's favor, organized a public protestation that seemed more like a riot. Malthanus, learning of this, advanced to Tarsus with a strong contingent; and in the struggle that ensued—at night or just before dawn—the Blues' προστάτης Damianus, a member of the city's boule, was killed. The Blues of the capital pressed Justinian to avenge the stain, but Leo succeeded in arranging things and Malthanes, summoned to court for an inquiry, was left unscathed, apart from a thrashing at the hands of the Blues administered in the palace area at the end of the hearing. Procopius draws from this adventure two rather contradictory conclusions: the appetite for gain is stronger for Justinian than considerations of allegiance to a faction; the factions enjoy a total license to do as they wish. For our purposes, it is more important to notice that Marthanius/Malthanes enjoys extended powers, especially in fiscal affairs and law and order, over both Cilician provinces (Cilicia Prima in Procopius's account of events shortly before 550, Cilicia Secunda in the acts of the council). In neither of our documents is there to be found either the name or even the suggestion of the existence of a governor, and it seems that the office has been emptied of almost all its significance as a result of the formation of local pressure groups by the city factions, who constitute a network throughout the empire, and of the high-handedness of senior military commanders to whom the role of representing the emperor is increasingly entrusted. Elsewhere Procopius discloses the miserable fate of Callinicus, governor of Cilicia Secunda, who having escaped assassination at the hands of the Blues was impaled on Theodora's orders (thus before 548), οὐδενὶ λόγῳ on the tomb of the culprits whom he had legally condemned to death.[18] In the novels, various administrative reforms give the impression, for the Cilicias and the *dioecesis Orientis*, that the power of the governors and of the *comes* was reestablished.[19] The texts we have examined disclose a different state of affairs toward the end of Justinian's reign: a soldier of Cilician origin "represents" the emperor and the state as *comes* in both Cilician provinces, thereafter as *magister militum* probably throughout the whole diocese of the Orient.[20] This is very close to the empire organized in Themes with *strategoi* representing the emperor ἐκ προσώπου.

In the "flash image" we possess in the Mopsuestia stone, as well as in the subtle conciliar ceremony of 550, we can see the professional soldier and the bishop holding comparable positions, as it were, on either side of the emperor; the provincial structure is doubtless not abrogated but has scarcely any reality except in terms of ecclesiastical hierarchy; as a result, the city is strengthened and provides its testimony, era, and the name of its *pater* instead of any reference to a governor.

Notes

1. J. D. Mansi, ed., *Sacrorum Conciliorum nova et amplissima collectio*, IX, 275–290.

2. Justinian, novs. 86, 128, 134; Justin II, nov. 149; *MAMA*, III, p. 125; cf. D. Claude, *Die byzantinische Stadt im 6. Jahrhundert* (Munich, 1969), pp. 118–121.

3. There are only three uncertain cases: those of Martyrius, of Olympius (a member of the clergy for fifty years, not fifty-five, according to one MS), and of the priest Paulus (aged fifty, not fifty-eight, according to one MS).

4. Justinian, nov. 123, 13: the age limits are a minimum of eighteen years for the readership, of twenty-five for the deaconate or subdeaconate, and of thirty-five for the priesthood. The rules definitely laid down at the council in Trullo are: subdeacons, twenty years; deacon, twenty-five; priest, thirty [G. A. Rallis, M. Potlis, *Syntagma ton theion kai ieron kanonon*, vol. 2 (Athens, 1856), pp. 337-338. On ecclesiastical tonsure, cf. V. Laurent, ed., *La vie merveilleuse de Saint Pierre d' Atroa* (Brussels, 1956), p. 71 and n. 5; Rallis and Potlis, *Syntagma* 2: 615-619 (Second Council of Nicaea, Fourteenth canon)]. The canon says: ἐπεὶ οὖν ὁρῶμεν ἐκτὸς χειροθεσίας νηπιόθεν τὴν κουρὰν τοῦ κλήρου λαμβάνοντάς τινας ... and forbids those who have been only tonsured to play the part of readers in the liturgy without having received the reader's ordination. The problem seems to be simple, but Balsamon, at the end of his commentary, complicates it considerably by referring to Justinian's Novel 123 and wondering if a child that a bishop ordained as a reader in his first age is to receive at the age of eighteen a "second seal." Balsamon wrote in the twelfth century, but it is obvious that entering into the clergy (νηπιόθεν), with a reader's ordination or not, was an old and definitive custom. For a Western comparison, cf. N. Duval (with the collaboration of Françoise Prévot), *Recherches archéologiques à Haïdra*, vol. 1, *Les inscriptions chrétiennes* (Paris and Rome, 1975): among the five readers mentioned, two are six years old and one is five; among the six *clerici*, one is four and the others are under eighteen. The term *clericus* seems here to describe those who have not yet received the reader's ordination.

5. For examples, see *MAMA*, III, 336, 463, 583, 682, 760; E. Wipszycka, *Les ressources et les activités économiques des églises en Egypte du IVe au VIIIe s.* (Brussels, 1972), pp. 163-167.

6. Paulinus and possibly the priest, Paulus. For Paulus, however, one MS gives a figure suggesting that he entered the clergy at the age of only twenty-two years.

7. For both offices, see details and bibliograpy in Claude, *Byzantinische Stadt*, pp. 114-116.

8. Cf. A. H. M. Jones, *The Later Roman Empire* (Oxford, 1964), p. 731 and nn. 41, 42. According to Justinian, nov. 128, 16, the πρωτεύοντες seem to be distinguished from and inferior to the κτήτορες, thus belonging to the class of οἰκήτορες.

9. Hypothesis of Jones, *Later Roman Empire*, p. 760.

10. An unpublished votive inscription of this period, preserved at Adana but possibly originating from Mopsuestia, mentions a certain Paul, τριβ-(οῦνος) νοτάριος. The *schola notariorum* performed a considerable administrative role in the provinces; cf. Justinian, nov. 8.

11. See for example the Corycus inscriptions in *MAMA*, III.

12. See Justinian, nov. 128, for the most interesting parallel.

13. This article is due to appear in a future issue of *Türk Tarih Kurumu, Beleten* (Ankara).

14. *CIG*, III, 4438: H. Grégoire, *Recueil des inscriptions grèques-chrétiennes d' Asie Mineure* (Paris, 1922), nos. 270, 307.

15. The inscription, which appears to be lost, was edited by Père Mouterde in *Mélanges de l'Université Saint-Joseph*, 8 (1922): 96-100.

16. The interpretation is difficult. First, because military titles such as *comes domesticorum* or *magister militum* may correspond to *vacant*, rather than effective, positions—in other words, they may be titles rather than functions, even if their holder has been given definite instructions. E. Stein, justly criticizing Père Mouterde's reconstruction of Marthanios's career and wrongly considering that the Marthanios of the council acts of 550 was the same as the Marthanès *comes rerum privatarum* of Novel 142, makes him a civilian and a *comes domesticorum vacans* [*Histoire du Bas-Empire*, vol. 2 (Paris, 1959), p. 761, n. 3]. This inscription leads to another reconstruction of his career that seems to me to prove the military character of the personage. Second, the term στρατηλάτης, at that time, either could have had a defined meaning and could have designated the holder of a *magisterium militum* (as in the code and the novels) or could have had the much vaguer sense of general or even military authority over a province (*dux*). On this point, any hesitation is dismissed by the very official character of the inscription and by the fact that another has been found in Phoenicia. It is possible, however, to imagine that Marthanios had an enormous military responsibility and a title with no geographic delimitation (*magister militum praesentalis?*).

17. Procopius, *Anecdota*, Loeb Classical Library (Cambridge, Mass., and London, 1935), chap. 29, secs. 28–38.

18. Ibid., chap. 17, secs, 2–4. As Callinicus was ἄρχων of Cilicia Secunda, this must have happened at Anazarbus.

19. Justinian, nov. 157 (542); commentary by Stein, *Bas-Empire*, 2: 750–752.

20. The post was no longer occupied by Belisarius after 550/551 (Stein, *Bas-Empire*, 2: 822). The fact that Cilicia served as winter quarters for the troops in the East is a contributory factor in the militarization of the area (Procopius, *Anecdota*, chap. 3, sec. 5).

Chapter 3

Titles of the Rulers of the Second Bulgarian Empire in the Eyes of the Byzantines

Ivan Djurić, *University of Belgrade*

The circumstances under which Symeon, the great founder of the First Bulgarian Empire, was crowned emperor, and particularly the Byzantine reaction to the coronation, as well as the form of the new empire, have been thoroughly discussed by historians. Although scholars have not agreed on many points, generally speaking, the fact that Symeon's title was recognized in Byzantium is no longer in dispute.[1] The existence of a new empire has never been doubted; however, its foundation, the content, and the epithets of the title of its first sovereign seemed to be rather blurred.

On the other hand, less attention has been paid to the imperial titles of the Bulgarian rulers of the Second Empire, and to the titles the Byzantines accorded these rulers. Nevertheless, these problems are of interest inasmuch as their clarification, even if it be a confirmation of what has already been expected or suspected, could throw some more light on both the formal and the real position and prominence of Bulgarian emperors within the Byzantine hierarchy of states. Moreover, the question of how the *Romaioi*—not only the emperor himself and the court officials—who thought themselves to be on the top of the Christian pyramid, regarded the neighboring, newly founded empire is worthy of inquiry. This is the more so, because the results of such an investigation could facilitate an interesting comparison with Byzantine attitudes toward the Serbian Empire, the younger of the two newly founded states that existed side by side with the successor of Rome. The imperial dignity of Stephen Dušan of Serbia, gained under dramatic circumstances, has aroused great scholarly interest (as has that of Symeon), so that today there are hardly any unknown facts concerning the nature, rank, and fate of Stephen Dušan's accession.[2] The treatment in this study is confined to the problem of Byzantine attitudes toward the imperial title in the Second Bul-

garian Empire. These titles differed a great deal in every respect in
the two Bulgarian empires. The difference was clearly established
and precisely defined by G. Ostrogorsky some forty years ago. It is
also useful to mention that a historian, when undertaking a research of any medieval intitulations, Byzantine in particular, must
bear in mind the distinction between the formal titles and epithets
and those used informally in general practice, the latter often out-
living the former.

Although unfortunately from a small number of sources, it is
known how the Bulgarian emperor referred to himself.[3] The evolution of the Bulgarian imperial dignity has already been treated
by scholars, and its similarity with the Byzantine imperial title,
after which it was modeled, has long been established.[4] Much
has been said about the attitudes assumed by Constantinople and
the West toward the new empire in the Balkans, but the formulas
used abroad when addressing the Bulgarian sovereign have not so
far been closely looked into. The official title of the Bulgarian
emperor tended, throughout its evolution, to become more extensive and pompous, always after its Byzantine models.[5] In its Slavonic version, the signature of Bulgarian rulers came much closer
to the Byzantine model than did the formulas used in neighboring Serbia. In short, in the course of its evolution, as the available sources record, the Bulgarian imperial signature distinguished
two main, very different types. The older was simply *H. tsr'
Bl'garom'* (or possibly *Bl'garom' i Gr'kom'*).[6] The other, more
complicated one was *H. v ha ba blgoveran' tsr' i samodr'žets'
vsiem Bl'garom' i Gr'kom'*.[7] The first formula had true translations both in Byzantine and Western official and unofficial forms
of address, whereas little remained of the second formula either in
the Greek or in the Latin language. Without going any further into
the matter, and in spite of the limited number of sources, it is
useful to point at two facts that have been rather neglected. First,
in Bulgaria, the title of autocrator or *samodržac* comes into use
during the rule of John Asen II, and not before 1230; that is, it
appears, after the battle of Klokotnica where the Bulgarians put
to rout the army of Theodore Angelus, emperor of Thessalonica,
and took him prisoner.[8] Shortly after this glorious victory, which,
at least for a while, seemed to bring John Asen II quite close to
the conquest of Constantinople, Nicaea agreed to sanction the
establishment of the Bulgarian Patriarchate in 1235. Since then,
all the rulers of Trnovo have included *"autocratoria"* in their
official signatures. We have every reason to believe that Emperor

John Stracimir of Vidin, who witnessed the collapse of Bulgarian medieval independence, did not include this dignity in his signature.[9] Besides autocrator, it is obvious that the rulers of Trnovo, starting with John Asen II, occasionally introduced the formula *tsr' Bl'garom' i Gr'kom'* so that, after 1347, it became a regular part of their official titles. Both John Alexander and John Šišman used it, but they changed the epithet *veran* into *blagoveran*, whereas neither John Stracimir nor the co-emperors of Trnovo mentioned "Greeks" in their formulas.[10] Something must have caused both these changes. What was it?

When we discuss the appearance of *autocratoria* in the official titles of the Bulgarian rulers, it is necessary to make a comparison with Serbia. If we draw such a parallel, we are of the opinion that the only valid information concerning the matter can be found in the official documents. It should not be overlooked that, in literary sources, for instance, the epithet *samodržac* was given to the (grand) župan (of Rascia) Stephen Nemanja although, as has long been known, it became part of the official title of the Serbian ruler after the coronation of Stephen the First Crowned, which was shortly followed by the recognition of the independence of the Serbian church.[11] The sequence of events in Bulgaria was quite similar. There too, political success was followed by the recognition of its church.

On the other hand, "Greeks" were mentioned with both Bulgarian and Serbian emperors in their respective formulas. In Serbia it was yet another sign of the success, ambition, and state ideology of Stephen Dušan, its first emperor. In Bulgaria, John Asen II, encouraged, among other things, by the fact that he had conquered Greek lands, adopted a similar usage after Klokotnica. Furthermore, it was not by chance that the year 1347 was a definite turning point. In spite of the limited number of available charters or other sources, the fact remains that it was in that year that the signature of John Alexander bore the formula "emperor of the Greeks" for the first time. Later on, John Šišman took over the same formula. They both used the new epithet *blagoveran*, too. It is quite possible that the change had something to do with the events that took place in Byzantium itself. There, the march of John VI Cantacuzenus into Constantinople meant the final defeat of the party of Empress Anne of Savoy, who had been supported by the Bulgarian sovereign. Moreover, a little prior to that, Stephen Dušan, having been crowned emperor, introduced into his title the notion that he ruled over "all Serbs and Greeks." The brother of John Alexander was the Serbian governor in Albania; the empress of Serbia was his sister.[12] It is also quite evident that the change within the title of 1347 brought along the epithet *blagoveran* to the rulers of Trnovo.

The comparison of this epithet with the same one as used in Serbia could produce some interesting results. The epithet *veran* first came into use when Stephen Dušan mounted the throne, or rather toward the end of the reign of Stephen Uroš III Dečanski, if the charter bearing his signature (1330) is not a counterfeit.[13] The epithet *blagoveran* was introduced by Stephen Dušan himself, but not before the conquest of "Greek lands" in the South.[14] In Serbia as in Bulgaria, there is considerable likelihood of an interdependence between the terms *Greek lands* and *blagoveran*. The epithet *blagoveran* or *veran* did not receive an adequate translation into Greek, which would have been *pistos* or *pistotatos* and which was, in fact, how the Emperor Stephen Dušan signed his name in that language.[15] The Byzantines used the general epithet *hypselotatos* instead, when they addressed a foreign ruler. By the way, this epithet has never been used in any Byzantine imperial dignity. If an equivalent for the adjective *blagoveran* was needed, the Byzantine diplomatic chancellery produced the epithet *eusebes* or *eusebestatos* which was almost solely reserved for foreign rulers, or better, emperors, the more so because it was rather unusual in Byzantine titles. A linguistically justified parallel for this Greek epithet in the Slavonic language would be *blagočastiv*. (These epithets are thoroughly discussed shortly.)

It is quite well known that the intitulations of Byzantine sovereigns, as well as those of Bulgarian and Serbian rulers, suffered considerable changes, abbreviations, and deformations in the West, where their meaning was often misunderstood. In the West, Bulgarian and Serbian imperial dignities were often intentionally or unintentionally reduced to the dignities of kings. In 1355, Charles IV, the German ruler and Western emperor, wrote to the Serbian emperor, Stephen Dušan, *"illustri principi domino Stephano Rassie regi,"* thus expressing his own ideas of both empire and the imperial dignity.[16] Rome assumed no different attitude toward the title of the Serbian ruler, because the popes were always rather hostile to any possible pretender to the imperial dignity, especially if he came from the East.[17] With the exception of the pope and the German emperor, the other Western states were more flexible where the Serbian Empire was concerned; yet none of them, not even the Ragusans, fully recognized Stephen Dušan's imperial title.[18] At best, Stephen Dušan was granted double reference depending on whom the documents were intended for. The Ragusans, the Venetians, and most probably the Bosnian rulers behaved in this way. They all had their own motives that are, at present, of no interest to us.[19] The West was also very hesitant about recognizing Bulgarian rulers. These were often deprived of recognition to a certain extent. Their position with both the Westerners and the pope was, however, different and essentially better than that of Serbian rulers. The longer tradition of the Bulgarian imperial dignity (in Serbia it was established in 1346) could, among other things, account for its more favorable position. In the beginning, the pope did not call the Bulgarian rulers anything but "kings." This attitude of the Roman Curia seemed to be resistant to even the most attractive offers for the union of the two churches coming from Trnovo.[20] To Pope Innocent III, Kalojan was only "*rex*" or, a bit more vaguely but with the same meaning, "*dominus Bulgarorum,*" although the ruler himself used the title *Calojoannes imperator Bulgarorum et Blachorum.*[21] An interesting view of the Bulgarian titles was taken by Henry of Flanders, the Latin emperor of Constantinople, who, in 1212, looked upon the sucessor of Kalojan as an ordinary usurper.[22] This also seems to indicate a certain continuity in the attitude of the rulers of Constantinople, both Latin and Byzantine, toward these titles. Juding by the international recognition of their ranks, the first rulers of the Second Bulgarian Empire were held in no greater respect by their Western contemporaries nor by the chroniclers of the period.[23]

A certain evolution in the treatment of the Bulgarian imperial dignity in the West did, however, take place. For example, in comparison with the Serbian imperial dignity, the Bulgarian emperor's title soon reached greater recognition among the Hungarians[24] and the Ragusans.[25] Even the attitude of the papal see was changing. In 1245, Pope Innocent IV addressed Koloman as "*illustri Colomano in Bulgaria imperante*";[26] a few decades later, a letter from Rome forwarded to George Terter read: "*magnifico principi Georgio imperatori Bulgarorum illustri.*"[27] The Bulgarian imperial dignity was recognized by the governor of Bari in his letter to Charles of Anjou in 1272, in which he referred to Constantine Tich as "*ad Imperatoris Bulgarorum.*"[28]

These examples, taken from abundant evidence, show how the Bulgarian, as well as the Serbian, imperial dignity was exposed to misunderstanding and misinterpretation that was, at times, deliberate. Nevertheless, it is obvious in both documents and narrative

sources that, in the West, the Bulgarian imperial title was held in
greater respect and considered more valid than the Serbian one.
Moreover, in the available Western sources, the Bulgarian titles
were defined both geographically and ethnically ("of Bulgaria"
and "of Bulgarians"), which was not the case with the Serbian
titles. The latter were defined solely in geographic terms, which
were less important than the ethnic ones.[29] It is also to be noted
that the rulers of Trnovo did not include in their title a list of
territories subject to their rule, as did some of the Nemanjids.[30]
This difference also weighs in favor of the Bulgarians. Their titles, more like the Byzantine one, tended to avoid any extensive
geographic description; the Byzantines assumed that such an
account within the title reduced it and limited the emperor's
grandeur.

The Byzantines undoubtedly recognized the imperial dignities
of the rulers of Trnovo, although not in the form in which these
rulers referred to themselves. This was not unnatural, for the Byzantines could not and would not accept the claim of some of the
rulers of Trnovo to rule over Greeks; only the Byzantine emperor
could have such a rule. The Byzantines granted to Bulgarian emperors a higher rank than to the Serbian rulers, however. In the
first place, the recognition of the Bulgarian imperial dignity was
broader and more consistent than was that of Stephen Dušan.
Bearing in mind the differences determined by the kind of source,
the Bulgarian emperor was accorded high rank both in literary
writings and in various documents. This is quite natural, for the
emperors of Trnovo made obvious efforts to imitate Byzantine
official titles; some of them even included mention of their rule
over the Greeks (besides that over the Bulgarians) in their titles
and they added the word *autocratoria* after 1230. The Byzantines,
however, acknowledged only Trnovo's imperial rule over Bulgarians. The reasons why Bulgaria and Serbia received such different treatment in the empire should be sought in the tradition
and origins of their respective imperial dignities. Both tradition
and legitimacy favor Bulgaria, whose emperor did not appear as a
usurper in the eyes of the *Romaioi*, although Byzantine recognition of his high rank was somehow delayed and unwilling.

It is no wonder, therefore, that John VI Cantacuzenus referred
to the Serbian ruler as "king of the Triballoi" and to John Alexander as "emperor of the Moesians."[31] Although Cantacuzenus
did not hide his essentially unfavorable and ironic attitude toward
the Bulgarian emperor's title, he did address Bulgarian rulers as
emperors. Cantacuzenus was no exception among Byzantine

authors. A rather similiar attitude was taken by Nicephorus Gregoras.
Earlier Byzantine authors also referred to Bulgarian emperors in
the same way. George Acropolites, for example, saw Kalojan as
"emperor of the Bulgarians" (*basileus Boulgarōn*),[32] and so did
other Byzantine writers. Manuel Philes, who seems to have been an
exception, provides a different example; he treated the Bulgarian
emperor Smiletz only as "*Smilos . . . ho kratōn ges Boulgarōn.*"[33]
The fact that the Byzantines accorded prestige and high rank to
the Bulgarian rulers should not surprise us, because the recognition of the Bulgarian patriarchate of 1235 secured the legitimacy
of their titles.[34] This recognition did not, however, do away with
the resentfulness toward the very idea of a barbarian emperor in
the neighborhood, a resentfulness expressed by Byzantine writers
as long as the empire existed. Some of these opponents, like
Nicephorus Gregoras, assumed a double attitude toward the Bulgarian rulers. Gregoras often treats John Alexander simply as
"*hegemōn* of the Moesians," whereas Maria, the wife of Andronicus IV Palaeologus was "daughter of Alexander, emperor
of the Moesians" to him.[35] Depending on the circumstances in
which he mentioned the Bulgarian ruler, the learned author of
Roman History granted him different ruler's epithets.

It must be mentioned that the attitude toward Bulgarian rulers
changes to some extent with the late Byzantine authors, inasmuch
as they did not witness any empire but the Byzantine one in the
Balkans. Bulgaria was rarely mentioned in the writings of that
period, so that any analysis of or conclusion drawn from these
sources about the attitude of the empire toward the Bulgarian
emperor's title has only relative value. All the same, the outlook
of certain Byzantine historians on Bulgarian and Serbian imperial dignities has changed. These authors granted Serbia more
space because of its fate as well as of the comparatively longer
existence of the empire of Stephen Dušan and of some of the
little states founded on its territory. It has been noted long ago
that some of these authors who witnessed the collapse of the
thousand-year-old empire favored the Slavs to quite an extent
because they saw them as bitter opponents of the mutual enemy
and at the same time as victims of the general danger.[36] Laonicus
Chalcocondyles best illustrates this view of the Balkan peoples.
Without hesitation, this chronicler of the Turkish victories almost
equalizes the titles of the Bulgarian and Serbian emperors. Michael
Šišman he calls "Μιχαῆλον τὸν Μυσῶν ἡγεμόνα"[37] or "Μιχαῆλον
. . . τὸν Μυσῶν ἡγεμόνα . . . καὶ τὰ βασίλεια ἐν Τρινάβῳ ποι-
ησάμενον,"[38] and John Šišman, more clearly, "Σούσμανον τὸν

τῶν Μυσῶν βασιλέα.³⁹ On the other hand, he refers to Stephen Dušan as "ὁ Τριβαλλῶν ἡγεμών" when he was crowned king and says that "Στέπανος ἐγένετο βασιλεὺς Τριβαλλῶν"⁴⁰ when he mounted the imperial throne. The Serbs were naturally more familiar to these *Romaioi* not only because the glory of their empire was still remembered by these authors but because of their longer and fiercer struggle to resist the Ottomans. The Bulgarian Empire, however, with all its might, belonged to the past as far as these authors were concerned, for it had definitely lost its glory and independence. The loss of prestige of the Bulgarian imperial dignity was most probably due to the premature decline of power and influence of the Empire of Trnovo, which had taken place before its physical end and long before Chalcocondyles. Half a century earlier, an anonymous chronicle, which dates from the period between 1392 and 1407, recorded a bygone event—the marriage of Theodore Vatatzes to "τῇ θυγατρὶ τοῦ ἄρχοντος τῶν Βουλγάρων τοῦ Ἀσάν, τῇ Ἑλένῃ ," which had taken place in 1235, when the Bulgarian patriarchate was acknowledged.⁴¹ Neither Chalcocondyles nor this chronicler produce evidence of the official attitude of the empire toward the Bulgarian state at the time of its existence, but they do explicitly represent Byzantine public opinion of the later period. Apart from these two chronicles, there is hardly any available narrative source, dating from the last days before the collapse of the empire, that provides more information on the subject.

Unfortunately, none of the Greek-language signatures of the Bulgarian rulers of the Second Empire have been preserved;⁴² however, Byzantine diplomatic materials contain casual references to the emperors of Trnovo. These references, in fact, could not be considered to be official and complete intitulations that originated from the imperial chancery. Furthermore, everything that is known about the treatment the Bulgarian emperor's title received in Constantinople has been drawn from the ecclesiastical, and not the imperial, administration. But in view of the fact that patriarchal models followed the form and rank of the imperial ones, the analysis of the former would be justified. This problem deserves attention especially because of the existence of a very useful Byzantine patriarchal manual for addressing both Byzantine and foreign heads of church and state, which thus provides valuable information. The manual in question is the so-called "Ekthesis nea." The body of the text dates from 1386, but a considerable number of additions were made in later versions. In this valuable textbook of instructions on how to write *pittakia*, a special kind of patriarchal letters, additions were also made to Chapter 5, which is on "the correspondence of metropolitans outside their dioceses."[43]

In the last additions to this part of the manual, the models for addressing John Stracimir (1365-1395), the emperor of Vidin, and John Šišman (1371-1393), the autocrator of Trnovo, are given. They are:

66. Ὅπως γράφει ὁ πατριάρχης καὶ ὁ μητροπολίτης πρὸς τὸν αὐθέντην Βυδίνης καὶ Βασιλέα τὸν Καντζιμηρόν· "Εὐσε-βέστατε καὶ φιλόχριστε, αὐτοκράτορ κράτιστε καὶ αὐθέντα Βυδίνης καὶ πάσης Βουλγαρίας, ἐν ἁγίῳ Πνεύματι αὐθέντα καὶ υἱέ τῆς ἡμῶν μετριότητος, ἢ ταπεινότητος."

67. Ὅπως γράφει ὁ μητροπολίτης πρὸς τὸν αὐθέντην καὶ Βασιλέα Βουλγάρων τὸν Σούσμανον· "Κράτιστε, εὐσεβέσ-τατε, φιλόχριστε, ὑψηλότατε βασιλεῦ τῶν Βουλγάρων, ἐν ἁγίῳ Πνεύματι γλυκύτατε καὶ ποθεινότατέ μοι αὐθέντα καὶ υἱέ."[44]

The chronology of the rule of the two men clearly shows that the models could have appeared only between 1386 (the year when "Ekthesis nea" was written) and 1393. An interesting comparison can be made between the intitulations of these two Bulgarian emperors, inasmuch as the formulas recorded in the manual are undoubtedly official and accurate reflections of the actual Byzantine concepts of state and jurisdiction, which we have discussed on several occasions.[45] It is noticeable that both John Stracimir and John Šišman are referred to as βασιλέα in the introductions to the formulas; this is, throughout the manual, a reference to their actual, more than to their formal, status. Now, the differences that appear in the titles mentioned in the "introductions" and the formulas of the manual should be pointed out. Constantine Dra-gaš, for example, is introduced as "πρὸς τὸν δεσπότην Σερβίας" in the heading, whereas the intitulation itself does not include these words.[46] Similiar examples of such differences can be found in many other sources. Thus, in the late narrative sources, for instance, many foreign feudal lords are honored with titles they never had. The so-called *Short Chronicles*, to mention these important texts only, set almost the same example. There, one can come across the title of "despot" (if we take it literally) given to Prince Lazar, Vaivode Mircea, and many others.[47] Con-

sequently, we conclude that in documents such as this patriarchal
manual (despite the differences between some of its versions)
only the intitulation itself provides reliable information for the
evaluation of dignities.

Proceeding from that assumption, it is significant that the imperial title of John Šišman was included in the formula, whereas
John Stracimir's was not. Instead of βασιλεῦ, the sovereign of
Vidin was to be addressed a bit vaguely as "αὐτοκράτορ κράτιστε
καὶ αὐθέντα," which essentially alters both the weight and meaning of the highest Byzantine title of *samodržac*, which had already
been granted to Stracimir. It is true that the *Romaioi* hesitated to
recognize imperial dignities of foreign rulers, particularly when the
title of autocrator was concerned;[48] therefore, Stracimir was to be
addressed only as "αὐτοκράτωρ" and not as "βασιλεὺς καὶ αὐτοκράτωρ," according to the manual. It is hardly possible that the
Byzantine emperor or the patriarch would have addressed either
the Bulgarian or the Serbian ruler as both basileus and autocrator
in any official document, whereas it is quite likely that they might
have used either emperor or *samodržac* but never both.[49] Justification for this assumption can be found in the other available
sources too. Unofficial documents and information and the titles
that "barbarian" rulers gave to themselves are a different thing.[50]
In other words, it becomes evident that the *Romaioi* made an obvious distinction between the rulers of Trnovo and those of Vidin,
so that only the imperial dignity of the former was recognized,
albeit to a certain extent only.

With reference to these titles, it stands out that, according to
the formulas of the manual, Stracimir was "Sovereign of Vidin
and all Bulgaria" (*Bydines kai pases Boulgarias*), whereas John
Šišman was "emperor of Bulgarians" (*tōn Boulgarōn*). It has
already been stated that the Byzantines distinguished between
titles that included ethnic terms and those that incorporated
geographic terms (the names of the territories subject to a ruler
or claimed by him). In "Ekthesis nea" itself, as well as in all its
versions, John Šišman appears to be the only one whose imperial dignity incorporated ethnic and not geographic terms. All
the other rulers are mentioned as rulers of certain countries,
cities, or islands. One of the additions to the manual contains a
seducing intitulation of the grand duke of Lithuania (*tōn Litbōn*),
which could easily be misunderstood as an ethnic term but is not.
It is a *pluralia tantum* whose nominative case is *Litbai*, which was
also the name of the metropolitanate. It is not unusual for the

titles of other feudal lords not to contain the name of the people subject to their rule. The "barbarian" rulers who were addressed by the patriarch and the metropolitans and thus mentioned in the manual were not entitled to such an inclusion because their tradition could not be compared with that of Trnovo. The only one who could have been compared with the emperor of Trnovo was the emperor of Serbia, who was no longer in existence.

We have already indicated the importance of the epithet *blagoveran* or *blagočastiv* within the titles of Bulgarian and Serbian emperors. It is characteristic that the epithet *eusebestatos* is used in the manual exclusively for persons of imperial blood. It is not used, however, for people who were often more powerful and more important but did not have the highest imperial dignity. Thus, "Ekthesis nea" omitted that epithet from the titles of Prince Lazar and Princess Milica, Francesco Gattilusio and Niccolo Gattilusio, Vaivode Mircea, Vaivode of Moldowallachia, Stephen IV and his wife Maria, and Constantine Dragaš. Naturally, this epithet does not exist in the forms of address to the Byzantine emperor and empress because special formulas were reserved to them. The manual suggests the use of *"eusebestates"* only for the "empress of Serbia" and her son, inasmuch as these were, according to the results of our previous research, Thomaide, the empress of Thessaly, that is, the widow of the emperor Symeon, half brother of Stephen Dušan,[51] and her son Stephen. Besides them, the patriarchal chancery used the same epithet only for the two Bulgarian rulers. To Stracimir it was, no doubt, a kind of oblique acknowledgment of his highest rank, inasmuch as the manual officially deprived him of the imperial title itself.

The list of Bulgarian rulers mentioned at the end of the *Synodicon of Tzar Boril* clarifies to quite an extent this interesting problem of the epithets included in the titles of the Bulgarian rulers of the Second Empire.[52] There, one finds four different epithets—*blagoveran*, *blagočastiv*, *veliki*, and *hristoljubiv*—which were exclusively used for Bulgarian rulers, their wives, and children. These four epithets refer to members of the imperial family only. The epithet *blagočastiv*[53] was most frequently used; *veliki* and *hristoljubiv* were less frequent; and the least frequent was *blagoveran*.[54] None of these epithets was used in the official documents of the Byzantine emperor. They were not included in his title either. "Ekthesis nea" clearly shows that they were not used in the intitulations of any member of the Byzantine imperial family.[55] Of the four epithets, neither the Byzantine state nor the patriarchal chanceries used the epithet *veliki* for Bulgarian rulers; the epithet *blagoveran* (*pistotatos*) was used by Bulgarian and Serbian rulers, although it does not appear in their Byzantine intitulations. The epithets *blagočastiv* (*eusebestatos*) and *hristoljubiv* (*philochristos*), however, do appear in the additions to "Ekthesis nea" and are used for Šišman and Stracimir. Besides these two Bulgarian rulers, "Ekthesis nea" says that among foreign rulers only the "despoina of Serbia" and her son were entitled to them. Comparing the *Synodicon of Tzar Boril* and the "Ekthesis nea," it becomes quite evident what epithets the Byzantine patriarchal chancery granted to emperors outside Constantinople. These Byzantine intitulations, logically, excluded the attribute *pistotatos* (for it bore too much resemblance to the signature of the Byzantine basileus) as well as the adjective *megas* (which is used, according to "Ekthesis nea," solely for "kings," "dukes," and "princes" and not for emperors).[56]

The available imperial and patriarchal documents produce no evidence on intitulations that include the epithets mentioned in the patriarchal manual. A much simplified version of intitulations was used instead. That version, however, agrees with the manual. In the diplomatic correspondence of the Byzantine state and patriarchal chanceries the epithet *preuzvišeni* (*hypselotatos*) was exclusively used when addressing Bulgarian rulers. Unfortunately, most of the information now available on Bulgarian rulers does not show the complete official address. Practically all known documents that originate from the Byzantine state or diplomatic chancellery do, however, refer consistently to the Bulgarian emperor as "ὁ ὑψηλότατος βασιλεὺς τῶν Βουλγάρων."[57] So, in 1355 John Alexander was addressed as "πρὸς τὸν ὑψηλότατον βασιλέα τῶν Βουλγάρων, ἐν Ἁγίῳ Πνεύματι γνησιώτατον υἱὸν τῆς ἡμῶν μετριότητος, κῦρ Ἰωάννην τὸν Ἀσάνι"[58] by Patriarch Callistos I. On the occasion of the nomination of the metropolitan of Vidin, in the so-called Praxis of Vidin of July 1381, John Stracimir is mentioned as "ὁ ὑψηλότατος βασιλεὺς τῶν Βουλγάρων, κῦρ Ἰωάννης ὁ Στραντζιμηρός,"[59] too, although this need not be taken as an official address because the emperor was not addressed directly, only referred to in the text.

Ljubomir Maksimović has long pointed out that there are no known Greek versions of the titles of Bulgarian rulers; thus it is impossible to compare the signatures of Bulgarian and Serbian emperors in the Greek language.[60] This statement remains true; there are no signatures of Bulgarian emperors in Greek, nor are there any official intitulations of the rulers of Vidin in the available documents of Byzantine origin. No more information can be found about the intitulations of the rulers of Trnovo. This does not mean that Bulgarian rulers were not at all mentioned in some diplomatic sources, but in order to compare them with the additions to the "Ekthesis nea," they should have included a direct address to the emperor; this they often lack because the emperor was not the person for whom the documents were intended.

In view of this situation we underline the value of the items of the "Ekthesis nea," believing that the intitulations or forms of address listed in this patriarchal manual can be treated as the most official extant ones when Bulgarian rulers are concerned. Furthermore, we are of the opinion that the evidence found in the "Ekthesis nea" represents an essential contribution to the knowledge of how the Byzantines regarded the titles of Bulgarian emperors. Like those of Serbian rulers, the documents of Bulgarian emperors in the Slavonic language are, naturally, quite different.[61] We do not intend to treat this problem at any length now, but it is necessary to mention that, in spite of the great insufficiency of diplomatic materials, it is evident that the titles of Šišman and Stracimir differed considerably. Thus, Šišman appears to have been "*Io Sisman' v ha ba Blgoveran' tsr' i samodr'žets' v'sem' Bl'garom' i Gr'kom',*" whereas Stracimir was simply "*Ioan' Srasimir' tsr' Blgarom'.*"[62] If the two contemporary emperors differed in their titles, there is no reason to doubt that the difference was appreciated and expressed by the Byzantines.

The titles of the Bulgarian emperors of the Second Empire have several times been compared with both Serbian and Byzantine imperial dignities. It has also been noticed that the rulers of Trnovo tended more consistently to imitate their Byzantine model than did Serbian rulers. Having analyzed the two main types of signatures of Bulgarian rulers, the simpler and the more complex one, it becomes evident that the epithet of autocrator was introduced into the titles of the rulers of Trnovo only after 1230, that is, after the collapse of the empire of Thessalonica. Since John Asen II, Bulgarian rulers occasionally included the formula "emperor of Bulgarians and Greeks" and the epithet *blagoveran*, which became general practice after 1347. This is likely to have been caused by the well-known changes and events that had taken place both in Byzantium and Serbia a little earlier. As in Bulgaria, so in the titles of Serbian rulers, there is an obvious interdependence between Greek lands and the epithet *blagoveran*.

As for the fate of the imperial dignity of Trnovo in the West, it was similar to that of the Serbian imperial title a century later; it was not recognized at the beginning. At first completely denied, the Bulgarian imperial dignity gradually gained more and more appreciation so that, in the fourth decade of the thirteenth century, the ruler of Trnovo started being addressed as an emperor even by the pope himself. The Serbian emperor's title was far less appreciated. A declared opponent of Stephen Dušan's imperial title was Hungary, which also disapproved of the imperial dignity of Trnovo. In its expressions of disapproval, however, Hungary was more discreet in the case of Trnovo, but it never failed to mention its seniority to the Bulgarian ruler.

Owing to its longer tradition and the more favorable circumstances under which it was established, the Bulgarian imperial dignity, if compared with the Serbian one, was, from the very beginning, more appreciated by the Byzantines. Even in the Byzantine literary sources, the mention of the imperial title of the rulers of Trnovo is hardly ever avoided. The Byzantines, who in principle resented the idea of the existence of any empire but their own, assumed, so to speak, a threefold attitude toward the rulers of Trnovo. Either they denied their imperial titles (such examples are most rare), or they acted according to the circumstances under which the Bulgarian emperor was mentioned (the example set by Nicephorus Gregoras, for instance), or they acknowledged, albeit in their own way, the imperial dignity of Bulgarian rulers (most frequent). The late Byzantine authors were much more tolerant toward the vanished Serbian Empire. They even equalized its rank with that of the Bulgarian Empire. Such an attitude is not unusual because Serbia became more important for Byzantium in the fifteenth century.

Until recently, the available sources could not secure a precise insight into how the Byzantines saw Bulgarian imperial dignities, for they did not include the official Byzantine forms of address used for Bulgarian rulers. In that respect, the new edition of the patriarchal manual for "pittakia" of 1386, the so-called "Ekthesis nea" with all its later versions, has made it possible to reach more accurate conclusions. In view of the fact that the models used by the patriarchal chancery were done after those of the imperial chancery, we have the true form of address to both the emperor of Trnovo and the ruler of Vidin (John Šišman and John Stracimir). The former was granted imperial dignity in both the formula and its introduction, whereas the latter was deprived of it in his formula, which gives evidence of the differentiation the Byzantines made between the two states. This differentiation is supported by the fact that Šišman appears to have been "emperor of the Bulgarians," whereas Stracimir was only "ruler of Vidin and all Bulgaria." The significance of the mention of people within the emperor's title on the one hand and of lands on the other is known from the rules of Byzantine title hierarchy. Although the ruler of Vidin was officially denied the emperor's title, the manual includes some strictly imperial epithets, used only for the emperor of Trnovo, and the "empress of Serbia" and her son, such as *eusebestatos*. The difference that appears in the manual between the two Bulgarian rulers is supported by their own signatures. There, too, the formula used by the ruler of Vidin appears considerably more modest.

Notes

1. Cf. G. Ostrogorski, "Avtokrator i samodržac," *Glas SKA* 164, 2d ser., 84 (1935): 122 ff. [repr. in G. Ostrogorski, *Vizantija i Sloveni* (Belgrade, 1970), pp. 303 ff.]; idem, "Die byzantinische Staatenhierarchie," *Sem. Kond.* 8 (1936): 45 ff. [repr. in G. Ostrogorski, *O verovanjima i shvantanjima Vizantinaca* (Belgrade, 1970), pp. 243 ff.]; F. Dölger, "Bulgarisches Zartum und byzantinisches Kaisertum," *Bulletin de l'Institut archéologique bulgare* 9 (1935): 57 ff.; W. Ohnsorge, *Das Zweikaiserproblem im früheren Mittelalter* (Hildesheim, 1947), p. 44.

2. Ostrogorski, "Avtokrator," pp. 152 (=330) ff.; M. Dinić, "Dušanova carska titula u očima savremenika," *Zbornik u čast šeste stogodišnjice cara Dušana* (Belgrade, 1951), pp. 87 ff.; idem, "Srpska vladarska titula za vreme Carstva," *ZRVI* 5 (1958): 9-19; Lj. Maksimović, "Grci i Romanija u srpskoj vladarskoj tituli," *ZRVI* 12 (1970): 61-78.

3. G. A. Ilyinskiy, *Gramoty bolgarskih cqrey* (repr. London, 1970); I. Ivanov, *B'lgarski starini iz Makedonia* (Sofia, 1931), pp. 577 ff. Cf. Ostrogorski, "Avtokrator," pp. 138 (=318) ff.; M. Laskaris, *Vatopedskata gramota na car Ivan Asena II* (Sofia, 1930); M. Lascaris, "Influences byzantines dans la diplomatique bulgare, serbe et slavo-roumaine," *Byzantinoslavica* 3 (1931): 500-510; P. Matufčiev, "K'm istoriata na Mesemvriiskite monastiri," *Sbornik v čest na V. N. Zlatarski* (Sofia, 1925), pp. 163-182; N. Mušmov, *Monetite i pečatite na b'lgarskite care* (Sofia, 1924); I. Gošev, *Trnovski carski nadgroben nadpis ot 1388 godina* (Sofia, 1945); A. P. Stoilov, "Svoden hrisovul za istoriata na Zografskia monastir," *Sbornik v čest na V. N. Zlatarski* (Sofia, 1925); I. Dujčev, "Prepiskata na papa Inokentii III s B'lgarite," *God. Sof. univ., Ist.-filol. fak.*, XXXVII, 3 (Sofia, 1942) (inaccessible to the author); I. Dujčev, *Proučavania v'rhu b'lgarskoto srednovekovie (Prepis ot zlatopečatnik na car Ivan Aleksandar)* (Sofia, 1945), pp. 122-129; P. Petrov, "K'm

v'prosa za avtentičnostta na Virginskata gramota i dostovernostta na s'd'ržas-cite se v nea svedenia," *God. Sof. univ., Filos.-ist. fak.*, t. I, 2, 1957; M. Andreev, *Vatopedskata gramota* (Sofia, 1965); G. Cankova-Petkova, "Vos-stanovlenie bolgarskogo patriaršestva v 1235 g. i meždunarodnoe položenie bolgarskogo gosudarstva," *Viz. Vrem.* 28 (1968): 136–150 (with partly collected earlier literature). In fact, there are only seven imperial charters of Trnovo available.

4. Cf. Ostrogorski, "Avtokrator," pp. 138–142 (=318–321); nn. 1, 3.

5. Ostrogorski, "Avtokrator," p. 141 (=320).

6. Those are the charters of John Asen II for the monastery of Vatopedi, for the Ragusans, and the well known inscription of Trnovo (Ivanov, *B'lgarski starini*, pp. 577, 578; F. I. Uspenskii, "O drevnostiah goroda Tirnova," *Izv. Russk. Arheol. Inst. v Konst*, VII, 1901). Cf. Ostrogorski, "Avtokrator," p. 138 (=318).

7. Such formulas came into use during the reign of John Alexander, start-ing in 1347 (Ivanov, *B'lgarski starini*, p. 594). Cf. Ostrogorski, "Avtokrator," p. 141 (=320).

8. Cf. G. Ostrogorsky, *History of the Byzantine State* (New Brunswick, N.J., 1969), 435 ff. (with bibliography).

9. The title of Stracimir is discussed later on. There is just one of his char-ters available, and he signed it modestly as *Ioan' Stracimir' tsar Blgarom'* (Ivanov, *B'lgarski starini*, p. 602).

10. The evidence for it is provided in the epitaph of the widow of John Asen, the brother and co-emperor of John Šišman, from 1388. Whereas the latter titled himself as "emperor of all Bulgarians and Greeks," the former was referred to by his wife only as "emperor of Bulgarians" (cf. Gošev, *Trnovski carski*). Cf. I. Dujčev, *Byzance après Byzance et les Slaves* [repr. in *Medioevo bizantino-slavo* 2 (Rome, 1968): 303].

11. Cf. Ostrogorski, "Avtokrator," pp. 141 (=322) ff.

12. The latest research on "Greeks" within the titles of Serbian rulers was undertaken by Maksimović, "Grci i Romanija," and it includes important earlier literature.

13. S. Novaković, *Zakonski spomenici srpskih država srednjeg veka* (Bel-grade, 1912), p. 645. Cf. Ostrogorski, "Avtokrator," p. 152 (=330).

14. Novaković, *Zakonski spomenici*, pp. 411, 474, 489, 681, etc.

15. A. Solovjev and V. Mošin, *Grčke povelje srpskih vladara* (Belgrade, 1936).

16. M. Kostić, "Zašto je osnovan slovenskoglagoljaški manastir Emaus u Pragu," *GSND* 2 (1927): 163. Cf. Dinić, "Dušanova titula," p. 104; O. Ha-lecki, *Un empereur de Byzance à Rome* (Warsaw, 1930), p. 47.

17. Cf. Dinić, "Dušanova titula," pp. 106–108.

18. Ibid., pp. 109–111. The treatment of Stephen Dušan's emperor's title in Dubrovnik depended on the relations of the Ragusans with Hungary, which permanently disapproved of the Serbian imperial dignity.

19. In November 1340 Stephen Dušan was, for the Venetians, "*dominus rex Raxie*" (Ljubić, *Listine*, III, 110), and in spring 1350 he was "*serenis-*

simus imperator Raxie et Romanie, dispotus Larte et Blachie comes" (Ljubić, *Listine*, III, 174). Nicolo Barbarigo, a Venetian and the duke of Dubrovnik, in 1355 refers to Stephen Dušan as "*lo emperador de Sclavonia*" (Ljubić, *Listine*, III, 270). These questions are thoroughly discussed by Dinić, "Dušanova titula."

20. Cf. Dölger, "Bulgarisches Zartum," pp. 57 ff.; V. N. Zlatarski, *Istoria na b'lgarskata država prez srednite vekove*, vol. 3 (Sofia, 1940): 149 ff.; Ostrogorsky, *History*, p. 420.

21. *PL* 214. 1113c, 1114c–1115a, 1116b. Pope Innocent III, in a letter to an unknown addressee, titles Kalojan as "*Rex quoque Blachorum et Bulgarorum cum Cumanis, Turcis et Graecis adversos Latinos pugnantes . . ." (PL* 215. 698c–d; cf. Zlatarski, *Istoria*, pp. 158–163, 220).

22. Boril was to him "*Borilus . . . qui similiter inter gentem Bulgarorum . . . imperiale nomen sibi cum singulis signis imperialibus usurpavit*" [J. B. Bouchon, *Recherches et matériaux pour servir à une histoire de la domination française aux XIIIe, XIVe et XVe siècles*, vol. 2 (Paris, 1840), p. 211; cf. Zlatarski, *Istoria*, p. 260].

23. The so-called Ansbert, for instance, says of Peter II, brother of Asen: "Kalopetrus, Blachorum et maxime partis Bulgarorum in hortis Tracie dominus, qui se imperatorem . . . et coronam imperialem regni Grecie ab eo sibi efflagitabat" [A. Chroust, *Quellen zur Geschichte des Kreuzzuges Kaiser Friedrichs I, MGH, SS.*, n.s., V, 58 (Berlin, 1928)]. In another instance the same author records: "*Kalopetrus, Blachorum domnus itemque a suis dictus imperator Grecie*" (Chroust, *Quellen*, p. 58). Robert de Clari, who wrote the famous description of the fall of Constantinople to the Crusaders in 1204, calls Kalojan simply "*Jehans li Blakis . . . roi de Blaquie*" and Boril "*Burus . . . rois de Blakie*" [Robert de Clari, *La Conquête de Constantinople*, trans. P. Charlot (Paris, 1939), chaps. 64–65]. To Villehardouin, Kalojan is "*Johannis, le roi de Blaquie et de Bogrie*" [G. de Villehardouin, ed. and trans. E. Faral, vol. 1 (Paris, 1938), chap. 252]. The chronicler Robert of Auxerre refers to Kalojan, almost like the pope, as "*Rex enim Blachorum et Bulgarorum cum Cumanis, Grecis et Turcis . . .*" (*Roberti canonici s. Mariani Antissiodorensis chronicon*, ed. Pertz, *MGH*, XXVI, 269). In Hungary, John Asen II was addressed: "*Johannis Asseni principis Bulgarorum*" [I. Dujčev, "Il francescanesimo in Bulgaria nei secoli XIII e XIV," *Medioevo bizantino-slavo*, vol. 1 (Rome, 1965), p. 398]. The same ruler was referred to, by the Western chronicler Albericus, in 1230 as "*Alsanus rex Bulgarie, frater Alexandri*" or, together with the emperor of Nicaea, John Vatatzes, as "*Vastachius et Alsanus duo reges potentissimi*," whereas Boril was to him "*Burillus . . . imperator est appellatus*" (*Chronicon Alberici monachi Trium Fontium . . .*, ed. Pertz, *MGH, SS.*, XXIII, 886, 927, 938). Cf. Zlatarski, *Istoria*, pp. 187, 48, 308.

24. It is known that Hungary, because of its protracted pretensions toward Serbia, which were expressed in the official titles of its kings, could not "allow Serbia to surpass it in rank in the hierarchy of states" (Dinić, "Dušanova titula," p. 108). As for Bulgaria, it should not be overlooked that, starting

with Bela IV, the Hungarian rulers included Bulgarian titles in their own [P. Nikov, B'lgaro-ungarski otnošenia ot 1257-1277 godina (Sofia, 1920), pp. 88-91]. Already in 1219, the Hungarian king Andrew II refers to the Bulgarian emperor, in a letter to Pope Honorius III, written on the occasion of the marriage of his daughter to the Bulgarian emperor, as "Azeno Bulgarie Imperatore . . ." [A. Theiner, Monumenta historica Hungariae, vol. 1 (Rome, 1859), 21; cf. Zlatarski, Istoria, p. 325]. An interesting example is found in a document from 1271 of the Hungarian king Stephen V in which Jacob Svetislav, the first Bulgarian despot, appears as his vassal but bears the title of emperor of the Bulgarians (Nikov, B'lgaro-ungarski otnošenia, pp. 175 ff.; Zlatarski, Istoria, pp. 539 ff.; B. Ferjančić, Despoti u Vizantiji i južnoslovenskim zemljama (Belgrade, 1960), pp. 141-144). No matter what made the Bulgarian despot assume such a title, the fact remains that the ruler of Hungary tolerated the emperor's title with the Bulgarian usurper as long as it did not threaten Bulgaria's vassal position.

25. The dignities of the rulers of Trnovo were not a stumbling block for the Ragusans, who were always flexible and practical. To them John Alexander was simply and logically dominus imperator Bulgarie, which they did not always recognize the Serbian ruler to be in Serbia (Ljubić, Monumenta spectantia historiam Slavorum meridionalium, III, 156-158). M. Lascaris quotes two documents of John Alexander in an Italian translation; he believes only the first of these documents to be original (Lascaris, "Influences byzantines," p. 503). Several times in 1340 the Ragusans referred to the ex-empress of Bulgaria, Anne, as "domina imperatrix de Bolgaria" (Ljubić, Monumenta spectantia, X, 135). Cf. A. Burmov, Izbrani proizvedenia, vol. 1 (Sofia, 1968) [Istoria na B'lgaria prez vremeto na Šišmanovci 1323-1396, God. na Sof. Univerz., Ist,-filol. fak., XLIII, 1947. 1-56, 1-20], p. 275.

26. Dujčev, "Il francescanesimo," p. 396.

27. Ibid., p. 402.

28. Zlatarski, Istoria, p. 525.

29. Maksimović, "Grci i Romanija," p. 64.

30. Cf. Dinić, "Dušanova titula"; Maksimović, "Grci i Romanija."

31. L. Schopen, ed., Ioannis Cantacuzeni eximperatoris Historiarum libri iv (Bonn, 1828), 1:394, 459, 468; the same author referred to Michael Šišman as "pros Michael ton basilea Mysōn" (ibid., 1. 284).

32. A. Heisenbere, ed., Georgii Acropolitae Opera (Leipsig, 1903), 21. The same author, however, uses the term archōn, too (ibid., 48-49, 152).

33. E. Miller, ed., Manuelis Philae carmina (Paris, 1855), p. 254. This poet, like Gregoras, sees Irene Palaeologina Asenina as basilis Boulgarōn Asanina [I. Dujčev, "Una poesia di Manuele File dedicata a Irene Paleologa Asenina," ZRVI 8, pt. 2 (1963): 91-99]; cf. E. Trapp, "Zur Genealogie der Asanen in Byzanz," Jahrbuch der österreichischen Byzantinistik 25 (1976): 163-177.

34. Cf. Ostrogorsky, History, p. 437.

35. Nicephorus Gregoras, Historia Byzantina, vol. 3, ed. B. G. Niebuhr (Bonn, 1855), pp. 149, 557. On the other hand, the same historian saw John Asen II as archōn only [ibid., vol. 1, ed. L. Schopen (Bonn, 1829), pp. 55-56].

36. Cf. N. Radojčić, "Grčki izvori za Kosovsku bitku," *GSND* 7–8 (1929–1930): 163 ff.

37. E. Darko, ed., *Laonici Chalcocandylae Historiarum demonstrationes*, vol. 1 (Budapest, 1922), p. 20.

38. Ibid., p. 26.

39. Ibid., pp. 20–23.

40. Ibid., p. 49.

41. P. Schreiner, *Die byzantinischen Kleinchroniken*, vol. 1 (Vienna, 1975), p. 680.

42. Maksimović, "Grci i Romanija," p. 73.

43. J. Darrouzès, "Ekthésis néa: Manuel des pittakia du XIVème siècle," *REB* 27 (1969): 58 ff.

44. Ibid., p. 62.

45. Cf. Djurić, "'Ekthesis nea'–vizantijski priručnik za 'pitakia' o srpskom patrijarhu i nekim feudalcima krajem XV veka," *Zbornik Filozofskog fakulteta u Beogradu* 12, no. 1 (1974): 415–432; "Les titulatures des métropolites dans l'Ekthésis néa et l'organisation de l'église dans l'Asie Mineure à la fin du XVème siècle," a communication given at the Fifteenth International Congress of Byzantine Studies, Athens, September 1976; "Titulature mitropolita u 'Ekthesis nea' i crkvena organizacija u Maloj Aziji krajem ZIV veka," *Zbornik Filozofskog fakulteta u Beogradu* 13, no. 1 (1976): 53–70; "Laička prosopografija 'Ekthesis nea'," *ZRVI* 18 (1977), in press.

46. Darrouzès, "Ekthésis néa," p. 62; cf. Djurić, "'Ekthesis nea' o patrijarhu i feudalicima," p. 430.

47. Schreiner, *Kleinchroniken*, pp. 380, 389, etc.; cf. Ferjančić, *Despoti*, pp. 3–8.

48. Cf. Ostrogorski, "Avtokrator," p. 121 (=302).

49. Ibid.

50. Cf. Maksimović, "Grci i Romanija," pp. 61 ff.

51. Darrouzès, "Ekthésis néa," p. 60; cf. Djurić, "'Ekthesis néa' o patrijarhu i feudalcima," pp. 422–427.

52. M. G. Popruženko, *Sinodik cara Borila* (Sofia, 1928).

53. Ibid., pp. 81 ff. Among other personalities, the emperors Theodore Svetoslav, George Terter, and Michael Šišman, as well as mothers, wives, and daughters of emperors, were entitled to have this epithet.

54. Popruženko, *Sinodik*, pp. 81 ff. The epithet "great" was used for Asen I, John Asen II, John Alexander, and John Šišman; *hristoljubiv* belonged to Asen I and Michael Asen, as well as to Maria, the wife of George Terter; *blagoverni* was shared by the emperor Koloman Asen and Maria, the wife of George Terter. Without epithet were left, among others, the feudal lords Strez and Alexios Slav.

55. Darrouzès, "Ekthésis néa," pp. 54 ff.

56. Ibid., pp. 57, 60–62; for the meaning of the term *megas basileus* in Byzantium, cf. Ostrogorski, "Avtokrator," p. 101 (=285) ff.

57. *Actes de Zographou, Actes grecs*, in W. Regel, E. Kurtz, and B. Korablev, eds., *Viz. Vrem.* 13 (1907), *Priloženie*, nn. 23, 26, 31; J. Zepos and P. Zepos, *Jus Graeco-Romanum*, vol. 1 (Athens, 1931), p. xxv, no. 139.

58. F. Miklosich and J. Müller, *Acta et diplomata graeca medii aevi sacra et profana*, vol. 1 (Vienna, 1860), p. 439.

59. Ibid., 2:28 (doc. 345).

60. Maksimović, "Grci i Romanija," p. 73.

61. Cf. Ostrogorski, "Avtokrator," pp. 303 ff.

62. Ivanov, *B'lgarski starini*, p. 602.

Chapter 4

Some Remarks on the Chronicle of Monemvasia

Ivan Dujčev, *University of Sofia*

Since the *Chronicon Monemvasiae* was first published around the middle of the eighteenth century, it has been the subject of numerous and often detailed investigations by well-known specialists, including Sp. Lambros, C. Hopf, N. A. Bees, S. Kugeas, and P. Lemerle. These scholars have already made important contributions toward the restoration of the text and the understanding of its contents.[1] During the last thirty years, Peter Charanis has been intensively occupied with this important, yet enigmatic, document. Thanks to his numerous publications, several fundamental problems of the *Chronicle of Monemvasia* can now be considered solved. In the course of the many years of research I spent in preparation for the recently published edition of the *Chronicle*, I profited much from these Charanis publications; it therefore seems fitting to discuss them here once again in a comprehensive way.

Already in 1946 in a short essay on the question of Hellenization of Sicily and southern Italy in the Middle Ages, Peter Charanis raised fundamental problems with regard to the *Chronicle*.[2] In the same year, there also appeared an article on the Byzantine emperor Nikephoros I (802–811) with special emphasis on his policy of colonization as a measure directed against Slavic and Bulgarian threats to the Balkan peninsula.[3] Some of the historical events described in the *Chronicle of Monemvasia* took place during the reign of this emperor, who fought bravely, but without much avail, against the Bulgarians. His unsuccessful invasion of Bulgaria in the early summer of 811 and his tragic defeat on the night of 25/26 July have cast a shadow on his historical image.[4] From the Byzantine viewpoint, he was one of the most vigorous rulers, and Charanis's study is concerned with the rehabilitation of this emperor, especially with regard to those of his measures that his contemporaries did not understand and that aroused resistance in the population.

51

Three years later, this Greek-American historian published two important reviews, of S. A. Pagulatos's doctoral dissertation (1947) and of a book published in 1945 by D. A. Zakynthinos, the noted Byzantinist from Athens.[5] At the same time, Charanis also published his contribution to the active debate in Greek medieval history over the Slavic migration into Greece.[6] In this connection, Charanis examined in detail the *Chronicle of Monemvasia*, which is one of the most important, but very controversial, historical sources for these events, and he published in 1950 a detailed and well-documented study of which it can be said (although a detailed discussion is impossible here) that it is one of the best contributions to the research into the *Chronicle* from a historical perspective.[7] Charanis's discussion with K. M. Setton,[8] an essay in 1953,[9] and two further studies in 1955[10] contributed— partly by the use of additional sources in the form of numismatic findings—new elements to a positive appreciation of the *Chronicle* as a historical source. Finally, the early Bulgarian migration of the sixth century was discussed in a later study.[11] Notwithstanding the critical remarks and reservations voiced by several scholars, today the conceptions propounded by Peter Charanis about the *Chronicle of Monemvasia*, its chronological data, and its general importance as a trustworthy historical source have won acceptance.

Obviously I found Charanis's research very useful in my own preparation of a new critical edition of the *Chronicle*. I am very much obligated to Peter Charanis for his opinions on numerous details as well as on fundamental problems of the *Chronicle*. Therefore I may be permitted, as a humble Antidoron, to dedicate to this excellent historian the following remarks, which complement my edition.

Naturally, this publication from my pen should not be considered the last word on the discussion of the complex problems presented by the *Chronicle of Monemvasia*. On the contrary, it is to be hoped that it will initiate further research on this historical and literary document. In the meantime several new and interesting contributions on the *Chronicle* have appeared, and I consider it necessary to discuss them in what follows.

* * *

J. Koder has tried in a short article to clarify the problem of the *Chronicle*'s authorship.[12] Koder, on the basis of the well-known study by P. Lemerle, assumed that the passage "(Νικηφόρου)

τοῦ Παλαιοῦ τοῦ ἔχοντος Σταυράκιον" (lines 139–140 in my edition) is a "later addition."[13] Therefore, "the *Chronicle of Monemvasia* should henceforth be dated between 806 (the death of the Patriarch Tarasios) and the year 932, when Arethas of Kaisareia incorporated a part of the *Chronicle of Monemvasia*, in a scholium from his own hand in the Chronicle of Patriarch Nikephoros."[14] Proceeding from this assumption, the Viennese Byzantine scholar, Gründe, suggests for consideration, "if only as a hypothesis," "whether Arethas himself is not the author of the *Chronicle of Monemvasia*, . . . although admittedly full certainty cannot be established, probably not even by stylistic comparison."[15] With this purpose, J. Koder has collected much important data on the life of Arethas of Kaisareia and has formulated a number of observations on the language of the *Chronicle*. Inasmuch as, in my commentary, I had intentionally avoided applying linguistic criteria to the text of the *Chronicle* in order to treat them separately in another study, I consider these linguistic observations very important. Nevertheless, I can hardly accept the following assertion:

> Following the modern historiographical fashion, the redactor (i.e., Arethas of Kaisareia), did not write a chronicle, but rather an expert's report summarizing all available information on the theme of 'The Slavs and the Erection of the metropolis of Patras'. This report could have served for example, as a basis for the negotiations of the metropolitan officials and for strengthening the position of Patras (possibly against that of the Archbishops of Corinth).

The author himself obviously does not consider his argumentation totally convincing, for at the end of his analysis he says:

> In conclusion, I must admit that positive proof that Arethas of Kaisareia was the author of the *Chronicle of Monemvasia* has not been established, and probably can never be established unless essentially new elements are added to the present body of source material. Nevertheless I believe that, on the basis of the arguments to determine the author's identity cited here, it is not only possible, but it is highly probable . . . *The Chronicle of Monemvasia* will thus continue to hold its value as a source for Slavic migration into the Peloponnese.[16]

As Koder himself acknowledges,[17] the hypothesis that Arethas of Kaisareia was the author of the *Chronicle* had already been formulated by S. Kyriakidis.[18] Obviously, setting such early dates— between 806 and 932—as has been previously proposed by P. Lemerle, is very tempting. I find it unacceptable, however, for both methodological and factual reasons. The method of explaining and especially of dating a historical document by reorganizing its text must be employed very cautiously. Obviously, it is always better to keep to the text rather than assume later additions or changes. The emendation proposed by Lemerle and adopted by Koder and others—to consider the mention of Staurakios as the son of Nikephoros I as a "later addition" and to distinguish him therefore from the emperor Nikephoros II Phokas (963–969)—allows one to date the first redaction of the *Chronicle* between 806 and 932. But this involves disregarding a very important element for the dating of the *Chronicle*, namely, the mention of the city of Sirmium (in Slavo-Bulgarian Srjam [Srěm]) as a city in Bulgaria (see lines 46–47 in my edition of the text). As I have already emphasized, the term *Bulgaria* is used here only in the sense of the Bulgarian state: "Il termine Bulgaria è qui usato evidentemente non nel senso geografico, ma technicamente, in referimento allo stato bulgaro."[19] Sirmium/Srěm was the last Bulgarian fortress, and with its capture by the Byzantines in 1018 the entire Bulgarian Empire fell to the Byzantine emperor Basileios II, the Bulgar Slayer (976–1025). The mention of Sirmium as one of the cities belonging to the Bulgarian Empire is therefore only possible up to 1018, which could also be the terminus ad quem for the creation of our *Chronicle*.

A few more remarks on Koder's study: As is already evident from the title, he uses—despite Lemerle's doubts—the name "Chronicle of Monemvasia" that is customary in scholarly literature, although with reservations.

In the passage "$τά$ $εὐγενῆ$ ... $ἔθνη$" (in my edition, lines 89, 106), Koder's emendation to $ἐγγενῆ$ is, I think, excellent.[20] Further, Koder quotes the passage "$τὴν$ $Ἀ(γ)χίαλον,$ $τὴν$ $νῦν$ $Μεσίνην$" of the *Chronicle* (my edition, line 71).[21] The interpretation of this passage has presented certain problems. A superficial reading would permit the identification of these two settlements, which is unacceptable.[22] Instead of assuming a gap in the text of the *Chronicle*, one must quite simply interpret it as a mention of two different settlements.

An important contribution to the investigation of our *Chronicle*

has been given by Otto Kresten, another representative of the Viennese school of Byzantine studies.[23] This specialist in the field of Greek palaeography and history has handled the question of the authenticity of the *Sigillion* of Emperor Nikephoros I on the elevation of Patras to a metropolitan see in a broad historical framework. In doing so, he at the same time offers an explanation of those passages in the *Chronicle* that provide us with information about the policies of this emperor vis-à-vis the Slavs in the area of Patras.[24]

In order to answer the question of the authenticity of this document, Kresten then analyzes the historical sources, namely, the mention in the *De administrando imperio* of Konstantinos VII Porphyrogenetos (Chapter 49); the mention in the synodical letter of 1084, of the patriarch of Constantinople, Nikolaos III Grammatikos (1084–1111); further, in the passage of the *Chronicle of Monemvasia* (lines 173 ff. of my edition); and finally the scholium of Archbishop Arethas of Kaisareia. Among the secondary sources, Kresten used primarily the article by Peter Charanis on the emperor Nikephoros. He thereby clearly accentuates the basic tendency of this study, which is "above all . . . an attempt to restore the reputation of the Emperor Nikephoros I, who was roughly handled in the Byzantine historiography of the ninth century."

Based on rich source materials, as well as archival, literary, and diplomatic arguments, Kresten has been able to refute the doubts expressed by S. Kyriakides about the document of Emperor Nikephoros I. In his view, "Kyriakides' method of proof . . . can in no way stand up to a diplomatic and historical critique." As an important argument for his interpretation, Kresten cites "the *dorea* of Emperor Justinianos II for the Church of St. Demetrios in Thessalonike in September 688, which has been preserved in an inscription."[25] "The meaning of such a measure is clear," he writes,

since in both cases what is involved is a conscious and clearly directed economic advancement of an institution that seemed to Justinianos II as well as to Nikephoros I to be a guarantee of the preservation of imperial Byzantine interests in the outpost of the Empire which was under Slavic threat—that is, the church or her hierarchy. The strengthening of the economic base of the church must have been seen by both emperors as the most appropriate means of following a

"Byzantine" policy in an area where for awhile there was no certainty of maintaining military control. The elevation of Patras to a metropolitan see . . . can also be viewed in the similar way.

If one accepts the authenticity of the *Sigillion* of Nikephoros I, the question of the exact dates of the document (805 or 807) still remains open.[26] Here Kresten proposes "end of 805/beginning of 806."

In considering Kresten's arguments, we should not forget that the struggle against the Slavs, and of course, against the Bulgarian Empire, which was closely allied with them, was the central problem of Nikephoros I's foreign policy, and that he sought to solve this problem with all available means—both military and peaceful. Anti-Byzantine rebellions of the Slavic population in the Peloponnesos or elsewhere in Byzantine territory occurred quite frequently, although not always in connection with the Bulgarian policies of expansion toward Slavic-occupied territories. In 805 the Bulgarian Khan Krum (802–814), was involved in a war against the Avars.[27] Thus, he had no possibility of rendering effective assistance to the rebellious Slavs. Being, doubtless, accurately informed of this, Emperor Nikephoros used the favorable moment to subdue the Slavic population in the environs of Patras. In addition to military actions, this aim was also served by the conversion of the Slavs to Christianity with the objective of gradual assimilation. Therefore, the Church of Patras had an important role to play in the control of the Peloponnesian Slavs, and this sufficiently explains the emperor's efforts to raise the hierarchical eminence of this church and to restructure its organization. The "Slavic problem" remained important for many years in this portion of the Byzantine Empire; for this reason, the Byzantine state and the Orthodox church repeatedly confirmed the privileges of Patras—with a firm economic foundation, it could more successfully perform its mission among the Slavs. This explains all the measures for the "economic strengthening of the newly established metropolitan see of Patras," as Kresten has admirably shown. In my opinion, this also provides a better "explanation of the comparatively large accumulation of privileges for the metropolitan see of the northwestern Peloponnese" than the conjecture that "such a density of sources . . . could be related to a legal situation so unstable in one way or another that it required repeated interference."

Finally, the study by the Viennese Byzantinist, which I have been examining, is to be evaluated as an important contribution to the investigation of the *Chronicle of Monemvasia*. Although Kresten forgoes to intervene "in the scholarly debate over the question of the Slavic settlement of the Peloponnese since the late sixth century or in the unsettled discussion of the importance of the *Chronicle of Monemvasia* as a source," it is clear from his whole presentation that he considers this *Chronicle* as an authentic and valuable historical source. On the whole, he follows the dating hypotheses of Lemerle and Koder. He calls Koder's conclusions about the *Chronicle*'s possible author "very plausible," although he states his position with great caution:

> It should be very deliberately avoided permitting the present study to result in a demand for rethinking from this point of view the hotly debated issue of the value of the *Chronicle of Monemvasia* as a source. But a plea that Arethas of Kaisareia was the author of the *Chronicle of Monemvasia* for its part would hardly take the text out of a highly emotional debate over the question of the Slavic settlement of the Peloponnese. The assertion in the source that wide areas of the Peninsula have been dominated by Slavs for 218 years will remain controversial, one side putting it in its "contexte historique" and the other perceiving it as a "légende."

The mention in the *Chronicle* of a Strategos descended from the Byzantine–Armenian family of Skleroi has presented problems to scholars (in my edition, lines 169 ff.).[28] In a monograph devoted to this family, W. Seibt has recently discussed this question.[29] As its first representative, he mentions a Skleros of about the year 805, with this observation: "The first person who appears explicitly as Skleros in the sources played an important role in the incorporation of large parts of the Peloponnese in the Byzantine Empire." He then gives as evidence the *Chronicle of Monemvasia* (in my edition, lines 144 ff.) and also the scholium of Arethas (ibid., lines 169 ff.) and adds: "Constantine VII Porphyrogenetos essentially confirms in his work, *De administrando imperio* (c. 49) the data in both sources about the events around the year 805 without naming the strategoi." In Seibt's opinion, "the success of Skleros in military and probably also in diplomatic areas . . . must have been very extensive, since the ecclesiastical new order of the Peloponnese dates from 805. In addition, the government worked hard to settle non-Slavic peoples with the Armenians specifically mentioned." The author names the Leon Skleros mentioned by Scriptor incertus in the year 811: "I see little reason to identify this Leon with the Skleros, who worked so successfully in the Peloponnese in 805 . . . ; he is much more probably his son or nephew, who was *persona non grata* after the catastrophe of 811."[30] The unequivocal identification of the Skleros mentioned in the *Chronicle of Monemvasia* is still not possible, even after Seibt's research, but I should still emphasize the fact that he considers and uses the *Chronicle* as an authentic and reliable historical source.

We have especially Peter Charanis's studies to thank, that modern historical research in general has come to such a positive evaluation of the *Chronicle of Monemvasia*. It is to be hoped that further research[31] will confirm this positive result.

Notes

1. See I. Dujčev, in *Cronaca di Monemvasia*. "Introduzione, testo critico e note," Istituto Siciliano di studi bizantini e neoellenici. Testi e monumenti pubblicati da Bruno Lavagnini, testi 12 (Palermo, 1976), in particular pp. ix–x.

2. P. Charanis, "The Hellenisation of Sicily and Southern Italy during the Middle Ages," *American Historical Review* 42, no. 1 (1946):74–86.

3. P. Charanis, "Nikephoros I The Savior of Greece from the Slavs (810 A.D.)," *Byzantina-Metabyzantina* 1 (1946):75–92.

4. For the details, see I. Dujčev, "La Chronique byzantine de l'an 811," *Travaux et Mémoires* 1 (1965):205–254.

5. P. Charanis, "Review," *Byzantinoslavica* 10 (1949):92–93 (with the conclusion, "That there is Slavonic blood in the modern Greeks there can be no doubt, but this does not mean that the modern Greeks are Slavs. They are Greeks.") and ibid., pp. 94–96.

6. P. Charanis, "On the Question of the Slavonic Settlements in Greece during the Middle Ages," *Byzantinoslavica* 10 (1949):254–258.

7. P. Charanis, "The Chronicle of Monemvasia and the Question of the Slavonic Settlement in Greece," *Dumbarton Oaks Papers* 5 (1950):139–166. A republication of this and other studies by Peter Charanis may be found in his book, *Studies on the Demography of the Byzantine Empire. Collected Studies* nos. 7, 10, 11, 14, 16 (London, 1972).

8. P. Charanis, "On the Capture of Corinth by the Onogurs and Its Recapture by the Byzantines," *Speculum* 27, no. 3 (1952):343–350.

9. P. Charanis, "On the Slavic Settlement in the Peloponnese," *Byzantinische Zeitschrift* 45 (1953):91–103.

10. P. Charanis, "The Significance of Coins as Evidence for the History of Athens and Corinth in the VII and VIII Centuries," *Historia* 4, nos. 2–3

(1955):163–172; idem, "Hellas in the Greek Sources of the Sixth, Seventh and Eighth Centuries," *Late Classical and Medieval Studies in Honor of A. M. Friend, Jr.* (Princeton, 1955), pp. 161–176.

11. P. Charanis, "Kouver, the Chronology of His Activities and Their Effects on the Regions around Thessalonica," *Balkan Studies* 11, no. 2 (1970):229–247.

12. J. Koder, "Arethas von Kaisareia und die sogenannte Chronik von Monemvasia," *Jahrbuch des Österreichischen Byzantinistik* 25 (1976):75–80.

13. P. Lemerle, "La Chronique improprement dite de Monemvasie: Le contexte historique et légendaire," *REB* 21 (1963):16 ff., 22, 26 ff.

14. Koder, "Arethas," p. 75.

15. Ibid., p. 76.

16. Ibid., pp. 79–80.

17. Ibid., p. 80 (supplementary remarks).

18. On this, see Dujčev, *Cronaca*, pp. xxi ff. and n. 59.

19. Ibid., pp. xliv ff.

20. Koder, "Arethas," p. 76.

21. Ibid., p. 77.

22. Cf. Dujčev, *Cronaca*, p. 21 and n. 63.

23. O. Kresten, *Zur Echtheit des Sigillion des Kaisers Nikephoros I für Patras*, in press. I thank O. Kresten very much for his permission to use his manuscript.

24. See Dujčev, *Cronaca*, lines 141 ff.

25. A. Vasiliev, "An Edict of the Emperor Justinian II, September 688," *Speculum* 18 (1943):1–13; H. Grégoire, "Un édit de l'empereur Justinien II, daté de Septembre 688," *Byzantion* 17 (1944/1945):119–124.

26. Cf. the statements in Dujčev, *Cronaca*, p. 21, n. 63.

27. Cf. V. N. Zlatarski, *Istorija na bŭlgarskata dŭržava prez srednite vekove.* I, 1 (Sofia, 1918), pp. 248 ff. For the diplomatic term *Keleusis* see my note: "Un passage obscure des 'Miracula' de St. Démétrius de Thessalonique," in Dujčev, *Medioevo bizantino-slavo*, vol. 1, *Saggi di storia politica a culturale* (Rome, 1965), pp. 45 ff.

28. Cf. Dujčev, *Cronaca*, p. 21, n. 61.

29. W. Seibt, *Die Skleroi: Eine prosopographisch-sigillographische Studie* (Vienna, 1976), pp. 19 ff.

30. *Scriptor incertus de Leonis Bardae* (Bonn), p. 336, 8 ff.

31. For the quotation from Evagrios (Dujčev, *Cronaca*, p. 5, n. 5) see now the French translation of A. J. Festugière: "Evagre, Histoire ecclésiastique," *Byzantion* 45, no. 2 (1976):413–414.

Chapter 5

Important Recent Research in Byzantine-Western Relations: Intellectual and Artistic Aspects, 500–1500

Deno J. Geanakoplos, *Yale University*

Intellectual history is primarily the history of ideas and, no less important, of the feelings and attitudes constituting the dynamics for those ideas. Ideas take on most meaning, it seems to me, when viewed in the total context of the life of the society that produces them. In discussing the intellectual side of Byzantine-Western relations, what complicates matters is that one has to deal with not one but two civilizations. It is therefore necessary to understand something not only of the internal dynamics of each society's cultural development but also of the qualities of attraction possessed by the donor culture and of the degree of receptivity on the part of the borrowing society. This latter consideration, involving attitudes of one culture toward another, I consider basic in seeking to delineate the history and significance of Byzantine-Western intellectual relations.

Among the many aspects of scholarship for which Peter Charanis has long been known is his acute judgment in reviewing books. My contribution here, an attempt to survey important recent works on Byzantine-Latin intellectual and artistic relations, may then not be out of place. In this paper, I shall consider books or monographs that have appeared in the last few years, citing articles only if they offer a unique contribution or seem necessary to mention for purposes of comparison. Actually, very few books have appeared devoted exclusively to my theme. I shall therefore take into account works of wider scope in the Byzantine-Latin encounter but focus attention on the particular portions of such works dealing with intellectual matters.

The primary carrier of ideas is, of course, language. Here two studies are worthy of note, the articles of H. and R. Kahane, "Cultural Criteria for Western Borrowing from Byzantine Greek,"[1] which deal with transmission of words (and thereby concepts) from East to West. They also document transformations in the form or meaning of the terms that may have occurred during the process of transmission [one example is the French word for silk, *samit* (English, "samite"), which comes from the Greek *hexamitos*, "six-threaded"].[2]

The question of ecclesiastical relations, especially negotiations for religious union, is technically outside this survey's scope; but something should be said about such works that belong also to the realm of thought and ideas. Special sections in B. Roberg, *The Union Between the Greek and Latin Churches at the Second Council of Lyons (1274)*,[3] and in the earlier work of Y. Congar, *After Nine Hundred Years*,[4] are concerned with difficult theological terms and problems caused between the two churches because of misunderstanding of the terms' precise meanings. Some examples are *prosopon, hypostasis, substantia, vicarius, aitia,* and *metanoia.*

The councils of Lyons and Florence provided opportunities for some intellectual and, in the case of Florence in particular, theological exchange. Certain Latin treatises written before the Council of Lyons at papal request have been the subject of recent works. Thus, the tract of Humbert of Romans, *Opus Tripartitum*, which affirms that for the Greeks the chief issue over union was not theological or ecclesiastical but rather the question of the empire—Greek resentment, that is, at Western recreation of the Roman Empire in disregard of Byzantine claims.[5] An unusual article by W. Ullman bears this out, as evidenced by a confidential communication sent by the Greeks at the Council of Florence to the pope, in which they express willingness to accept papal supremacy provided the Byzantine ruler be recognized as the one true Roman emperor—a remarkably anachronistic view, revealing the unrealistic thinking persisting in certain quarters of the Greek East as late as the fifteenth century.[6] In a section of my recent study, "Bonaventura, the Two Mendicant Orders, and the Greeks at the Council of Lyons (1274)," I quote from Humbert's tract, which affirms that Western churchmen should become familiar not only with Greek theology and church history but, in particular, with Greek canon law—a remarkable suggestion I have seen expressed in no other Latin document.[7] H. Wolter and H. Holstein have translated much of Humbert's tract into French and incorporated some of Humbert's ideas into their discussion.[8]

Although I eschew reference to textual editions, mention of one such work is useful, V. Laurent's remarkable edition of the Byzantine Syropoulos's *History of the Council of Florence*.[9] This work provides for the first time a truly accurate edition of this much maligned and misunderstood Byzantine historian, who, despite his anti-Latin bias, alone gives us intimate glimpses into the innermost thoughts of the Greek delegation at the Council of Florence.

The Orthodox Churches and the West, a volume containing the papers read at the British Ecclesiastical History Society in 1975, includes several pertinent articles.[10] One is by Peter Brown, "Eastern and Western Christendom in Late Antiquity: A Parting of the Ways,"[11] in which he attributes the initial cause of the growing East-West cleavage primarily to differing views of, and emphases on, what he terms "the holy" and its relationship to the "secular"—views very similar to those he propounded in his cogent article on the causes of the iconoclastic conflict,[12] but here expressed rather less convincingly. The same volume also includes my study referred to above on Bonaventura and the Greeks at Lyons.

I turn now to political history, but only where the emphasis is on political ideology or has some connection with intellectual thought. D. Nicol's *The Last Centuries of Byzantium*, combining an emphasis on political and ecclesiastical considerations, faithfully, if at times mechanically, summarizes the views of the many monographs on this most complex of all Byzantine periods, the Palaeologan era.[13] Nicol's account could have been enriched, however, had he also discussed the changing attitudes of both societies of East and West toward each other and their cultural interrelationships—connections themselves bound up closely with political and religious developments in a period when East-West interaction was at its height.

A valuable collection of essays that has the merit of pointing out at least some such mutual attitudes for our period is *Relations between East and West in the Middle Ages*, edited by D. Baker.[14] K. Leyser's essay provides 'some speculation regarding the impact of Theophano and her Byzantine entourage on the Germany of Otto II and III, but it makes no mention of possible connections between Gerbert of Aurillac (who loomed so large in Western cultural developments of that time) and any of the Greeks who came with Theophano.[15] A. Bryer's fascinating contribution to the same volume, stresses, among other things, what he calls Byzantine "subcultures" in Serbia, Hungary, and southern Italy, in all of which certain cultural exchanges took place, some of which are still little known.[16] Bryer also (as I too do in comparing Greek attitudes to Western in my work *Interaction of the Sibling Cultures*) utilizes R. Southern's suggestion that it was only in the second generation of the twelfth century that Western intellectuals began to feel comfortable about their command of the achievement of their past.[17]

Another volume, actually a textbook but containing insights on cross-cultural intellectual phenomena, is P. Whitting, editor, *Byzantium: An Introduction*.[18] Though political and ecclesiastical events constitute the framework for the book, included also is some treatment of mutual attitudes. Thus A. Bryer's "The First Encounter with the West, 1050-1204"[19] and J. Gill's "The Second Encounter with the West, 1204-1453,"[20] examine the sharpened hostility of the two peoples during the early crusades and the fateful events of 1204 and thereafter. Bryer quotes the words of the Byzantine patriarch Nilus who, as early as the late twelfth century, could say—and I think this clearly prefigures the pro-Turkish (more accurately, less anti-Turkish than anti-Latin) attitude of Lucas Notaras before the fall of Constantinople in 1453—that subjugation to the Muslims would not force conversion to Islam, but "under Frankish rule and union with the Roman church, I may have to separate myself from my God."[21]

In the broad context of political-religious relations, I cite the vast project edited by K. Setton, *The Crusades*. Volume 3, which came out in 1975, contains two chapters of mine, "Byzantium and the Crusades, 1261-1354," and "Byzantium and the Crusades, 1355-1453,"[22] which I include here because the emphasis throughout is on delineation of the changing attitudes of the two Christian communities toward the crusades and toward each other. The failure of the last crusades of the fourteenth and fifteenth centuries was, I believe, at bottom due to Western refusal to accept papal reorientation of the crusading objective from recovering Jerusalem to saving Constantinople from the Turks, and, certainly, no less, to the inability of most Byzantines to consider a Western crusade, ostensibly coming to save them, as anything but another predatory expedition to reconquer their empire and to recatholicize them. As the Byzantine monk Joseph Bryennios put it succinctly in the early fifteenth century: "Let no one be deceived by delusive hopes that the Italian allied troops will come to save us. If they pretend to rise to defend us, they will take arms only to destroy our city, our race, and our name."[23]

On political ideology and the last period of Byzantine history, pertinent is A. Vakalopoulos, *The Origins of the Greek Nation*, volume 1, which propounds the thesis, accepted by other modern historians and especially Greek scholars, that the emergence of modern Greece as a nation dates from the first appearance of a Greek ("Hellenic") ethnic sentiment, as distinguished from a Byzantine ("Roman") one, especially after the Latin expulsion from Constantinople and the Byzantine restoration under Michael VIII in 1261.[24] I might add that a chapter of my work *Sibling Cultures* entitled "Religion and Nationalism in the Byzantine Empire" deals, in its last section, with the rise of a sense of "Greek" ethnicity in the context of the antagonism that had developed between Byzantium and the West.[25] H. Ahrweiler's little volume, *The Political Ideology of the Byzantine Empire,* sets forth much the same sort of view for this last Palaeologan period, though in the earlier part of her book she discusses various crises undergone by Byzantium from 330 onward in facing external dangers, and the Byzantine ideological response to them from a political viewpoint.[26] Both books, that of Vakalopoulos and that of Ahrweiler, are full of provocative ideas, hers concentrating purely on ideology, his offering a much fuller picture of the increasing pessimism and wretchedness of life in the last two centuries of Byzantium's existence—a fact that is to be contrasted with the amazing Palaeologan revival of the same period, the so-called Palaeologan Renaissance, of Byzantine culture. To this Palaeologan revival, its genesis and remarkable intellectual and to a lesser extent artistic influence on the West, a large section of my book *Sibling Cultures* is devoted.[27]

Obolensky's book, *The Byzantine Commonwealth*, though focusing on Byzantine-Slavic relations, articulates the significant psychological phenomenon of the Slavs' deep attraction to Byzantine culture on the one hand, and on the other, their hesitancy to come too close to Constantinople for fear of losing their own sense of ethnic identity—in other words, what he calls the qualities of "attraction and repulsion."[28]

Regarding the church, the most influential institution in the medieval period, H. Beck has an erudite chapter, "Intellectual Life in the Late Byzantine Church," in the German *Handbook of the Church* series.[29] Among other things he refers to the changed views toward Greek classical learning on the part of Byzantine churchmen and even monks in the late Palaeologan period, stressing that it was no longer so remarkable for monks, even Hesychasts, to show interest in classical letters. He shows how this attitude developed in the context of Byzantine rivalry with, and hostility to, the Latin West.

The transmission of institutions from East to West or vice versa falls into my purview because changes in mental attitudes and patterns of thought are particularly involved. Again, in my book *Sibling Cultures*, I try to analyze the phenomenon and meaning of the momentary but surprising appearance in Byzantine Nicaea of the Germanic Western institutions of ordeal by fire and judicial duel.[30] And this despite Byzantium's long tradition of Roman law. Byzantine reception of these institutions, even if not lasting, not only indicates the increasing degree of Latin influence on certain classes of the East but helps to disprove the general belief that cultural influences always flowed from East to West. In another chapter in the same book, I try to set forth the rather intensive Western theological influences of Scholasticism on Byzantine thought in the thirteenth and fourteenth centuries and the even more surprising, but less pervasive, influences of Latin classical learning on some Byzantine intellectuals such as Maximos Planudes in these same centuries. Elsewhere in my book, I set forth the limited but not insignificant influences of the Latin Church Fathers on the early Byzantine period and also on the Palaeologan era, during which time certain Byzantine Fathers were first translated or first printed in the West.[31]

D. Jacoby's article, "The Encounter of Two Societies: Western Conquerors and Byzantines in the Peloponnesus after the Fourth Crusade," deals with social and legal aspects of the Byzantine-Latin encounter in one particular Greek area occupied by Western feudal lords. The author concludes with the hope that "further study [will] seek to discover the mental patterns underlying the attitudes and behavior of individuals and classes reacting to each other in conquered areas." I could not agree more.[32]

Vogel's survey of Byzantine science in the *New Cambridge Medieval History*, although exhaustive, does not deal much with Byzantine-Western interaction in this sphere.[33] But Rose's study "Humanist Culture and Renaissance Mathematics," credits the Byzantine cardinal Bessarion with promoting the study of Greek mathematics in the Italian Renaissance, especially the works of Archimedes. Rose shows that so great was Bessarion's influence on Western humanists and mathematicians such as Regiomontanus that, during the later fifteenth century and subsequently, mathematics became in effect an integral part of the *studia humanitatis*—a view obviously in contradiction to the usual one that science held little or no appeal for Western humanists.[34]

On engineering, nothing recently has been written as useful as the older article of Keller, on the plan of Bessarion to send young Greeks to the West to learn new techniques of ship building and iron working in order to help revive the moribund Byzantine state.[35] F. Lane's even older book, *Venetian Ships and Shipbuilders of the Renaissance*, refers to a competition held in fifteenth-century Venice for the submission of new ideas for warships—a competition won by a young Byzantine who presented a plan based on the ancient Athenian *dromon*.[36] As Lane wrote, "The finest galleys built in the early 15th century were still heirs to Byzantium."[37] With respect to science and technology, it might be pointed out that Bessarion was well aware of Western advances over the Byzantine East in this respect and wanted to utilize such techniques to aid the Byzantine Empire.

With respect to education, Speck's book, *The Imperial University and the Question of the Higher School in 9th and 10th Century Byzantium*, shows that no state-supported university as such ever existed in Byzantium in the time of Photius, Constantine VII, or Constantine IX.[38] Thus the idea must be abandoned that the Byzantine state had any official educational policy. According to Speck's view, therefore, both the so-called university and patriarchal schools owed their creation and maintenance to private initiative. It has of course long been clear that the organization of the college and degree system of the modern university find their origins in the Western medieval university, certainly not in Byzantium.

Weiss's book, *Byzantine Officials and Administration as Seen Through the Works of Psellus*, fortifies Speck's conclusions, pointing out in particular that Psellus, the eleventh-century state official and professor, did not instruct in a public university but was a private teacher who enjoyed imperial protection.[39] Comparing the eleventh-century Byzantine bureaucracy with the Western, Weiss concludes that the unique character of Byzantine bureaucracy probably prevented it from having much influence on later Western bureaucratic developments.

In the increasingly studied area of the veneration of relics, nothing so important as Riant's *Exuviae Sacrae Constantinopolitanae* has been published.[40] Unfortunately, the interesting book of N. Herrmann-Mascard focuses entirely on social and legal aspects of the cult of relics *within* the West and says little of the East.[41] Geary's interesting *Sacra Furta*, now in press, will, I believe, include some discussion of the Byzantine provenience of certain relics, along with how this provenience affected the kind of reception accorded Eastern relics in various Western communities.[42]

Intellectual interaction was not always confined to the more literate classes but can at times also be discerned with respect to the lower classes. In a chapter of my *Sibling Cultures*, views of the common Greek population as well as of the Latin are analyzed as expressed probably in a hypothetical colloquy between a Greek cleric and a Latin.[43] Why, asks the Greek of the Latin, do the Latins take the cross and move about carrying it from place to place (a popular Greek misinterpretation, it seems, of the Latin practice of the stations of the Cross)? An indication of popular Greek misunderstanding of the Western cult of Mary in this period is reflected in the question of the Greek as to why the Latins call Mary "Santa Maria" ("merely a Saint," as the Greek puts it) instead of "Mother of God" (*Theotokos* in Greek). Greek scorn and spite is certainly reflected in the remarks of the Greek that Latin monks sleep all night with a woman, then in the morning make her get up, kneel before them, and entreat forgiveness for sinning. The bias of the Byzantine is so transparent as to need no comment.

Humanism, the study of Latin and Greek classical works, was probably the area in which the greatest amount of intellectual interaction took place and also the sphere most of us would think of first with respect to intellectual relations. P. Lemerle's *Le premier humanisme byzantin*, which analyzes the activities of Photius, Arethas, and Constantine VII, concentrates brilliantly on internal Byzantine cultural developments in the ninth and tenth centuries but devotes little attention to intellectual relations with the West.[44] He does, of course, mention Anastasius, the Greek-speaking librarian of the papacy,[45] and the transmission westward of the works of Pseudo-Dionysius with Maximos the Confessor's commentary, a collection referred to commonly in the West as the Dionysian Corpus.[46]

On the so-called Comnenian period of Byzantine humanism in the twelfth century, the only good, truly analytical recent work I know of is Browning's article, "Byzantine Scholarship," in which at the end he seeks to establish parallels between Byzantine developments and the French Renaissance in the twelfth century.[47] He concludes that, though there may well have been connections, developments were clearly in diverging directions. One wonders how much impact the popularity of John of Damascus's works in

the West had at this time and also what influence and effects on
the West the presence in the court at Constantinople of such
Western scholars as Burgundio of Pisa and his brother, Hugo Eter-
ianus, had.

The last Byzantine renaissance of humanism, that of the Palaeologan period, is certainly the most significant from the viewpoint
of intellectual relations with the West. Runciman's very useful
book, *The Last Byzantine Renaissance*, summarizes some of what
is known on the development of the internal aspects but makes no
effort toward integrating any of these facts with the development
of the Italian Renaissance.[48] On the question of Byzantine scholars
in the Italian Renaissance, after the work of K. Setton and myself,[49] more light has recently been shed, particularly on the
careers of several Greek scholars in Florence, Venice, or Rome,
though the last-named center and its cultural ambience await
fuller elucidation. One Byzantine intellectual repeatedly discussed
is Bessarion, on whose library L. Labowsky has published several
studies and has a book forthcoming.[50] A recent conference in
Rome on Bessarion and his influence yielded several articles, including those of Coccia and Schirò, which, although useful on his
career, provide very few new insights into the development of his
thought. Mioni's monograph on Musurus's library, on the other
hand, is of considerable value for its analysis of the significance of
his manuscripts for the Italian Renaissance.[51] In my recent book,
Sibling Cultures, I have published the complete text, with analysis
and commentary, of the discourse of the Byzantine humanist,
Demetrius Chalcondyles, on the inauguration of Greek studies at
Padua University in 1463.[52] The discourse, one of the few Byzantine to survive from the Renaissance period, throws light on this
unknown episode in the life of that university as well as on the
career of Chalcondyles himself. Chalcondyles points out to his
Venetian and Paduan audience the intellectual and political benefits the chair of Greek would have for the Venetian state and,
then, as a Greek patriot, beseeches the Venetian Signoria to aid
"prostrate Greece, suffering under the Turkish yoke like the
damned in Dante's Inferno." (This is the only Byzantine reference
I have ever been able to find to Dante's masterpiece.) Did the
Byzantines not know of Dante (something I find hard to believe),
or was it their overriding interest in the ancient Greek literature
that made them ignore a work written not even in Latin but in the
vernacular Italian?

An article by J. Seigel,[53] another by myself,[54] and a third by E.

Garin[55] discuss the career of Argyropoulos, probably the most influential Byzantine humanist in Renaissance Italy along with Chrysoloras and Bessarion. All three works emphasize that, although Argyropoulos was called to the Florentine Studium to teach Aristotelian philosophy and rhetoric, through his private teaching of the Platonic dialogues, he played a major, if not the main, role in reorienting Florentine humanism from an emphasis on rhetoric to one on Platonic metaphysics, thus paving the way for the work of Marsilio Ficino. Garin's study, focusing primarily on Argyropoulos's Florentine student Donato Acciaiuoli, after analyzing Politian's *Miscellanea* affirms that it was Argyropoulos who first revealed to the Florentines and especially to Politian the *totality* of ancient Greek thought and civilization. P. Mastrodimitri, a Greek professor, has recently written a careful, detailed biography of another Greek scholar in Italy, the little-known but active Byzantine interpreter at the Council of Florence, Nicholas Secundinos.[56]

An area of intellectual relations only now beginning to be studied is the restoration to the West of the texts of the Greek Church Fathers. In the final chapter of my *Sibling Cultures*, I make an attempt to synthesize the process of development in this restoration.[57] I concentrate on the activities of various Greek refugee scholars in Italy who edited and printed liturgical works as well as works of the Fathers, and also on Western humanists, stressing the particular reasons for Western humanistic preference (of Erasmus, for instance) for certain Greek Fathers in translating, editing, and preparing them for the press. It is no accident, I believe, that the first work of a Greek Father to be widely disseminated in the early Renaissance and subsequently to be published was Leonardo Bruni's translation of Saint Basil's *Advice to the Christian Youth on the Study of Greek Literature*, which offered support, even if qualified, for the Italian humanists' defense of their study of pagan literature.[58] Much work on the *fortuna* in the West of other writings of the Greek Fathers (as well as of the Latin) remains to be done.

The very learned and well-documented biography by J. Monfasani on George of Trebizond shows that George's notorious reputation for mistranslation of Greek classical and patristic works is largely unjustified.[59] Demonstrating the significance for Western humanism of the many translations George made for the papacy (Ptolemy's enormously important *Astronomy* from the original Greek, for example), Monfasani suggests, convincingly I believe, that Trebizond's trimming of the text of Eusebius's *De preparatio evangelica* was done on papal orders in order to extirpate the Arianism of the original.[60] More important, Monfasani shows that Trebizond's own work, *Rhetoric in Five Books*, so influenced Italian humanistic scholarship as to become the principal model for Italian and Northern humanist rhetoricians in the succeeding period. The recent work of A. Patterson on rhetoric is very disappointing from the standpoint of Byzantine-Western relations, containing no mention whatever of the provenience of Hermogenes from the Greek East and completely ignoring any Byzantine rhetorical influence on the West.[61] A chapter in the book of S. Camporeale on Lorenzo Valla convincingly proves that Valla, impressed by the Greek humanist rhetorical method as demonstrated in arguments at the Council of Florence, became convinced of the inadequacy of the Western Scholastic method and of the need to substitute for it an exegetical theology based primarily on the philology and rhetorical analysis of the biblical text, but derived, in the Byzantine manner, from the patristic commentaries. As is well known, Valla preferred the purity of Latin to the ancient Greek, which he affirmed (in the preface to his *Elegantia Latinae*) had no standard form and too many dialects.[62] Finally, an illuminating recent book by Charles Stinger on the monk Ambrogio Traversari,[63] the first Italian Renaissance scholar, apart from Bruni, to become interested in the Greek Church Fathers (he translated more than twenty Greek patristic works into Latin), shows that Traversari learned Greek not from Chrysoloras, as is usually believed, but from Demetrius Scaranus,[64] a virtually unknown Byzantine monk living in Traversari's Florentine monastery. Traversari's work not only benefited the Roman Church and furthered humanist interest in the Greek Fathers for the sake of a better understanding of the New Testament, but it helped to recover for the West a large part of the original heritage of a united Western and Greek Christendom.[65]

P. Stadter's learned article, "Planudes, Plutarch, and Pace of Ferrara," demonstrates, contrary to general belief, that the Byzantine scholar Manuel Planudes did in fact have several pupils in Byzantium as well as in Italy and therefore did exert some influence on the development of Italian humanism.[66] P. Kristeller's two masterful essays on the Renaissance and Byzantine learning in his recent volume, *Renaissance Concepts of Man*, mention, among other things, that the Italian humanist Leonaro Lianori taught Greek at Bologna University, to whose library he left some of his Greek manuscripts.[67] This fact shows, contrary to widely held belief, that even the great Scholastic university of Bologna had its circle of early humanists interested in the *studia humanitatis*.

On the subject of the Greek Diaspora to the West, the only recent work of any genuine significance known to me is Hassiotes, "The Greek Colony of Naples," in which he clearly shows that the Neapolitan Greek community, in contrast to that of Venice, had little interest in humanistic studies.[68]

Turning now more briefly to artistic relations between East and West, the one book entirely devoted to the subject is O. Demus's *Byzantine Art and the West*, which offers carefully worked-out theories on practically all questions of artistic interaction between East and West.[69] Although I cannot here consider each of his views, I might comment only on the vital question of possible Byzantine influence on Giotto and vice versa and of the rise, almost concurrently, of "realism" in both Western and Byzantine art. I think, with respect to this particular matter, that Demus, despite his usually very objective approach, somewhat overestimates Byzantine influence on the West. On this question I prefer the more cautious views of Kitzinger as expressed in his penetrating study, "The Byzantine Contribution to Western Art of the Twelfth and Thirteenth Centuries," recently republished in a collection of his essays.[70] He draws a fine distinction between the massive "direct" influences of Byzantine art and aesthetic concepts on Italian art in the twelfth century, and what he calls the more "indirect" Byzantine influences (the *maniera greca*, which he terms "a series of living impulses") that played an important, though indirect, part in bringing Italian medieval art to its great climax in Giotto. I could not agree more with Kitzinger's observation that "the whole vast problem of East-West artistic relations in the late medieval and early Renaissance period is a psychological problem of the senses and of views toward the world which encompass the whole problem of the Greek and Western world in their estrangement as well as in their kinship."

Recent general works on Byzantine art inevitably include sections on Western connections. T. Rice's *Byzantine Painting: The Last Phase* contains a short but fascinating discussion of Theophanes the Greek's bold use of highlights to express the inner light corresponding to Hesychastic belief in the uncreated light of Mount Tabor, as compared to the techniques of El Greco to express the mystical realities of the spiritual world.[71] In sections of his new book, *Byzantine Style and Civilization*, one of his best, S. Runciman attempts to combine approaches to history, art history, and aesthetic theory.[72] Thus Runciman discusses, among other problems, the interrelationships and influences between Byzantine and Western art, providing, I believe, a very effective treatment of the artistic considerations involved in the wider context of Byzantine civilization.

In C. Mango's *The Art of the Byzantine Empire: Sources and Documents, 312–1453*, I especially liked the selection about the Byzantine viewer of a Western painting who could not (apparently *would* not) understand it, because, as he affirmed, it was done in the Western (realistic) manner.[73] This observation may help us to understand better why the Macedonian and Constantinopolitan-metropolitan styles (to use the terms now in vogue) of the thirteenth and fourteenth centuries did not endure longer than they did in Byzantium.

M. Baxandall's interesting article, "Guarino, Pisanello, and Manuel Chrysoloras," discusses the influences on Italian artists of the period of Chrysoloras's ideas on art and aesthetic theory—a point that brings to mind that of Byzantine inspiration for certain of Ghiberti's sculptures in the Florentine Baptistry of which those of Solomon and Sheba are considered to symbolize the Latin and Greek Churches.[74] A. Megaw's "Notes on Recent Work of the Byzantine Institute in Istanbul" makes the striking observation (I suspect adversely adjudged by both Western and Byzantine art historians) that the art of the medieval Gothic window glazier, the technique of making stained glass, was anticipated by the Byzantines.[75] The evidence consists of pieces of stained glass remaining from the Pantocrator monastery in Constantinople. One wonders, of course, *if* this thesis is correct, why the Byzantines discontinued the use of this lovely art form, and why there seems to be no mention whatever of such a remarkable artistic achievement in any Byzantine source. To conclude, I make only an allusion to P. Underwood's massive four-volume work on the art of the Chora (*The Kariye Djami*) in which he discusses, among other things, the works of Theophanes the Greek and his school.[76] Included in the volumes are several articles by other scholars on related historical and aesthetic considerations. The best of these in my judgment are the articles by I. Ševčenko and by Meyendorff, both with many references to connections between Byzantium and Western intellectuals and theologians.[77]

In conclusion, I should like to make a few more analytical remarks on my own recent book,[78] with respect to its scope and methodology, which I believe is new (at least with regard to the prologue and epilogue) in its interdisciplinary approach of utilizing criteria both of sociology and of history. The book seeks basically to trace the development of attitudes between the two Christian societies—attitudes being the key, as I noted above, to understanding the acceptance or rejection of cultural influences on that part of each of the two societies. With Byzantine culture up to the twelfth century far more advanced than the Latin, it is not surprising that Byzantine influences were far more numerous on the West than the reverse. From 1204 and especially 1261 onward, however, despite the virtual parity finally achieved by Latin culture with Greek, and even despite the greater advance of the West in social organization, dynamism of theological speculation, and technological know-how, the Byzantines refused to take virtually anything from the West. This was primarily owing to the almost paranoid Byzantine fear, especially on the part of the lower, middle, and part of the upper classes, of renewed Latin military and ecclesiastical domination.

Among the Byzantine common people this fear manifested itself in an extremely tenacious clinging to the very roots of their cultural tradition—the writings of the Greek Church Fathers and the pronouncements of the seven ecumenical councils. The reaction of some of the upper class expressed itself differently, in a remarkable and surprising revival of interest in *ancient* Greek learning, but more intense and systematic than ever before, something which made many Byzantines, for the first time in their history, now look back on the ancient Greeks (Hellenes) as their forebears. A much smaller group, of the intellectual elite, calling to mind the original unity of Christendom with the two cultures as "siblings" (that is, fraternal heirs to the ancient Christian Roman tradition with the rivalry as well as the attraction of siblings), desired not only religious union with Rome but, in effect, the creation of a synthesis based on amalgamation of Byzantine *and* Latin cultural elements. Especially important in this respect was what these Byzantines considered to be the more dynamic Western use of Aristotle and his ancient Greek philosophical heritage. But this latter group of *Latinophrones* was too distrusted by most Greeks to affect the views of the Byzantine masses, with the result that, despite Western offers of aid—always tied however to demands for ecclesiastical union—very few Latin influences, and those only temporary, were able to affect the East.

Byzantine preoccupation with the problem of "Latinization," that is, fear of assimilation to, and even perhaps, finally, absorption by Latin society and culture, was primarily responsible, I believe, for depriving the Byzantine East of what could have been certain beneficial influences from the now more technically advanced West. The attempt to delineate such attitudes by sociologic as well as historical methods and to show the effect of these attitudes on the receptivity toward, and rejection of, cultural influences on the part of the two sibling societies throughout the course of their histories, serves as the framework for the book.

Notes

1. H. Kahane and R. Kahane, "Cultural Criteria for Western Borrowing from Byzantine Greek," in *Homage to A. Tovar* (Madrid, 1972), pp. 205–229, and articles in their *Abendland und Byzanz: Sprache* (Amsterdam, 1977).

2. Kahane and Kahane, "Cultural Criteria"; also cited in D. Geanakoplos, *Byzantine East and Latin West* (Oxford, 1966), p. 40.

3. B. Roberg, *Die Union zwischen der griechischen und der lateinischen Kirche auf dem II. Konzil von Lyon (1274)* (Bonn, 1964).

4. Y. Congar, *After Nine Hundred Years: The Background of the Schism between the Eastern and Western Churches* (New York, 1959), p. 31.

5. Humbert de Romans, *Opus Tripartitum*, in Mansi, vol. 24, cols. 109–136. Cf. A. Michel, *Das opus tripartitum des Humbertus de Romanis O. P.* (Graz, 1926).

6. W. Ullman, "A Greek Démarche on the Eve of the Council of Florence," *Journal of Ecclesiastical History* 26 (1975):37–52.

7. D. Geanakoplos, "Bonaventura, the Two Mendicant Orders and the Greeks at the Council of Lyons (1274)," in *The Orthodox Churches and the West: Studies in Church History*, ed. D. Baker (Oxford, 1976), pp. 183–211.

8. H. Wolter and H. Holstein, *Lyon 1er et Lyon 2e* (Paris, 1965).

9. V. Laurent, *Les "Mémoires" de Sylvestre Syropoulos sur le Concile de Florence (1438–1439)* (Paris, 1971).

10. Baker, ed. *The Orthodox Churches.*

11. P. Brown, "Eastern and Western Christendom in Late Antiquity: A Parting of the Ways," in ibid., pp. 1–24.

12. P. Brown, "A Dark Age Crisis: Aspects of the Iconoclastic Controversy," *English Historical Review* 346 (1973):2–34.

13. D. Nicol, *The Last Centuries of Byzantium* (New York, 1972).

14. D. Baker, ed., *Relations between East and West in the Middle Ages* (Oxford, 1973).

15. K. Leyser, "Byzantine-Western Relations in the Tenth Century," in ibid., pp. 29–63.

16. A. Bryer, "Cultural Relations between East and West in the Tenth Century," in ibid., pp. 77–94.

17. Bryer, "Cultural Relations," p. 79, citing R. Southern, *The Making of the Middle Ages* (London, 1953), pp. 210, 220.

18. P. Whitting, ed., *Byzantium: An Introduction* (New York, 1971).

19. A. Bryer, "The First Encounter with the West, 1050-1204," in ibid., pp. 83-110.

20. J. Gill, "The Second Encounter with the West, 1204-1453," in ibid., pp. 111-134.

21. Bryer, "First Encounter," p. 103.

22. K. Setton, *The Crusades*, vol. 3, *A History of the Crusades* (Madison, 1975), chap. 2, pp. 27-68, and chap. 3, pp. 69-103.

23. See in N. Kalogeras, *Mark Eugenikos and Cardinal Bessarion* (in Greek) (Athens, 1893), p. 70. Cited in D. Geanakoplos, *Interaction of the Sibling Byzantine and Western Cultures in the Middle Ages and Italian Renaissance* (New Haven, 1976), p. 16, which also cites such other views.

24. A. Vakalopoulos, *The Origins of the Greek Nation: The Byzantine Period, 1204-1461* trans. I. Moles (New Brunswick, N.J., 1970).

25. Geanakoplos, *Sibling Cultures*, chap. 2, pp. 36-54.

26. H. Ahrweiler, *L'idéologie politique de l'Empire byzantin* (Paris, 1975).

27. On the Palaeologan Renaissance, see Geanakoplos, *Sibling Cultures*, esp. Prologue and Epilogue, pp. 17-22 and 284-287; also, passim.

28. D. Obolensky, *The Byzantine Commonwealth: Eastern Europe, 500-1453* (New York, 1971).

29. H. Beck, "Intellectual Life in the Late Byzantine Church," in *Handbook of the Church*, ed. H. Jedin et al., vol. 4 (New York and London, 1970), pp. 505-512. Other chapters by Beck, on more strictly theological and ecclesiastical matters, are included.

30. See Geanakoplos, *Sibling Cultures*, chap. 7, "Ordeal by Fire and Judicial Duel at Byzantine Nicaea (1253): Western or Eastern Legal Influence?" pp. 146-155.

31. Geanakoplos, *Sibling Cultures*, esp. chap. 4, "Western Influences on Byzantium in Theology and Classical Latin Literature," pp. 95-117, and chap. 14, "The Last Step: Western Recovery and Translation of the Greek Church Fathers and Their First Printed Editions in the Renaissance," pp. 265-280; also in the Epilogue.

32. D. Jacoby, "The Encounter of Two Societies: Western Conquerors and Byzantines in the Peloponnesus after the Fourth Crusade," *American Historical Review* 78 (1973) esp. 891, 903 ff. For comment on Jacoby's statement see Geanakoplos, *Sibling Cultures*, pp. 306-307.

33. K. Vogel, "Byzantine Science," in *New Cambridge Medieval History*, vol. 4, pt. 2, chap. 28 (Cambridge, 1967) pp. 265-306.

34. P. Rose, "Humanist Culture and Renaissance Mathematics: The Italian Libraries of the Quattrocento," *Studies in the Renaissance* 20 (1973):48-105. See also his "The 'Mechanica' in the Renaissance," *Studies in the Renaissance* 18 (1971):76 ff.

35. A. Keller, "A Byzantine Admirer of Western Progress: Cardinal Bessarion," *Cambridge Historical Journal* 11 (1953-1955):343 ff.

36. F. Lane, *Venetian Ships and Shipbuilders of the Renaissance* (Baltimore, 1934).

37. Ibid., p. 56.

38. P. Speck, *Die kaiserliche Universität von Konstantinopel: Präsierungen zur Frage der höherischen Schulwesens in Byzanz im 9. und 10. Jahrhundert* (Munich, 1974).

39. G. Weiss, *Oströmische Beamte im Spiegel der Schriften des Michael Psellos* (Munich, 1973).

40. P. Riant, *Exuviae Sacrae Constantinopolitanae*, 3 vols. (Geneva, 1877–1904).

41. N. Herrmann-Mascard, *Les reliques des saints: Formation coutumière d'un droit* (Paris, 1975).

42. P. Geary, *Furta Sacra: Theft of Relics in the Central Middle Ages* (Princeton, 1978). I have not yet seen the published book.

43. Geanakoplos, *Sibling Cultures*, chap. 8, pp. 156–171.

44. P. Lemerle, *Le premier humanisme byzantin* (Paris, 1972).

45. Some scholars now believe that Anastasius was not Greek.

46. On Maximos the Confessor's commentary on the Pseudo-Dionysius's works, see now Geanakoplos, "Maximos the Confessor and His Influence on Eastern and Western Theology and Mysticism," *Sibling Cultures*, chap. 6, pp. 133–145.

47. R. Browning, "Byzantine Scholarship," *Past and Present* 28 (1964): 3–20.

48. S. Runciman, *The Last Byzantine Renaissance* (Cambridge, 1970).

49. K. Setton, "The Byzantine Background to the Italian Renaissance," *Proceedings of the American Philosophical Society* 100 (1956):1–76, and D. Geanakoplos, *Greek Scholars in Venice: Studies in the Transmission of Greek Learning from Byzantium to the West* (Cambridge, Mass., 1962), repr. as *Byzantium and the Renaissance: Greek Scholars in Venice* (Hamden, Conn., 1973).

50. L. Labowsky, "Bessarion Studies," *Medieval and Renaissance Studies* 5 (1961):108–162. On another aspect of Bessarion's career, see the careful, scholarly work of Z. Tsirpanlis, *To Klerodotema tou Kardinaliou Bessarionos gia tous Filenotikous tes Benetokratoumenes Kretes (1439–17os aionas)* (Thessalonica, 1967).

51. E. Mioni, "La biblioteca greca di Marco Musuro," *Archivio Veneto* 43 (1971):5–28.

52. D. Geanakoplos, "The Career of the Byzantine Humanist Demetrius Chalcondyles at Padua, Florence, and Milan," chap. 13 in *Sibling Cultures*, pp. 231–253; Latin text on pp. 296–304 and English trans. on pp. 254–263.

53. J. Seigel, "The Teaching of Argyropoulos and the Rhetoric of the First Humanists," in *Action and Conviction in Early Modern Europe*, ed. T. Rabb and J. Seigel (Princeton, 1969) pp. 237 ff.

54. D. Geanakoplos, "The Italian Renaissance and Byzantium: The Career and Influence of the Byzantine Humanist John Argyropoulos in Florence and Rome (1415–87)," in *Conspectus of History*, vol. 1-1, *Focus on Biography* (Muncie, 1974) pp. 12–28.

55. E. Garin, "Donato Acciaiuoli, Citizen of Florence," in *Portraits from the Quattrocento*, chap. 3, trans. V. Velen and E. Velen (New York, 1973).

56. P. Mastrodimitri, *Nikolaos Sekoundinos (1402-1464). Life and Work* (in Greek) (Athens, 1970).

57. Geanakoplos, *Sibling Cultures*, chap. 14, "The Last Step: Western Recovery and Translation of the Greek Church Fathers and Their First Printed Editions in the Renaissance," pp. 265-281.

58. Ibid., pp. 270-271.

59. J. Monfasani, *George of Trebizond: A Biography and a Study of his Rhetoric and Logic* (Leiden, 1976).

60. Compare the similarities in Geanakoplos, *Sibling Cultures*, p. 272.

61. A. Patterson, *Hermogenes and the Renaissance: Seven Ideas of Style* (Princeton, 1970).

62. S. Camporeale, *Lorenzo Valla: Umanesimo e Teologia* (Florence, 1972).

63. C. Stinger, *Humanism and the Church Fathers: Ambrogio Traversari (1386-1453) and Christian Antiquity in the Italian Renaissance* (Albany, 1976).

64. On Scaranus, see also Geanakoplos, *Sibling Cultures*, pp. 60, 267.

65. Geanakoplos, *Sibling Cultures*, chap. 14, pp. 265-281.

66. P. Stadter, "Planudes, Plutarch, and Pace of Ferrara," *Italia medioevale e umanistica* 16 (1973):137-162.

67. P. Kristeller, *Renaissance Concepts of Man* (New York, 1972), pp. 64-110.

68. J. Hassiotes, "Hellenikoi Epoikesmoi sto Basileio tes Neapoles," *Hellenika* 22 (1969):116-162.

69. O. Demus, *Byzantine Art and the West* (New York, 1970).

70. E. Kitzinger, "The Byzantine Contribution to Western Art of the Twelfth and Thirteenth Centuries," *Dumbarton Oaks Papers* 17 (1963): 25-48.

71. T. Rice, *Byzantine Painting: The Last Phase* (New York, 1968). Cf. further on Theophanes and the light of Mount Tabor in Geanakoplos, *Sibling Cultures*, p. 90, and especially p. 311, n. 39.

72. S. Runciman, *Byzantine Style and Civilization* (Harmondsworth, 1975).

73. C. Mango, *The Art of the Byzantine Empire: Sources and Documents, 312-1453* (Englewood Cliffs, N.J., 1972), especially pp. 253-254.

74. M. Baxandall, "Guarino, Pisanello, and Manuel Chrysoloras," *Journal of the Warburg and Courtauld Institutes* 28 (1965):197 ff.

75. A. Megaw, "Notes on Recent Work of the Byzantine Institute in Istanbul," *Dumbarton Oaks Papers* 17 (1963):333-372.

76. P. Underwood, *The Kariye Djami*, 4 vols. (New York, 1966-1975). See vol. 4, *Studies in the Art of the Kariye Djami and Its Intellectual Background* (1975).

77. I. Ševčenko, "Theodore Metochites, the Chora, and the Intellectual Trends of His Time," in Underwood, *Kariye Djami*, 4:17-91, and J. Meyendorff, "Spiritual Trends in Byzantium in the Late Thirteenth and Early Fourteenth Centuries," in ibid., pp. 93-106. See also the articles of J. Meyendorff,

"Society and Culture in the Fourteenth Century," and of I. Ševčenko, "Society and Intellectual Life in the Fourteenth Century," in *Actes du XIVe Congrès International des études byzantines, 6-12 Septembre 1971* ed. M. Benz and E. Stefanescu (Bucharest, 1974), pp. 144 ff. and 81 ff., respectively.

78. Geanakoplos, *Sibling Cultures*.

Chapter 6

Two Letters of Athanasius I, Patriarch of Constantinople: An Attempt at Reinterpretation

A. P. Každan, *Dumbarton Oaks*

Two Letters of Patriarch Athanasius I, Numbers 103 and 94 in A.-M. Talbot's Edition[1]

Letter 103

The subject of Letter 103 is the great crime, or fault ($\tau o \tilde{v}$ $\sigma \varphi \acute{\alpha} \lambda \mu \alpha \tau o \varsigma$ $\tau \grave{o}$ $\pi o \lambda \acute{v}$), committed by a certain Glykys and his associate, who have provided a most despicable creature ($\tau \tilde{\omega}$ $\dot{\alpha} \nu \alpha \iota \delta \varepsilon \sigma \tau \acute{\alpha} \tau \omega$) with means of escape. The patriarch asks for the emperor's clemency toward the two men, who had been led astray by carelessness and had not fully understood the wicked deeds of the impious fellow. V. Laurent[2] has identified Glykys (Mr. "Sweet") as the impostor John Drimys (Mr. "Bitter"), who had organized a conspiracy around 1305, claiming to be a descendant of the Lascarids. According to Laurent, Athanasius had given Drimys this name *féru d'antonymie*—a pun, I may remark, which would not have been typical of our writer. Talbot, following her teacher, Ihor Ševčenko, rejects this identification with good reason.[3] In her turn, she identifies Drimys—about whom Athanasius writes in Letter 81—with the associate of Glykys, that is, with the anonymous traitor of Letter 103. Talbot's identification is based upon five similarities that she finds between Drimys and the unnamed traitor, and which I will reproduce in the author's order:

1. Both men received many benefits from the emperor but ungratefully turned against him.
2. Both men were connected with the Lascarid party: Drimys pretended to be a descendant of the family, and Glykys appears to be a ward of John II Lascaris.
3. Both men disregarded sworn oaths.
4. The anonymous traitor had "mocked at divine things," whereas Drimys claimed to be a priest.
5. Athanasius used the same phrase to describe the treachery in the two letters.

These five "similarities" do not appear to be well founded. The similarities mentioned in the first and third points appear to be mere fortuities, inasmuch as the events mentioned here are rather trivial. Fortuitous, too, is the last purported similarity. The two sentences cited by Talbot coincide in only one modified quotation from the Gospel of John 13:18: πτέρναν ἐπάραι, a phrase that may also be found in other of Athanasius's letters.[4] Points 2 and 4 refer to simply illusive similarities. To mock at divine things and to pretend to be a priest (Point 4) are not at all similar things. In Point 2, Talbot establishes a similarity, not between Drimys and the anonymous partner of Glykys, but between Drimys and Glykys himself, thus committing an apparent *mutatio elenchi*. Even this mutated collation does not work, for Mr. "Bitter" claimed to be a descendant of the Lascarids, whereas Mr. "Sweet" was no more than a ward of the last Lascarid emperor. The case of Glykys has nothing in common with the conspiracy of Drimys.

There is, however, another of Athanasius's letters that does display a real parallelism to the epistle concerning Glykys. That is Letter 51, in which the patriarch asks for the emperor's clemency toward the men who inadvertently allowed the Christianized Turk Paxes to escape from prison. It is easy to see that the crime, or fault, of Glykys and his unnamed partner was quite the same: they allowed an enemy to escape. Letters 103 and 51 have not only a similarity in general content but also a number of identical details, phrases, quotations, and epithets. Thus, Athanasius cites 3 Kings 21:42: ἄνδρα ὀλέθριον, "a man appointed to destruction" (Letter 51.3), which Talbot has conveyed as "abominable fellow" in Letter 103.4, without reference to the Biblical text; in both letters, Athanasius stresses that he is undertaking his mission on behalf of the culprits together with the bishops (Letters 51.9, 103.40–41). The escaped convict is described in both letters as βδελυρός ("abominable man") (Letter 51.13) or "an object of abomination" (Letter 103.27). This abominable fellow disregarded the many favors he had received: πολλῶν τῶν εὐεργεσιῶν (Letter 51.24) or τοσούτων εὐεργετημάτων (Letter 103.28); this wretch mocked holy baptism: τοῦ θείου λουτροῦ ἐκμυκτηριστὴν ἀναφανέντα (Letter 51.25) or τῷ θείῳ λουτρῷ ἀναιδευσάμενον (Letter 103.28). In both letters, Athanasius cites a long quotation (although with some differences) from 2 Pet. 2:22, comparing this apostate to a sow who loves to wash by wallowing in the mire and to a dog who loves to take his fill of his loathsome vomit (Letters 51.26–28 and 103.29–30, 32–33). According to Athanasius, in both cases discussed in the two letters, the well-disposed servants have not discovered the malice of the apostate: δόλον . . . μὴ ὡς δέον φωράσαντας (Letter 51.15) or τὸν δόλον . . . μὴ φωράσαντα (Letter 103.35–36).

In sum, we may suppose that Glykys, a good servant (εὔνουν δοῦλον in Letter 103.34–35), was one of the good servants (θεράποντας ἀγαθούς) mentioned in Letter 51.13. Caught up in lethargy and torpor (Letter 103.6–7), or in ignorance and drunkenness (Letter 51.15), he allowed the barbarian Paxes to escape from prison. He was not involved in the conspiracy of Drimys.

Letter 94

According to the editor of Athanasius's letters, Letter 94 presents several difficulties. She tries to struggle with them through an unusual number of emendations, which seem to be necessary if grammatical sense is to be made of the text. If I am not mistaken, these emendations appear mostly in the English translation, not in the Greek text. As far as the text is concerned, there is, except for a normal erasure of a duplicated τούτου (line 15), only an addition of πάσας (line 16), which does not seem necessary to me. The original οὐδὲ μόνη μιᾷ τῶν τότε πληγῶν, ἀλλὰ πάσαις ἐξικνουμένην is comprehensible, if not grammatically correct: certainly, in classical Greek, ἐξικνέομαι governed the accusative, but Athanasius might use it with the dative as well.[5] Although in the Greek text there is this unique—and far from obligatory—emendation, one will find nine additions, corrections, and question marks in the English translation. Let us inquire whether all of these are necessary and whether they help provide the correct interpretation of the letter.

The beginning of the letter is quite clear. Athanasius, after comparing the emperor to Moses (which is traditional in Byzantine rhetoric),[6] entreats him to deliver the Orthodox people from the grim tyranny of the Sicilian (lines 10–14). The word "Sicilian" refers, according to Talbot, to the Catalan leader Roger de Flor.

Talbot interprets, with some reservations, the key section of the letter (lines 17–26) as follows: "I (or: he) possess no other defense against the frightful death that awaits him, against the merciless and cruel <angel> which is going to hasten him to the separation of his soul, than to grasp my (or: his) beard in my (or: his) hands, and to say to <the angel>, 'This gray hair, which you see,

O angel of God, I made white, anointed and broadened with patriarchal excommunications and curses.'"[7] And the angel brings to
the Sicilian the following <verdict>: "Thou, aged 'fool, in this
night' (I mean in the darkness surrounding him), 'thy soul shall
be required of thee.' And then 'whose shall be' the things which
you thought to appropriate for yourself?"

The angel's response includes a quotation from Luke 12:20,
with the addition of the word "aged," and a short commenting
phrase: "I mean, in the darkness surrounding him." Talbot's
translation of this phrase seems to me preferable to Laurent's
paraphrase, "Celui qui a entouré cet autre de ténèbres" (Laurent
means God).[8] The Greek text says: τῷ περιέχοντι τοῦτον σκότῳ.
Talbot interprets περιέχοντι as a participle agreeing with σκότῳ,
whereas Laurent understands σκότῳ as a dative depending on
περιέχω ("surround with darkness").

Talbot's interpretation of the above section meets with an ob-
stacle the editor herself has already noted: if this interpretation
is correct, then Roger de Flor is described as an old man, although in reality he was a young man when he perished. The
editor's explanation, that Athanasius was foreseeing Roger's
death in old age, sounds strained. One might further ask whether
the entire scene, in which the patriarch shows his beard to the
angel or even grasps the angel's (!) beard, makes any sense. Let us
attempt to understand this section otherwise, as a dialogue, not
between the patriarch and the angel of God, but rather between
the patriarch and the messenger (ἄγγελος) of the Sicilian, whom
Athanasius ironically calls an angel of God. In this case, the tenor
of the text would be approximately the following: I possess no
other means (ἐφόδιον), wrote the patriarch, against his forthcoming (or: appointed) frightful marching out (τῆς προκειμένης
φρικτῆς ἐκείνου ἐξόδου), which is going to urge (κατεπείξειν) the
separation of the soul in the merciless and cruel future (πρὸς τὸν
μέλλοντα . . . ἀσυμπαθῆ καὶ ἀπότομον).

Let us consider the two interpretations of Athanasius's text.
If my understanding is correct, death has been menacing not the
Sicilian ("awaits him," as has been translated by Talbot), but the
patriarch himself. In this case, there is no longer any need to add
"angel" in the translation, and the words "merciless and cruel"
appear to agree with τὸν μέλλοντα, "the future."

Thus, the patriarch wrote that he possessed no other means
against his own death but to grasp his beard in his hands. It is
to be understood that the patriarch pointed at his gray beard,

entreating for clemency or sympathy. To the Byzantines, the beard was "a most . . . manly symbol."[9] and grasping one's beard would naturally be a gesture of beseeching. This interpretation of the phrase can be confirmed by the exchange between the patriarch and the "angel." Athanasius reminds the "angel of God" of the excommunications and curses that have made his beard white, enriched, and broad—in other words, gray and neglected. Athanasius continued that the "angel" will answer, giving no way to clemency, "You aged fool, in this night you will die (literally: Thy soul shall be required of thee)." This quotation from the Gospel ($\tau\dot{\eta}\nu$ $\psi\upsilon\chi\dot{\eta}\nu$ $\sigma\upsilon$ $\dot{\alpha}\pi\alpha\iota\tau\upsilon\tilde{\upsilon}\sigma\iota\nu$ $\dot{\alpha}\pi\dot{o}$ $\sigma\upsilon\tilde{\upsilon}$), is closely connected to the above-mentioned threat of the separation of the soul ($\tau\tilde{\omega}$ $\delta\iota\alpha\chi\omega\rho\iota\sigma\mu\tilde{\omega}$ $\tau\tilde{\eta}\varsigma$ $\psi\upsilon\chi\tilde{\eta}\varsigma$). The only word added to the quotation, except for the short comment, is "aged" ($\gamma\eta\rho\alpha\lambda\acute{\epsilon}\epsilon$), and this addition stresses that the man threatened with death was old, in all probability the patriarch himself.

Thus, even if one identifies the Sicilian of Letter 94 with Roger de Flor (I cannot say anything pro or contra this identification), it is clear that this letter does not contain any hint of the forthcoming murder of the Catalan leader.

Notes

1. Alice-Mary M. Talbot, *The Correspondence of Athanasius I, Patriarch of Constantinople: Letters to the Emperor Andronicus II, Members of the Imperial Family, and Officials*, Dumbarton Oaks Texts, 3 (Washington, D.C., 1975).

2. V. Laurent, *Les regestes des actes du Patriarcat de Constantinople*, vol. 1, *Les actes des Patriarches*, fasc. 4 (Paris, 1971), no. 1637.

3. Talbot, *Correspondence*, p. 431.

4. Cf. ibid., Letter 61.79.

5. In this sentence, I should like to connect $\tau\iota\nu\dot{\alpha}$ with $\tau\tilde{\omega}\nu$ $\pi\lambda\eta\gamma\tilde{\omega}\nu$, and translate, not "comparable to the plagues," but "comparable to one of the plagues." This, however, is a trifle.

6. Cf. Talbot, *Correspondence*, p. 445.

7. Talbot has understood the Greek $\dot{\epsilon}\lambda\acute{\iota}\pi\alpha\nu\alpha$ to mean "anointed," which does not make any sense. It is better to translate "enriched": cf. "nourrie," in Laurent, *Regestes*, no. 1608.

8. Laurent, *Regestes*, no. 1608.

9. Eustathius of Thessalonica, quoted in Ph. Koukoules, *Vie et civilisation byzantines*, 4: 358.

Chapter 7

Saints and Society in the Late Byzantine Empire

Angeliki E. Laiou-Thomadakis, *Rutgers University*

The period of the late-thirteenth and the fourteenth centuries was one in which seminal changes were taking place in the Balkans. At the economic and social level, the spread of quasi-feudal relations and the existence of a dependent peasantry is a common characteristic in the Greek, Serbian, and Bulgarian lands.[1] At the same time, there is still an active economy of exchange, supported on the net of commercial relations that developed in the eastern Mediterranean under the leadership and influence of Italian merchants. At the political level, the two most important sets of events are the progressive decentralization of political authority and, after the 1340s, the spread of Ottoman domination in the Balkans. All of these developments created a fluid situation, which in the church was reflected in a series of crises, the most important being the dispute over church union with Rome and the Hesychast controversy.

The period was also one in which a considerable number of people attained sainthood. Both the question of church union and the practice of and dispute over Hesychasm created Orthodox martyrs or apologists, some of whom were later canonized. Furthermore, this was a time in which monastic life was active, and a number of monastic establishments were founded; the founders of monasteries were often canonized in the Byzantine Empire. A considerable number of saints' Lives, both published and unpublished, have survived from this period and are very useful sources for social history. The richness of this type of source both for Byzantine and for Western medieval history has long been recognized. Saints' Lives are a relatively popular literary genre, and they are concerned not only with the thoughts and beliefs but also with the actions and activities of saints. Therefore, they give a precious insight into everyday life and can provide valuable information about social conditions. Also, the description of saints' activities is a valuable guide to the norms of their society, for, in the Middle Ages, saints were considered as individuals who had attained the highest level of perfection. Direct information about saints, that is, who they were, and how and why they became saints, is as important as the indirect information the sources provide about social matters.

This study is limited to the Balkans of the late-thirteenth, fourteenth, and fifteenth centuries and is based primarily on the lives of sixteen saints.[2] Three of these (Athanasios, patriarch of Constantinople; Meletios; and Germanos Haghiorites) were born early enough in the thirteenth century to have lived through the period of the unionist policy of Michael VIII; one, Damianos, died in 1281, before the pro-unionist policy was reversed. Most of the other saints were active in the fourteenth century. Four of them (Romylos, Athanasios of Meteora, Dionysios Athonite, and Niphon) lived in the second half of the century, Saint Niphon dying in 1411. Saint Philotheos lived in the late-fourteenth and first half of the fifteenth century. These Lives provide information for the late period, which is rather poor both in narrative and in documentary sources, and are particularly valuable for this reason. All of the saints studied here were monks, most of them— with the exception of Saint Meletios and possibly of Saint Philotheos—spending at least some time on Mount Athos. Several also founded monastic establishments, either small ones, like that founded by Athanasios, patriarch of Constantinople, or more ambitious ones. Dionysios and Athanasios of Meteora founded two major monasteries, Dionysiou on Mount Athos and Meteora, respectively. Saint Gregory of Sinai was responsible for the establishment and growth of a large monastic community in Paroria, in Bulgarian territory.[3] A few of the saints attained high positions in the ecclesiastical hierarchy: Saint Athanasios became patriarch of Constantinople twice (1289-1293 and 1303-1309). Saint Isidore also was patriarch of Constantinople (1347-1350), whereas Saint Gregory Palamas was archbishop of Thessaloniki, and Arsenios was metropolitan of Veroia. The domination of Mount Athos over the spiritual and religious life of the Byzantine Empire, and to some extent over the rest of the Balkans, is immediately obvious.

Usually, the first piece of factual information given in a saint's Life concerns his country or city of origin and his parentage. For the most part, the saints we are concerned with originated from Thrace, Macedonia, and other areas in the southern Balkans. Saint Gregory Palamas was born in Constantinople, although

his parents were from Asia Minor. Saint Philotheos the Athonite
was born in Chrysopolis, in Macedonia, east of Kavalla; but his
parents also were refugees from the town of Elateia in Asia Minor
and had fled to Macedonia for fear of the Turks. Thessaloniki,
the second city of the empire, could boast of three of the most
important Hesychast saints, Savas the Young, Germanos, and
Isidore, whereas Saint Athanasios, patriarch of Constantinople,
was born in Adrianople. More outlying provinces of the empire
and small towns also produced some saints: Niphon was born in
the small village Loukove in Epirus; Dionysios came from the village Korysos near Kastoria; Athanasios of Meteora was born in
Neopatras, in Greece proper. Meletios and Maximos were from
Asia Minor, from Theodotou, a small and little-known town on
the Black Sea coast, and from Lampsakos, respectively. Gregory
of Sinai was also born in Asia Minor, in a town near Klazomenes.
Romylos was born in Vidin of a Greek-speaking father and a
Bulgarian mother; we do not know the birthplace of another
Bulgarian saint, Kosmas.[4] The authors of saints' Lives tried to
specify their hero's birthplace and to glorify it as much as possible. The patriarch of Constantinople Philotheos Kokkinos (1353–
1354, 1364–1376), who wrote the Lives of Gregory Palamas,
Savas the Young, Germanos, and Isidore, could justly wax enthusi-
astic about the renown of Constantinople and Thessaloniki. The
latter city in particular, being Philotheos's own birthplace, was
glorified by his pen as the mother of great men—military, civil,
and religious leaders, intellectuals, and monks. Concerning Adrianople, the biographer of Saint Athanasios of Constantinople
could say that this city had, of old, been a populous one, and
therefore, worthy of his subject. But Meletios's biographer was
forced to admit that the saint's birthplace had been unknown
before his birth and received its glory only through him.[5]

The Lives also commonly give some information about the
parents and family of the saint. This kind of information lends
itself to hagiographic commonplaces, so that one might regard
it with some suspicion. For the saints' Lives of this period, however, suspicion would be entirely unjustified. These are true accounts about men who were still remembered by contemporaries,
and although some of the hagiographers (specifically Philotheos)
would much prefer their subjects to stem from the aristocracy,
they do not let this predilection interfere with historical truth.
Where the information can be checked from other sources, it
proves to be accurate. The only commonplace seems to concern

the saints' parents' moral character—they are invariably good men and women.

A surprising number of saints come from highly placed families. Gregory Palamas's parents were, we are told, very rich; they were noble (*eugeneis*), his father was a member of the Constantinopolitan Senate, and the young man himself had easy access to the palace and came under the protection of Emperor Andronikos II after his own father's death.[6] The father of Saint Germanos Maroules was a high official in Thessaloniki, performing both financial and judicial functions. It is possible that he came from Asia Minor, with the victorious Nicene armies, and he may even have functioned as governor of the city. The family itself was a well-known, aristocratic one.[7] Saint Savas's parents also formed part of the upper class of Thessaloniki, whereas Saint Isidore sprang from a clerical family, originally from Chios; although he does not seem to have been as rich as the other saints mentioned above, the family was comfortable and well-known.[8] The family of Athanasios of Meteora appears also to have belonged to the provincial aristocracy of Greece; we are told that his parents were illustrious, and greater than their contemporaries.[9] Meletios's parents, in Asia Minor, are described as particularly pious and philanthropic. Their acquisition of wealth and prominence (his father became an official in the army) is attributed to their piety. This may be an indication that the family was not, originally, a rich one but became so in the course of time.[10] As for the great Hesychast saint, Gregory of Sinai, his family too is said to have commanded both wealth and prominence in Asia Minor.[11] On the other hand, the biographers of Maximos and Kosmas refer to their subject's "noble" parents with a vagueness that may suggest that the nobility is somewhat less pronounced than the author would want it to be.[12]

If several saints originated among the aristocracy, a few others came from families that are commonly described as living "in conditions of self-sufficiency" (*en autarkeia*). This is specifically said of Saint Romylos and Saint Dionysios, of whose parents we are also told that they made their living from the land. Saint Athanasios of Constantinople was clearly a poor man, and his biographer, Kalothetos, was moved to remind his audience that the rich will not enter the kingdom of heaven. Niphon's father was a priest. We do not know the condition of Saint Philotheos's family while his parents were still living in Asia Minor; but when they moved to Macedonia, they led a very harsh life, being "strangers

and *paroikoi*," and without protector after the father had died.
The term *paroikoi* may here be taken either in its technical sense
("dependent peasants"), or in a more general sense that would
describe the family's rootlessness in the area.[13]

The most striking fact that may be observed here, is that, with
the possible exception of Philotheos, none of the saints originated
from very poor families, or from the largest segment of the population, the dependent peasantry. We do know that dependent
peasants became monks and entered the monasteries of Mount
Athos, but they do not seem to have become conspicuous enough
to reach the summit of their world, sainthood. To some extent
this is due to the fact that a number of the saints were canonized
because of their active role in the ecclesiastical controversies,
where a certain education was necessary. This is particularly true
of the Hesychast saints, of whom Saint Gregory Palamas is the
most obvious example: he was well educated and well connected,
and thus his defense of Hesychasm could have a strong impact
both in the church and in the imperial circles. The same is true
of saints who served as advisers of emperors: Saint Isidore and
Saint Savas, like Saint Maximos, were men who were close to
John VI Kantakouzenos and John V, who advised them on important matters and foretold the future to them.[14] Is it by chance
that Kantakouzenos, the representative of the highest aristocracy
and a man with a most clear class consciousness, used as his advisers some of the most aristocratic of saints?[15]

As for the companions and disciples of the saints, their background was, perhaps, more variegated than that of the saints
themselves. Once again, we find a number of members of the
aristocracy or, more generally, of good families. Saint Germanos
had with him his nephew, a doctor who studied at Constantinople
and who shared his aristocratic background. With Gregory Palamas,
we find Dionysios, a man from the Constantinopolitan upper
class (*tōn eupatridōn*) who had become a Hesychast monk.[16] Saint
Gregory of Sinai had in his entourage people from different social
backgrounds: Gerasimos was from a rich and noble family of
Nigroponte; his compatriot, Joseph, a highly educated man, also
appears to have come from a rich family. On the other hand, there
was a man named Markos, from Klazomenes, who, we are told,
was so humble that even in his venerable old age he preferred to
work in the kitchen and the bakery at Mount Athos. There was
also a Bulgarian named Klemes, who had been a shepherd, and in
his simplicity had been blessed with visions of the divine light. He

is described in very positive terms as a simple man, with no intellectual curiosity, whose only concern was with God, and who became a good Hesychast monk. This is one of the rare cases in which a poor and ignorant man is presented as being a disciple of an important saint.[17]

The information about the family background of saints includes some facts of demographic significance. The number of cases is not sufficiently large, nor is the information itself complete enough, to be of true statistical significance. Nevertheless, some indicators may be discerned. First of all, it may be noticed that saints have a longer-than-average life span, with two extreme cases dying at the ages of ninety-six (Niphon) and nearly one hundred (Athanasios of Constantinople).[18] This is clearly the result of a bias selection in the sources; to become a monk on Mount Athos, a man had to be at least in late adolescence, as he had to have a beard; and in order to become a priest, he had to be at least thirty years old. By then, he was past the most dangerous years, those of infancy and early childhood, and his chances of surviving to old age had improved over those of the population as a whole. Furthermore, to become a patriarch, or a saint, a man had to be old enough to have acquired renown; the saints are drawn from a pool of people that was distinct from that of the population at large, being composed of men who had reached a relatively advanced age.

The saints' families, however, were subject to the same problems as the rest of the population. Several of the saints lost one or both of their parents while they were still children or adolescents. The father of Athanasios, patriarch of Constantinople, died when the saint was an adolescent, as did Saint Philotheos's father; Athanasios of Meteora lost his mother at his birth and his father soon thereafter. A monk named Euthymios, who was a disciple of Athanasios of Constantinople, was also orphaned while he was still a baby. Saint Gregory Palamas lost his father when he was seven years old; his mother died much later, when he himself was little over thirty.[19] His parents had had four children after him, in the space of seven years: there were three boys and two girls in the family. One brother and one sister died when Palamas was in his early thirties; they themselves must have been just over or just under thirty years old; his last sister, Theodote, died sometime between 1338 and 1341, when Palamas was between forty-two and forty-five years old; she was in her mid- or late thirties.[20] This family history is not far removed from the fourteenth-century

demographic patterns observable elsewhere;[21] what is exceptional
is the fact that Palamas's family became extinct, for all five children of Constantine and Kallone lived a monastic life and never
married. Other saints too came from large families. Thus, Isidore
had four brothers and five sisters, all younger than himself, and
Germanos had seven siblings, three male and four female. Presumably, even more children were born but did not survive long
enough to be counted; Isidore himself almost died in early childhood.[22]

The Lives also provide some interesting information about the
education the saints received, and thus about the educational
system in the cities and provinces of the Byzantine Empire. In
Thessaloniki, Constantinople, Vidin, even in Asia Minor in the
first half of the fourteenth century, the children of the upper
class were sent to teachers (*grammatistai, paideutai*), who taught
them grammar, poetry, history, rhetoric, and logic.[23] Teaching
was done not only privately but also in schools. The Lives of
Saint Romylos and Saint Isidore discuss such schools, in which,
it seems, the majority of the students was as interested in creating
mischief as in studying. Saint Isidore taught at such a school,
which was attended, we are told, not by poor children, but rather
by the sons of rich and renowned families.[24] Saint Gregory of
Sinai, in his small Anatolian town, managed to read widely in the
Scriptures and became a calligrapher, an art he later practiced on
Mount Sinai; but we know nothing more specific about his education. Saint Philotheos learned his sacred letters only when he
entered a monastery.[25]

A curriculum of studies is discussed in the Life of Saint Isidore;
it may be a somewhat atypical one because he was the son of
a priest. First he learned his sacred letters, an education that
lasted until he was sixteen years old. Then he studied "profane
wisdom," that is, rhetoric, grammar, and poetry. His biographer,
Philotheos Kokkinos, was particularly interested in the details
of Isidore's education, as well he might be; for he himself had
studied in the same city of Thessaloniki, under the learned Thomas
Magister.[26]

Education, however, was quite expensive: two of the saints,
Athanasios of Meteora and John, bishop of Heracleia, had to
listen secretly to the teachers who were giving lessons to the
children of the upper class.[27] In the countryside, or in small
provincial towns, and for the children of poor parents, secular
education was not easily accessible. They were taught a few letters,

mostly from and for reading sacred books. A poor early education was not an absolute barrier to advancement in the church, or to sainthood; but it was considered a misfortune, which some individuals tried to correct. Thus, Saint Maximos, although we are told that his parents were important people, had learned some sacred letters but was weak in grammar. When he appeared at the court of Andronikos II and began to astound his audience with his knowledge of the Scriptures, he was scorned by Theodore Metochites, one of the most learned men of his day; the saint then abandoned the palace and sought the company of the patriarch, Athanasios I, himself a poor man who had read much theology but who had little secular education and was, according to his own testimony, corroborated by that of his contemporaries, rather uncultured in his speech and his writings. Others, like Theodosios, the brother of Saint Dionysios, acquired their education later in life; he went to Constantinople at the time of Andronikos II, when intellectual activity was substantial, and there he acquired both a sacred and a profane education, which allowed him to become metropolitan of Trebizond.[28] The first half of the fourteenth century was a period characterized by such intense intellectual activity that it has been called the Palaeologan Renaissance. It is, therefore, not surprising that the education of the young should seem important to the society and that it should be easily available. Nevertheless, it was an education that was concentrated in the cities and that was limited to boys of the upper class. Girls did not go to the same schools as boys, and there is no evidence of how they learned their letters. It is obvious that some rich ladies did manage to get an education: the patriarch Philotheos of Constantinople complains of Constantinopolitan ladies of high birth who took part in discussions and arguments and who showed a sceptical attitude with regard to miracles.[29]

Life in the Byzantine Empire and the southern Balkans, especially in the second half of the fourteenth century, is to be seen against a background of insecurity created by the invasion of hostile peoples and by a growing political instability. The Lives of saints of the period give a picture of almost unrelieved gloom, a picture that becomes progressively bleaker as the century draws to its close. Because this study is limited to the Balkans, Asia Minor is not discussed, although the hagiographic sources for this area, too, are interesting and show the Christian population living in difficult conditions and exposed, among other things, to piratical raids, razzias, and enslavement.[30]

In the early fourteenth century, the relative peace of the reign of Andronikos II was shattered by the incursions of the Catalans who, with their Turkish allies, devastated Thrace and then (after 1307) Macedonia before moving to Thessaly. Men fled before their onslaught; cities and villages were emptied of their inhabitants. Andronikos II, unable to send an army to Mount Athos, wrote to the monks asking them to leave the unfortified monasteries and either enter those that were protected or go to the cities; the road to Thessaloniki from Mount Athos was almost entirely closed because of the incursions and the threat of further attacks.[31] Thus it was that Saint Savas, unable to return to his native city, left by sea for a long pilgrimage to Jerusalem. Many monks left the Holy Mountain, to go to islands, cities, or mountains as they would do with increasing frequency in the course of the century.

The only other important political event of the reign of Andronikos II that is reported in our hagiographic sources is the capture of the city of Neopatras by the Catalan leader, Alfonso Fadrique, in 1319. At that time, Saint Athanasios of Meteora was a young boy; he was captured by a "Frank," who was taken by his handsome and pleasant demeanor and wanted to send him to his homeland—presumably as a slave. This is a concrete example of the fact, known from other sources, that Catalans used to send Greeks captured at war to Italy and Sicily as slaves.[32]

Piracy was active in the Aegean in the fourteenth century. Striking evidence of its importance early in the century is given in the life of Saint Athanasios of Constantinople. When, after his second abdication, in 1309, he tried to get from the city to his monastery in Xerolophon, he barely escaped a piratical attack just outside the walls of the capital.[33] Whereas in the early fourteenth century most of the pirates had been Greeks or Italians, the Turks begin to replace them within a few decades.

The first mention of Turkish attacks on Mount Athos (not counting the joint Catalan-Turkish enterprise) comes in 1325. The Turks came suddenly, presumably by sea, attacking the monks, especially those who lived outside the monasteries, and taking many prisoners. Several monks then left; among them was Saint Gregory Palamas, who went to Thessaloniki with eleven others. Among them also was Saint Gregory of Sinai with his disciples, including his biographer Kallistos, and Saint Isidore. Gregory Palamas and his friends, as well as Gregory of Sinai, planned to sail to Jerusalem. But instead, Palamas stayed in Thessaloniki, while Gregory of Sinai and Kallistos left for Chios after two months; then they sailed to Lesbos, and finally to Constantinople, where they were well received by Emperor Andronikos II. Six months later, they sailed to Sozopolis and from there went to Paroria. At the time of this raid, Saint Germanos left his hermitage and entered the monastery of Lavra, which was fortified.³⁴ A similar raid took place in 1335, at which time some monks, among them Athanasios of Meteora, left Mount Athos for good; he went to Thessaloniki and then to Veroia and Servia. It was probably on this occasion that Gregory of Sinai, who had returned to Mount Athos, found it necessary to seek refuge in the walled premises of the Great Lavra. Feeling uncomfortable with the cenobitic life, he left again and went to Paroria where he built his monastic community.³⁵

In Paroria, too, the presence of the Turks was soon felt. In the early 1340s, the Byzantine governor of Skopelos, near Saranta Ekklesies in eastern Thrace, wrote to the monks who were living in the monasteries built by Saint Gregory of Sinai in Paroria to leave or to hide in fortified places because the Turks were coming to hunt; five years later, the Turks came again, attacked the town, and stole the animals of the monks; at this point, the monks left, burning the tower, while Saint Romylos went further into Bulgaria, where he would feel safer.³⁶

In the late 1340s and the 1350s, a number of piratical Turkish incursions are attested against Mount Athos. Their aim seems to be plunder, and the capture of hostages, some of whom were important personalities. Thus Theodosios, the *higoumenos* of the monastery of Philotheou, was seized on 25 March 1348, was taken to Brusa, and was later ransomed. In 1354, the Turkish pirates took many captives in Mount Athos, and, outside Gallipoli, they captured Gregory Palamas, who spent some time in Asia Minor, and has left us some very important documents from his captivity. The ransom that was demanded for him seems to have been very high; it was paid either by John VI Kantakouzenos, who was no longer emperor, or by unnamed Serbs.³⁷

The battle of the Maritsa, on 26 September 1371, was a watershed for the history of the Balkans. The Ottoman attacks now became massive, on land and by sea. For Mount Athos, it was the death of John Uglješa, who had restored the Serbian church to the patriarchate of Constantinople, and who had kept a measure of peace in western Macedonia, that seemed threatening. The monks became apprehensive, and many of the hermits began to leave. It was at this time that Saint Romylos went to Valona, where he tried to instill some Christian love into the souls of the inhabitants, whom his biographer calls "raw and beastly." The fears of the monks were far from misplaced: in 1372 or 1373, the Ottomans launched a great attack against the Holy Mountain; they brought a number of ships, and machines for besieging the fortified monasteries. The grand *primmikerios* John, who was charged with the defense of the area, did not dare to attack the Turks; he only came to the defense of the monks when three Venetian ships arrived and struck an alliance with him. It may be on the strength of this common action that his brother Alexios later requested, and received, Venetian citizenship.[38] It is, of course, indicative of the decline of the Byzantine Empire that, at a moment of great danger, Mount Athos could only be rescued by the Venetians, not by the Byzantines themselves. A further Turkish invasion, in the early summer of 1378, resulted in the capture of the still-small monastery of Dionysiou; the monks and their possessions were carried away, and its founder, Saint Diony-sios, was forced to go to Asia Minor and ransom his brothers, using the money given him by Alexios III, emperor of Trebizond, for the needs of the monastery.[39]

In the late-fourteenth century, too, the Turks began the prac-tice of *devshirme*: they collected Christian boys, converted them to Islam, educated them into Turkish customs, and used them in the army. Saint Philotheos and his brother, whose family had fled Asia Minor to escape the Turks, were now taken into captivity, although soon thereafter they managed to escape and flee to a town named Neapolis, where they entered a monastery. At the time, the boys were young enough to be called *paides* by the hagiographer; presumably, they were around fifteen years old. If the editor of the Life is correct in her assumption that Philotheos's family had arrived in Macedonia sometime before 1380 or 1387, then the capture must have taken place at the latest in 1395 or 1402, and probably earlier than that. Thus, this text is one of the earliest sources for the history of the *devshirme*.[40] The mechanics of the collection of child-tribute are also interesting, for the Life claims that normally one boy was taken from each family, whether the family had two, three, or even ten children. Even so, says the hagiographer, there was difficulty in collecting the tribute, since apparently the relatives were able to raise objections, sometimes successfully. It was the saint's particularly unpleasant fate to have no close male relatives to protect him, and thus it was that both he and his brother were taken. The text also indicates that young boys could find refuge from the *devshirme* in monasteries, as Saint Philotheos and his brother did; this was a double monastery, and their mother was soon able to join them. Saint Philotheos had one further recorded encounter with the Turks when, much later, a Turkish ship tried to attack him and his three students in their habitation, near the monastery of Dionysiou; but the saint prayed, and there was a storm that confused and dispersed the enemies.[41]

The hagiographic sources do not give much more information about the Turkish conquests of the late-fourteenth and fifteenth centuries. They do record the martyrdom of Arsenios, the metropolitan of Veroia, who was killed by the Turks when they captured his city. This event must have taken place during one of the several occasions in which the Turks took and retook Veroia, that is, in 1386, or in the period between 1389 and 1394, or sometime around 1430; but it is not possible to be more precise about the date.[42]

The ravages wrought by the Turks were supplemented by disorders and incursions wrought by others. The attacks of the Serbs on Byzantine Macedonia are mentioned only twice: in 1331, the Serbs made several incursions in the area near Veroia, taking many prisoners and burning villages; in 1347, the victorious Stephen Dushan went to Mount Athos to persuade Gregory Palamas to join him, offering the saint many churches, cities, and revenues.[43] There is, too, an allusion to a possible Bulgarian attack on Thrace.[44]

Brigandage was endemic in this period, particularly in frontier areas or in areas remote from centers of power. The region of Paroria was infested with particularly unscrupulous robbers and murderers, who terrorized the monks and hermits living there. A peculiar story, recounted in the Life of Saint Gregory of Sinai, shows the brigands in the pay of a monk, a rival of the saint, who paid them to capture Saint Gregory and his disciples. This must have taken place during the saint's first trip to the area, after 1325. When he returned, several years later, to build his monastic community, he once again found "many robbers and thieves," who apparently carried out their work completely unhindered. The monks were very frightened, and many were forced to disperse. It was Ivan Alexander, tsar of Bulgaria (1331–1371), who was finally able to bring the brigands under control. He built a great tower in the area, and threatened the brigands with military action. The monks also received from him landed possessions, lakes and fisheries, oxen and sheep and beasts of burden, which apparently they were able to enjoy for a while, unmolested by the brigands.[45]

Brigands were also active in Greece; the monks who lived in Meteora were constantly attacked, despite their great poverty.[46] Later in the century, we find the area around Valona described as a barbarous, wild place, whose local leaders (*toparchai*) were unjust and murderous. The political anarchy that prevailed in the countryside is evident: both the area around Meteora and the Dalmatian coast were governed by local lords, with no evidence of any kind of central control.[47] The provinces in general, outside Thrace and Macedonia, are described as barbarous. Thus, Saint Savas, passing through Athens, sought in vain to find in this poor and barbarized town evidence of its ancient glory. The poverty of Greece was thought to extend to religious matters as well. Gerasimos, the disciple of Saint Gregory of Sinai, spread the practices involved in Hesychasm to Greece, much as though he were importing a new doctrine to a backward area. He was, we are told, particularly appropriate for this kind of work because he was familiar with the dialect of the people of Greece. The inhabitants of Lemnos, also, were considered to be "barbarous in mores," and uncultivated; at least this was how Gregory Palamas found them, and during his stay there he tried to civilize and correct them. Among the provinces, only the Morea appears in the hagiographic sources as a rich, populous civilized area.[48]

Natural disasters add to this picture of decline and insecurity. Apart from occasional poor crops, two more serious famines are attested. Sometime between 1335 and 1346, the monks who lived in Paroria could find nothing to eat except some rye, which they boiled in water. Another time the monks, who lived in solitude on Mount Athos and who depended on the various monasteries for their sustenance, were in great need of food. We are told that there was a great famine, but this is probably not true; for it seems that the monks inside the monasteries had bread at least, and so did those who held *adelphata* from the *monasteries*. At that time, Saint Romylos sent his disciples to *buy* food, which suggests that food, although scarce, was in fact, available. This second crisis seems to have taken place sometime just after the civil war between John VI Kantakouzenos and John V Palaiologos, when the agricultural production of Macedonia was destroyed.[49] A major plague hit Lavra sometime in the middle of the fourteenth century, killing such a great number of monks that Saint Niphon was called into the monastery from his cell to serve as a priest because there were very few priests left. This is a reference either to the Black Death itself or to a recurrence of it a few years after its original outbreak in 1347.[50] There was a great plague in Lemnos in 1349 and another one at Mount Athos several years later.[51]

It will be noticed that many of the man-made and natural disasters that are mentioned in the hagiographic sources fall in the second half of the fourteenth century. This is also the conclusion that one can reach from other sources. It is primarily with the civil war between Kantakouzenos and John V, and with the installation of the Turks on Byzantine soil, that conditions in the southern Balkans become dangerous and extremely uncertain. The earlier period, despite some famines and incursions, is one of perhaps chronic but not acute crisis. This is evident, among other things, from the fact that individuals could, in the early period, communicate or travel over long distances with relatively little difficulty. The travels of fourteenth-century monks and saints were so extensive that they could easily form the subject of an entire study. A few points may be retained here. In the second half of the thirteenth century and the early part of the fourteenth, monks travel easily, over great distances. Athanasios I was able to go from Adrianople to Thessaloniki and Mount Athos, and from there to sail to Jerusalem. On his way back, he visited several monasteries in Asia Minor: Mount Latros (near Miletus), Mount Auxentius, Mount Galesion (near Ephesus), and Ganos in Thrace. Then he reached Constantinople.[52] At about the same time, Saint Meletios went from his small Pontic village to Palestine, Mount Sinai, Syria, and returned from Galesion to Constantinople by boat; John, later bishop of Heracleia, traveled from his own town in the Black Sea to Nicaea and then, after 1261, to Constantinople.[53]

Saint Savas was probably the most widely traveled of the saints. Leaving Mount Athos soon after 1307, he sailed to Lemnos, Lesbos, Chios, Patmos, Cyprus, Jerusalem, and then went to Mount Sinai, Damascus, and Antioch; returning to Constantinople, he was shipwrecked in Crete and spent some time traveling in Nigroponte, Peloponnesos, Athens, and Patras. Then he took a ship to Tenedos and found his way to Constantinople and Mount Athos. He sailed again to Constantinople in 1342, at the time of the Hesychast controversy; on both his trips to the capital, he found there a number of people from his native city of Thessaloniki.[54]

Almost as widely traveled was Gregory of Sinai. After being freed from his captivity in Laodicea, he went to Cyprus and afterward to Mount Sinai, where he stayed for three years, then traveled to Jerusalem, Crete, and Mount Athos. When he was forced out of the Holy Mountain by the Turkish attacks, he sailed to Constantinople and then to Sozopolis. Communication between Constantinople and Mount Athos in the 1320s and 1330s took place primarily by sea, as did communication between Sozopolis and Constantinople. It was even possible—although highly unpleasant—to sail from Constantinople to Mount Athos in the deep of winter.[55]

Traveling by sea from the Morea to Constantinople seems to have been relatively easy in the period from 1341 to the end of 1344, when Isidore was bishop-elect of Monemvasia. A number of people from his diocese went to Constantinople, mostly, it appears, for trading purposes, although some may have served in the fleet as sailors. They were able to bring him three hundred gold coins as partial payment of the revenues of his see. His biographer insists on the importance of the commercial activities of these Moreots; we are, perhaps, seeing here those Monemvasiot merchants, known from other documentation, still able to function in the 1340s.[56]

There is also evidence of some travel between Epirus, Greece, and Macedonia. Nicholas, disciple of Saint Gregory of Sinai, traveled from Athens to Mount Athos early in the fourteenth century; Saint Niphon traveled from Epirus to Mount Athos sometime after 1335; Saint Athanasios went to Meteora at the same time; an old man traveled from Meteora to Constantinople in the 1340s. Job, who had been *higoumenos* of Lavra, found refuge in Greece after his resignation, sometime after 1281.[57]

After the 1340s, there is no more evidence of long trips such as those undertaken by Savas or Gregory of Sinai. Within the Byzantine Empire, it is clear that, at least until 1371, communications remained open between Constantinople and the provinces. Monks seem to have moved freely and fairly regularly throughout Macedonia and Thrace, but much of this travel was caused by the need to find a haven against invaders, and much of it was interrupted by pirates. Saint Romylos and his friends were almost constantly on the move between Trnovo and Paroria in the period 1335–1346, chased by famine and brigands. He settled down on Mount Athos but in 1371 was on the move again, first to Valona and then to Ravanica, in Serbia. Even after the catastrophe of 1371, he was able to send a letter from Valona to an old man in Constantinople and get an answer. Saint Athanasios of Constantinople had already been attacked by pirates after 1309; in 1354, Saint Gregory Palamas was captured by them; Saint Dionysios was harassed by them on his travels from Constantinople to Trebizond in the 1370s.[58]

The social and economic structure of the late Byzantine Empire is, to some degree, visible in the saints' Lives. This was a highly stratified society, in which the differences between the poor and the rich were becoming greater and more visible. The church functioned both as the richest institution and as the institution that occasionally tried to relieve the worst effects of poverty through the distribution of alms or of justice.

The social history of the late Byzantine Empire is dominated by the spread of feudal or quasi-feudal relationships, and social relations are primarily those between great landlords and peasants. But there were also economic relations that were not primarily feudal, as there were groups that did not make their living from the land. In the late-thirteenth century, we are told of various groups of people in need who went to visit Saint Meletios in Mount Auxentius: soldiers, peasants, shepherds, hunters, fishermen. The interesting point in this list is, of course, the inclusion of some soldiers (*stratiotai*) among the poorer social groups; these people do not have the privileged position the term usually implies.[59] The existence of hired agricultural labor in the Balkans in the second half of the thirteenth century is specifically attested in the Life of Saint Germanos. His father, who was a rich man, lived in Thessaloniki but had vineyards outside the city. He hired laborers, whom he paid—presumably in cash—and who appear to have lived in Thessaloniki (perhaps even at his house) and set out for the fields in the morning.[60]

Among the trades, that of builder is mentioned fairly frequently. Michael VIII, we are told, asked the people of Constantinople to work to extend and strengthen the seawalls in case of an attack from the West (1269–1270). The laborers who worked there, even the unskilled ones, were paid in cash.[61] Builders are also mentioned in the Life of Saint Meletios, and in the 1370s, when they are hired to build the monastery of Dionysiou. Smaller huts and cells on Mount Athos and in the monasteries of Saint Gregory of Sinai were built with the labor of the monks themselves.[62] Tailors are mentioned, from villages near Mount Athos, and a man who worked gold and silver into the sacred garments; he exercised his profession in Thessaloniki.[63]

The extensive economic activity that the Black Sea area witnessed during the fourteenth century is illustrated by the Life of Saint John the Young. Saint John was a Greek merchant from Trebizond, who traveled, for trade, on a "Frankish" ship and landed in the Cimmerian Bosporus. There he was handed over to the Tatars by the captain of the ship and was later executed. The date of this event is approximately 1344/1345. The saint's profession and his travel aboard an Italian ship confirm what we know from documentary sources. Commerce in the Black Sea area was very brisk in this period and was dominated by the Venetians and the Genoese. Greeks from the towns of the littoral, however, did participate in that trade, either on their own or in cooperation with the westerners. Of course, in this particular case, the cooperation broke down rather violently.[64]

Living conditions in the Byzantine Empire of this period were harsh for a large part of the population; at times of wars and invasions, crisis conditions prevailed. One of the worst famines attested for Constantinople broke out during the winter of 1306/1307, and the biographers of Athanasios I describe the terrible spectacle of people lying in the streets of the city, dying of famine. They describe also the patriarch's efforts to alleviate the famine by running soup kitchens and distributing clothing to the poor. In general, Athanasios I was deeply concerned with the poor of the city and with the oppression practiced by the rich, the aristocracy, the friends and relatives of the emperor.[65]

Social conditions in the empire in general, and in Constantinople itself, deteriorated further during the civil war of 1341–1347. The biographer of Patriarch Isidore provides a good summary of some of the most important effects of the war. The state and the people had been much impoverished, for taxes had not been collected, lands had lain uncultivated, and property had been destroyed. There was permanent damage, that is, the destruction of people and property and the loss of lands to the Serbs and the Turks. There was also damage that in theory was reversible, that is, the loss of revenues.[66]

Not only did the productive resources of the empire decline during and after the war; there had also taken place a certain redistribution of properties and incomes among the people who had been active during the conflict. With the advent of peace, those who had seen their properties seized and confiscated wanted them back, whereas those who had profited from the war did not want to lose what they had gained. This created disorder among the aristocracy, or, as Philotheos put it, among the army and the members of the senate. It is clear that these people pressed increased claims upon a state whose resources had been considerably diminished.[67]

In these circumstances, the patriarch was supposed to play a double role. For one thing, he was expected to act as a mediator among people with conflicting claims; a graceless task, which, apparently, gained Isidore no friends. On the other hand, the patriarch also assumed the by-now-familiar role of judge and protector of the poor. We are told that he not only gave alms but tried to protect the orphans and the widows from the unjust acts of the rich, the imperial officials, and even of the emperor himself. Poverty seems to have been very widespread at this time. Although the church itself, in its role as landowner, was responsible for much of the poverty, especially in the countryside, in the cities individual churchmen, and particularly the patriarch, were trying to minimize social conflict by dispensing justice and alms.[68] In these conditions, begging was frequent and to some degree organized: we hear of the existence of permits for begging, which were granted by Athonite monks for legitimate causes.[69]

As might be expected, the Lives of fourteenth-century saints provide a certain amount of interesting information concerning life in the monasteries, the economic basis of monasticism, and the particularities of the Hesychast experience. Much of this information is deliberate. For example, it is a commonplace that saints, and monks in general, had an extremely poor diet and few clothes and that the Hesychast monks lived a life full of privations. Nevertheless, some important points appear, along with the commonplaces.

In terms of the economic organization of monastic life, the most important element to be found in the saints' Lives has to do with the difference between the activities of monks living in monastic communities and those monks who preferred to live in solitude, outside the monasteries. That the Byzantine monasteries, and especially those of Mount Athos, formed important economic units with extensive interests in agriculture and commerce is well known. A little information concerning these activities can be found in the Lives. The rich monastery of the Great Lavra is specifically mentioned as an institution in which lay concerns were of the first order of importance. The patriarch Philotheos, biographer of Saint Germanos, discusses the activities in which the monks of Lavra had to engage because the monastery itself

was a large and populous one and was, from the beginning, one
that cared not only for the spiritual but also for the bodily life of
its members. The monks of Lavra engaged in agriculture; they
traded, by land or by sea, in small numbers or in groups; they
"ruled over" lands and small towns, whose taxes they collected;
and they found it necessary to send embassies to emperors and
other rulers. In the late-thirteenth century, the *higoumenos* of
Lavra, Job, tried to reform the polity of the monks, and according to the Life of Saint Germanos, his reforms had the aim of
reducing the worldly concerns of the monastery. For this reason,
the reforms were opposed by the monks who lived outside the
monastery and by a group of those inside, who thought that the
innovations would lead to catastrophe.[70]

Not only Lavra, but all monasteries, were involved in worldly
activities. Saint Dionysios, who had himself been a solitary monk
on Mount Athos, when his disciples increased in number, found
for them a cultivable area in which they built their cells and a
church and started to cultivate vineyards. Soon they acquired a
small boat with which to import wheat and other necessities.
With funds furnished by some monks and especially by some
laymen, Dionysios built a tower to protect his monks from the
Turks. By 1366 the small monastery already had some landed
possessions, which later increased. Saint Athanasios, the founder
of Meteora, who had been a Hesychast monk, found it necessary to distribute some vineyards to his monks; but he did not
allow them to possess money or to sell their surplus of wine,
wheat, or oil.[71] Saint Gregory Palamas, the apologist of Hesychasm, voiced a certain amount of opposition to the ownership
of wealth, not by monasteries so much as by individual monks.
Monastic wealth, expressed in terms of great warehouses filled
with wheat and wine, he considered to be God's treasure house;
but wealth owned by individual monks, he considered to be
totally incompatible with a monastic life.[72]

Many of the monks living in solitude, whether in Mount Athos
or elsewhere, in theory and sometimes in practice rejected ownership of anything for themselves. Some, like Saint Maximos Kausokalybes, who was considered a trifle unbalanced by his contemporaries, spent years foraging for food; he is said to have spent ten
years eating nothing but chestnuts, acorns, and weeds. Other
monks occasionally brought him food: bread, wine, fish, octo-
pus.[73] A poor monk (*penes*) once brought Saint Niphon some
millet, the most meager gift of food possible. Gifts of oil and

fish always seemed welcome to the solitaries.[74] The Hesychast monks expected to be fed either through the labor of their disciples or through the charity of the monasteries. Thus, Saint Romylos spent a great deal of time fishing for the food of his superiors; another of the solitary monks of his day used to send his disciple to work in the bakery of a monastery in exchange for bread. Saint Dionysios spent three years on Mount Athos begging for food, as did Saint Athanasios of Meteora for an undetermined length of time. Some monks who lived outside the monasteries were supported through the grant of *adelphata*; but Saint Romylos was not able to get one from Lavra because he had only recently arrived there.[75]

It is clear from the sources that, if some solitary monks did, in fact, practice poverty, there were others who did not. The Life of Saint Maximos mentioned a number of monks who had a certain amount of cash; one had sixty *hyperpyra* and another one, ninety ducats, both fairly considerable sums of money. Others appear to have practiced a trade on Mount Athos itself and received pay for their work. Such was Saint Germanos, who was a calligrapher, was paid for his labor, and according to his *Vita*, kept nothing for himself, giving all the money to his superior to distribute to the poor. This latter statement, however, may well be a hagiographic *topos*.[76] Even from these sources, whose concern is to show the sanctity and the otherworldliness of the saints, it is clear that the monasteries of the fourteenth century had an active economic life, a monetized one, and one that produced a considerable surplus.

We have discussed above some aspects of life in the late Byzantine Empire as they appear in hagiographic sources. As important is the ideology these sources project, especially the class attitudes that can be attributed either to the saints themselves or to their biographers. The ideology of the monks, and specifically of the Hesychasts, was one that glorified poverty.[77] In most of the Lives, the personal poverty of the saint is stressed as an example of his withdrawal from worldly affairs. Individual poverty—as opposed to the wealth of monastic institutions—is upheld as a virtue, and in some instances monks are specifically castigated for owning money. Yet if poverty is a monastic and saintly virtue, in the rest of society it is wealth and power that are admired. The saints' Lives almost invariably take a positive view of wealth when discussing the saint's family background. The hagiographers are also interested in pointing out that their heroes influenced the upper classes, and they specifically mention visits paid to the saints by members of the aristocracy, imperial officials, or rich and powerful individuals.[78] The class divisions of late Byzantine society, and the developing class consciousness of the aristocracy are evident in these sources.

Particularly important in this connection are the four published Lives written by Philotheos Kokkinos. Philotheos was not, himself, a member of the aristocracy. He was born in Thessaloniki of poor parents and paid for his education by serving as a cook for Thomas Magister. Nevertheless, this man, who became patriarch, had a highly developed class consciousness, a respect and admiration for the aristocracy, and fear and contempt for the people. This is most evident in the Life of Saint Savas and that of Saint Isidore, in both of which he describes the civil war of 1341–1347 and its aftermath. The Zealots of Thessaloniki he qualifies as a mob, specifying that they were neither of the aristocracy nor of the "second and middle" class. The war itself he describes as a tempest (*trikymia*), and as an irrational (*paralogon*) struggle; irrationality (*alogiston*) is a quality he ascribes to the people, as opposed to the aristocracy. Elsewhere, speaking of the persons who visited Saint Germanos, he says in some surprise that the saint welcomed them all, even if they were "from among the vulgar and coarse ones, and those who make their living from the land. . . ."[79] Even in their performance of miracles, the saints of Philotheos favored the aristocracy: the great majority of their miracles were performed for members of the upper class. This is particularly the case with Saint Gregory Palamas and Saint Isidore, both of whom served as high members of the secular clergy, lived in cities, and were in close contact with the Byzantine aristocracy. Saint Gregory Palamas performed a number of miracles—mostly cures—for aristocratic families from Thessaloniki and from the rest of Macedonia, Adrianople, and Thessaly; one particularly rich and powerful family from Veroia, that of Tzimiskes, was honored with three miracles. Only in one case was the recipient of the saint's benevolence a poor woman.[80] Saint Isidore was somewhat less selective. He was kind to the poor, distributed money to them, and tried to soften the exactions and injustice to which the poor were subjected. After his death, he was able to cure a poor priest and a poor woman who was paralyzed and was so indigent that both she and her children were in danger of dying of hunger. But most of his important miracles were primarily reserved for the rich and powerful, such as the bishop of Rhodes, a nun, and the empress herself.[81] His most interesting miracles were performed for a man from Peloponnesos, named Nikolaos.

Nikolaos was a member of the aristocracy who had moved to Constantinople along with his family and who became one of the supporters of John VI Kantakouzenos during the civil war. To this man Isidore sent some olive oil, given to him by a Monemvasiot (? a Peloponnesian, anyway) merchant. In a not unusual miracle, the oil increased so much that it spilled out of the jars and out of the house and into the streets, where people collected it! At the time of the civil war, and before John VI had entered Constantinople, Nikolaos went out of the city to join him. According to Philotheos, what happened then was that the people, moved by their usual "irrational," thoughtless impulse, surrounded Nikolaos's house and tried to set it on fire. Philotheos is particularly offended by the fact that this punishment was to be meted out without a court decision, and not by soldiers, but by the people themselves. The fire was set, and the people were urged by their leaders (or demagogues, according to the text) to enter the house. But at this point Isidore arrived, and through the intercession of the Virgin the mob suddenly came to its senses, did not destroy the house, and dispersed.[82]

This "miracle" is interesting for a number of reasons. First, it has the elements of a true story. Presumably, Nikolaos was a well-known supporter of Kantakouzenos, and the opponents of Kantakouzenos were either trying to capture him or else to punish him by destroying his possessions. The fact that the people did not enter the house probably means that they realized he was no longer there or that they did not want to attack those who were still left in the household. But what is of particular importance is the role of the saint and Philotheos's view of it. It seems that Isidore, then still bishop-elect of Monemvasia, took it upon himself to protect the property of a rich man, and a supporter of Kantakouzenos. Philotheos, on the other hand, describes the incident in considerable detail, appears to condone Isidore's action entirely, and seizes the opportunity to express his own position on these matters: his contempt for the people, their motives, and their leaders is obvious; and it is, perhaps, significant that in his eyes only miracles could be invoked against the irrational actions of the "mob."

These last observations may serve as a reminder of the great political, social, and ideological power wielded by the Byzantine church in the late period. The monasteries in particular, with their solid economic basis, produced bishops and patriarchs who supported and in many ways supplemented the functions of the disintegrating imperial authority. The Lives of the saints of this period illuminate important aspects of this phenomenon and illustrate the ideology behind it.

Notes

1. From the extensive bibliography I shall cite only G. Ostrogorskij, *Pour l'histoire de la féodalité byzantine* (Brussels, 1954); A. P. Každan, *Agrarnye otnošenija v Vizantii XIII–XV vv* (Moscow, 1952); P. Charanis, "On the Social Structure and Economic Organization of the Byzantine Empire in the Thirteenth Century and Later," *Byzantinoslavica* 12 (1951): 94-153; n.a., *Le Féodalisme à Byzance*, in *Recherches internationales à la lumière du Marxisme*, no. 79-2/1974.

2. These saints are: (a) Romylos (d. after 1371). There are two published versions of his Life, one Greek [published by F. Halkin, "Un ermite des Balkans au XIVe siècle: La vie grecque inédite de St. Romylos," *Byzantion* 31 (1961): 116-145; cf. also I. Dujčev, "Un fragment grec de la vie de St. Romile," *Byzantinoslavica* 7 (1937/1938: 124-127] and one Slavic [pub. P. A. Syrku, "Monaha Grigorija Žitie prepodobnago Romila," *Pamjatniki drevnej pismennosti i iskusstva*, no. 136 (St. Petersburg, 1900)]. The Greek text, which is considered as the original one, has been used in this article. On this, cf. P. Devos, "La version slave de la vie de St. Romylos," *Byzantion* 31 (1961): 148-187. (b) Maximos Kausokalybes (b. 1270 or 1285; d. 1365 or 1380). Two versions of his Life are published by F. Halkin, "Deux vies de St. Maxime le Kausokalybe, ermite au Mont Athos (XIVe s.), *Analecta Bollandiana* 54 (1936): 38-112 (hereafter, Halkin, "St. Maxime," I, and Halkin, "St. Maxime," II). (c) Niphon (1315-1411), whose Life was published by F. Halkin, "La vie de Saint Niphon, ermite au Mont Athos (XIVe siècle)," *Analecta Bollandiana* 58 (1940): 5-27. (d) Gregory Palamas (b. 1296; d. 14 November 1359). Two *enkomia*, written by the patriarchs of Constantinople Philotheos Kokkinos and Nilos, are published in *PG* 151: 551-656 (hereafter, Philotheos, "Enkomion"), 656-678 (hereafter, Nilos, "Enkomion"). (e) Savas the Young (fl. in first half of the fourteenth century), whose life, written by Philotheos, appears in A. Papadopoulos-Kerameus, *Analekta Hierosolymitikes Stakhyologias* (St. Petersburg, 1898), 5: 191-359 (hereafter, Papadopoulos-Kerameus, *St. Savas*). (f) Germanos (ca. 1252-ca. 1336). His Life, also written by Patriarch Philotheos, was published by P. Ioannou, "Vie de St. Germain l'Hagiorite par son contemporain le Patriarche Philothée de Constantinople," *Analecta Bollandiana* 70 (1952): 35-115 (hereafter, Ioannou, "St. Germain"). Cf. the critical notes by V. Laurent, "La vie de St. Germain l'Hagiorite; quelques observations," *REB* 10 (1950): 113-123. (g) Isidore, patriarch of Constantinople (1347-1350). His Life by Philotheos is published by A. Papadopoulos-Kerameus, *Žitija dvuh vselenskih patriarhov*

XIV v, in *Zapiski istoriko-filologičeskago Fakuljtet imperatorskago S. Peterburskago universiteta* 76 (1905): 52–156 (hereafter, Papadopoulos-Kerameus, *St. Isidore*). (h) Athanasios I, patriarch of Constantinople (b. ca. 1230–1235; d. after 1310; patriarch, 1289–1293; 1303–1309). There are two extant Lives: one by Theoktistos the Studite, published in ibid., pp. 1–51 (hereafter, Papadopoulos-Kerameus, *St. Athanasios*), and in H. Delehaye, "La vie d'Athanase, Patriarche de Constantinople," *Mélanges d'archéologie et d'histoire de l'école française de Rome* 17 (1897): 39–75; the other written by Joseph Kalothetos. This latter Life was published by A. Pantokratorinos, "Calotheti Vita Athanasii," *Thrakika* 13 (1940): 56–107; on this edition, see the critical notes by E. Kourilas, *Theologia* 24 (1935): 283–303. On Athanasios, see also Alice-Mary M. Talbot, *The Correspondence of Athanasius I, Patriarch of Constantinople*, Dumbarton Oaks Texts, 3 (Washington, D.C., 1975). (i) Damianos (d. 1281). Life in K. Doukakis, *Megas Synaxaristes*, 23 February (hereafter, Doukakis, *St. Damianos*). (j) Kosmas Zographites (d. 1423). Ibid., 22 September (hereafter, Doukakis, *St. Kosmas*); I have not been able to find I. Dujčev, "La vie de Kozma de Zographou," *Hilandarski Zbornik* 2 (1971): 59–68. (k) Gregory of Sinai (d. 1346). Life by Kallistos, patriarch of Constantinople, published by I. Pomjalovskij, "Žitie iže vo svatyh otsa našego Grigorija Sinaita," *Zapiski istorikofilologičeskago fakuljtet imperatorskago S. Peterburskago universiteta* 35 (1896): 1–64 (hereafter, Pomjalovskij, "Žitie"). (l) The neomartyr Arsenios, metropolitan of Veroia (d. late fourteenth or early fifteenth century). G. Chionides, *Anekdotos Akolouthia tou Neomartyros Arseniou Metropolitou Veroias* (Thessalonica, 1971) (hereafter, Chionides, *Arsenios*). (m) Philotheos Athonite (b. late fourteenth century; d. mid-fifteenth century). Life by Daniel, monk of Dionysiou, published by Basilike Papoulia, "Die Vita des Heiligen Philotheos vom Athos," *Südost Forschungen* 22 (1963): 259–280 (hereafter, Papoulia, "Philotheos"); cf. idem, *Ursprung und Wesen der "Knabenlese" im Osmanischen Reich* (Munich, 1963), pp. 78 ff. Cf. also F. Halkin's review of the edition of the Life in *Analecta Bollandiana* 83 (1965): 454–455. (n) Dionysios Athonite (ca. 1308/1313–1382/1389). Life by Metrophanes, published by B. Laourdas, "Metrophanous bios tou hosiou Dionysiou tou Athōnitou," *Archeion Pontou* 21 (1956): 45–76 (hereafter, Laourdas, "St. Dionysios"). Cf. N. Oikonomidès, *Actes de Dionysiou*, in *Archives de l'Athos* (Paris, 1968). (o) Athanasios, founder of Meteora (ca. 1305–ca. 1383). Life published by N. A. Bees, "Symbole eis ten historian tōn monōn tōn Meteōrōn," *Byzantis* 1 (1909): 237–261 (hereafter, Bees, *St. Athanasios*). A modern Greek version may be found in Sp. Lampros, "Symbolai eis tēn historian tōn monōn tōn Meteōrōn," *Neos Hellenomnemōn*, 2:51–87. Cf. D. M. Nicol, *Meteora: The Rock Monasteries of Thessaly* (London, 1963). (p) Meletios (d. 1286). Life published by Sp. Lavriotes in *Gregorios ho Palamas* 5 (1921): 582–584, 609–624; *Ho Athōs* 2, nos. 8–9 (1928): 9–11 (hereafter, Lavriotes, *St. Meletios*). Other saints' Lives, used less extensively because they concern Asia Minor, are (q) Michael, Life written by Theodore Metochites and published in *AASS*, November, IV, 669–678 (hereafter, "St. Michael"); (r) Niketas the Young, Life published by H. Delehaye in *Mélanges offerts à M. Gustave Schlumberger*, vol. 1 (Paris, 1924), pp. 208–211 (hereafter, Delehaye, "St. Niketas"); and (s) John, metropolitan of Heracleia, Life written by his nephew, Nicephorus Gregoras, and published by V. Laurent, "La vie de Jean, metropolite d'Héraclée du Pont," *Archeion Pontou* 6 (1935): 29–63, with commentary.

3. For the highly disputed geographic location of Paroria, see G. Ajanov, "Stari monastiri v Strandža," *Izvestija na B'lgarskija arheologičeski Institut'* 13 (1939), 253–264, who places it in the southeastern frontier of Bulgaria and the Byzantine Empire. See also N. A. Bees, "Ein Buchgeschenk an das Madonna-Katakekryomeni-Kloster," in *Byzantinisch-Neugriechische Jahrbücher* 15 (1939): 187–195.

4. Philotheos, "Enkomion," pp. 553–554; Papadopoulos-Kerameus, *St. Savas*, p. 193; Ioannou, "St. Germain," p. 51; Papadopoulos-Kerameus, *St. Isidore*, pp. 54–56; Papadopoulos-Kerameus, *St. Athanasios*, p. 2; Pantokratorinos, "Calotheti Vita Athanasii," p. 61; Halkin, "St. Niphon," p. 12; Laourdas, *St. Dionysios*, p. 46; Bees, *St. Athanasios*, p. 239; Lavriotes, *St. Meletios*, p. 583; Halkin, "St. Maxime," I, p. 43; II, 67–68; Pomjalovskij, "Žitie," p. 3; Halkin, "St. Romylos," p. 116; Doukakis, *St. Kosmas*, p. 369; Papoulia, "Philotheos," p. 273.

5. Papadopoulos-Kerameus, *St. Isidore*, p. 55; Papadopoulos-Kerameus, *St. Athanasios*, pp. 2–3; Lavriotes, *St. Meletios*, p. 583.

6. Philotheos, "Enkomion," pp. 553, 558–559; cf. J. Meyendorff, *Introduction à l'étude de Grégoire Palamas* (Paris, 1959), pp. 45–46.

7. Ioannou, "St. Germain," pp. 51–52; cf. Laurent, "Vie de St. Germain," pp. 113–116, and idem, "Légendes sigillographiques et familles byzantines," *Echos d'Orient* 30 (1931): 481–484.

8. Papadopoulos-Kerameus, *St. Savas*, pp. 192, 195; idem, *St. Isidore*, pp. 56–57.

9. Bees, *St. Athanasios*, p. 239; cf. Nicol, *Meteora*, pp. 88 ff.

10. Lavriotes, *St. Meletios*, p. 583.

11. Pomjalovskij, "Žitie," p. 3.

12. Halkin, "St. Maxime," II, p. 68; Doukakis, *St. Kosmas*, p. 369.

13. Halkin, "St. Romylos," p. 116; Laourdas, *St. Dionysios*, p. 46; Pantokratorinos, "Calotheti Vita Athanasii," p. 62; Halkin, "St. Niphon," p. 12; Papoulia, "Philotheos," p. 273.

14. Halkin, "St. Maxime," I, p. 45; II, p. 93; Papadopoulos-Kerameus, *St. Savas*, pp. 339–347; idem, *St. Isidore*, pp. 115 ff. Cf. *Ioannis Cantacuzeni eximperatoris historiarum libri IV*, vol. 3 (Bonn, 1832), pp. 176–177. The biographer of Saint Maximos adds that Saint Gregory of Sinai influenced, through his letters, "the emperors of the world: Andronikos [III, 1328–1341], Alexander [Ivan Alexander of Bulgaria, 1331–1371], Stephen [Dushan of Serbia, 1321–1355], and Alexander" [whom Halkin identifies with Alexander I, of Wallachia, 1338–1364]: Halkin, "St. Maxime," II, p. 90.

15. On Kantakouzenos, see G. Weiss, *Joannes Kantakuzenos—Aristokrat, Staatsmann, Kaiser und Mönch* (Wiesbaden, 1969).

16. Philotheos, "Enkomion," p. 597.

17. Pomjalovskij, "Žitie," pp. 7, 15 ff., 20–30. Gerasimos is said to have been a relative of the "king" of Negroponte, "Fatzos." This can only have been Boniface of Verona, husband of Agnese, dame of Karystos (1294–1317): C. Hopf, *Chroniques gréco-romanes*, (Berlin, 1873), p. 479.

18. Maximos died at ninety-five and Philotheos at eighty-four: Halkin, "St. Maxime," II, pp. 95, 101; Papoulia, "Philotheos," p. 279.

19. Papadopoulos-Kerameus, *St. Athanasios*, p. 4; Bees, *St. Athanasios*, p. 240; Philotheos, "Enkomion," pp. 558, 572; Papoulia, "Philotheos," p. 273.

20. Philotheos, "Enkomion," pp. 573, 592–593; Meyendorff, *Palamas*, p. 71.

21. A. E. Laiou-Thomadakis, *Peasant Society in the Late Byzantine Empire: A Social and Demographic Study* (Princeton, 1977), chap. 7.

22. Papadopoulos-Kerameus, *St. Isidore*, pp. 55–56; Laurent, "Vie de St. Germain," p. 114. Saint Germanos's sister was between nineteen and twenty-one years old when she married: he went to Mount Athos at the age of eighteen, after the marriage of his eldest sister: Ioannou, "St. Germain," pars. 7, 8, 30.

23. Papadopoulos-Kerameus, *St. Savas*, pp. 197 ff.; Philotheos, "Enkomion," pp. 559–560; cf. Nilos, "Enkomion," p. 660; Ioannou, "St. Germain," pp. 53, 55, 58; Lavriotes, *St. Meletios*, p. 583; Halkin, "St. Romylos," par. 2. Romylos and Kosmas were bilingual in Greek and Bulgarian: Halkin, "St. Romylos," pp. 171–172; Doukakis, *St. Kosmas*, p. 282.

24. Papadopoulos-Kerameus, *St. Isidore*, p. 68; Halkin, "St. Romylos," pp. 171–172.

25. Pomjalovskij, "Žitie," p. 67; Papoulia, "Philotheos," p. 274. On this, cf. R. Browning, "Literacy in the Byzantine World," *BMGS* 4 (1978): 46–49.

26. Papadopoulos-Kerameus, *St. Isidore*, pp. 58–60; cf. V. Laurent, "Philothée Kokkinos," in *Dictionnaire de théologie catholique*, col. 1500. Cf. also Halkin, "St. Niphon," pp. 12–13.

27. Bees, *St. Athanasios*, p. 240 (in Thessaloniki, after 1319); Laurent, "Jean d' Héraclée," p. 46 (in Constantinople, in 1274–1282); cf. V. Laurent, "La personnalité de Jean d' Héraclée (1250–1328), oncle et précepteur de Nicéphore Grégoras," *Hellenika* 3 (1930): 297–315.

28. Halkin, "St. Maxime," I, p. 43; II, pp. 68, 71; the *Vita* (p. 71) refers to a grand logothete who was also *epi tou kanikleiou* in 1289–1293 or in 1303–1309. This does not accord with the *cursus honorum* of either Theodore Metochites or Nikephoros Choumnos: cf. I. Ševčenko, *Études sur la polémique entre Théodore Métochite et Nicéphore Choumnos* (Brussels, 1962). It is, however, almost certain that the reference is to Metochites, inasmuch as it is his title of grand logothete that is stressed. The other references are to: Papadopoulos-Kerameus, *St. Athanasios*, pp. 3–4; Pantokratorinos, "Calotheti Vita Athanasii," par. 10; Talbot, *Athanasius I*, pp. xxviii–xxxi, and Letters 73, 86; Nicephorus Gregoras, *Byzantina Historia* (Bonn, 1829), 1: 180; Laourdas, *St. Dionysios*, pp. 47, 48, 50.

29. Saint Germanos went to school with his elder brother but not with his elder sister: Ioannou, "St. Germain," p. 53; Philotheos, "Enkomion," p. 642.

30. Pomjalovskij, "Žitie," p. 4; Delehaye, "St. Nikétas," passim; "St. Michael," pp. 669 ff.

31. Papadopoulos-Kerameus, *St. Savas*, pp. 210-211, 213.

32. Bees, *St. Athanasios*, p. 240; Lampros, *St. Athanasios*, p. 65; Nicol, *Meteora*, p. 88; K. M. Setton, R. L. Wolff, and H. W. Hazard, *A History of the Crusades*, vol. 3 (Madison, Wis., 1975), p. 187.

33. Pantokratorinos, "Calotheti Vita Athanasii," p. 101.

34. Philotheos, "Enkomion," p. 569; Papadopoulos-Kerameus, *St. Isidore*, pp. 77 ff.; Pomjalovskij, "Žitie," pp. 33-36; Ioannou, "St. Germain," p. 98. For the date, see Meyendorff, *Palamas*, p. 53. For the walled and unwalled monasteries, see Pantokratorinos, "Calotheti Vita Athanasii," p. 66.

35. Bees, *St. Athanasios*, p. 243. Date: he was over thirty years old; because he had been born ca. 1305, the raid must have taken place ca. 1335. Cf. Pomjalovskij, "Žitie," pp. 38-39. Cantacuzenus, I, 455, mentions a Turkish attack on Mount Athos; it involved about sixty ships and took place ca. 1330. Oikonomidès, *Dionysiou*, pp. 8-9, considers that the worst Turkish attack took place in the second quarter of the fourteenth century.

36. Halkin, "St. Romylos," pars. 11-12. Date: the second attack took place while Saint Gregory of Sinai was still alive, that is, before 1346; the first attack had taken place at least five years earlier. Cf. Meyendorff, *Palamas*, pp. 78, 79, 117, 353. On Turkish attacks in Thrace in the 1340s, see Gregoras, II, 683; he speaks of the capture of men, women, and beasts, and of the fact that because of these invasions the land lay fallow and uncultivated. On the Turkish presence in Thrace in the later part of the fourteenth century, cf. Irène Beldiceanu-Steinherr, "La conquête d'Andrinople par les Turcs: La pénétration turque en Thrace et la valeur des chroniques ottomanes," *Travaux et Mémoires* 1 (1965): 439-461.

37. Laourdas, *St. Dionysios*, pp. 58 ff.; Halkin, "St. Niphon," p. 19; the Life of Saint Maximos talks of the monks' fear of invasion, ca. 1350: Halkin, "St. Maxime," I, p. 48; Philotheos, "Enkomion," pp. 627 ff.; cf. Meyendorff, *Palamas*, pp. 157 ff.; G. Georgiades-Arnakis, "Gregory Palamas among the Turks and Documents of His Captivity as Historical Sources," *Speculum* 26 (1951): pp. 104 ff., and P. Wittek, "Chiones," *Byzantion* 21 (1951): pp. 421 ff.

38. Halkin, "St. Romylos," par. 22; Halkin, "St. Niphon," pp. 24-25; G. M. Thomas, *Diplomatarium Veneto-Levantinum* (Venice, 1899), vol. 2, nos. 98-99; N. Oikonomidès, "Monastères et moines lors de la conquête turque," *Südost Forschungen* 35 (1976): 2-3. One Venetian ship was given to Lavra, presumably to help the monastery's future defense. Cf. I. Dujčev, "Le patriarche Nil et les invasions turques vers la fin du XIVe siècle," *Medioevo Bizantinoslavo* 2: 253-261, who mentions Nilos's general references to Turkish invasions in 1380-1388. On Uglješa, cf. H. Hunger, "Kaiser Johannes V. Palaiologos und das Heiligen Berg," *BZ* 45 (1952): 363-365.

39. Laourdas, *St. Dionysios*, p. 68; Oikonomidès, *Dionysiou*, p. 12. In Halkin, "St. Niphon," pp. 26-27, we find a monk collecting money for ransoming some monks from the Turks.

40. Papoulia, "Philotheos," p. 269; cf. Speros Vryonis, Jr., "Isidore Glabas and the Turkish Devshirme," *Speculum* 31 (1956): 433–443.

41. Papoulia, "Philotheos," pp. 278–279.

42. Chionides, *Arsenios*, pp. 23, 29; K. Stathopoulou-Asdracha, "The Turkish Captures of Veroia (14th and 15th Centuries) and the Privileges of a Christian Family" (in Greek), *Epitheōrēsē Technēs* 11 (1965): 152–157; A. Vakalopoulos, *A History of Macedonia* (in Greek), (Thessalonica, 1969), pp. 40–41, 109–111.

43. Philotheos, "Enkomion," pp. 574, 614; Cantacuzenus, *Historiarum libri IV*, 1: 454 ff. Cf. Meyendorff, *Palamas*, pp. 136–137, and U. Bosch, *Andronikos II. Palaiologos: Versuch einer Darstellung der byzantinischen Geschichte in den Jahren 1321-1341* (Amsterdam, 1965), pp. 91 ff.

44. Philotheos, "Enkomion," p. 597; Meyendorff, *Palamas*, pp. 78–79, n. 55.

45. Pomjalovskij, "Žitie," pp. 36–38, 40–41; Halkin, "St. Romylos," pp. 124–126.

46. In the late 1330s: Bees, *St. Athanasios*, p. 247; Halkin, "St. Romylos," pp. 197–199; cf. Nicol, *Meteora*, pp. 94 ff.

47. Cf. Bees, *St. Athanasios*, pp. 247, 250; Halkin, "St. Romylos," pp. 197–199; Nicol, *Meteora*, pp. 54–69.

48. Papadopoulos-Kerameus, *St. Savas*, pp. 290–291; Pomjalovskij, "Žitie," pp. 15–16; Philotheos, "Enkomion," p. 616; Papadopoulos-Kerameus, *St. Isidore*, pp. 98 ff.

49. Philotheos, "Enkomion," p. 583; Halkin, "St. Romylos," pp. 124, 187–188. On the *adelphata*, cf. Oikonomidès, "Monastères," pp. 6–8, and Mirjana Živojinović, "Adelfati u Vizantiji i srednjovekovnoj Srbiji," *ZRVI* 11 (1968): 241–270.

50. Halkin, "St. Niphon," pp. 14–15. On the date of the first plague: it took place about sixteen years after he was first ordained as a priest; this latter event occurred in 1335 (cf. pp. 8, 14). On the Black Death, see Gregoras, II, 797–798 and Cantacuzenus, III, 49–52.

51. Philotheos, "Enkomion," p. 616; Halkin, "St. Niphon," p. 19.

52. Pantokratorinos, "Calotheti Vita Athanasii," pp. 79–80 (between 1250/1255 and 1260/1265). For another example of extensive travels, in search of knowledge this time, cf. the travel of the philosopher Joseph from his native Ithaki to Thessaloniki to Constantinople: M. Treu, "Der Philosoph Joseph," *BZ* 8 (1899): 7, 8, 18.

53. Lavriotes, *St. Meletios*, pp. 611–617; Laurent, "Jean d'Héraclée," pp. 33–39. St. Maximos traveled from Lampsakos to Ganos, Papikion, Mount Athos, and Constantinople in the late-thirteenth or early-fourteenth century: Halkin, "St. Maxime," I, p. 43; II, pp. 69–72.

54. Papadopoulos-Kerameus, *St. Savas*, passim; Gregoras, II, 620; Meyendorff, *Palamas*, p. 100.

55. Pomjalovskij, "Žitie," pp. 33–40. Saint Germanos went from Mount Athos to Constantinople on a small boat: Ioannou, "St. Germain," p. 66.

56. Papadopoulos-Kerameus, *St. Isidore*, pp. 85–88. For the date, see Meyendorff, *Palamas*, pp. 90, 105–106, 109–115.

57. Halkin, "St. Niphon," p. 13; Bees, *St. Athanasios*, pp. 244–245; Ioannou, "St. Germain," p. 75; (for Job's dates, see Laurent, "Vie de St. Germain," p. 120); Pomjalovskij, "Žitie," pp. 16 ff.

58. Halkin, "St. Romylos," passim; Laourdas, *St. Dionysios*, pp. 62–64. The travels of other individuals may be mentioned here: Saint Athanasios of Meteora went from Neopatras to Thessaloniki, to Mount Athos, to Crete, and back to Mount Athos after 1319; he traveled to Thessaloniki, Veroia, Serbia, and Meteora after 1335: Bees, *St. Athanasios*, passim. Saint Dionysios and his brother went to Trebizond by boat from Constantinople in 1374: Laourdas, *St. Dionysios*, p. 60; some time in the second half of the fourteenth century, we find that a monk from Serres went to see Saint Maximos at Mount Athos; two monks sailed from Lavra to go to Constantinople on a ship from Thessaloniki; and a secretary (*grammatikos*) went from Constantinople to Lavra: Halkin, "St. Maxime," I, pp. 49, 57–59; before Dionysiou was built, a poor monk from Trebizond found his way to Mount Athos (Halkin, "St. Romylos," par. 15); Saint Gregory Palamas keeps traveling from Thessaloniki to Mount Athos, to Veroia, to Constantinople, and gets to Lemnos: Philotheos, "Enkomion," passim.

59. Lavriotes, *St. Meletios*, p. 616.

60. Ioannou, "St. Germain," par. 6.

61. Laurent, "Jean d'Héraclée," p. 39; cf. Georgius Pachymeres, *De Michaele Palaeologo* (Bonn, 1835), p. 364.

62. Lavriotes, *St. Meletios*, p. 624; Laourdas, *St. Dionysios*, p. 62. The fact that the monks themselves built small cells is mentioned in various places in the Lives of Romylos, Gregory of Sinai, and Maximos.

63. Halkin, "St. Maxime," I, pp. 54, 57; Philotheos, "Enkomion," pp. 629–630. Tailors are mentioned in Halkin, "St. Maxime," I, p. 54; II, p. 98.

64. P. Nasturel, "Une prétendue oeuvre de Grégoire Tsamblak: Le martyre de Saint Jean le nouveau," *Actes du premier Congrès international des études balkaniques et sud-est européennes* 6 (1971): 345–351. For documentary evidence of Black Sea trade in the mid-fourteenth century, see, among others, Giovanna Balbi and Silvana Raiteri, *Notai Genovesi in Oltremare: Atti rogati a Caffa e a Licostomo (sec. XIV)* (Bordighera: Istituto Internazionale di Studi Liguri, 1973) and Geo Pistarino, *Notai Genovesi in Oltremare; Atti rogati a Chilia da Antonio di Ponzo (1360–61)* (Bordighera: Istituto Internazionale di Studi Liguri, 1971).

65. Papadopoulos-Kerameus, *St. Athanasios*, pp. 33–35; Pantokratorinos, "Calotheti Vita Athanasii," p. 101; A. Laiou, "The Provisioning of Constantinople during the Winter of 1306–07," *Byzantion* 37 (1967): 91–113.

66. Papadopoulos-Kerameus, *St. Isidore*, pp. 124–126.

67. The redistribution of property among the followers of the opposing armies in the civil war is evident in the documents that have survived in the archives of Mount Athos; for one particular case, see, for example, P. Lemere, "Un praktikon inédit des archives de Karakala (Janvier 1342) et la

situation en Macédoine orientale au moment de l'usurpation de Cantacuzène," *Charisterion eis Anastasion K. Orlandon*, vol. 1 (Athens, 1965), pp. 278–298.

68. Papadopoulos-Kerameus, *St. Isidore*, p. 125. Some imperial officials, who happen to be close relatives of saints, appear, in the Lives, to be just in their dealings with the poor. Examples are the father of Germanos (Ioannou, "St. Germain," p. 52) and Constantine Palamas, father of Gregory, who did not hesitate to accuse Constantine, the son of Andronikos II, of taking money away from a widow (Philotheos, "Enkomion," p. 555). This last action is hardly a case of helping the poor, however, because the widow had lost—and recovered, through Palamas's intervention—the rather considerable sum of three hundred *hyperpyra*.

69. Halkin, "St. Romylos," pp. 93–94; Halkin, "St. Maxime," I, p. 59; II, p. 101.

70. Ioannou, "St. Germain," pp. 78–79, 82–85; on the wealth of Lavra, cf. Laiou-Thomadakis, *Peasant Society*, passim. In 1361 or 1376, the emperor John V asked Lavra and Vatopedi to furnish his uncle with wood and artisans to rebuild a building in Lemnos: Hunger, "Kaiser Johannes V," p. 369.

71. Laourdas, *St. Dionysios*, p. 55; Oikonomidès, *Dionysiou*, no. 3 and pp. 5, 10; Bees, *St. Athanasios*, pp. 250–251; Nicol, *Meteora*, pp. 98–101.

72. Philotheos, "Enkomion," pp. 512–513.

73. Halkin, "St. Maxime," I, pp. 44, 54. Despite his poverty and his perhaps voluntary air of madness, many *archontes* came to him for advice: ibid., I, pp. 45–46, 48, 60–61; II, pp. 93 ff., 67. Philotheos ate bread and salt every other day: Papoulia, "Philotheos," p. 278.

74. Halkin, "St. Niphon," p. 21; Doukakis, *St. Kosmas*, pp. 282–286.

75. Laourdas, *St. Dionysios*, p. 52; Halkin, "St. Romylos," pars. 6, 7, 10, 13, 20; Bees, *St. Athanasios*, pp. 243, 256; cf. Ioannou, "St. Germain," par. 9. In the Life of Saint Romylos, the *adelphata* seem to be granted without payment.

76. Halkin, "St. Romylos," pars. 9, 16; Ioannou, "St. Germain," pp. 65, 80; Halkin, "St. Maxime," I, pp. 50–51; II, p. 96.

77. Saint Maximos was the most extreme in this matter. He owned nothing (Halkin, "St. Maxime," II, pp. 79, 88), and every so often he used to burn his hut.

78. For example, see ibid., I, pp. 45–46, 48, 60–61; II, pp. 93 ff., and Papadopoulos-Kerameus, *St. Isidore*, pp. 101–103. In his biography of Saint Savas, Philotheos says that, ten years before the civil war, a certain important Thessalonian named Andrew (presumably, Palaiologos) had gone to visit the saint, who refused to see him because he had foreseen the "beastly" role he would play in the coming conflict: Papadopoulos-Kerameus, *St. Savas*, pp. 326–331.

79. Papadopoulos-Kerameus, *St. Savas*, pp. 193–194, 329; idem, *St. Isidore*, p. 104; Halkin, "St. Germain," p. 107.

80. Philotheos, "Enkomion," pp. 636 ff., 647 ff.

81. Papadopoulos-Kerameus, *St. Isidore*, pars. 76, 77, 78, 64, 66. In his will, dated February of the third indiction (1350), Isidore mentions his

life-long concern with the poor and disclaims any personal interest in wealth. He leaves his personal property to poor members of the clergy, to poor nuns, and to the poor of Constantinople: F. Miklosich and J. Müller, *Acta et diplomata Graeca medii Aevi* vol. 1 (Vienna, 1860), pp. 287–294.

82. Papadopoulos-Kerameus, *St. Isidore*, pars. 40, 41, 42. Later, Nikolaos named his son Isidore after the patriarch: ibid., par. 43.

Chapter 8

Monastic Stability: Some Socioeconomic Considerations

Ernest W. McDonnell, *Rutgers University*

The ample *Regula Magistri* (RM),[1] but more specifically, the concise and magisterial rule of Saint Benedict of Nursia (RB),[2] by transmitting to Western monastic literature the fourfold classification of monks (two desirable—cenobites and anchorites—and two reprehensible—Sarabaites and gyrovagues), codified, in the light of Roman concepts of *militia* and *stabilitas*, qualifications that can be traced back directly through patristic lineage at least to the last quarter of the fourth century. Partly in response to personal conviction seasoned with eremitic experience at Subiaco,[3] partly determined by contemporary socioeconomic needs and thereby made acceptable to the body politic and ecclesiastical structure alike, Benedict's classification nevertheless continued to inform monastic tradition long after the original frame of reference had been outgrown.[4]

Combining respect for tradition with a lawyer's penchant for definition, Isidore of Seville (d. 636), however, expanded these four kinds of monks to six. In addition to cenobites, who claimed as ancestor the primitive Jerusalem community, he distinguished as acceptable both hermits—foreshadowed by Elijah and John the Baptist—and anchorites, who, having been conditioned in community life, were qualified to seek perfection through contemplation in their individual cells. To counterbalance these were three unacceptable kinds: (1) the counterparts of true anchorites who, as Cassian put it, disdained in their lukewarmness obedience and humility; (2) the Circumcellions who, borrowed from Augustine, now represented in general the gyrovagues, caricatures of true eremitism; and (3) the Sarabaites (or, after Jerome, the Remoboth), whose commercialism vividly recalled Ananias and Sapphira, thereby making their integrity suspect.[5]

The genesis, growth, and perpetuation of this concept of *genera monachorum* exemplify how vocabulary and metaphor that are

characteristic of monastic tradition build up by accretion and are
transmitted with the aid of scriptural prototype, evangelical coun-
sel, and patristic authority venerated as the *praecepta* and *instituta
maiorum*. The matter-of-fact record of conciliar legislation, then,
is personalized in hagiography, embellished in no small degree by
folklore, amplified by legend, and colored by didactic concern.
Scholarship treating the relationship of RB and RM has often been
preoccupied with linguistic and textual questions[6] as well as with
the development of official worship in liturgy; or the scholarship
has been geared to moral or polemical ends, slighting, if not avoid-
ing historical vicissitudes in favor of matters of spiritual import.
Nowhere is this more apparent than in the handling of the Sarabaites and gyrovagues whom Benedict summarily dismissed as
unworthy of closer examination. RM, on the contrary, was not
loathe to dilate on the errant ways of the gyrovagues.[7] Although
Sarabaites and gyrovagues were often confused from the outset as
well as in subsequent monastic comment, efforts were made,
above all in the West, to distinguish two distinct types. Cassian
followed his lengthy critique of the Sarabaites with the curt observation that an itinerant element had recently (*nuper*) appeared.
Although Sarabaites, motivated by expectation of material gain,
did not offer a convincing example of austerity, were they not, in
the absence of structure, ascetics—quasi-religious or self-ordained,
chiefly in an urban setting—whose inability or failure to observe
total renunciation and continued involvement in worldly affairs
laid them open to suspicion of lukewarmness? As for the gyrovagues, the moralist saw in these pseudomonks the epitome of
hypocrisy, if not a threat of heresy. The proponent of unity in
church and state detected in their presence only subversion of a
well-ordered society. What is barely hinted at are the socioeconomic crises of the late Roman Empire that, together with the
impact of the barbarian invasions, created a floating population,
even as state regimentation and church institutionalization were
fashioning a temper for *stabilitas* and definition of both structure
and doctrine. If not victims of these crises, did not certain gyrovagues recall either civil disturbances, especially in Eastern cities,
or the individualism of itinerant preachers, prophets, ascetics, and
miracle workers of the early church? While RM and RB identified
the gyrovagues with a parasitic element ever on the move, eager
to exploit hospitality and charity, the term, with numerous synonyms, encompassed any kind of vagabondage in the Middle
Ages.[8]

Moreover, this classification constitutes a chapter in early comparative monasticism that embraces and evaluates, within the cadre of a theology of history, the different kinds of religious life. Into the Carolingian period these were essentially eremitical and cenobitic with variants. Then, with the particularizing of that life in the proliferation and variety of religious orders (*religiones*) from the eleventh century on, comparative monasticism considers the relative merits or claims of these diverse congregations with respect to origins, sources, observances, discipline, objectives, and polity. Whereas such an approach pertains to Western monachism within a predominantly rural society, comparative monasticism must also concern itself with diversity between West and East where, in addition to deep-seated eremitism, monks often insinuated themselves into the political life of cities. Even as comparative monasticism offers case studies in differentiation and assimiliation, to the customary threefold division of religious vocation (*ordo monasticus, ordo canonicus,* and *ordo fratrum*), each with distinctive features, yet all built on a common evangelical core, must be added, as evidence of increasing articulation of lay spirituality within a revitalized urban context, the study of innumerable extra-regular or quasi-religious associations. The sociocaritative or penitential impulses of these associations were frequently enlisted by the church through absorption into one of these *ordines*, with a predilection being exhibited for tertiaries under aegis of the friars. The merits of these developments were to be measured in juridical terms in relation to local ordinaries; to traditional, well-established monachism; or to fresh reform efforts that confronted monastic preserves and objectives with austerity and rigorism, whether by a more literal interpretation of RB, by prescriptions contained in the so-called Augustinian rule, or by the logic of scripture itself. Specifically, such a study focuses attention on espousal of a *vita arctior* in place of a *vita laxior*, an espousal that first involved transfer from one teacher to another, then from one house to another, finally from one order to another, in search of greater austerity and more complete solitude.

Finally, the stature now accorded to RM on the strength of editions equipped with critical apparatus presents to Benedictine studies a new dimension of which earlier scholarship was unaware,[9] although the uniqueness of RB continues to be underscored by its proponents.

RM and RB may be regarded as the first consolidation of ascetic observances in the West in a methodical, systematic, and comprehensive manner that—especially in the case of RB—suggests a juridical setting. Although this juridical nature has at times been minimized in preference to the initial charisma of an abbot, as the abbatial office hardened into administrative importance, its spiritual or pneumatic character diminished abruptly. To under-score his rule as a code of law and to make a plea for utility, with-out concern for speculative theology, Benedict complemented a laconic style with an intensely practical approach, predicated, in deference to human frailty and natural variables, on such recurrent clauses as *si fieri possit, si expediat, si loci necessitas exegerit* as well as on spelling out the daily and seasonal horarium to minutiae. Despite Gregory the Great's promotion of Saint Benedict's cultus and despite the missionary zeal of Anglo-Saxon monks under Roman auspices,[10] assurance of blanket application of the Benedic-tine prescriptions for the Latin Church had, nevertheless, to await Carolingian sponsorship of a unitary monastic society in what might be termed the second, and decisive, period of consolidation. Only at the beginning of the ninth century, with Benedict of Aniane (d. 821) as the chief architect of a projected monastic reform, with Inden (Cornelimünster) as its focus, and with the *Concordia Regularum*, together with the *Codex Regularum*, pro-viding the instruments along with the cadre presented by the *Capitulare monasticum* of Aix-la-Chapelle (817), did the RB begin to enjoy centralization of publicity and unrivaled celebrity as an effective agency of Romanization as well as the acknowledged index of religious stability.[11]

Monasticism is full of paradoxes. The very term signifies oneness, yet its fulfillment was found in community endeavor. Critical of contemporary lifestyle, it kept alive through diversity, individual-ism, and a spirit of protest, acting as the conscience of the church in a plea for periodic reform, if not disavowal, of the social organ-ism; yet in the West it became a staunch and consistent supporter of the established order, even developing quickly into a powerful instrument in consolidating and extending the claims of Roman jurisdiction. In the period under consideration, monasticism offered no religious orders or congregations; yet however diverse the exercises, observances, and objectives, not unaccompanied with a spirit of rivalry and even animosity, it constituted an *ordo monasticus*, rooted in a common ideal of evangelical perfection and appropriating for its own peculiar use the terms *conversio* and *religio*. It introduced *ascesis* and *eremus* to the Latin tongue;[12] yet it availed itself of Roman juridical concepts, heavily freighted with emotional overtones, and with feudal terminology, the whole vocabulary, to be sure, subject to eschatological coloration. Without confusing claustration (*clausura*) with stability, monasticism was erected on *stabilitas* in the dual sense of perseverance of profession and permanence of residence; yet monks frequented spiritual teachers, served as couriers, conducted routine affairs outside the cloister, journeyed to distant shrines, lent yeoman service in the conversion of pagans, and despite limitations on *transitus*, moved from one monastery to another, even indulging in order-jumping in the high Middle Ages. Monasticism registered disdain for the world, both kin and property, seeking a life of renunciation in such inaccessible places as deserts, mountains, and valleys. Yet, from the outset, urban monks were not uncommon either in East or West, extending hospitality to pilgrims and travelers as well as alms to the destitute.[13] The antithesis of civilization, which it so heartily spurned in the fourth century, monachism had become by the ninth century the very palladium of classical letters and patron of the arts. Between spiritual claims and mundane activity, monasticism postulated a sharp demarcation, couched in concepts often encrusted with clichés or clouded by exaggerated metaphor; yet it was ever responsive to fresh needs and ready to adapt itself—not without compromise or deference to specialization of function—to new circumstances whether in an agricultural society, feudal custom, the crusade epoch, or (but with far less alacrity and success) the recrudescence of urban life. It championed egalitarianism not only within its own ranks but also by courageous defense of popular grievances; yet it created its own administrative hierarchy and through selective recruitment identified itself with the outlook of the nobility. To accentuate repudiation of worldly interests, monasticism exacted personal poverty; yet acknowledgment of collegiate wealth inspired claims to political prerogative and special privilege that corroded essential monastic values. In short, monasticism began as a lay movement, eschewing bishops and women alike;[14] yet through its own clericalization as well as regularization of the secular clergy, it claimed spiritual elitism.[15] However much this elitism might be recorded in expression of competition, it bore rich fruit on behalf of the church as a whole by enlargement of liturgical experience and creation of schools of spirituality. How unique religious experience was regarded even in the eyes of secular authority was voiced by Justinian: "Monastic life is so honorable and can render the man who embraces it so acceptable to God that it can remove him from all human blemishes, declare him to be pure and submissive to natural reason, enriched in knowledge, and superior to others by reason of his thoughts. Hence, where anyone who intends to become a monk is lacking in theological erudition and soundness of discourse, he becomes worthy, obtaining both by his change of condition."[16]

Juridical and patristic heritage facilitated the clericalization of monastic status whereby ecclesiastical authority methodically channeled and adapted to its structure and mission the fruits of lay reform impulses.[17] Despite an ahistorical frame of reference, these impulses aimed at moral regeneration, whether within or apart from contemporary society, by seeking to recapture, on the strength of renunciation of the world as illustrated by the prophets of the Old Testament[18] or as counseled in the Gospels,[19] the immediacy and freshness of the apostolic life (*imitatio apostolorum/ Christi*),[20] postulated for the Jerusalem community as described in the Book of Acts.[21] If natural affection was discountenanced,[22] fraternal spirit summarized in the formula *unum cor et una anima*[23] was to be cultivated within the context of egalitarianism whereby all things were held in common and distribution was made to each according to his need. Far from being an expression of mere nostalgia for the idyllic past, what was termed *simplicitas* and *rusticitas* in the patristic age became a slogan for reform from the eleventh century on[24]—the *vita apostolica* that demanded a return to the early church, poor, humble, simple, and penitential.[25] It was a cult of primitivism, idealized and subject to legend, but all the more potent for the reformer. On the other hand, if expectation of the imminent end of the world removed incentive to earn one's livelihood, Saint Paul, relying on his Jewish heritage, took pride in manual work[26] from which one derived his wages.[27] In place of enthusiasm of the apocalyptic strain,[28] he demanded purposeful activity through physical labor in service to one's neighbor,[29] as well as for one's own subsistence or as a penitential act, rather than as a mere deterrent to idleness and ennui. To support stability in the sense of maintaining the *status quo*,[30] Saint Paul provided the corollary that one should abide in the vocation to which he is called,[31] a proposition that underlay the medieval organic conception of society in its defense of conservatism. If for Saint Paul every Christian was indiscriminately a *miles Christi*,[32] Tertullian applied the designation to martyrs and confessors as a special kind of soldier, and Origen did likewise for ascetics.[33] As martyrdom yielded to ascesis, with its sturdy advocacy of chastity, monasticism constituted preeminently the *militia Christi*, rooted in self-discipline and governed by obedience to a superior.[34]

Again, many an early monk enjoyed status among his contemporaries as a miracle worker or prophet, thereby never losing completely the charismatic gifts of the apostles.[35] In a conspectus that owed less to historical roots than to theological speculation, the role of the patriarchs, prophets, and apostles was continued by men who, in addition to preaching and teaching, founded monasteries.[36] As if to underscore the essential unity of Judeo-Christian tradition in answer to Manichaean disavowal of the Old Testament, but more precisely, to trace the inherent idea of the unfolding of that tradition within a severe ascetic context and with an appeal to primitivism, whether of *eremus* or the Jerusalem community, Jerome postulated with individual flavor what became the formula of monastic succession with eremitical foundation: Elijah–Elisha–John the Baptist–Antony–Paul of Thebes.[37] Despite the limitation imposed by such a lineage, Jerome's own mature view became cenobitic and practical, more attuned to a Pachomian community than to the individualism of Paul the protohermit described in the brief Chalcis period.

Jerome, no less than Athanasius, Eusebius of Vercelli, Evagrius of Antioch, Rufinus of Aquileia, Cassian, Sulpicius Severus through the vehicle of Postumianus, and Augustine who had to rely on a literary tradition, transmitted Egyptian asceticism to the West whether through his problematical *vita* of Paul the Hermit or his Epistle 22. 33–35 to Eustochium, both written prior to personal experience in the Nile Delta; through the sounder *vita* of Hilarion (2, 3) (A.D. 390), the Epistle 108. 14 (A.D. 404) also addressed to Eustochium, or his Epistle 125. 11, 13 to Rusticus (A.D. 411); or through the translation of Pachomian materials in A.D. 404 from a Greek text rendered in turn from the Coptic.[38] The first discernible step toward the Benedictine classification was taken by Jerome, who allowed a growing personal dislike of cities, with their distractions and encouragement to compromise essentials of asceticism, to color his judgment of urban monks. His letter to Eustochium, written in 384, reports that an example of avarice in Nitria provided the occasion for a digression on three classes of monks in Egypt: cenobites, the most numerous; anchorites; and an offensive kind that he labeled Remnuouth or Remoboth. The last, he adds acidly, is the chief, if not the only, sort in his own province.[39]

Monastic stability involves a twofold obligation: *stabilitas professionis*, which exacts perseverance in monastic vocation until death,[40] and *stabilitas loci*, which requires permanent abode in the monastery in which the profession is made.[41] In the three requisites for salvation counseled by Antony—always to walk in the presence of God, to abide by Scripture, and to maintain residence in one place[42]—may be discerned in germ the three activities prescribed by RB: *Opus Dei, lectio divina*, and *labor manuum*, which assures *stabilitas*. Despite informality and multiplicity, Egyptian monasticism recognized in essence *stabilitas loci* inasmuch as spiritual perfection can best be attained by a cell ascesis that, contrary to pastoral care, consists of constant meditation on one's sins and prayer for public good.[43] From Jerome comes the classic formula, elevated to legal stature in the *Decretum*, that the function of the monk is not to teach but to weep, a theme already well coursed in the *Apophthegmata Patrum*:[44] "Monachus autem non doctoris habet, sed plangentis officium; qui vel se, vel mundum lugeat, et Domini providus praestoletur adventum."[45] The converse for the priest is not stated so succinctly.[46] If education puts the monk in peril of pride, ignorance is the surest guarantee of stability in the state that he has chosen. Despite scriptural and patristic injunction, in practice, movement and stability, change and residence, were no more mutually exclusive than culture and holiness. Although the *Life of Antony* considered a monk outside his cell like a fish out of water,[47] Antony himself went to Alexandria to preach against the Arians[48] and to lend assistance to defendants in the court of law.[49] Nor did the rule of Pachomius confuse strict claustration with separation from the world, inasmuch as the latter could be mitigated by family circumstances.[50] John Moschus (d. ca. 619) demonstrates, in his own life as well as in the *Pratum Spirituale*, mobility within the world of asceticism, whether in search of spiritual perfection or under pressure of invasion.[51]

Monachism, like worldly existence itself, was viewed as a pilgrimage, in both the figurative and the literal sense. Pilgrimage in a figurative sense involved monks putting a premium on local stability out of respect for the bond to a particular abbey and abandoning self, family, and property, rather than homeland. In a literal sense, pilgrimage could be seen in the Irish, whose compulsion to wander eventually promoted the apostolate across the Channel and prepared the way for the more systematic missionary endeavors of Anglo-Saxon monks.[52] Although claustration might be challenged in the formative period by the *peregrinatio* of Irish hermits, Columbanus exacted geographic stability, *unius loci habitatio*, from his followers.[53] Similarly, Irish monastic legislation expressed concern at vagabondage as a flouting of obedience. An alleged Patrician saying contained in the collection of canons called Hibernensis declared that a monk who moved about aimlessly without abbatial permission ought to be excommunicated.[54] How closely *stabilitas* must be equated with livelihood by *labor manuum* is made explicit in a Celtic *vita*: "Cultivate the soil and work well," runs Luan's instructions at Clonfert, "so that you may have enough food, drink, and clothing. For where the servants of the Lord have sufficiency, there is stability; where there is stability, there is religion."[55]

To implement rigorous asceticism, the Irish monk, with Abraham as his prototype,[56] considered this life a voluntary exile, a pilgrimage, with himself as "a guest of the world," to whom the Hebrides and Orkneys beckoned as "a desert in the sea." The member of a clan, he was conscious of no continuing *civitas* and was thus unfamiliar with Roman diocesan organization.[57] To sever his connections with his own land as an act of penance (nor did the beauties of the Irish countryside escape the hagiographer),[58] "for the love of God," and "in order to gain the heavenly fatherland," the Irish monk was willing to become a *peregrinus*, not in the sense of a pilgrim, but as an expatriate who took what was tantamount to a vow that he would remain absent from his native land for a prolonged period, if not for life.[59]

Despite disparity in austerity and discipline, the coexistence of RB and the Columban rule in the same continental abbey need not suggest tensions, such as those Bede records in a monastery Colman planted with Irish and Anglo-Saxons. A dispute arose in the summer when the Irish wandered off into regions familiar to them instead of assisting at harvest. Then, as winter approached, they came back and expected to share whatever the English had gathered. To resolve the altercation, the latter were transferred to Mag éo (Mayo).[60] In this episode it appears to be a question of *monachi dispersi vagantes* more reminiscent of *monachi gyrovagi* than customary *peregrinatio*.[61]

When Irish hospices in Frankland were being seized in the middle of the ninth century, the inmates were often reduced to mendicancy. "Moreover, the hospices of the Irish (*hospitalia Scotorum*), which holy men of that race built in this kingdom and endowed with property bestowed on them because of their sanctity, have been entirely alienated from that service of hospitality; and not only are newcomers not received in those hospices, but even the very men who from infancy have in the same places been serving the Lord in religion are sent forth and compelled to beg from door to door."[62] To rectify this lamentable condition the Council of Meaux (845), with the cooperation of Charles the Bald, took steps to reestablish Irish foundations.

If Caesarius of Arles (503–543) defined stability in the dual sense as a condition of monastic life,[63] Benedict fortified and spread it in the West by requiring formal obligations in the style of written and signed promises to be preserved in the monastery.[64] For the postulant, he prescribed a triple vow of stability (*stabilitas*), a way of life (*conversio/conversatio morum*),[65] and obedience (*militia*). *Stabilitas*, equated with livelihood through *labor manuum*, both confronts the waywardness of the gyrovagues and injects structured asceticism into the informality of more settled urban monks; *morum conversatio*, which encompasses chastity and personal poverty, combats the lukewarmness of the Sarabaites and for gyrovagues underscores the necessity of self-abnegation as the prerequisite for the religious state; *militia* chastens not only disreputable monks but also the acceptable anchorite whose self-righteousness, accompanied by remissness in discipline, might engender untoward pride. The coenobium whose inhabitants serve under a rule and an abbot (*militans sub regula vel abbate*) provides the training from which the eremite, or more precisely, the anchorite, may move on to achieve greater spiritual perfection in solitude and tranquillity. Thus the workshop in which the tools of good works may be used is most properly the enclosure of the monastery with stability in the community.[66] While Sarabaites were at least self-sustaining, gyrovagues posed an essentially threefold problem: bringing them to accept perseverance in monastic profession with the minimal contact with the outside world; change of habitation or transfer (*transitus*) from one monastery to another subject to the approval of a superior; and self-support rather than dependence on mendicancy and social responsibility rather than a parasitic existence.

Admission to and departure from a monastery involved practical questions. To regularize acceptance, the candidate was expected to undergo a probationary period to judge his worthiness for full profession. Such impediments as marriage, slavery, military service, and public affairs must receive proper consideration.[67] In the second instance, what was to be done with the property that a monk had brought to his abbey, should he wish to leave? RB[68] and RM[69] are explicit that whatever property is donated to the monastery upon profession must remain in its possession, even in event of transfer to another monastery.[70] Although loss of civil status was accompanied by divestment of individual proprietary right, that the monastery as a corporate body was allowed to accumulate substantial property through endowment and productivity presented the real prospect of a *vita laxior*, which the serious inhabitant would find unconscionable, inducing him, therefore, to transfer to a reformed house.

Anchorites and cenobites, whose mode of life met with general approval, had been adumbrated respectively by Antony and Pachomius together with Basil. Although cenobitism was epitomized by Benedict as the *genus fortissimum* with the terse, yet heavily freighted, definition "hoc est monasteriale, militans sub regula vel abbate" (a qualification that consistently receives precision throughout the Rule in the spelling out of the requisites of obedience and stability), the anchorites were accorded sufficient attention to pose the perennial question of whether contemplation in seclusion or the active life, even extending to the *cura animarum* and other socially constructive tasks, offered the more certain path to achieving spiritual perfection. The advantages of eremitism were clearly acknowledged, subject to conditioning in a coenobium. Jerome had informed Rusticus that he wished to see come from the palaestrae of the monasteries only soldiers who had no fear of arduous training, who had long given proof that they could endure this kind of life.[71] For Cassian, too, the coenobium was a training school that, after instilling a practical knowledge of ascesis, prepared for that theoretical level of contemplation that can but be achieved in solitude.[72] Without composing a monastic rule or writing a formal treatise on asceticism, Cassiodorus (ca. 485–ca. 580) nevertheless addressed himself to the specific needs, above all intellectual, of a monastic community. Not without issuing a caveat with respect to semi-Pelagian teaching,[73] the ex-governor of Lucania and Bruttium was not loathe to express indebtedness to Cassian in the elaboration of the twofold monastery on his domain: at the foot of Mount Moscius near Squillace, the coenobium, called Vivarium, whose natural amenities and ambiance invited pilgrims and refugees alike; and on the side of Mount Castellum, the isolated cells, "encompassed by ancient walls" (*muris pristinis ambientibus*),[74] for hermits whose spiritual progress had been sufficiently advanced in community endeavor to justify a larger measure of austerity and self-reliance through withdrawal. Whether by juxtaposition or in a Palestinian-type laura, eremitism reacted vigorously against formalism in the eleventh century. Influenced by Romuald, founder of the Camaldulese, Peter Damian (1007–1072) was convinced that Benedict had exhorted monks to rise beyond community life to a higher state where spiritual struggles are harder and more continuous but where the triumphs are more glorious.[75] Consequently, the relative merits of these two kinds of monks became the staple of an extensive, but not infrequently pedantic, literature. In practice, however, it was admitted that along with the contemplative and active life is a composite (*vita mixta*), for the contemplative life must not omit duty to neighbor, nor must active life neglect contemplation of God.[76]

Inherent in eremitism was the danger of excessive individualism, unmitigated by obedience to rule or superior, owing its impetus to lay spirituality, and at times compounded by claims to a gift of prophecy. Cultivation of exaggerated mortification, frequently in a spirit of rivalry, engendered a feeling of pride or self-righteousness that could lead to a patronizing of clergy or fellow solitaries.[77] Coenobium, no less than cell or desert, offers the possibility of surrender to *acedia*, weariness or idleness of spirit, which results in despondency, in diffusion rather than concentration of thought and energy, thereby driving the monk from his vocation.[78] In the absence of fellowship, the hermit may create for himself a world of fantasy, nourished by illusion and distortion of true values. Out of disgust with cell and neglect of manual work, he may adopt an impulsive lifestyle that ends in social parasitism.

Not only were hermits accepted as an essential component of medieval society, provided they did not build isolated cells without abbatial consent,[79] but eremitism was to flower periodically and, by compelling self-examination, to rejuvenate, with examples of renunciation, simplicity, contemplation, and penitence, the entire ecclesiastical organism. Particularly responsive to the demands of lay piety, it generated reform impulses that often resulted in the foundation of monasteries and orders.[80] On the other hand, cenobitism, at once assuring security and mutual assistance within a familial relationship but also structured and attuned to ecclesiastical requirements, only too quickly identified itself through compromise with the established order. Respectability and strength, acquired through acceptability, are purchased at the price of declension from early enthusiasms and integrity. In the fourth century, eremitism reacted against externalism of the church as well as the moral decay and insecurity that accompanied the tottering Roman Empire; in the eleventh and twelfth centuries, its recrudescence in the West took the measure of monachism committed to feudal obligations.

That socioeconomic factors should be stressed as a primary determinant for the espousal of the monastic vocation or for the creation of an abbey is understandable. Although monastic literature, with its eschatological orientation and didactic intent, normally puts the accent on interior experience, it nevertheless is equally easy to exaggerate material ends in explaining motivation underlying religious decisions. For the pagan Rutilius Namatianus, the hermits inhabiting the islands of Capraria and Gorgon epitomized social maladjustment by shunning the world with its delights as well as its responsibilities;[81] for Smaragdus, the true hermit seeks solitude for prayer and not because of antisocial tendency or fear of life.[82] Yet how many relics were amassed, how many monasteries founded or endowed, for the salvation of one's soul, not to mention the economic opportunities such investment afforded! The habit clearly did not make the monk, but what benefits it conferred upon him! To what extent impetus for community life came from liturgical observance and collective prayer or from the search for mutual security and subsistence through cooperative manual work depends in no small measure on the relative importance that personal predilection assigns to these factors.[83] Yet material considerations obtrude themselves relentlessly, only too often reducing religious motivation to the status of an excuse. In RB the *raison d'être* of the coenobium lies in the *Opus Dei*:[84] Benedict gathered his monks for official prayer seven times a day and once at night as was common in the East.[85] If work groups, for Basil, provided not only protection but an opportunity to render psalmody,[86] so, in Benedict's eyes, absence from the oratory, occasioned by labor requirements, would not interfere with the *Opus Dei*.[87] Indeed, divine office and *lectio divina* must alternate with the *opus laboris*, the length and nature of which will be determined by geographic and economic considerations.[88] Because of human frailties, Benedict readily acknowledged that prolonged prayer, like excessive toil, can be self-defeating.[89] Nevertheless it was not merely as a deterrent to idleness (*otiositas*), as an ascetic exercise, or for therapeutic advantage that work found its justification: local conditions and need for sustenance required harvesting, with Benedict himself lending his own hand in the field.[90] Continuity between the Old Testament and the New Testament is assured by the Pauline work ethic, which became an indispensable component of official monasticism.[91]

Notwithstanding the constant intrusion of the miraculous, the *Vitae Patrum* of Gregory of Tours, no less than his *Historia Francorum*, portrays for Merovingian Gaul the same harsh, frontier conditions that Gregory the Great suggests for the Italian scene in both the *Dialogi* and his correspondence. When the recluse Calupan, who withdrew to the monastery of Méallet in Auvergne, weakened himself by excessive abstinence to such a point that he was unable to work with his brethren, they chided him, "as is the custom of monks," that unless he worked he would not eat.[92] In the region of Bourges, Ursus (d. ca. 510), a native of Cahors, illustrates by the mill he constructed at one of his monasteries how solicitude for economic well-being turned monks to technological innovation to find labor-saving devices.[93]

In place of Jerome's formula of *nuditas* as ultimate renunciation even in the midst of urban society, Benedict, in his communal blueprint, postulated *sufficientia*, predicated on collegiate property but personal poverty.[94] Not only was the abbot to provide necessities for his charges, but Benedict, albeit ever the moralist, advocated for the monastery what was tantamount to economic self-sufficiency, if still primarily intended as a prerequisite for spiritual well-being. "Monasterium autem, si possit fieri, ita debet constitui, ut omnia necessaria, id est, aqua, molendinum, hortus, vel artes diversae intra monasterium exerceantur, ut non sit necessitas monachis vagandi foris, quia omnino non expedit animabus eorum."[95] Given different socioeconomic conditions, however, nothing prevented prudence or *providentia*, ably assisted by purposeful *labor manuum*, from translating economic autarky into material affluence and from converting the expendable into the indispensable, as when an ample cartulary evinced well-being in copious charters, testaments, and acts of donation or when an impressive physical complex testified to confidence and prosperity having taken the place of self-effacement and renunciation or the mere need for security. The desirability of manual work was enhanced by the presence of recruits drawn from slaves, freedmen, peasants, and artisans whose crafts would prove beneficial the more they were plied.[96] To live in community, attuned both to subsistence (*stabilitas*) and charity while cultivating the worldly entanglements implicit in corporate ownership and administration of wealth, nevertheless offered advantages that strictly spiritual interests would find hard to resist.

RB[97] and RM[98] both provided for journeys outside the cloister, even as pilgrim monks and refugees might be expected to seek hospitality.[99] Nor did Benedict discourage a monastery, staffed with craftsmen, from selling their products to the public. He merely insisted that, for the sake of humility and to avoid the sin that Ananias and Sapphira (i.e., as Sarabaites) had incurred, they should undersell the competition in the world.[100] RM spells out this work ethic more fully. The monastery may dispose of a surplus of manufactured goods only at a lower price than that commanded by laymen, so that the religious may be separated from laymen by the distance of deeds ("spiritales a saecularibus actorum distantia separari"). For the sake of altruism, the rule forbids profit beyond the just price.[101] If monks ply their trades diligently, they are motivated not by avarice but by a desire to utilize the work period most effectively and to avoid idleness.[102] Given the imperative of food, the growth of the community, and the obligation to care for pilgrims and alms seekers, collegiate property could not be renounced.

To illustrate the advance of an agricultural economy in the sixth century, Pope Gregory relates that when a monastery was faced with a failure of the olive crop, the abbot decided to allow his charges to seek employment in neighboring orchards in return for a share of the oil. They were deterred, however, by the dangers that would befall monks who sought employment outside their claustral precincts.[103] Otherwise the *Dialogues* are replete with examples of monks engaged in labors requisite for survival: tending gardens,[104] clearing briers,[105] building walls,[106] baking bread,[107] and mowing hay.[108] RM,[109] on the other hand, provided for the leasing of land so that field work, care of property, grievances of tenants, and disputes with neighbors would fall on lay managers.

As spiritual director of such well-born, affluent Roman matrons as Paula with her daughter Eustochium and as Marcella, who turned her Aventine residence into a religious retreat, Jerome was acquainted with that informality of early monastic vocation to be expected in urban centers, both East and West. Although himself the product of educational and religious opportunities that Rome, Treves, Aquileia, Antioch, Constantinople, Jerusalem, and Caesarea afforded, the so-called irascible hermit whose eremitic experience occurred but briefly in Chalcis—and then not without contacts with the outside world—nevertheless aired with vehemence the distractions found in city life.[110] What monks found in rural life was peace and tranquillity, the *secreta ruris*,[111] which, far from Gaul, made Bethlehem, that "corner of the earth,"[112] so attractive in Jerome's maturity and old age.[113] Here for about forty years he occupied a cell in or near the monastery.[114] No longer inured to harsh austerity, he partook of a simple fare and, to avoid conspicuousness, counseled neatness of attire.[115] Such a moderate regimen particularizes through personal experience traditions that classical letters had cherished and that may be said to have culminated in Horace's apostrophe to *rus*.[116] For the ancients considered withdrawal (*otium*) from what is transient, above all from anything urban in character, as the *summum bonum* of this existence, not only for peace of mind, but in pursuit of philosophical contentment.[117] When Jerome undertook to convince Marcella of the advantages of provincial living, he contrasted the idyllic simplicity of the countryside in seasonal change with the tumult, depravity, and insincerity of Rome, not omitting a jibe at her own *senatus matronarum*.[118] Abundant as Rome was in relics and shrines, as Jerome well knew from boyhood Sunday excursions to the catacombs, and even though the capital bore the fiat of Petrine authority, its ostentation and size, the ever-present throngs wooed by its distractions, rendered it unpalatable for monastic seclusion.[119] Much better, it would be, for Eustochium, while still a resident there, to seek intercession of martyrs in her own quarters instead of appearing in public.[120] Far from fostering idleness, withdrawal from the world, now translated to a spiritual plane, makes possible concentration in silence, that oneness of person indispensable to prayer and study alike.[121]

Such considerations must have informed Jerome's strictures leveled at the Remnuoth, "a very inferior and despised kind" of monk who lived together in twos and threes, seldom in larger numbers, and followed their own will and direction.[122] Like early monks and nuns who lived in their own homes or under the parental roof, the Sarabaites (as Cassian came to call Jerome's pseudomonks because "they set themselves apart from the communities and provided, each for himself, for their own needs") are generally found in cities and villages.[123] Contrary to normal prescriptions to monks, what they sold commanded a high price, for "their workmanship, not their life, is sanctified." Admittedly, a portion of their earnings was earmarked for a common fund that provided food for all. Although they deserved to be commended for self-support through *labor manuum*, their motivation was vitiated by a desire to "live unto themselves." Absence of discipline and obedience to a superior encouraged competition in both secular occupation and religious practices, the result being ostentation in conduct and habit. Because of visibility, tonsure, like garb, was singled out as decisive evidence of deception.[124]

When Jerome warned Rusticus, a monk in Toulouse, in A.D. 411 of the dangers that attend the solitary life, not only did he detail willfulness and overweening pretensions that accompany excessive independence in eremitism but he appears to have had in mind the Sarabaite who preferred to the secluded cell the informal habitation afforded by the city: in the presence of his brethren he feigns aloofness but actually prefers to rub shoulders with the crowd in the street.[125] More pointed is the reference to monks who, inveigled by the profit motive, are unable to break from their crafts and trades that they had previously plied. Despite swarms of servants about them, they still call themselves hermits (*solitarii*). Only such an environment could breed the monk "as rich as Croesus," who, by exploiting the alms collected by the city for the poor, amassed a fortune for himself that will then be bequeathed to his heirs.[126] Moreover, Jerome considered women particularly susceptible to the blandishments of pseudomonks.[127]

Cassian regarded Sarabaites as the counterfeit of cenobitism; even as true cenobitism owed its origins to the primitive Jerusalem community described in Acts 4, so the Sarabaites, by withholding a part of their property for themselves, must claim Ananias and Sapphira as their progenitors.[128] This pair epitomized, for early church fathers,[129] hypocrisy through mendacity, but it was not until late in the fourth century that their duplicity was associated with what was considered a baneful trend in monachism. Whereas Jerome continued to inveigh in general terms against their greed,[130] it is in his commentary on Saint Matthew that withholding a portion of their property came to represent a declension from that spiritual perfection that the new asceticism promised in return for unqualified poverty.[131] Unlike Cassian, Benedict did not directly identify the couple with Sarabaites in RB 1, but, as noted above, in RB 57 he warns that when the handiwork of craftsmen in a monastery is sold, Ananias and his wife must be constantly kept in mind lest monastic property be handled dishonestly. Hereafter identification of this couple with pseudomonks who refused full renunciation recurs in medieval literature, if not in art.[132] Deprived of fellowship in community life, the avaricious monk labors day and night to the exclusion of prayer, fasting, or vigils.[133]

In treating undesirable kinds of monks, Eastern sources put considerable emphasis on the attractiveness of urban environment to the itinerant element. Isidore of Pelusium (ca. 360–435 or 449) compared vagabond monks to the hare that had no settled lodging and would depart at a whim.[134] To wander from one monastery to another exploiting hospitality merited vigorous disapproval.[135] A proponent of asceticism in moderation,[136] Isidore would not impose a rule on neophytes too rigorously lest they become faint-hearted. Similarly, monks were advised to abstain from excessive fasting.[137] In avoidance of self-gratification,[138] the desert offered advantages the city did not: in short, an urban setting with its turmoil and distractions is incompatible with monastic life.[139] If, for Benedict, Sarabaites appear to represent urban monks too much inured to commercialism and gyrovagues to represent a floating, parasitic element, no clear distinction between these kinds is yet to be discerned in Isidore.

Saint Nilus (d. ca. 430), abbot of a monastery near Ancyra, complained with equal fervor about pseudomonks whose uniquitous, pointless wandering combined with mendicancy, above all in urban centers, discredited the whole monastic state.[140] Although Nilus the moralist attributes desertion of cell ascesis to instability of character, to an unwillingness to submit to discipline,[141] he did glimpse a socioeconomic motivation behind the soliciting of food albeit under the pretense of religion.[142] After all, it was not unusual for laymen to provide ascetics with regular sustenance.[143] Yet by persisting in prayer and psalmody within monastic precincts, the inhabitants would not become a burden to the laity and would be able to provide for their needs.[144] Even as cenobites are to be preferred to anchorites,[145] so *stabilitas loci* alone makes possible spiritual concentration.[146] On the other hand, the Syrian stylites, sedentary as they were, invited distrust, for how does self-elevation engender humility?[147] Specifically, observance of stability prevents untoward conduct by forbidding spiritual direction in the houses of pious women.[148] With age, a monk can ask to be immured in a cell provided he returns to the community when pride or temptations assail him.[149] Monasteries should be built outside of cities; it is a specious argument to claim that, because towns offer more obstacles to ascetic practices, the urban locale therefore offers greater sanctification.[150] Urban monks are called *columbae*, whereas those in the desert are *turturae*, because the former are intent on making a public spectacle of their virtue.[151] Nilus discouraged visitation of relatives, although assistance in time of need is recommended if unaccompanied by natural affection.[152]

Pachomius forbade monks of other monasteries to partake of

the fare at Tabennisi except in transit. To gain admission to the community, a three-year probationary period was required.[153] How restlessness in mind or body posed dangers for the solitary life received a classic analysis from John Climacus (579–649).[154] Bishop Synesius of Cyrene (ca. 365–ca. 414) had exhibited concern less for vagabond monks than for vagrant or discharged priests.[155] Without a closer definition of the term *anchorite*, Sulpicius Severus (through the mouth of Postumianus) attests to the presence of an early itinerant element in Nitria. A number of monks "live in the desert without roofs over their heads, whom people call anchorites. They subsist on the roots of plants, they settle nowhere in any fixed place, lest they should frequently have men visiting them; wherever night compels them they choose their abode."[156] Called to Constantinople in 511, Abbot Sabas (d. 531) was at first denied entry to the palace by the *silentiarii*, who mistook him for a beggar because of his rags, which the hagiographer hastens to add, he had donned out of humility.[157]

To turn to the West, although Ambrose was most familiar with cenobitism in an urban environment, he acknowledged the ancestry of Elijah, Elisha, and John the Baptist.[158] More specifically, as bishop of Milan, Ambrose, toward the end of his life, denounced to the bishop of Vercelli, Sarmatio, and Barbatianus as two renegade monks who had fled their monastery in his see and espoused what Ambrose loosely labeled Epicurean teaching.[159] That descendants of Old Testament solitaries included an undisciplined, itinerant element evoked strictures from Jerome,[160] and Paulinus of Nola[161] before their presence induced Cassian to elevate them to the status of a fourth, nondescript kind of monks who had just appeared as the counterpart of anchorites grown cold in fervor.[162] Elsewhere, he was critical of defections from fixed abodes out of preference for vagabondage as well as feigned humility.[163]

Augustine's own classification in *De moribus ecclesiae catholicae et de moribus Manicheorum* (A.D. 388), embracing only anchorites and cenobites, was designed to refute the Manichaeans' claim that, by virtue of their ascetic prowess, crystallized in chastity, they alone constituted the elect.[164] The former were associated by him chiefly with Egypt and the East, with details that bear close resemblance to Jerome's.[165] Observing personal poverty, they obtained livelihood by the work of their hands and assigned the fruits of their labor to *decani*, who were charged with administration of individual and community needs under the guidance of a "father."[166] In strict claustration, women, too, spun and wove woolen cloth, which they exchanged with the brethren for food.[167] For the cenobite, both male and female, Augustine could draw upon direct experience in the West, above all, in Milan and Rome.[168] Interest in monasticism being whetted by Pontinianus's account of Saint Antony,[169] Augustine, together with his associates, once back in Africa, led a communal life at Tagaste.[170] Then, successfully blending priestly duties with ascesis,[171] he was to be regarded as the founder of the canons regular and to lend his name to the rule that purports to rest on Epistle 211 and the *Regula ad servos Dei*.[172] It was not his purpose to describe those who had withdrawn to desolate places for a vocation of austerity because, in some quarters, with insufficient understanding to be sure, they were considered to have exceeded propriety by eschewing social responsibility.[173]

Nevertheless it remained for Augustine to focus attention on the vagabond element even though his strictures largely assumed the form of an excursus dictated by special socioeconomic conditions in North Africa. In *De opere monachorum*, written at the request of Aurelius, bishop of Carthage, about A.D. 400,[174] Augustine registered stern disapproval of vagrant monks who endeavored to circumvent the Pauline injunction to work in return for food and clothing by appealing, with no thought of the morrow, to the double metaphor of birds of the air and lilies of the field.[175] To add to the onus of receiving alms, they flouted another Pauline directive[176] by wearing their hair long.[177] Whether these strictures concerned more than local conditions at Carthage is not clear.

In rebuking Ecdicia for excessive religious zeal, which threatened to destroy her marriage, Augustine was particularly harsh in chastising her liberality, for without her husband's approval, she had entrusted the family fortune to two wandering monks (*transeuntibus monachis*) as if alms were being distributed to the poor. By insinuating themselves into a private dwelling, they had preyed upon the woman's credulity.[178] Not only did such pseudomonks travel about without authorization, never stationary, stable, or settled, but exploitation of religious relics offered them too tempting a business prospect.[179] After distinguishing properly conditioned anchorites, Jerome, with his own saints' Lives written a generation earlier in mind, added that they were too conscientious to invent monstrous tales of struggles with demons, as some foolish men do in order to cause amazement among the ignorant and thereby to extort money.[180] Basil had already frowned upon the prevalence of commercial transactions at martyrs' shrines,[181] and Jerome grudgingly admitted that Vigilantius's criticism of these popular practices carried some cogency.[182] Ambrose[183] and Cassian[184] alike record the disturbances that often accompanied the desire to possess relics. No better illustration of growing religiosity within a sturdy ascetic context is to be found than the veneration of saints by Paulinus of Nola (crystallized in his cult of Saint Felix) and the explicit faith in the curative virtues of their relics. If drunken orgies previously inspired among the local populace by Venus and Bacchus were now being expiated by the feast of Felix, cast as the spiritual physician,[185] Paulinus's credulity nevertheless was put to severe strain by the worldly behavior of the faithful at vigils.[186] Trafficking in relics attracted the attention of government circles as well. Theodosius decreed that a buried body was not to be transferred to another site and that the relics of a martyr should not be sold; over the grave of a saint, a martyry might be erected, however, in veneration of the saint.[187]

Similarly, the presence of Donatists and Circumcellions in Numidia and Mauretania called forth from Augustine an invective against floaters and dissenters who eventually would be identified with gyrovagues.[188] Despite efforts to associate these movements, with emphasis on religious dissent, socioeconomic problems would appear to have contributed decisively among landless, migrant workers who, faced with heavy taxation and insecurity, were driven to violence in seeking the means of livelihood.[189]

By involving themselves in city politics in behalf of the socially dispossessed, Eastern monks attracted attention from official quarters as potential fomenters of sedition and riot. Because religious dissent cannot be easily disentangled from social and economic discontent, the emperors viewed its incidence as a treasonous act, disruptive of political unity, an effrontery to God and emperor alike. Monks were required in 390 to inhabit desert places and inaccessible solitudes.[190] Two years later, however, this law was repealed, allowing them to return to towns without denying the right to interpose an appeal within statutory time limits.[191] In 398 the emperor condemned clerics and monks who had committed crimes of disorder to aid individuals under arrest.[192] To prevent possible disturbance Theodosius II in 431 ordered Candidianus of the imperial guard to expel from Ephesus lay strangers and monks who had assembled in the city presumably to observe the council.[193] It remained for the Council of Chalcedon (451) to formalize the status of monachism as a significant component of the ecclesiastical fabric by forbidding monks to wander aimlessly in cities, disturbing under pretext of religion either church or civil affairs, or even to found monasteries for themselves. Henceforth those espousing asceticism must be subject to episcopal jurisdiction. Without specific commission by the bishop, they were to observe *stabilitas loci* and refrain from wordly entanglements.[194] Though bishops had already assumed the right of surveillance by virtue of *ratione peccati*, Canon 4 set the scope of episcopal jurisdiction.[195] In 471 Emperor Leo I (457-474) again forbade monks to leave their precincts for cities; necessary business was to be transacted through agents (*apocrisarii*), that is, monks who were entrusted with the business affairs of their houses.[196] That vagabond monks continued to be proscribed in the *Novellae* suggests how persistent the problem was.[197]

Identified either with itinerant clerics or wayward monks, gyrovagues in the West presented a constant theme in monastic literature. Peter Damian denounced their kind, who were always on the road, attracted attention by slovenly attire, and felt a compulsion to engage without commission in apostolic ministry.[198] At a time when lay piety was being voiced by itinerant preachers, Bruno admonished his charges at the Grande Chartreuse: Stay where you are and flee like a pestilence the unhealthy band of laymen who peddle their writings, uttering what they do not understand and what they contradict by word and deed. As gyrovagues, they reject rule and obedience.[199] Abelard was likewise disturbed by monks who wandered alone or in small bands outside their abbeys in town and countryside.[200] In a poem entitled *De falsis heremitis qui vagando discurrunt*, composed about 1130, Payen Bolotin spoke indiscriminately and with the usual clichés of false pilgrims, suspected hermits, gyrovagues, and "pretenders in religion," with those in white habit—presumably Cistercians—being singled out for their innovations.[201] Yet Cistercians with their respect for *stabilitas loci* must not be confused with "false hermits" who refused to remain cloistered.

Bolotin's strictures parallel those made by Ivo of Chartres in a letter to the Benedictine monks of Coulombs (diocese of Chartres), written before 1116. A staunch defender of the canonical life, the bishop nevertheless hastened to disclaim any censure of eremitism, especially of anchorites who, trained in monasteries under the discipline of a rule, withdraw to the desert with the permission of their superiors (*ordinabiliter ad eremum secedunt*). Living from the work of their hands they pursue an active life or refresh their minds in contemplation. "But when I see," he continues, "men leave their calling and, covered with sheep skins, wander in all directions through towns, castles, and cities, aiming by the negligence of their garments and the coarseness of their food, to dazzle the public with their merits and ambitions, and to become masters without ever being disciples. . . . These men I do not consider solitaries or cenobites, they are gyrovagues or Sarabaites."[202]

Localism as a compound of geographic isolation and constitutional autonomy contributed much to monastic diversity as well as to relaxed discipline both during the evolution of eremitism and cenobitism and in the centuries when community life was endorsed and stabilized by the Benedictine rule. In the eleventh century older monachism, which had become a territorial and political force tightly enmeshed with feudalism, was challenged in various quarters within its own domain: the revival of eremitism in emulation of the Desert Fathers, the renewal of cenobitism by recapturing the pristine purity of the Rule, the emergence of canons regular subscribing to the Augustinian Rule, and early manifestations of lay piety. In the thirteenth century, values that had enlisted the support of Augustine in *De opere monachorum* and of other early monastic proponents were reversed. Instead of withdrawal in pursuit of contemplative delights in solitude, the religious life, though predicated on a keen sense of penitence, now represented affirmation of the world around through apostolic endeavor. In place of *stabilitas loci*, which was meaningful for a rural society and local autonomy, the friars put the accent on *mobilitas*, transcending diocesan limits and taking the world as their parish. Whereas crystallization of monastic principles in the West had coincided with contraction to an agricultural economy, the friars adopted methods and objectives that not only met the conditions of an urban environment but also encompassed expanding horizons, geographic and intellectual alike. Consciously espousing a social program responsive to the needs of townsmen, the Franciscans, in particular, achieved through tertiaries an intermeshing of religious and secular life. Without looking askance at *labor manuum*, the friars nevertheless put a premium on mendicancy in an effort to maintain collegiate as well as personal poverty. Sarabaites who appear to have been urban monks in the fourth century, unable or unwilling to separate themselves completely from ordinary daily affairs, must not have differed appreciably from tertiaries or extraregulars who, as laymen in urban centers in the fourteenth century, endeavored to leaven ordinary daily commitments with meaningful religious practices. Similarly, gyrovagues at first included itinerant preachers, teachers, and prophets, then became synonymous with lay piety that was suspected of excessive individualism or with vagabondage that was aimless and parasitic. With the creation in the thirteenth century of a veritable spiritual infantry, subject to close discipline, *mobilitas*, on the contrary, came to involve, in the pursuit of apostolic poverty under papal auspices, the promotion of evangelical mission at home and far afield together with a dedication to social work.

Notes

1. Adalbert de Vogüé, ed., *La Règle du Maître*, 3 vols. in *SC*, nos. 105–107 (Paris, 1964–1965); H. Vanderhoven and F. Masai, eds., *La Règle du Maître: Edition diplomatique des manuscrits latins 12205 et 12634 de Paris*, in *Les Publications de Scriptorium*, no. 3 (Brussels and Paris, 1953).

2. Adalbert de Vogüé and Jean Neufville, eds., *La Règle de Saint Benoît*, 6 vols., in *SC*, nos. 181–186 (Paris, 1971–1972). Although priority of RM, an anonymous compilation of uncertain date (now attributed to the first decades of the sixth century) and provenance (presumably from the Roman Campania) with consequent adaptation by RB, is now widely accepted, such a stance, evoking much soul searching in Benedictine scholarship, has generated a voluminous literature since Dom Augustin Genestout raised the question of relationship in 1937. For a bibliography and history of this multifaceted problem, see Bernd Jaspert, *Die Regula Benedicti—Regula Magistri—Kontroverse* (Hildesheim, 1975); idem, "Regula Magistri—Regula Benedicti, Bibliographie ihrer historisch-kritischen Erforschung 1938–1970," *Studia monastica* 13 (1971):129–171; G. Penco, "Origini e sviluppi della questione della Regula Magistri," in *Antonius Magnus Eremita*, Studia Anselmiana, no. 38 (Rome, 1956), pp. 283–306; Adalbert de Vogüé, "Scholies sur la Règle du Maître," *Revue d'ascétique et mystique* 44 (1968):121–160, 261–292; David Knowles, *Great Historical Enterprises: Problems in Monastic History* (London, 1963), pp. 135–195.

3. Gregory the Great *Dialogi* 2. 3, ed. Umberto Moricco (Rome, 1924), pp. 84–85.

4. Gregorio Penco, "Il capitolo *De generibus monachorum* nella tradizione medievale," *Studia monastica* 3 (1961):241–257.

5. Isidore of Seville *De eccl. offic.* 2. 15. 2–10, *PL* 83. 794–799; *Etymologiae* (7. 13. 2–4, *PL* 82. 293–294) recognizes only the three good kinds; *Regula monachorum*, PL 83. 867–894. Cf. K. S. Frank, "Isidor von Sevilla, das "Mönchskapitel" (*De ecclesiasticis officiis* II 16) und seine Quellen," *Römische Quartalschrift* 67 (1973):29–48, esp. 32–41; Paul Séjourné, *Saint Isidore de Séville, son rôle dans l'histoire du droit canonique* (Paris, 1929), pp. 210–218. In his *De genere monachorum*, Valerio of Bierzo (d. after 695) grafted on Isidore's categories a "seventh kind of monk, recently added and worse than the former ones." These were the product of proprietary churches in Visigothic Spain, specifically the northwest part of Astorga, the site of several of Fructuosus's monasteries with which Valerio himself was later

associated. The treatise attacks the practice of obliging coloni or serfs to become monks in order to populate a monastery and to assure economic security, thereby enabling the proprietor to collect revenues from endowment of the monastery [*Dicta de genere monachorum*, incorporated by Benedict of Aniane in the *Concordia Regularum, PL* 103. 750-754; cf. Consuelo Maria Aherne, *Valerio of Bierzo, an Ascetic of the Late Visigothic Period* (Washington, D.C., 1949), pp. 51-55; 183, n. 130].

6. Cf. François Masai and Eugene Manning, "Les états du ch. ler du Maître et la fin du Prologue de la règle bénédictine," *Scriptorium* 23 (1969):393-433; idem., "Recherches sur les manuscrits et les états de la *Regula Monasteriorum* (II-III)," *Scriptorium* 20 (1966):193-214; 21 (1967):205-226; 22 (1968):3-19.

7. RM 1. 13-74; cf. RB 1. 12.

8. Martin Bechthum, *Beweggründe und Bedeutung des Vagantentums in der lateinischen Kirche des Mittelalters* (Jena, 1941); Helen Waddell, *The Wandering Scholars* (Boston and New York, 1927).

9. David Knowles, "The Monastic Life of the Master's Rule," *Studia patristica*, 13, in *TU*, no. 116 (1975), pp. 471-478; P. Tamburrino, "La Regula Magistri e l'origini del potere abbaziale," *Collectanea Cisterciensis*, 28 (1966): 160-173; Adalbert de Vogüé, *La communauté et l'abbé dans la Règle de Saint Benoît* (Bruges, 1961); idem., "Travail et alimentation dans les règles de Saint Benoît et du Maître," *Revue bénédictine* 74 (1964):242-251; A. Böckmann, "Akzentuierungen der neutestamentlichen Armut nach der Regula Benedicti" (Second International Congress on the Rule of St. Benedict, Maria Laach, 1975) *Regulae Benedicti studia* 5 (Hildesheim, 1977), 141 ff.

10. J. Wollasch, *Mönchtum des Mittelalters zwischen Kirche und Welt* (Munich, 1973), pp. 24-40; Arnold Angenendt, *Monachi Peregrini: Studien zu Pirmin und den monastischen Vorstellungen des frühen Mittelalters* (Munich, 1972); C. de Clercq, *La législation religieuse franque de Clovis à Charlemagne (507-814)*, (Louvain and Paris, 1936), 1:119 f., 124.

11. P. Schmitz, "L'influence de S. Benoît d'Aniane dans l'histoire de l'ordre de S. Benoît," in *Il monachesimo nell'alto medioevo* (Spoleto, 1957), pp. 401-415; Josef Narberhaus, *Benedikt von Aniane: Werk und Persönlichkeit*, Beiträge zur Geschichte des alten Mönchtums und des Benediktinerordens, 16 (Münster i. W., 1930), pp. 19-22, 51-67.

12. L. T. A. Lorié, *Spiritual Terminology in the Latin Translations of the Vita Antonii with Reference to Fourth and Fifth Century Monastic Literature*, Latinitas Christianorum primaeva, 11 (Nijmegen, 1955), pp. 51-58, 65-70.

13. Peter Charanis, "Monk as Element of Byzantine Society," *Dumbarton Oaks Papers* 25 (1971):63-84, esp. 64 f.; D. J. Chitty, *The Desert a City: An Introduction to the Study of Egyptian and Palestinian Monasticism under the Christian Empire* (Oxford, 1966).

14. Cassian *Inst.* 11. 18, ed. M. Petschenig, in *CSEL*, vol. 17 (Vienna, 1888), 203; cf. ibid. 11. 14 (*CSEL* 17:201).

15. Cassian *Conl.* 24. 26, *CSEL*, 13: 704 ff.; Fourth Council of Toledo (633), can. 50 (Mansi, X, 631 = Causa, XIX, q. 1, c. 1). Can. 45 (Mansi, X, 630 = Causa, XXIII, q. 8, c. 5), however, prescribed monasteries as houses of detention for seditious clergy.

16. Justinian nov. 5, *De monachis*, praef., trans. S. P. Scott, *The Civil Law*, vol. 16, coll. I, tit. 5, praef. (Cincinnati, 1973), p. 24.

17. Terence P. McLaughlin, *Le très ancien droit monastique de l'Occident: Etude sur le développement général du monachisme et ses rapports avec l'église séculière et le monde laïque de Saint Benoît de Nursie à Saint Benoît d'Aniane* (Ligugé and Paris, 1935), pp. 111–171.

18. Cf. Heb. 11:37–38.

19. Matt. 10:21–22. 19:21; Luke 9:3, 23; Mark 10:21.

20. Karl Suso Frank, "Vita Apostolica: Ansätze zur apostolischen Lebensform in der alten Kirche," *Zeitschrift für Kirchengeschichte* 82 (1971):145–166; idem, "Vita Apostolica und Dominus Apostolicus," in *Konzil und Papst, historische Beiträge zur Frage der höchsten Gewalt in der Kirche: Festgabe für Hermann Tüchle* (Munich, 1975), pp. 19–41; M. H. Vicaire, *L'imitation des apôtres, moines, chanoines et mendiants, IVe–XIIIe siècles* (Paris, 1963); H. Bacht, "La loi du 'retour aux sources' (De quelques aspects de l'idéal monastique pachômien)," *Revue Mabillon* 51 (1961):6–25, esp. 7–16.

21. Acts 4:32, 34–35; cf. 2:44–47.

22. Matt. 19:29; Luke 14:26.

23. Acts 4:32.

24. Rudolf Eiswirth, *Hieronymus' Stellung zur Literatur und Kunst* (Wiesbaden, 1955), pp. 34–36, 69 f.; P. Antin, "'Simple' et 'simplicité' chez S. Jérôme," *Revue bénédictine* 71 (1961):371–381; also pub. in *Recueil sur Saint Jérôme*, Collection Latomus, 95 (Brussels, 1968), pp. 147–161; Paul Lehmann, "Die heilige Einfalt," *Historisches Jahrbuch* 58 (1938):305–316; H. Hagendahl, "Piscatorie et non Aristotelice: Zur einem Schlagwort bei den Kirchenvätern," *Septentrionalia et Orientalia studia Bernhardo Karlgren dedicata* (Stockholm, 1959), pp. 184–193; P. C. Bori, *Chiesa primitiva: L'immagine della communità delle origini—Atti 2. 42-47, 4. 32-37—nella storia della chiesa antica* (Brescia, 1974); O. Hiltbrunner, *Latina Graeca: Semasiologische Studien über lateinische Wörter im Hinblick auf ihr Verhältnis zu griechischen Vorbildern* (Bern, 1958), pp. 85–105.

25. E. W. McDonnell, *The Beguines and Beghards in Medieval Culture with Special Reference to the Belgian Scene* (New Brunswick, N.J., 1954).

26. 1 Cor. 4:21; 1 Thess. 2:9; 2 Thess. 3:4.

27. 1 Tim. 5:17–18; 1 Cor. 3:8.

28. 2 Thess. 2:2, 3:8–12.

29. Eph. 4:28; cf. Acts 20:35.

30. Luke 10:7.

31. 1 Cor. 7:20, 24.

32. 2 Tim. 2:3; cf. Eph. 6:10–18.

33. Lorié, *Spiritual Terminology*, p. 103.

34. Edward Malone, *The Monk and the Martyr: The Monk as the Successor of the Martyr* (Washington, D.C., 1950); résumé in *Antonius Magnus Eremita*, Studia Anselmiana, 38 (Rome, 1956), pp. 201–228; A. Harnack, *Militia Christi, die christliche Religion und der Soldatenstand in der ersten drei Jahrhunderten* (Tübingen, 1905); Linus Hofmann, "Militia Christi: Ein Beitrag zur Lehre von den kirchlichen Ständen," *Trierer Theologische Zeitschrift* 63 (1954):76–92.

35. Acts 2:43; cf. Peter Brown, "The Rise and Function of the Holy Man in Late Roman Society," *Journal of Roman Studies* 61 (1971):80–101.

36. Gregory of Tours *Vitae patrum* 18, *PL* 71. 1084.

37. Jerome assigned to anchorites illustrious progenitors: his own hero, Paul of Thebes, introduced this way of life ("huius, i.e., monasticae, vitae auctor Paulus, illustrator Antonius," Ep. 22. 36, *PL* 22. 421; "princeps vitae monasticae," *Vita Pauli*, prol. *PL* 23. 17 f.), whereas Antony popularized it [Jerome admitted that contemporaries even doubted Paul's very existence (*V. Hilarionis* 1, *PL* 23. 29)] and John the Baptist served as the prototype [Ep. 22. 36, *PL* 22. 421; "sicut sacerdotum principes sunt apostoli, sic monachorum princeps Johannes Baptista est," *De principio Marci* 1. 1–12, in G. Morin, ed., *Anecdota Maredsolana* III. 2 (Maredsous, 1897), p. 321; *Homilia in Iohannem* 1. 1–14, in ibid., p. 387] in his abandonment of urban centers (*Tractatus in Marci Evangelium* 1. 1–12, in ibid., p. 321. According to Jerome, who had apostolic origins in mind, Philo called early habitations in Egypt monasteries (*De vir. illustr.* 11, *PL* 23. 625/627).

38. Amand Boon, *Pachomiana latina, règle et epîtres de S. Pachôme, epître de S. Théodore et "Liber" de S. Orsiesius* (Louvain, 1932).

39. Jerome's province was Pannonia; Stridon, obliterated during the invasions, was his birthplace [F. Bulic, "Stridone luogo natale di S. Girolamo," *Miscellanea Geronimiana* (Rome, 1920), pp. 253–350; F. Cavallera, *Saint Jérôme, sa vie et son oeuvre* (Louvain and Paris, 1922), 1. 2. 68–70]. Although neighboring towns had their coteries of ascetics—Aquileia, those gathered about Bishop Chromatius (d. 407) (Jerome, Eps. 6–9); Haemona (Ljubljana), a cluster of ascetic women with whom Jerome corresponded (Eps. 11–12), and Concordia, renowned for its venerable Paul (Eps. 5. 2, 10)—Jerome lashed out fiercely at delinquent clerics in his homeland (Ep. 7. 5).

40. RB prol. 50; RM ths. 46; cf. Lorié, *Spiritual Terminology*, pp. 114 f.

41. RB 60. 8–9; 61. 5.

42. *Verba seniorum* 1. 1, *PL* 73. 855a.

43. Ibid., 7.24, *PL* 73. 897c–900a; M. Rothenhäusler, "Ältestes Mönchtum and klösterliche Beständigkeit," *Benediktinische Monatschrift* 3 (1921): 87–95, 223–237; Peter Nagel, *Die Motivierung der Askese in der alten Kirche und der Ursprung des Mönchtums*, *TU*, 95 (Berlin, 1966), pp. 96–98; J. McMurray, "Monastic Stability," *Cistercian Studies* 1 (1966):209–224; Emilio Herman, "La 'stabilitas loci' nel monachismo bizantino," *Orientalia Christiana periodica* 21 (1955):115–142.

44. *Verba seniorum* 3, *PL* 73. 860–864; A. Wallis Budge, *The Paradise or Garden of the Holy Fathers*, 2 vols. (London, 1907), 2:31–35.

45. Jerome *Liber contra Vigilantium* 15, *PL* 23. 351 = Causa, XVI, q. 1, c. 4; cf. Rufinus *Hist. mon.* 1, *PL* 21. 397ab; cf. Leo I, Ep. 119. 6, *PL* 54. 1046a; Ep. 120. 6, *PL* 1054b.

46. Jerome *Comm. in Ezech.* 13, c. 44, v. 22, *PL* 25. 441a; cf. *Comm. in Aggaeum* 2, vv. 11 ff., *PL* 25. 1407ab.

47. Athanasius *V. Ant.* 85, *PG* 26. 961c; Sozomen *Historia ecclesiastica* 1. 13, *PG* 67. 899a; the metaphor is based on Isa. 50:2; for the metaphor of barrenness of a frequently transplanted tree, *Verba seniorum* 7. 36, *PL* 73. 902; in criticism of itinerant monks, Theodore Studite refers to sheep outside the fold (*Sermones catechetici* 72, *PG* 99. 605).

48. *V. Ant.* 69. After referring to this incident, Theodoret (*Historia ecclesiastica* 4. 24) observed that the monks adapted themselves as the occasion demanded, whether it involved remaining inactive or leaving the desert for towns.

49. Athanasius *V. Ant.* 46.

50. P. Ladeuze, *Etude sur le cénobitisme pakhômien pendant le IVe siècle et la première moitié du Ve* (Fontemoing, 1898; repr. Frankfurt, 1961), pp. 292 f.

51. John Moschus, *Le Pré spirituel, SC,* 12 (Paris, 1946); cf. N. H. Baynes, *Byzantine Studies and Other Essays* (New York, 1955), pp. 261-270.

52. John Ryan, *Irish Monasticism: Origins and Early Development* (Dublin, 1931), pp. 256-263; J. P. Fuhrmann, *Irish Medieval Monasteries on the Continent* (Washington, D.C., 1927), pp. 2, n. 7, 41-53; P. W. Finsterwalder, "Wege und Ziele der irischen und angelsächsischen Mission im fränkischen Reich," *Zeitschrift für Kirchengeschichte* 47 (1928):203-226; L. Gougaud, *Christianity in Celtic Lands*, trans. Maud Joynt (London, 1932), pp. 219-231; Hans von Campenhausen, *Tradition and Life in the Church*, trans. A. V. Littledale (Philadelphia, 1968), pp. 231-251.

53. O. Seebass, "Ordo sancti Columbani de vita et actione monachorum," *Zeitschrift für Kirchengeschichte* 14 (1894):78-92, esp. 87; idem., "Regula monachorum," can. 8 in ibid., 15 (1895):374-386, esp. 382 f.

54. "Patricius ait: Monachus inconsulto abbate vagus ambulans in plebe debet excommunicari" (cited by Gougaud, *Christianity in Celtic Lands*, p. 170, cf. p. 169). In like fashion, transfer to a stricter monastery was subject to regulation [H. Wasserschleben, *Die irische Kanonensammlung* (Leipzig, 1885; repr. Aalen, 1966), xxxix, 9, p. 151; xxxix, 7, p. 150].

55. "bene colite terram, et bene laborate, ut habeatis sufficientia cibi et potus et vestitus! ubi enim sufficientia erit apud servos Domini, ibi stabilitas erit; et ubi stabilitas in servitio divino fuerit, ibi religio erit" [*AASS,* 4 August, I, 353 n. f.; cf. *Vita S. Luani,* can. 6, 43 (ibid., 352)].

56. Gen. 12:11; Heb. 11:8-9.

57. F. O. Briain, in *Dictionnaire d'histoire et de géographie ecclésiastique* (1956), 13:316; Helen Bittermann, "The Influence of Irish Monks on Merovingian Diocesan Organization," *American Historical Review* 40 (1935): 232-245.

58. "Dulce solum natalis patriae" (*Vita Mariani* 32, *AASS,* 9 February, II, 372).

59. *Vita Findani* 5. 6, *MGH, SS,* XV. 1. 504.

60. Bede, *Ecclesiastical History of the English People,* ed. B. Colgrave and R. A. B. Mynors (Oxford, 1969), IV. 4, pp. 346, 348.

61. Campenhausen, *Tradition and Life,* p. 244.

62. Council of Meaux (845), can. 40 (Mansi, XIV, 827 f.); cited by Gougaud, *Christianity in Celtic Lands,* p. 179.

63. Caesarius of Arles *Regula ad virgines,* c. 1, *PL* 67. 1107b; *Regula ad monachos,* can. 1, *PL* 67. 1099b.

64. RB 58. 17-18; RM 89. 3-16; cf. C. Butler, *Benedictine Monachism: Studies in Benedictine Life and Rule* (London, 1910), pp. 122-145.

65. P. Steidle, "De conversatione morum suorum," *Studia Anselmiana* 44 (Rome, 1959):137-144; O. Lottin, "Le voeu de 'conversatio morum' dans la Règle de Saint Benoît," *Recherches de théologie ancienne et médiévale* 26 (1959):5-16; J. Chapman, *Saint Benedict and the Sixth Century* (London,

1929), pp. 206-231; for the development of *conversio* and *conversatio*, see C. Mohrmann, *Etudes sur le latin des chrétiens* 2 (Rome, 1961):341-345; Lorié, *Spiritual Terminology*, pp. 82, 84-85.

66. RB 4. 78: "Officium . . . claustra sunt monasterii et *stabilitas in congregatione*"; cf. RB prol. 50; 58. 17; 60. 9; 61. 5. Without Benedict's telling formula in RB 4. 78, the *ars sancta*—detailed in RM 3. 1-77, with a list of spiritual tools to be cultivated (RM 4) and vices to be avoided (RM 5)—concludes with "officina . . . monasterium est in qua ferramenta cordis in corporis clusura reposita opus divinae artis diligenti custodia perseverando operari potest" (RM 6); cf. RM 79. 27-28; 88. 1; 89. 1, 33-34; for those unwilling to observe *stabilitas loci*, i.e., *firmare*, see RM 79. 29-34.

67. Norman F. McFarland, *Religious Vocation, Its Juridic Concept* (Washington, D.C., 1953), pp. 71-78.

68. RB 58. 24-29; cf. Cassian, *Inst.* 4. 5.

69. RM 87. 33-39.

70. Cf. Justinian nov. 5. 7; cf. 4-6.

71. Jerome Ep. 125. 9, *PL* 22. 1077.

72. Cassian, *Conl.* 18. 16, *CSEL*, 13:531.

73. Cassiodorus *De institutione divinarum litterarum*, c. 29, *PL* 70. 1144; *An Introduction to Divine and Human Readings*, trans. L. W. Jones (New York, 1946), pp. 131 f.

74. Cassiodorus *De institutione*, c. 29, *PL* 70. 1144c; cf. A. van de Vyver, "Cassiodore et son oeuvre," *Speculum* 6 (1931):244-292.

75. Damian Ep. 12, *PL* 144. 392-396; cf. *Opusc.* 15, *PL* 145. 336-337. See articles in *L'Eremitismo in Occidente nei secoli XI e XII: Atti della seconda internazionale di studio Mendola, 30 agosto-6 settembre 1962* (Milan, 1965); L. Gougaud, *Ermites et reclus: Études sur d'anciennes formes de vie religieuse* (Liguçé, 1928).

76. Augustine *De civ. Dei* 19. 19, *PL* 41. 647. To Basil, Gregory of Nazianzus assigned responsibility for reconciling what appeared to be two incompatible ways of life (*Oratio* 2. 29, *PG* 35. 437/438b), one fraught with pride, the other endangered by turbulence (*Oratio 43, In laudem Basilii Magni* 62, *PG* 36. 577/578b; cf. ibid., 81, *PG* 36. 603/604b; cf. *Oratio 21, In laudem Athanasii* 19, *PG* 35. 1101/1104a). For the moralist such reconciliation of diverse lifestyles illustrates how monasticism is characterized by steadfastness of disposition rather than mere physical withdrawal (ibid., 20, *PG* 35. 1103/1104b).

77. "armentque linguas suas, vel clericis, vel aliis monachis detrahendo" (Jerome Ep. 130. 17, *PL* 22. 1121; cf. Ep. 125. 9, *PL* 22. 1077.

78. Cassian *Inst.* 10, 1-8, *CSEL*, 17:173-182.

79. Council of Vannes (465), can. 7 (Mansi, VII, 954). This canon, together with cans. 5, 6, 8, was reproduced verbatim by the Council of Agde (506), can. 38 (ibid., VIII, 331). The Fourth Council of Toledo (633) decreed that "religiosi propriae regionis qui nec inter clericos nec inter monachos habentur, sive hi qui per diversa loca vagi fuerint" were subject to episcopal discipline (can. 53, ibid., X, 632). Cf. the Council of Orleans (511), can. 22 (ibid., VIII, 355 = Caus. XVIII, q. 2, can. 14); the Seventh Council of Toledo (646), can. 5 (Mansi X, 769 f.); the council in Trullo (692), cans. 41-42 (ibid., XI, 963-964), which, by stipulating a three-year training in a monastery as a prerequisite for the solitary life, distinguished between cenobitism and eremitism and yet provided for a complementary role. Not uncommon was the

special form of reclusion, its devotees, singly or in pairs, pursuing solitude in a cell (*cellula, reclusorium, reclusagium, inclusarium*) adjacent to a monastery, cathedral, collegiate church, or chapel. In any case, they "dwelt under the eaves of the church" [*The Ancren Riwle: A Treatise on the Rules and Duties of Monastic Life*, ed. James Morton, Camden Society, 57 (London, 1853), p. 143]. The Seventh Council of Toledo, can. 5, spelled out the procedures for its adoption subject to episcopal and abbatial consent. The Council of Frankfurt (794) completed the legislation governing reclusion (can. 12, Mansi XII, 908; *MGH, Leg.* 3, *Concilia* 2. 168), and Grimlaic composed the *Regula Solitariorum* in the ninth century (*PL* 103. 573-661). In addition to Gougaud (*Ermites et reclus*), see O. Doerr, *Das Institut der Inclusen in Süddeutschland* (Münster i.W., 1934), 24-70.

80. "Vita eremitica, quae est radix vitae monasticae vel coenobiticae" (Hildegarde of Bingen, *Vita S. Disibodi* 3. 29, *PL* 197. 1106ab); cf. J. Leclerq, "L'érémitisme en Occident jusqu'à l'an mil," in *L'Eremitismo in Occidente*, pp. 27-44, esp. 42.

81. Rutilius *De reditu suo* (ca. A.D. 417), vv. 439-452, 515-526; cf. J. Vessereau, *Cl. Rutilius Namatianus* (Paris, 1904), pp. 280-289.

82. Smaragdus *Commentaria in reg. S. Benedicti* 1, *PL* 102. 725b.

83. de Vogüé and Neufville, *Règle de Saint Benoît, SC*, 185:664-671; Armand Veilleux, *La liturgie dans le cénobitisme pachômien au quatrième siècle*, Studia Anselmiana, 57 (Rome, 1968); A. Van der Meensbrugghe, "Prayertime in Egyptian Monasticism (320-450)," *Studia Patristica*, 2, *TU*, 64 (1957), pp. 435-454.

84. "nihil Operi Dei praeponatur" (RB 43. 3).

85. RB 16.

86. Basil *Reg. fus. tr.*, 37, *PG* 31. 1009/1016.

87. RB 50; RM 61.

88. RB 48. 1; cf. RM 50. 107.

89. RB 48. 7-9.

90. Gregory the Great *Dial.* 2. 32, ed. Moricco, p. 124; cf. RB 48. 7-8.

91. W. Harold Mare, "The Pauline Work Ethic," in *New Dimensions in New Testament Study* (Grand Rapids, Mich., 1976), pp. 357-369; Arthur T. Geoghegan, *The Attitude towards Labor in Early Christianity and Ancient Culture* (Washington, D.C., 1945), pp. 93-228; Walther Bienert, *Die Arbeit nach der Lehre der Bibel, eine Grundlegung evangelischer Sozialethik* (Stuttgart, 1954), pp. 187-378; Hermann Dörries, "Mönchtum und Arbeit," in *Wort und Stunde* 1 (Göttingen, 1966):277-301.

92. Gregory of Tours *Vitae Patrum* 11, *PL* 71. 1059a; cf. S. G. Luff, "A Survey of Primitive Monasticism in Central Gaul (c. 350-700)," *Downside Review* 70 (1952)180-203.

93. Gregory of Tours *Vitae Patrum* 18, *PL* 71. 1085-1086.

94. RB 33; RM 16. 58-61.

95. RB 66. 6-7. Containment is similarly recommended in RM 95. 17-18: "Omnia vero necessaria intus intra regias esse oportet, id est furnus, macinas, refrigerium, hortus vel omnia necessaria, ut non sit frequens occasio, propter quam fratres multotiens feras egressi, saecularibus mixti" (cf. de Vogüé and Neufville, *Règle de Saint Benoît, SC*, 182: 660 f., n. to 6-7). Much the same physical complex, accompanied with moral directives, was spelled out for the monastery headed by Isidore a century earlier (*Historia monachorum* 17, *PL* 21. 439c). Cf. A. Werminghoff, "Die wirtschaftstheoretischen Anschauungen

der Regula sancti Benedicti," in *Historische Aufsätze Karl Zeumer als Fest-gabe* (Weimar, 1910), pp. 31–50; for the East, see L. Daloz, *Le travail selon Saint Jean Chrysostome* (Paris, 1959).

96. Augustine, *De opere monachorum* 22, *PL* 40. 568.

97. RB 50, 51, 67.

98. RM 66–67.

99. RB 61; RM 72.

100. RB 57: "In ipsis autem pretiis non subripirat avaritiae malum, sed semper aliquantulum vilius detur quam ab aliis secularibus dari potest. . . ." Cf. Cassian, *Inst.* 7. 25, *CSEL.* 17, 146 f.; *Verba Seniorum* 6. 11, *PL* 73. 890.

101. RM 85. 2–7; cf. RM 17. 16 (de Vogüé and Neufville, *Règle de Saint Benoît, SC,* 106, 87, n. 16).

102. RM 86. 18–22. To minimize commitment to the world, cultivation of a garden was adjudged most important (RM 86. 27).

103. Gregory the Great *Dial.* 1. 7, ed. Moricco, p. 46. Cf. Ferdinand Anton-elli, "De re monastica in Dialogis S. Gregorii Magni," *Antonianum* 2 (1927): 401–436, esp. 432 ff.

104. Gregory the Great *Dial.* 1. 3; 3. 14.

105. Ibid., 2. 6.

106. Ibid., 2. 9–11.

107. Ibid., 1. 11.

108. Ibid., 1. 4.

109. RM 86. 1–2.

110. P. Antin, "La ville chez Saint Jérôme," *Latomus* 20 (1961) 293–311, repr. in *Recueil sur Saint Jérôme,* Collection Latomus, 95 (Brussels, 1968), pp. 375–389; cf. J. N. D. Kelly, *Jerome, His Life, Writings, and Controversies* (London, 1975).

111. Jerome Ep. 112. 18, *PL* 22. 928.

112. "in hoc terrarum angulo " (*De vir. illustr.,* praef., *PL* 23. 603c).

113. "de extremis Galliae finibus in Bethleemitico ruro latitantem " (Ep. 110, praef., *PL* 22. 981); "juxta Bethleemitica forsitan rura suspiras (i.e., Fabiola)" (Ep. 64. 8, *PL* 22. 612); "ob conscientiam peccatorum Bethlemi-tici ruris saxa incolimus" (Ep. 75. 4, *PL* 22. 688).

114. Ep. 105. 3, *PL* 22. 835.

115. Ep. 52. 9, *PL* 22. 535; Ep. 60. 10, *PL* 22. 594 f.; Ep. 79. 4, *PL* 22. 657.

116. Horace *Sat.* 2. 6, 60–62.

117. Jean-Marie André, *L'otium dans la vie morale et intellectuelle romaine* (Paris, 1966), pp. 455–527; cf. Jacques Fontaine, "Valeurs antiques et valeurs chrétiennes dans la spiritualité des grands propriétaires terriens à la fin de IVe siècle occidental," *Epektasis, Mélanges patristiques offerts au Cardinal Jean Daniélou* (Beauchesne, 1972), pp. 571–595.

118. Ep. 43. 3, *PL* 22. 479. That *matronarum senatus* may be derived from Porphyry's lost book on chastity is suggested by *Comm. Is.* 3. 12, *PL* 24. 66c, where Jerome refers to Porphyry's allusion to *mulieres* and *matronae* as a "*senatus.*" For an analysis of this passage in light of common rhetorical devices, see David S. Wiesen, *St. Jerome as a Satirist: A Study in Christian Latin Thought and Letters* (Ithaca, N.Y., 1964), pp. 28 f., esp. n. 38.

119. Ep. 46. 12, *PL* 22. 491; cf. Ep. 22. 16, 27–28, *PL* 22. 403 f., 412–415.

120. Ep. 22. 17, *PL* 22. 404; cf. Ep. 25, *PL* 22. 411.

121. *Otium* must not be confused with jejuneness (*Apol. adv. libros Rufini* 3. 22, *PL* 23. 473c).

122. In Ep. 22. 34, Jerome utilized certain qualifications (*deterrimum atque neglectum, hi bini vel terni, suo arbitratu ac dicione viventes*) that became common coin in subsequent references to the Sarabaites: Bede, *Expositio Actuum Apostolorum et Retractatio*, ed. M. L. W. Laistner (Cambridge, Mass., 1939), p. 27; John of Salisbury *Policraticus* 7. 23, ed. C. C. I. Webb (Oxford, 1909), 2:203; *De unitate ecclesiae conservanda* 42, *MGH, Libelli de lite* 2. 276, 279 f.; and Ratherius of Verona, in *Studien und Mitteilungen zur Geschichte des Benediktiner-Ordens* 44 (1926):82: "Vae Sarabaitis, id est, aut sub monachico habitu, aut in aliqua reclausura sibi viventibus, id est, suam voluntatem facientibus, et regularem disciplinam accipere renuentibus." How the term *renuitae* was equated with Sarabaites is illustrated by Odo of Cluny (*Collat.* 3. 23, *PL* 133.607b).

123. Cassian *Conl.* 18. 7, *CSEL*, 13:513-516; cf. ibid. 18. 1, *CSEL*, 13: 506; *Inst.* 5. 36, *CSEL* 17: 108.

124. RB 1. 7; RM 1. 6 adds that, were it not for the tonsure, Sarabaites should be called laymen.

125. Jerome Ep. 125. 9, *PL* 22. 1077.

126. Ep. 125. 10, 16, *PL* 22. 1077, 1082.

127. See, for example, Ep. 22. 28, *PL* 22. 414.

128. Acts 5:1-11. Cassian *Conl.* 18. 5, 7, *CSEL*, 13:509 f., 513; ibid., 18. 30, *CSEL*, 13:606. Since poverty can be retained only if one observes claustration, content with food and clothing alone (Cassian *Inst.* 7. 29, *CSEL*, 17:148), the covetousness exemplified by Ananias and Sapphira must be avoided (ibid., 7. 19, 25, 30, *CSEL*, 17:143, 146, 148).

129. Tertullian *Pud.* 21. 4. 12, *PL* 2. 1024a, 1025b; Clement of Alexandria *Stromata* 1. 23, *PG* 8. 899/900b; Ambrose *De officiis ministrorum* 3. 11, 74, *PL* 16. 166c; cf. Ambrose *De offic. min.* 30, 146, *PL* 16. 66a. See Migne's commentary for Acts 5:1-11 in *Scripturae Sacrae cursus completus* 23 (Paris, 1840):1169-1171.

130. Ep. 14. 5, *PL* 22. 350; Ep. 18. 4, *PL* 22. 963; Ep. 130. 14, *PL* 22. 1118. Cf. Caesarius of Arles *Sermo* 71. 2, in ed. G. Morin, *Corp. Christ. Ser. Lat.*, 103:300-302.

131. *Comm. in evang. Matt.* 19:21, *PL* 26. 137b.

132. Without mention of Sarabaites, Gregory the Great Ep. 1. 33, *MGH Epp.*, I, 46; Ratherius of Verona *Dial. confes.* 23, *PL* 136. 412-414. For paucity of Ananias-Sapphira iconography, see H. Leclercq, in *Dictionnaire d'archéologie chrétienne et de liturgie*, 1. 2 (1907), 1896f.

133. Cassian *Inst.* 4. 13-15 *CSEL*, 17:55-57.

134. Isidore Pelusiotae Ep. 1. 41, *PG* 78. 207/208c.

135. Ep. 1. 314, *PG* 78. 363/364cd; for work, Ep. 1. 49, *PG* 78. 211c/ 214a.

136. Ep. 1. 258.

137. Ep. 2. 45.

138. Ep. 1. 260.

139. Ep. 1. 92, 220; cf. 1. 25.

140. Nilus, *Liber de monastica exercitatione*. 8-9, *PG* 79. 727/728; Ep. 1. 292, *PG* 79. 189/190; Ep. 1. 295, *PG* 79. 190/191; Ep. 2. 136, *PG* 79. 257/ 258; Ep. 3. 119, *PG* 79. 437/438; cf. Karl Heussi, *Untersuchungen zu Nilus dem Asketen*, in *TU*, 42. 2 (Leipzig, 1917), pp. 103-113; M. T. Disdier, in *Dictionnaire de théologie catholique*, 11. 1 (1931), 670-671; J. M. Besse,

Les moines d'Orient antérieurs au Concile de Chalcédoine (451) (Paris, 1900), pp. 50-52.

141. Wandering is occasioned not because of necessity but out of faintheartedness (Ep. 1. 295, *PG* 79. 189/192; cf. Ep. 2. 56, *PG* 79. 223/224; Ep. 2. 62, *PG* 79. 227/228.

142. *Liber de monastica exercitatione* 8-9, *PG* 79. 727/728.

143. Ep. 1. 129, *PG* 79. 137/138; Ep. 2. 60, *PG* 79. 225/228; Ep. 2. 84, *PG* 79. 239/240; Ep. 2. 105, *PG* 79, 245/248; Ep. 2. 157, *PG* 79, 273/276; whereas provision is made for monks, Eusebius, himself one of their number, roams about towns, never quiet (Ep. 2. 136, *PG* 79. 257/258; Ep. 3. 119, *PG* 79. 437/438.

144. Ep. 3. 58, *PG* 79. 417/418.

145. Ep. 3. 72, *PG* 79. 412/422; *Tractatus ad Eulogium* 31, *PG* 79. 1133/1136.

146. Ep. 2. 56, *PG* 79. 223/224; Ep. 2. 71-72, *PG* 79. 231/232; Ep. 2. 117, *PG* 79. 241/242; Ep. 2. 140, *PG* 79. 263/264; *De monachorum praestantia* 26, *PG* 79. 1091/1092; *Liber de monastica exercitatione* 60-61, *PG* 79. 791/794.

147. Ep. 2. 114-115, *PG* 79. 249/250.

148. Ep. 2. 46, *PG* 79. 217/218. This problem elicited attention both East and West. Consecrated virgins generally remained under the parental roof, occupied houses of their own, observed a "spiritual marriage" by living as *subintroductae* [Labriolle, "Le 'Mariage spirituel' dans l'antiquité chrétienne," *Revue historique* 138 (1921):204-225; H. Achélis, *Virgines subintroductae* (Leipzig, 1902); *agapetae* (Antoine Guillaumont, "Le nom des Agapètes," *Vigiliae Christianae* 23 (1969):30-37], or lived as *sorores* with members of the clergy. This time-honored practice provoked considerable criticism (Jerome Ep. 22. 14, *PL* 22. 402-403; cf. Ep. 17. 1, 4, 9, *PL* 22. 953 ff.). Chrysostom contributed to the issue two treatises, *Adversus eos qui apud se habent virgines subintroductas*, *PG* 47. 495-514, and *Quod regulares feminae viris cohabitare non debeant*, *PG* 47. 513-532.

149. *Tractatus ad Eulogium* 32, *PG* 79. 1135/1136; Ep. 2. 129-130, *PG* 79. 255/256ab; Ep. 3. 243, *PG* 79. 529/530b.

150. *De monachorum praestantia* 1, *PG* 79. 1061/1062.

151. Ibid., 26, *PG* 79. 1091/1092bc.

152. Ep. 3. 290, *PG* 79. 527/528a.

153. Palladius *Historia lausica* 32. 5; for the role of the xenodochium, see Boon, *Pachomiana, Prae.* 48-51, pp. 25-27.

154. John Climacus *Scala Paradisi*, gradus 27, *PG* 88. 1095-1102.

155. "Vagantur quidam apud nos vacantivi" [Synesius of Cyrene, Ep. 67, *PG* 66. 1427c; *The Letters of Synesius of Cyrene*, trans. A. Fitzgerald (Oxford, 1926), pp. 158 f.)].

156. Sulpicius Severus *Dial.* 1. 15, *CSEL*, 1:167. Cf. R. Gregoire, "Saeculi actibus se facere alienum: Le 'mépris du monde' dans la littérature monastique latine médiévale," *Revue d'ascétique et de mystique* 41 (1965):251-287.

157. Festugière, *Les moines d'Orient*, vol. 3, pt. 2, *Les moines de Palestine* (Paris, 1962), p. 68.

158. Ambrose Ep. 63. 67, *PL* 16. 1207b.

159. Ibid., Ep. 63. 7-9, *PL* 16. 1191 f.

160. Jerome Ep. 50. 1, *PL* 22. 511; *In Gal.*, praef. to Lib. 2, *PL* 26. 356; *In Ps.* 145, in ed. Morin, *Anecd. Mared.*, III, 2, p. 293.

161. Paulinus of Nola *Carmen* 24, lines 325–332, ed. Hartel, *CSEL*, 30:217.

162. Cassian *Conl.* 18. 8, *CSEL*, 13:516 f.

163. Cassian *Conl.* 7. 23, *CSEL*, 13:202; *Conl.* 18. 11, *CSEL*, 13:544 f.; Cassian *Inst.* 10.6, *CSEL*, 17:177.

164. *De moribus ecclesiae* 1. 31. 65–68, *PL* 32. 1337–1339.

165. "Quis enim nescit summae continentiae hominum christianorum multitudinem per totum orbem in dies magis magisque diffundi, et in Oriente maxime atque Aegypto" (*De moribus ecclesiae*, 1. 31. 65).

166. Ibid., 1. 31. 67, *PL* 32. 1338 f.

167. Ibid., 1. 31. 68; cf. ibid., 1. 33. 70, *PL* 32. 1340.

168. Ibid., 1. 33. 70–73, *PL* 32. 1339–1341. A. Zumkeller, *Das Mönchtum des heiligen Augustinus* (Würzburg, 1950); P. Monceaux, "Saint Augustin et Saint Antoine: Contribution à l'histoire du monachisme," *Miscellanea Agostiniana* 2 (Rome, 1931):61–89; U. Moricca, "Spunti polemici di S. Agostino contro i nemici e i falsi interpreti del suo ideale monastico," ibid., pp. 933–975.

169. Augustine *Conf.* 7. 13–15, *PL* 32. 754–756.

170. Possidius *Vita* 2–3, *PL* 32. 35–36.

171. Ibid., 11, cf. ibid. 5, *PL* 32. 42, 37.

172. P. Schroeder, "Die Augustinerchorherrenregel," *Archiv für Urkundenforschung* 9 (1926):271–306; L. Hertling, "Kanoniker, Augustinusregel und Augustinusorden," *Zeitschrift für katholische Theologie* (1930):335–359; Luc Verheijen, *La règle de Saint Augustin*, 2 vols. (Paris, 1967).

173. *De moribus ecclesiae* 1. 31. 66, *PL* 32. 1337 f.

174. Aurelius was himself solicitous for the well-being of ascetics (Augustine Ep. 22. 9, *PL* 33. 93–94).

175. *De opere monachorum* 1. 2, *PL* 40. 575; cf. *Retractationes*, 2. 21, *PL* 32. 638–639, where emphasis is put on violent quarrels that ensued. Matt. 6:25–34.

176. 1 Cor. 11:14.

177. *De opere monachorum* 31–32, *PL* 40. 571 f.

178. Augustine Ep. 262. 5, *PL* 33. 1079; cf. ibid., 6, *PL* 33. 1079 f.

179. "tam multos hypocritas sub habitu monachorum usquequaque dispersit, circumeuntes provincias, nusquam missos, nusquam fixos, nusquam stantes, nusquam sedentes. Alii membra martyrum, et tamen martyrum, venditant; alii fimbrias et phylacteria sua magnificant . . ." (*De opere monachorum* 28. 36, *PL* 40. 575 f.).

180. Jerome Ep. 125. 9, *PL* 22. 1077.

181. Basil *Reg. fus. tr.* 40, *PG* 31. 1019 f.

182. Jerome *Adv. Vigil.* 1, 4, 5, 9, *PL* 23. 341 f.

183. Ambrose Ep. 22. 2, 10–13, *PL* 16. 1019, 1022 f.; Paulinus *Vita di S. Ambrogio* 14, ed. M. Pellegrino (Rome, 1961), pp. 70 ff.; P. Courcelle, *Recherches sur les Confessions de Saint Augustin* (Paris, 1950), pp. 139–155.

184. Cassian *Conl.* 6. 1, *CSEL*, 13: 153–154.

185. Paulinus *Carm.* 19, lines 164–229, *CSEL*, 30: 124–126.

186. Ibid., 27, lines 542–567, *CSEL*, 30: 286–287.

187. *Cod. Theod.*, IX, 2. 7 (A.D. 386).

188. "Maxime in agris territans, ab agris vacans, et victus sui causa cellas circumiens rusticanas, unde et circumcellionum nomen accepit" (Augustine *Contra Gaudentium* 1. 28. 32, *PL* 43. 725; cf. ibid., 1. 26. 29; 1. 29. 33; 1. 38. 51); "nam circumcelliones dicti sunt, quia circum cellas vagantur; solent enim ire hac, illac, nusquam habentes sedes, et facere quae nostis, et quae illi norunt, velint, nolint" (*Enarratio in Psalmum* 132. 3, 6, *PL* 37. 1730, 1732 f.); *De haeresibus ad Quodvultdeum* 69, *PL* 42. 43; *Contra Cresconium* 3. 42, 43, 45, 47, 48, 63, *PL* 43. 521-525, 534; Possidius *Vita S. Aug.* 10, *PL* 32. 41 f.; 12. 43). For socioeconomic and religious interpretations that the Circumcellions have elicited, see Emin Tengström, *Donatisten und Katholiken: Soziale, wirtschaftliche und politische Aspekte einer nordafrikanischen Kirchenspaltung* (Göteburg, 1964), pp. 24–78; J. J. Gavigan, *De vita monastica in Africa Septentrionali inde a temporibus S. Augustini usque ad invasiones Arabum* (Rome, 1962), pp. 232-233, 239-240; W. H. C. Frend, *The Donatist Church, a Movement of Protest in Roman North Africa* (Oxford, 1952), pp. 172-178, 256-258, passim; idem., "The Cellae of the African Circumcellions," *Journal of Theological Studies* 3 (1952): 87-89; F. Martroye, "Une tentative de revolution sociale en Afrique: Donatistes et Circoncellions," *Revue des questions historiques* 76 (1904): 353-416, and 77 (1905): 5-53; idem., "Circoncellions," *Dictionnaire d'archéologie chrétienne et liturgie* 3. 2 (1914): 1692-1710; C. Saumagne, "Ouvriers agricoles ou rôdeurs de celliers? Les circoncellions d'Afrique," *Annales d'histoire économique et sociale* 6 (1934): 351-364; T. Büttner-E. Werner, *Circumcellionen und Adamiten: Zwei Formen mittelalterlicher Haeresie* (Berlin, 1959), pp. 1-72.

189. A.D. 412, *Cod. Theod.*, XVI, 5. 52.

190. *Cod. Theod.*, XVI, 3. 1; cf. ibid., XVI, 4. 1-4.

191. *Cod. Theod.*, XVI, 3. 2.

192. *Cod. Theod.*, IX, 40. 16 (A.D. 398); ibid., XI, 30. 57.

193. C. J. Hefele, *Histoire des conciles*, trans. and rev. H. Leclercq, 2. 2 (Paris, 1910), pp. 313 ff., 342 ff.

194. Can. 4 (ibid., pp. 779-782); Heinrich Bacht, "Die Rolle des orientalischen Mönchtums in den kirchenpolitischen Auseinandersetzungen um Chalkedon (431-519)," *Das Konzil von Chalkedon, Geschichte und Gegenwart*, 2 (Würzburg, 1953), pp. 193-314, esp. pp. 241 ff.; Leon Ueding, "Die Kanones von Chalkedon in ihrer Bedeutung für Mönchtum und Klerus," ibid., pp. 569-676, esp. pp. 607-616. Whereas Canon 3 envisaged involvement on a wider scale through sociocaritative activity (Hefele, *Histoire des conciles*, 2. 2, pp. 775-779 = *Corpus Juris Canonici*, dist. 86. 26), Canon 23 concerns monks, as well as clerics, who had caused disturbance in Constantinople (Hefel, *Histoire des conciles*, 2. 2 pp. 809-810 = Causa, XVI, q. 1, c. 17). For unruly monks in the time of Chrysostom, see Sozomen, *Historia ecclesiastica* 8. 9, *PG*, 67, 1540 f.

195. Whereas in the West a monastery could not be erected without the consent of the diocesan bishop (Synod of Agde, 506, can. 27, Mansi, VIII, 329) and monks were subject to their abbots while the abbots were in turn subject to episcopal authority (First Synod of Orleans, 511, can. 19, Mansi, VIII, 354 f.), such a policy was to be counteracted by papal reaction under Gregory the Great [Ep. 1. 12 (A.D. 590), *MGH*, Epp., I, 13] and eventually by the development of monastic exemption (cf. Fourth Council of Toledo,

633, can. 51, Mansi, X, 63; Council of Hereford, 673, can. 3, Mansi, X, 129).

196. *Corpus Juris Civilis*, vol. 2, *Codex Justinianus*, 1, 31. 29, ed. P. Krueger (Berlin, 1880), p. 22.

197. Ibid., vol. 3, nov. 5. 7; 123. 42, ed. R. Schoell and G. Kroll (Berlin, 1895), pp. 33, 623.

198. Peter Damian *Opusc.* 12. *Apologeticum de contemptu saeculi* 9–14, 20–25, *PL* 145. 260–267, 271–279; *Apologeticum* 17–19, *PL* 145. 269–270; *Apologeticum* 22–32, *PL* 145. 279–289.

199. *PL* 152. 419b. Cf. Ernst Werner, *Pauperes Christi: Studien zu sozial-religiösen Bewegungen im Zeitalter des Reformpapsttums* (Leipzig, 1956), pp. 79 ff.

200. Abelard Ep. 8, *PL* 178. 265c.

201. W. Meyer, "Zwei Gedichte zur Geschichte des Cirstercienser Ordens," *Nachrichten von der königlichen Gesellschaft der Wissenschaften zu Göttingen, Philologisch-hist. Kl.* (Berlin, 1908), pp. 386–395; reed. J. Leclercq, "Le poème de Payen Bolotin contre les faux ermites," *Revue bénédictine* 68 (1958): 77–84; for analysis, pp. 52–77, 85–86; cf. Orderic Vitalis *Historia ecclesiastica* 8, 24, *PL* 188. 636bc.

202. Ivo of Chartres Ep. 192, *PL* 162. 198 ff.; Ep. 256, *PL* 162. 260–262, esp. 261a; cf. G. Morin, "Rainaud l'Ermite et Yves de Chartres: Un épisode de la crise du cénobitisme au XIe-XIIe siècle," *Revue bénédictine* 40 (1928): 99–115. Corruption at Saint Paul's in Verdun was also attributed to Sarabaites and gyrovagues (Laurentius, *Gesta Episcoporum Virdunensium* 32 (A.D. 1134), *MGH, SS,* 10: 510.

Chapter 9

A Contribution to the Historical Geography of the Island of Kythira during the Venetian Occupation

Chryssa Maltezou, National Research Institute, Athens

After the Fourth Crusade of 1204 Kythira fell under the influence of the Republic of Venice which a few years later granted the island in fief to the patrician family of Venier.[1] During their domination of the island (variously referred to as Cerigo or the Isola de Venere in Venetian sources),[2] the Venier brothers adopted a conciliatory policy toward the inhabitants, appearing to be acting at least somewhat independently of Venetian rule.[3] When they supported the revolt of the feudal lords in Crete against Venice in 1363, the Republic put an end to Venier rule in Kythira, placing the island under direct Venetian control. The Venier brothers eventually reacquired part of their property, confiscated in the meantime,[4] but the administration of the island remained under the jurisdiction of the castellan-proveditor, sent directly from Venice and changed every two years.[5] The Venetian occupation of Kythira lasted, with the exception of the years 1715 to 1718 when the island was held by the Turks, until 1797 when the Republic of Venice was dissolved.[6]

The purpose, here, is to contribute to the study of the historical geography of Kythira during the Venetian occupation. The work is based on archival sources (such as reports addressed by the Venetian officials to the senate and censuses taken by the Venetian authorities), on contemporary maps, and on travelers' descriptions.[7] The information contained in this material permits us to identify events and place names, helping us to trace more accurately the markings of the past.[8]

Castles and Ports

The castles and ports of each Venetian colony were of primary interest to the Republic, for on them depended both its

Figure 1. The castle of Kapsali (State Archives of Venice, "Atlante Mormori," c. 53).

defense and its trade. Kythira, lying between Crete and the Peloponnesos, was fundamental for Venetian control of the Aegean against Turkish and pirate incursions.[9] The island is often referred to in contemporary documents as the "eye of Crete,"[10] *il passo de tutto il Levante,*[11] *chiave et antemurale del regno da questa parte,*[12] *fanale e lanterna dell'arcipelago, e la lingua e la spia di tutti gli andamenti Turcheschi.*[13] The Venetian governors always gave detailed descriptions of the island's castles and ports, pointing out the need for repairs and new fortifications.[14]

Until the middle of the sixteenth century Kythira had three castles: Ayios Dimitrios (San Dimitri), Kapsali, and Mylopotamos. The castle of Ayios Dimitrios, which guarded the Byzantine city of the Eudaimonoyiannis family, was completely destroyed in 1537[15] after the invasion by Khayr al-Din Barbarossa.[16] The fortifications were not rebuilt, partly because of the cost and partly because the Venetians feared that Barbarossa, having captured the castle once, would do so again. The possibility of asking the Venier to pay for redoing the fortifications was considered, for the adjoining land belonged to them and they would have benefited had the inhabitants returned to cultivate it, but this suggestion was not acted upon.[17] The region was deserted, and eventually its name was forgotten. It came to be known as *Paliochora,*[18] a toponymic often used in the

Figure 2. The castle and port of Kapsali (State Archives of Venice, "Provveditori alle Fortezze," B. 43, dis. 197).

Greek language to indicate deserted villages or cities.[19] It is interesting to note here that whereas the Byzantine city of Ayios Dimitrios came to be known as *Paliochora* (old village), the ancient city of Kastri was known, at least in the sixteenth century, as *Paliopoli* (old city).[20] Thus, in the small area of Kythira, two cities, abandoned far apart in time, have been kept in the memory of the local inhabitants by new place names.

The castle of Kapsali was built on a particularly advantageous site, with the sea to the southeast and Mount Palamida to the west. A low valley between the castle and Palamida sheltered animals when Kapsali was under siege. In times of danger, the proveditors of Kythira communicated with the Regimen of Canea by signal fires on the castle, visible in Gramboussa and Cape Spathi in Crete.[21] The *borgo*, at the foot of the castle, was surrounded by a wall in the sixteenth century after the inhabitants appealed to the Venetian Senate.[22] Documents of the eighteenth century distinguish between the *borgo* and the *borgo serrato*.[23] According to the proveditor reports, there were from three to five cisterns in the *borgo*.[24] On Kythira, as in most of the Aegean Islands, the traditional *kastro-chora, fortezza-borgo,* housing pattern has developed, the houses clinging to the top of a hill on which there is a castle. The *chora* consists of a group of houses, often abutting the walls of the castle, and small twisting streets that form a spiral around the fort. This traditional housing pattern holds the village in a very limited area.[25]

The castle of Mylopotamos, although surrounded only by a low wall, was secure against attack. Fifty families lived there in 1545, having returned after the war to cultivate the lands that belonged to the *Dominio Veneto*.[26]

Kythira's two major ports were Kapsali and Ayios Nikolaos of Avlemonas.[27] In the middle of the sixteenth century, Kapsali could accommodate ten galleys, but its natural capacity was far greater. In 1620 the general proveditor Marc'Antonio Venier recorded in his report to the Venetian Senate the works needed to harbor a total of fifty galleys.[28] Ayios Nikolaos of Avlemonas was a smaller port, overlooked by a promontory on which, reported the proveditor Zuanne Soranzo in 1545, a castle could be built relatively inexpensively to protect it from the enemy.[29] According to the description of V. Coronelli, the port was admirably suited for ships, for it had virtually a natural pier. It could accommodate forty galleys and, furthermore, it could be protected by drawing a chain across the entrance.[30] Both ports were uninhabited.[31] The steep rocky coasts of the island are inhospitable,[32] but the main reason the islanders preferred to live inland was to be as far away as possible from pirate raids.[33]

Population

The information contained in Venetian documents regarding the population of Kythira reveals some aspects of the island's social and economic situation during the Venetian occupation. Kythira's low population was a major concern of the Venetian authorities, who often referred to the island as semideserted land.[34] The main reasons for the population being low were raids, the arid soil, and the bad living conditions of the dependent peasants (*parichi*).

Its strategic location on the trade sea routes made Kythira the target of frequent attack. As early as the tenth century, according to the Life of Ayios Theodoros of Kythira, the island was reported as having been abandoned because of attacks by the Saracens of Crete.[35] The Venetian sources during the following centuries are full of accounts of attacks against the island by Catalans, Turks, Genoese, and pirates in general.[36] Local tradition reports that Barbarossa captured 7,000 inhabitants in the middle of the sixteenth century. Clearly, this is an exaggeration for an island often described as semideserted, but it does indicate the extent of the damage wrought by Barbarossa's attack.[37] Moreover, the various Venetian-Turkish wars of the sixteenth and eighteenth centuries were a major factor in inhibiting population growth.[38]

The barrenness of the island kept it from being accepted as a suitable place to settle by the groups of refugees who fled there from the Turks. In 1383, the people of Tenedos, leaving their homes in accordance with the Treaty of Turin, chose Crete over Kythira as a place of emigration.[39] In 1501, the inhabitants of Koroni came to the island as refugees but soon moved on to settle in Cephallonia.[40] In 1540, after Monemvasia fell to the Turks, the Monemvasiots asked the Venetian authorities not to be sent there, as the land was rocky and dry.[41] A number of Cretans who came to Kythira, after the occupation of Crete by the Turks, soon moved on to the more fertile Ionian Islands.[42]

In contrast to the method of governing its other possessions, Venice administrated Kythira as a feudal territory. The Republic did not levy a tax but received an income (instead of the *decima* it demanded the *terzaria*). The proveditor Maffeo Baffo reported in 1547 that the Venier family rented the income (*entrada*) to the local powerful families (*potenti*), who in turn oppressed the inhabitants in order to profit on their investment as much as possible.[43] The abuse of this system contributed at least as much to keeping the population down as did aridity of the soil and the various attacks upon the island. Despite Venice's promise of tax exemption to all new settlers on the island, most people refused to go to Kythira because of this exploitation by the local nobles.[44] Baffo suggested that Venice correct the situation by leasing the incomes directly within the framework of a paternalistic policy. The senate, however, did not act upon this proposal.[45] The Venetian dignitary supported his proposal by describing the oppression of the inhabitants in detail, adding his opinion that this was the main reason for the island's abandonment and desertion.[46] The bad living conditions of the peasants are also indirectly referred to in the letter written in 1540 by the archbishop of Monemvasia, Mitrofanis, to his people, warning the Monemvasiots not to settle in Kythira for fear that their children would become *parichi*.[47]

The island was divided into five administrative districts (*distretti* or *territorii*): Fortezza and Borgo, Livadhi, Kastrissianika, Potamos, and Mylopotamos. The unpublished censuses recently found in the local historical archives of Kythira and the proveditor reports inform us about the island's population throughout the entire

Venetian occupation. This information is given in detail, down to
the number of inhabitants in each district, for the eighteenth
century. In Table 1, I have assembled the data for the population
of Kythira from 1470 to 1814.[48]

Table 1 shows that the districts of Livadhi and Potamos were the
most heavily populated; the population in the districts of
Kastrissianika and Mylopotamos gradually increased; the population in the district of Fortezza and Borgo increased in the sixteenth
century, decreased in the early eighteenth, and remained comparatively stable throughout the remainder of the eighteenth
century. The island's total population increased in the seventeenth
century and decreased in the early eighteenth. The population
increase was caused by the influx of refugees from the Venetian-
Turkish war, particularly after Crete fell to the Turks, when many
Cretan refugee families fled to safety in neighboring Kythira.[49] On
the other hand, the population decrease in the early eighteenth
century was caused by the island being occupied in the years
1715–1718 by the Turks, who removed two hundred Kythirian
families to Africa.[50]

Social Composition

There were two social classes in the small island of Kythira:
the class of the *cittadini* and the class of the *popolani*. The local
council, decreeted in 1572, according to a decision by Daniel
Venier, general proveditor of Crete, was composed only of *cittadini*
and not of nobles (*nobili*).[51] When the council first met, it consisted of 30 members, but at the end of the eighteenth century, it
had as many as 168 members. This increase was caused in part by
the influx of refugees, coming from different parts of the Turkish-
occupied Greek world, who belonged to various social classes.[52]
The eighteenth-century censuses inform us of the distribution of
the social classes in the island's five administrative districts. The
cittadini were mostly grouped in the castle and the *borgo*, where
the Venetian authorities also lived and where public events were
held. Most of the *popolani*, whose number increased throughout
the eighteenth century, were gathered in the districts of Livadhi
and Potamos,[53] and, finally, most of the priests (*religiosi*), who
formed a category apart, lived in Livadhi.

Table 2 shows the population distribution in each district according to social class in the years 1733 and 1788. Table 3 shows the
number of inhabitants in each class during the period from 1733 to
1788.

Table 1. **Population of Kythira (1470–1814)**

	1470	1545	1553	1579	1590	1620	1724	1733	1753	1765	1772	1773	1784	1788	1814
Fortezza and Borgo				1,719			840	872	805	989	688	816	756	823	965
Livadhi							1,365	1,186	1,311	1,509	1,334	1,590	1,742	1,677	2,369
Kastrissianika					1,443[a]		861	783	942	1,059	944	1,123	1,226	1,308	1,609
Potamos							1,146	1,349	1,320	949	1,175	1,475	2,081	2,340	2,252
Mylopotamos							652	731	1,008	1,677	880	1,025	1,153	1,277	1,284
Total	500	1,850	3,300	3,162	4,000	7,500	4,864	4,921	5,386	6,183	5,021	6,029	6,958	7,425	8,479[b]

[a] This number represents the total population for the districts of Livadhi, Kastrissianika, Potamos, and Mylopotamos.
[b] Absent: 751 (men 686, women 65).

Table 2. **Social Classes by District (1733 and 1788)**

	Priests		Cittadini		Popolani		Aged		Women		Children	
	1733	1788	1733	1788	1733	1788	1733	1788	1733	1788	1733	1788
Fortezza and Borgo	29	15	92	85	157	161	24	19	440	332	130	211
Livádhi	53	55	29	58	294	386	54	63	545	573	211	542
Mylopótamos	17	40	4	6	189	310	40	55	361	438	120	428
Kastrissiánika	18	24		16	195	319	42	67	383	481	145	401
Potamós	18	32	4	3	397	607	56	78	636	826	238	794

Table 1. **Population of Kythira (1470–1814): Sources**

1470: Chronicle of Giacomo Rizzardo [cf. J. Ghikas, "Dhyo venetsianika chronika ghia tin alossi tis Chalkidas apo tous Tourkous sta 1470," *Archeion Evoikon Meleton* 6 (1959): 231; Vakalopoulos, *Istoria tou neou Ellinismou*, 2:122].

1545: Relation of Giovanni Soranzo, proveditor of Kythira (Sathas, *Documents*, 6:289).

1553: Relation of Andrea Vicenzo Querini, proveditor of Kythira (cf. Leonhard, *Insel Kythera*, p. 34).

1579: Biblioteca Marciana (Venice), *Cod. Marc. It.*, VII, 1190, coll. 8880, fol. 303, Description of Crete by Petros Kastrophylakas [cf. also A. Xirouchakis, *I venetokratoumeni Anatoli, Kriti kai Eptanissos* (Athens, 1934), p. 175; A. Andreadis, "Meletai peri tou plythismou tis Eptanissou: O plythismos ton Kythiron (kat' anecdhotous pigas"), *Oikonomiki Ellas* (1911), p. 546].

1590: Relation of [Giovanni Garzoni], proveditor of Kythira (cf. Leonhard, *Insel Kythera*, p. 35).

1620: Relation of [Pietro da Molin], proveditor of Kythira (cf. Leonhard, *Insel Kythera*, p. 35).

1724: Local historical archives of Kythira, census of 1724 ("Anagrafi del 1724"), taken under the proveditor Paolo Donà.

1733: Local historical archives of Kythira, register of Antonio Marin, proveditor of Kythira, fol. 20 ff.

1753: Local historical archives of Kythira, census of 1753, taken under the proveditor [Giorgio Loredan] (in the same register with the census of 1772).

1765: Biblioteca Marciana (Venice), "Anagrafi di tutto lo stato della republica di Venezia comandata dal senato ed eseguita dal magistrato dei deputati ed aggiunti sopra la provisione del danaro, Venezia 1768" (cf. Leonhard, *Insel Kythera*, p. 35; Andreadis, "Meletai," p. 547).

1772: Local historical archives of Kythira, census of 1772, taken under the proveditor [Vincenzo Diedo].

1773: Local historical archives of Kythira, census of 1773, taken under the proveditor [Marco Cicogna].

1784: Local historical archives of Kythira, census of 1784 ("Anagrafi osia descrizione di tutti li componenti la popolazione di Cerigo, formata per ordine del' Illustrissimo et Eccellentissimo Signor Daniele Trivisan, Proveditor e Castellano di dita isola, l'anno 1784").

1788: Local historical archives of Kythira, census of 1788, taken under the proveditor [Giovannandrea Catti].

1814: Local historical archives of Kythira, census of 1814, taken under the governor, Philip Newton.

Table 3. **Number of Inhabitants by Class**

	1733	1772	1773	1784	1788
Priests	135	143	163	178	166
Cittadini	129	141	155	139	168
Popolani	1,232	1,399	1,652	1,715	1,783
Aged	216	196	257	255	282
Women	2,365	2,550	2,969	3,443	2,650
Children	844	592	833	1,228	2,376

Settlements

The earliest references to place names in Kythira are in the proveditor reports, in the *Antique memorie dell'isola di Cerigo*, and in the *Description of Crete* by Petros Kastrophylakas. Place names are mentioned in the first two sources only indirectly. The Venetian officials were primarily concerned with strategic matters and named settlements only as areas to be protected (Mylopótamos, Potamós, San Zorzi, and Theódoros, this last exactly in the center of the island).[54] The chronicler of the *Antique Memorie*, probably writing at the end of the sixteenth century, gives an account of the Venier period and describes the division of the island into lots, mentioning the place names Mitáta, Goniá (east of Mitáta), Orthólithos (west of Logothetiánika), and the regions Finikiá and Gabriglianà (a name derived from Gabriel Venier).[55] The first systematic list of settlements on Kythira is given in the 1583 manuscript of Petros Kastrophylakas.[56] Kastrophylakas's list is particularly valuable because seven settlements (those in italics) of the fourteen he names are not mentioned in any other source. The transcription of the place name *Allicangri* is uncertain.

Kastrophylakas's List

casal S. Dimitri	*casal Coniana*
casal Mittata	casal Cusunari
casal Catto Chiperi	*casal Platano*
casal Apano Chiperi	*casal Biotica*
casal Callamutades	*casal Allicangri*
casal Pizanades	*casal Arcario*
casal Grisoti	castel Milopotamo[57]

The eighteenth-century censuses were taken by parish (*parochia*). According to the method used by the Venetians—a method not much unlike the one used by today's statisticians—all the island parishes are listed together with the name of the village in which each parish was located. From the eight registers, covering the period 1724–1814, I have grouped the names of the villages and settlements by district.[58] It should be added that most of these names derive from the name of the family living there (e.g., Arónis = Aroniádhika, Lourándos = Lourandiánika, Semitékolos = Semitekoliánika, Státhis = Stathiánika, Kendrotís = Kendrotiánika).

Villages and Settlements by District (1724–1814)

Fortezza and Borgo

Chalepáki
Sfakianá
Yiofýri

Livadhi

Alexandhrádhes
Dhrymónas
Fatsádhika
Goudhiánika
Kakopétri
Kalokairnés
Kamária
Karavochorió
Karbonádhes
Karteriánika
Káto Chorió
Katoúni
Keramotó
Kominiánika
Kondoletoú
Kondoliánika
Koútsaka
Kyriakádhika
Levounári
Likouvára
Livádhi
Lourandiánika
Magonesiánika

Manitochóri
Mesarakiánika
Pitsiniánika
Poúrko
Samiádhika
Semitekoliánika
Skorpouliánika
Stathiánika
Strapódhi
Tsikalaría

Mylopotamos

Aréi
Dhókana
Frátsia
Kendrotiánika
Lendarakiánika
Mylopótamos
Petrochiliánika
Písso Pigádhi
Raftakiánika
Raisiánika
Rísa
Semiánika
Viarádhika

Kastrissianika

Aloisiánika
Aroniádhika

Dhrymonári
Douriánika
Kastrissiánika
Káto Kíperi
Kíperi
Mitáta
Perlengiánika
Pitsinádhes
Yerakitiánika
Yiorgádhika

Potamos

Christoforiánika
Fardhouliánika
Gouría
Karavás
Katsouliánika
Koroniánika
Koussounári
Logothetiánika
Melitiánika
Panaretiánika
Potamós
Priniádhika
Trifylliánika

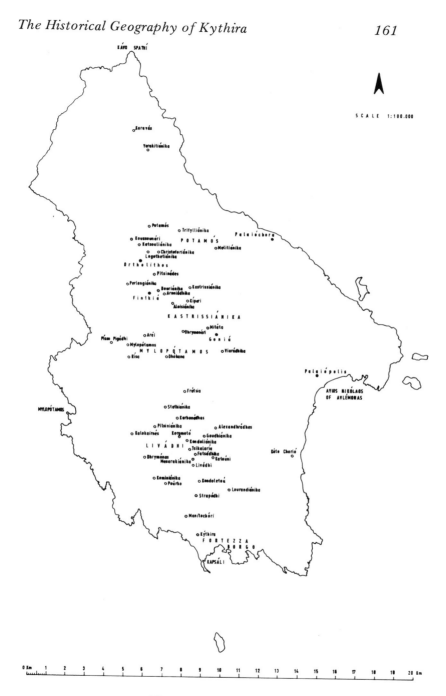

Figure 3. Map of Kythira.

Churches and Monasteries

Kythira has a great number of Byzantine and post-Byzantine churches. Unfortunately, although many of these churches are remarkable both for their architecture and paintings, not all of them have been studied.[59] The local historical archives offer much important information for the identification, dating, and location of these churches, for most of which the eighteenth-century censuses are our only written record. Tables 4–8 give in alphabetical order the names of the churches with their locations. The dates indicate the years of the censuses in which each church has been registered.[60] An asterisk by the church name indicates that the church is mentioned in the bibliography given at the end of each table.[61]

It should be added that the study of the Kythirian archives will also contribute to our knowledge about the Latin monasteries and churches of the island, such as the monastery of San Giovanni Battista alla Grotta,[62] the *altare di rito latino* in the monastery of Beata Vergine Maria di Martiri in Myrtidhia, and the churches of the Madonna in Aroniadhika and the Madonna in Fortezza, all *di ius patronato di sua Serenità.*[63]

Most of the material presented here is based on the unpublished documents preserved at the local historical archives of Kythira. Further research in these recently discovered archives will bring to light considerable information, not only concerning the local history of the island, which because of its significant geographic position was a major link in Venice's chain of possessions in the Levant, but also the general history of the southern part of the Venetian Romania.

Table 4. **Fortezza and Borgo**

Church	Census
Sant'Anna in Borgo	1724 1753 1772 1773 1784 1788 1814
Sant'Antonio a Yiofýri	1733 1753 1773
Santa Croce episcopale in Borgo	1724 1733 1753 1772 1773 1784 1788 1814
*San Giovanni Battista in Fortezza	1724 1733 1753 1772 1773 1784 1788 1814
*San Giovanni Chrysostomo in Borgo Serrato	1724 1772 1773 1784 1788 1814

Table 4 (continued)

San Giovanni Evangelista (Theologo) in Borgo	1724	1733	1753	1772	1773	1784	1788	1814
*Madonna Messochoritissa in Borgo Serrato	1724	1733	1753	1772	1773	1784	1788	1814
*Madonna Orfani in Fortezza	1724	1733	1753	1772	1773	1784	1788	1814
Altare di San Nicolò nella chiesa di Sant'Anna in Borgo, ius patronato dei signori Levuni			1753	1772	1773	1784	1788	1814
*Omnipotente in Fortezza		1733	1753					
*San Salvatore Caluci in Borgo Serrato	1724	1733	1753	1772	1773	1784	1788	1814
San Salvatore in Borgo a Sfakianá	1724	1733	1753	1772	1773	1784	1788	1814
San Salvatore in Fortezza	1724			1772	1773		1788	1814
Tre Santi Gherarchi in Borgo								1814
*Santa Trinità in Borgo	1724							
*Tutti i Santi in Borgo	1724	1733	1753	1772	1773	1784	1788	1814
*San Zorzi Caluci in Borgo Serrato	1724	1733	1753	1772	1773	1784	1788	1814
*San Zorzi detto Lombardo sto Chalepáki (vescovato vecchio)	1724	1733	1753	1772	1773	1784	1788	1814

BIBLIOGRAPHY: Lazaridis, *Archaiologikon Deltion* 20 (1965): B_1, 184–185; 22 (1967): B_1, 204; 24 (1969): B_1, 166; Chatzidakis, ibid., 21 (1966): B_1, 22; Orlandos, ibid., 24 (1969): B_1, 14; Vokotopoulos, "Vyzantini Techni," p. 163.

Table 5. **Livadhi**

Church	Census							
*Sant'Andrea a Livádhi (Karavochorió) (ius patronato di Megaloconomo Cardarà)	1724	1733	1753	1772	1773	1784	1788	1814
Sant'Andrea a Magonesiánika (Tsikalaría)		1733		1772	1773	1784	1788	1814
Sant'Antonio a Dhrymónas			1753	1772	1773	1784	1788	1814

Table 5 (continued)

	1724	1733	1753	1772	1773	1784	1788	1814
Sant'Ascensione a Manitochóri								1814
San Cosma (Santi Anargiri) a Manitochóri				1772	1773	1784	1788	1814
San Cosma a Fatsádhika	1724	1733	1753	1772	1773	1784	1788	1814
San Costantino a Livádhi (Mesarakiánika)	1724	1733	1753	1772	1773	1784	1788	1814
Santa Croce a Keramotó (Pitsiniánika)		1733	1753	1772	1773	1784	1788	1814
Santa Croce a Lourandiánika	1724							
San Demetrio a Kyriakádhika	1724	1733	1753	1772	1773	1784	1788	1814
*San Demetrio a Poúrko	1724		1753	1772	1773	1784	1788	1814
Sant'Elia a Karbonádhes	1724	1733	1753	1772	1773	1784	1788	1814
Santa Erini a Katoúni (Livádhi)	1724	1733	1753	1772	1773	1784	1788	1814
Sant'Eustathio a Karbonádhes (Stathiánika)	1724	1733	1753	1772	1773	1784	1788	1814
San Giovanni a Alexandhrádhes	1724	1733	1753		1773	1784	1788	
San Giovanni a Keramotó			1753		1773		1788	1814
San Giovanni a Kominiánika				1772	1773		1788	1814
San Giovanni a Kyriakádhika		1733						
San Giovanni a Likouvára	1724	1733	1753	1772	1773	1784	1788	1814
San Giovanni a Strapódhi	1724	1733	1753	1772	1773	1784	1788	1814
San Leone a Alexandhráhes	1724	1733						1814
San Liberal a Manitochóri	1724		1753	1772	1773	1784	1788	1814
Madonna a Kakopétri (e convento)	1724	1733	1753	1772	1773	1784	1788	1814
Madonna a Karbonádhes	1724	1733	1753	1772	1773	1784		
Madonna a Karteriánika		1733	1753		1773	1784	1788	
Madonna a Katoúni (Semitekoliánika)	1724	1733		1772	1773	1784	1788	1814
Madonna a Kominianika	1724	1733	1753	1772	1773		1788	1814
Madonna Kondoletoú	1724	1733	1753	1772	1773	1784	1788	1814
Madonna a Kondoliánika	1724	1733	1753	1772	1773	1784	1788	1814
Madonna Paliopirghiotissa	1724	1733	1753	1772	1773	1784	1788	1814
Santa Marina a Dhrymónas	1724	1733	1753	1772	1773	1784	1788	1814
San Michiel Arcangelo a Alexandhrádhes	1724	1733	1753	1772	1773	1784	1788	1814

Table 5 *(continued)*

San Nicolò a Karbonádhes	1788							
San Salvatore a Keramotó	1724	1733	1753	1772	1773	1784	1788	1814
San Salvatore a Livádhi (Koútsaka)	1724	1733	1753	1772	1773	1784	1788	1814
San Spiridione a Kalokairnés	1724	1733	1753	1772	1773	1784	1788	1814
Santa Trinità a Alexandhrádhes	1724	1733	1753	1772	1773	1784	1788	1814
Santa Trinità a Keramotó (Skorpouliánika)	1724	1733	1753	1772	1773	1784	1788	1814
Santa Trinità a Levounári (Livádhi)	1772	1784	1788	1814				
Tutti i Santi a Alexandhrádhes (Goudhiánika)	1724	1733	1753	1772	1773	1784	1788	1814
San Zorzi a Kamária (Alexandhrádhes)	1724	1733	1753	1772	1773	1784	1788	
San Zorzi a Karbonádhes	1724	1733	1753	1772	1773	1784	1788	1814
San Zorzi a Káto Chorió	1733	1772	1773	1784	1788	1814		
*San Zorzi a Lourandiánika	1724	1733	1753	1772	1773	1784	1788	1814
San Zorzi a Samiádhika	1724	1733	1753	1772	1773	1784	1788	1814

BIBLIOGRAPHY: Soutiriou, "Messaionika mnimeia Kythiron," pp. 318–320, 323–325; Lazaridis, *Archaiologikon Deltion*, 20 (1965): B₁, 186–187; Chatzidakis, ibid., 21 (1966): B₁, 22–23; 24 (1969): B₁, 167–168; Orlandos, ibid., 24 (1969): B₁, 14; Vokotopoulos, "Vyzantini Techni," p. 163.

Table 6. **Mylopotamos**

Church	Census							
*Sant'Athanasio nel castello di Mylopótamos	1724	1733	1753	1772	1773	1784	1788	1814
San Charalambo a Frátsia (Petrochiliánika)	1773	1784	1788	1814				
San Demetrio a Frátsia	1772	1773	1784	1788				
*San Demetrio a Mylopótamos	1724	1733	1753	1773	1784	1788	1814	
*Sant'Elia nel castello di Mylopótamos	1724	1733	1753	1772	1773	1784	1788	1814
*San Giovanni nel castello di Mylopótamos	1724	1753	1772	1773	1784	1788	1814	
San Giovanni a Frátsia (Lendarakiánika)	1772	1773	1784	1814				

Table 6 (continued)

San Liberal a Dhókana	1724	1733	1753	1772	1773	1784	1788	1814
Madonna a Aréous	1724	1733	1753	1772	1773	1784	1788	1814
Madonna a Frátsia	1724	1733	1753	1772	1773	1784	1788	1814
*Madonna Messochoritissa nel castello di Mylopótamos	1724	1733	1753	1772	1773	1784	1788	1814
Madonna Myrtidhiotissa a Frátsia (Raisiánika)	1733	1772	1773	1784	1788	1814		
Madonna a Viarádhika	1724	1733	1753	1772	1773	1784	1788	1814
San Nicolò a Mylopótamos	1753	1772	1773	1784	1788	1814		
*San Pantaleone a Frátsia (Raftakiánika)	1724	1733	1753	1772	1773	1784	1788	1814
San Salvator a Kendrotiánika	1724	1733	1753	1772	1773	1784	1788	1814
*San Soso a Mylopótamos	1724	1733	1753	1772	1773	1784	1788	1814
Santa Trinità a Písso Pigádhi (Mylopótamos)	1772	1773	1784	1788	1814			
*Tutti i Santi a Frátsia	1724	1753	1772	1773	1784	1788	1814	
San Zorzi a Lendaraki-ánika	1724	1733	1753	1772	1773	1784	1788	1814
San Zorzi a Semiánika (Rísa)	1772	1773	1784	1788	1814			

BIBLIOGRAPHY: Lazaridis, *Archaiologikon Deltion* 20 (1965): B_1, 188–192; Chatzidakis, ibid., 21 (1966): B_1, 23–24; 22 (1967); 17: Vokotopoulos, "Vyzantini Techni," p. 166.

Table 7. **Kastrissianika**

Church	Census							
*Sant'Antonio a Kastrissiánika	1724	1733	1753	1772	1773	1784	1788	1814
*Sant'Athanasio a Pitsinádhes	1724	1733	1753	1772	1773	1784	1788	1814
San Charalambo a Yerakitiánika	1772	1773	1784	1788	1814			
San Demetrio a Mitáta	1724	1733	1753	1772	1773	1784	1788	1814
San Giovanni a Douriánika	1784							
Madonna a Aroniádhika	1724	1733	1753	1772	1773	1784	1788	1814
Madonna a Kíperi (Káto Kíperi)	1724	1733	1753	1772	1773	1784	1788	1814
Madonna a Perlengiánika	1784							

Table 7 (continued)

*Madonna a Pitsinádhes	1753	1772	1773	1784	1788	1814		
*San Michel Arcangelo a								
Aroniádhika	1724	1733	1753	1772	1773	1784	1788	1814
San Nicolò a Dhrymonári	1753	1772	1773	1784	1788	1814		
San Salvatore a								
Aroniádhika	1724	1733	1753	1772	1773	1784	1788	1814
San Theodoro a								
Aloisiánika	1724	1733	1753	1772	1773	1784	1788	1814
*San Theodoro								
cathedra episcopale	1724	1733	1753	1772	1773	1784	1788	1814
Santa Trinità a Kíperi								
(Káto Kíperi)	1724	1733	1753	1772	1773	1784	1788	1814
Santa Trinità a Mitáta	1724	1733	1753	1772	1773	1784	1788	1814
Santa Trinità a								
Yiorgádhika	1724	1733	1753	1772	1773	1784	1788	1814
San Zorzi a Mitáta	1724	1733	1753	1772	1773	1784	1788	1814

BIBLIOGRAPHY: Sotiriou, "Messaionika mnimeia Kythiron," pp. 315–316; Orlandos, "Sphendonion," pp. 401–405; Lazaridis, *Archaiologikon Deltion* 20 (1965): B_1, 194–196; Oikonomidis, "Vios tou ayiou Theodorou," pp. 267–271, 279, 280, 288–289; Vokotopoulos, "Vyzantini Techni," pp. 169–170.

Table 8. **Potamos**

Church	Census							
San Charalambo a Karavás	1814							
*San Charalambo a								
Potamós	1814							
San Cosma a								
Panaretiánika	1724	1733	1753	1772	1773	1784	1788	1814
San Demetrio a Gouría	1724	1733	1753	1772	1773	1784	1788	1814
San Giovanni Battista a								
Koroniánika	1753	1772	1773	1784	1788	1814		
*San Giovanni a								
Trifylliánika	1724	1733	1753	1772	1773	1784	1788	1814
Madonna (B.V. Despina)								
a Karavás	1788							
Madonna Lariotissa (a								
villa grande)	1724	1733	1753	1772	1773	1784	1788	1814
Madonna a Melitiánika	1724	1733	1753	1772	1773	1784	1788	1814
Madonna (Pandanassa) a								
Fardhouliánika	1724	1733	1753	1772	1773	1784	1788	
Madonna a Priniádhika								
(Logothetiánika)	1724	1733	1753	1772	1773	1784	1788	1814

Table 8 (continued)

San Mina (San Martino?) a Logothetiánika	1724	1733	1753	1772	1773	1784	1788	1814
San Nicolò a Gouría (Koussounári)	1724	1733	1753	1772	1773	1784	1788	1814
Omnipotente a Potamós (villa grande)	1733	1753	1772	1773				
San Salvatore a Potamós (villa grande)	1724	1784	1788	1814				
Tre Gherarchi (S. Basilio) a Christoforiánika	1772	1784	1788	1814				
Santa Trinità a Katsouliánika	1753	1772	1773	1784	1788	1814		
Santa Trinità a Potamós (villa grande)	1724	1733	1753	1772	1773	1784	1788	1814
San Zorzi a Fardhouliánika	1733							

BIBLIOGRAPHY: Lazaridis, *Archaiologikon Deltion* 20 (1965): B_1, 198.

Notes

1. F. Thiriet, *La Romanie Vénitienne au Moyen Age: Le développement et l'exploitation du domaine colonial vénitien (XIIe–XVe siècles)* (Paris, 1959; repr. 1975), p. 87; idem, "A propos de la seigneurie des Venier sur Cerigo," *Studi Veneziani* 12 (1970): 199–210. See the family tree of the Venieri in C. Hopf, *Chroniques gréco-romanes inédites ou peu connues* (Berlin, 1873), pp. 526–527; cf. C. Sathas, ed., *Documents inédits relatifs à l'histoire de la Grèce au Moyen Age,* vol. 6 (Athens and Paris, 1884), p. 308.

2. For names given to Kythira in Western sources, see in general, O. Markl, *Ortsnamen Griechenland in "fränkisher" Zeit* (Graz and Cologne, 1966), p. 40; cf. also Thiriet, "A propos de la seigneurie des Venier," p. 201.

3. Twice members of the Venier family married daughters of Byzantine *archontes* who continued to rule the island. In 1238, Marco Venier, Marino's son, married the daughter of Nikolaos Monoyiannis (Eudaimonoyiannis), while between the years 1295 and 1300 Bartolomeo Venier married the daughter of a Byzantine official who governed the island in the name of the emperor Andronikos [see Thiriet, "A propos de la seigneurie des Venier," pp. 202–203; cf. Judith Herrin, "Byzantine Kythera," in *Kythera: Excavations and Studies conducted by the University of Pennsylvania Museum and the British School at Athens,* ed. J. N. Coldstream and G. L. Huxley (London, 1972), p. 49]. On the philhellenic attitude of the Venier family, see Thiriet, "A propos de la seigneurie des Venier," pp. 203 ff.

4. The four brothers divided the island into twenty-four *carati* (lots) and took six each. After the Cretan uprising of 1363, Venice beheaded the

traitors and confiscated their property. Later, however, the Republic returned thirteen of the twenty-four *carati*, but withheld the rest: A. Andreadis, *Peri tis oikonomikis dioikisseos tis Eptanissou epi venetokratias*, vol. 2 (Athens, 1914), p. 250; cf. Herrin, "Byzantine Kythera," p. 49.

5. Sathas, *Documents*, 5 (1883): 50. For the list of names of the castellans and proveditors of Kythira, see Hopf, *Chroniques gréco-romanes*, pp. 410–413. Until 1669, the year Candia fell to the Turks, the castellans and proveditors depended from the Regimen of Crete. The castellan of Kythira was elected by the duke of Candia and was moreover paid from the treasury of Crete: see F. Thiriet, *Régestes des délibérations du Sénat de Venise concernant la Romanie*, vol. 2 (Paris and The Hague, 1959), p. 151, no. 1636; idem, *Délibérations des Assemblées vénitiennes concernant la Romanie*, vol. 2 (Paris and The Hague, 1971), no. 905, p. 71; nos. 929, 930, p. 76; cf. Chryssa Maltezou, "*Eptanissa*," in *Istoria tou Ellinikou Ethnous*, vol. 10 (Athens, 1974), p. 220.

6. The bibliography concerning the history of Kythira during the Venetian occupation is very poor. Among the earlier publications, see N. Stai, *Raccolta di antiche autorità e di monumenti storici riguardanti l'isola di Citera oggi Cerigo in senso fisico, morale e politico* (Pisa, 1847), and R. Leonhard, *Die Insel Kythera: Eine geographische Monographie*, Petermanns Mitteilungen, n. 128 (Gotha, 1889); among the more recent, see "Kythira" by S. Stathis in *Megali Elliniki Engyklopaideia*, 15:342, and the articles by D. S. Alvanakis in *Kythiraiki Epetiris* (Kythira, 1909), pp. 19 ff.; see also M. Petrocheilos, *Istoria tis nissou Kythiron* (Athens, 1940), pp. 34–43; J. Kassimatis, *Apo tin palaia kai synchroni kythiraiki zoi* (Athens, 1957), pp. 74–102; A. Philippson, *Die griechischen Landschaften*, vol. 3, *Der Peloponnes*, pt. 2, *Der Westen und Süden der Halbinsel* (Frankfurt am Main, 1959), pp. 509–517; Maltezou, "*Eptanissa*," 10:215 ff., 11 (1975): 212 ff. On Byzantine Kythira, see N. Oikonomidis, "O vios tou ayiou Theodorou Kythiron," in *Proceedings of the Third Panionian Congress*, 1 (Athens, 1967): 264–291; Herrin, "Byzantine Kythera," pp. 41–48.

7. Up to now, our documentation was based mainly on the archival sources of the State Archives of Venice. Recently, however, valuable archival material was found in the local historical archives of Kythira. On the importance of these archives for historical research, see Chryssa Maltezou, "Les Archives Vénitiennes de Cythère: Un fonds historique négligé," *Byzantinische Forschungen* 5 (1977): 249–252 (Symposion Byzantinon, Strasbourg, September 1973); idem, "To notariako archeio Kythiron," *Deltion tis Ioniou Akadimias* 1 (1976): 15–84. Apart from the already known maps, stamps, and designs of Kythira to be found in the works by C. Buondelmonti, T. Porcacchi, M. Boschini, V. Coronelli, and A. L. Castellan, as well as by other travelers and cartographers, relevant unpublished material is preserved at the Archivio di Stato of Venice (see "Atlante Mormori," c. 53; "Provveditori alle Fortezze," B. 43, dis. 197; "Archivio privato Correr," no. 81; "Provveditori da Terra e da Mar," Filza 783).

8. On the nature, problems, and methodology of historical geography, see,

in general, Hélène Ahrweiler, "Les problèmes de la géographie historique byzantine," in *Proceedings of the Thirteenth International Congress of Byzantine Studies, Oxford 1966* (London, 1967), pp. 465 ff.; cf. Association internationale des études byzantines, "Géographie historique: Rapports des comités nationaux," *Bulletin d'Information et de Coordination* 8 (1975–1976): 79–106.

9. In his report (relazione) of 1545, Zuanne Soranzo, proveditor of Kythira, referring to the *grandissima importantia* of the island, notes that between Zakynthos (Zante) and Crete (a distance of over 350 *migliari*) Kythira was the only place where ships could seek refuge in time of need (Sathas, *Documents*, 6:286).

10. Cf. St. Spanakis, "Benetto Moro, Ritornato di Provveditor General del Regno di Candia, Relazione letta in Pregadi a 25 Giugno 1602," in *Mnimeia tis Kritikis Istorias*, vol. 4 (Irakleion, 1958), pp. 61–62.

11. See Proveditor Maffeo Baffo's relation of 1547 (Sathas, *Documents*, 6:290).

12. Archivio di Stato of Venice, "Provveditori da Terra e da Mar," Filza 783, no. 51 (relation of Marc'Antonio Venier, proveditor general, 1620).

13. Statement by privateer Cigala in the middle of the sixteenth century: F. Braudel, *The Mediterranean and the Mediterranean World in the Age of Philip II*, trans., vol. 2 (London, 1973), p. 877, n. 191.

14. Already in 1398 the castellan of Kythira received the order to repair the fortress of the island so as to render it secure against Turkish invasions: Thiriet, *Régestes*, vol. 1 (1958), no. 943, p. 220.

15. *"fu expugnato et ruinato al tempo delle guerre passate per infedelli . . ."* (see Zuanne Soranzo's relation of 1545 in Sathas, *Documents*, 6:286; cf. idem, 5:59).

16. On the life and the activity of Barbarossa, see, in general, E. Bradford, *The Sultan's Admiral: The Life of Barbarossa* (London, 1969); cf. Braudel, *Mediterranean*, pp. 116 ff.; Elizabeth Zachariadou, "Symvoli stin istoria tou Notioanatolikou Aigaiou (me aformi ta patmiaka firmania ton eton 1454–1522)," *Symmeikta*, vol. 1 (Athens, 1966), p. 188.

17. See Zuanne Soranzo's relation of 1545 (Sathas, *Documents*, 6:287).

18. On Paliochora of Kythira there is an architectural study by D. Zaglanikis [*Paliochora* (Zakynthos, 1962)], which unfortunately I have been unable to find; cf. summary of this study in *Kythira: To nissi tis Ouranias Aphroditis* (n.d., n.p.), pp. 149–156.

19. I mention here as an example the Paliochora of Aegina [see N. Moutsopoulos, *I Paliachora tis Aeginis; istoriki kai morfologiki exetassis ton mnimeion* (Athens, 1962)]. On the place names composed with the adjective *palios* (old), see Hélène Antoniadis-Bibicou, "Villages désertés en Grèce: Un bilan provisoire," in *Villages désertés et histoire économique (XIe-XVIIIe siècle)* (Paris, 1965), p. 357, n. 3.

20. The manuscript of the Biblioteca Marciana (Venice) entitled: "L'antique memorie dell'isola di Cerigo, ridotte in questi scritti," in *Documents*, ed. Sathas, 6:299–300, mentions the ancient city "*Scandea, città all'hora*

principale et maritima, vicina al porto della Vlemona, hor detta Paiopoli. . . ."

21. See Zuanne Soranzo's relation (Sathas, *Documents*, 6:286). The inscription with a bas-relief of Saint Marc's lion (*Pax tibi Marco Evangelista meus MDLXV*), preserved on the gate of the fort, reveals that in that year (1565) repairs must have been made there (cf. Kassimatis, *Kythiraiki zoi*, p. 85).

22. Zuanne Soranzo's relation (Sathas, *Documents*, 6:287).

23. See below, list of churches.

24. Zuanne Soranzo's relation (Sathas, *Documents*, 6:287); see also the relation of Marc'Antonio Venier, proveditor general, 1620, no. 50 (cited above, n. 12).

25. On that type of habitat, see E. Y. Kolodny, *La population des îles de la Grèce*, vol. 1 (Aix-en-Provence, 1974), pp. 262–263.

26. Zuanne Soranzo's relation (Sathas, *Documents*, 6:287).

27. In contemporary maps, the harbors of Kythira are noted by the names Porto Delfino (Kapsali), Porto Tine, and San Nicolò. Leonhard (*Insel Kythera*, p. 34) identifies Porto Tine with Platia Ammos.

28. Relations of Zuanne Soranzo (1545) and Maffeo Baffo (1547) (Sathas, *Documents*, 6:288, 295) and of Marc'Antonio Venier (1620) (no. 51, cited above, n. 12). In his report of 1545, the proveditor proposes the construction of *"un navilio li appresso il scoglio ditto San Zorzi, il che in vero seria una cosa bonissima et molto utile a tanti che anderanno per mar."*

29. Zuanne Soranzo's relation (Sathas, *Documents*, 6:288); cf. Herrin, "Byzantine Kythera," p. 50.

30. Coronelli mentions also a smaller port, that of San Nicolò de Modari [see *Description géographique et historique de la Morée reconquise par les Vénitiens . . . par le père Coronelli, cosmographe de la Republique de Venise* (Paris, 1686), p. 70]. But in the Isolario [*Isolario dell'Atlante Veneto*, vol. 2 (Venice, 1696), p. 189], Porto Tine is identified with San Nicolò's harbor.

31. Coronelli (*Description géographique*, p. 70) mentions in 1682 that there was no habitat in Kapsali.

32. According to information offered by the relations of the proveditors, *"l'isola è tutta montuosa et tutte le marine grebanose"* (Maffeo Baffo's relation, Sathas, *Documents*, 6:291), *"il monte da ascender è asprissimo"* (Zuanne Soranzo's relation, *ibid*, p. 286), *" . . . essendo tutto il terreno di sasso vivo . . ."* (Marc'Antonio Venier's relation, no. 50, cited above, n. 12).

33. On the retreat of the population to the mountains, see A. Vakalopoulos, "La retraite des populations grecques vers des régions éloignées et montagneuses pendant la domination turque," *Balkan Studies* 4 (1963): 265–276; cf. Antoniadis-Bibicou, "Villages désertés," p. 380. The verses below, preserved in the folklore of Kythira, illustrate the islanders' fear of pirate invasions, a fear so great that they avoided even going down to the coast: "Δὲ σοῦ τό᾽ πα γὼ Ἑλένη / στὸ γιαλὸ μὴ κατεβαίνεις; / Καί σ᾽ἁρπάξουνε οἱ κουρσάροι / γιά᾽να γιλο γιά᾽να ψάρι" (see Kassimatis, *Kythiraiki zoi*, p. 101). In free translation: *"Helen, didn't I tell you / not to go down to the beach? / For the pirates might take you away / for no reason at all?"*

34. The Venier brothers had invited old Leo Kassimatis to settle in Kythira

with his family, because the island was sparsely populated (see *L'antique memorie dell'isola di Cerigo*, in *Documents*, ed. Sathas, 6:302). "The population of Kythira," noted C. Buondelmonti in 1420, "is for reasons unknown to me very small" [see E. Legrand, *Description des îles de l'archipel grec (1420) par Christophe Buondelmonti* (1897; repr. Amsterdam, 1974)]. B. Bordone, who traveled to Kythira in 1526, mentioned that the island was *"mal habitata e quasi deserta"* [see *Isolario di Benedetto Bordone, nel qual si raggiona di tutte l'isole del mondo*... (Venice, 1534); cf. Kolodny, *La population*, 1:154]. Finally, Maffeo Baffo, in his report to the Venetian authorities in 1547, stated that *"è un gran peccato che la* [isola] *non sia habitata"* (Sathas, *Documents*, 6:292).

35. Oikonomidis, "Vios tou ayiou Theodorou," pp. 266, 271.

36. Cf. Thiriet, *Régestes*, vol. 1 (1958), no. 62, p. 35; no. 103, p. 43; vol. 2 (1959), no. 1,174, p. 50; vol. 3 (1961), no. 2,899, p. 178; idem, *Assemblées* (Paris and The Hague, 1966), vol. 1, no. 538, p. 212; vol. 2, no. 1,435, p. 186. On the pirate invasions see, in general, A. Vakalopoulos, *Istoria tou neou Ellinismou*, 2d ed., vol. 2 (Thessalonica, 1976), p. 120. See also: Ἀκολουθία τῆς ὑπεραγίας Δεσποίνης ἡμῶν Θεοτόκου καὶ Ἀειπαρθένου Μαρίας τῆς Μυρτιδιότισσας ... συντεθεῖσα μὲ (sic) παρὰ ... Σωφρονίου ἐπισκόπου Κυθήρων τοῦ Παγκάλου ... (Venice, 1789), p. 20, where reference is made to a pirate attack against the monastery in Myrtidhia.

37. *L'antique memorie dell'isola di Cerigo*, p. 307.

38. Petrocheilos, *Istoria tis nissou Kythiron*, p. 44; Stathis, "Kythira," p. 343, where reference is made to the capture and massacre of inhabitants in the years 1569, 1571, 1715, 1756.

39. Thiriet, *Régestes*, vol. 1 (1958), no. 631, pp. 154-155; no. 662, pp. 160-161; no. 666, p. 162; idem, *Assemblées*, vol. 2, no. 842, p. 52; no. 857, p. 57.

40. A. Vakalopoulos, *Istoria tou neou Ellinismou*, vol. 3 (Thessalonica, 1968), p. 82.

41. Cf. Chryssa Maltezou, "Agnostoi eidisseis (1539-1540) peri Mitrofanous Monemvassias ek tou archeiou tou douka tis Kritis," *Thesaurismata* 5 (1968): 39, 42.

42. Cf. Maltezou, "I simassia tou Istorikou Archeiou Kythiron ghia tin istoria tis Kritis sti diarkeia tis Venetokratias," in *Proceedings of the Fourth International Cretological Congress* (Irakleion, 1976), in press.

43. *"sono da ditti affituali tiranizati, strusiati* ... (Sathas, *Documents*, 6:292).

44. *"per non esser suggetti a tal tirani"* (ibid.).

45. Sathas, *Documents*, 6:293.

46. On the deplorable condition of the peasants, see also *L'antique memorie dell'isola di Cerigo*, p. 302.

47. "καὶ μετὰ τῶν ἄλλων καὶ τοῦτο ξῆ μεῖζον πάντων κακόν, τὸ ἐς παροικίαν πεσεῖν. εἰ γὰρ καὶ μὴ καταρχὰς οἱ πάντ᾽ ἐλεύθεροί γε ἡμεῖς, ἀλλ᾽ οὖν οἱ παῖδες ἡμῶν ἐς τὸν μετέπειτα ἀναμφιβόλως πεσοῦνται, μέλλοντες τοῖς ἐκεῖ παροίκοις γάμῳ νομίμῳ διαζευχθῆναι" (cf. Maltezou, "Agnostoi eidisseis," p. 43).

48. I included the census of 1814 both because it is unpublished and because it was taken only about twenty-five years after the last known Venetian census. On the population of the Ionian Islands, see, in general, the articles by A. Andreadis in *Oikonomiki Ellas* (1911); cf. also V. Panayotopoulos, "I dimografiki katastassi tou neou Ellinismou," in *Istoria tou Ellinikou Ethnous,* vol. 11 (Athens, 1975) pp. 152–158.

49. See the lists with the names of the Cretan refugee families who received an allowance from the Venetian treasury in Chryssa Maltezou, "Prosfyges apo tin Kriti sta Kythira: Agnostes plirofories apo to Archeio ton Kythiron," *EEBS,* 39–40 (1972–1973): 519 ff., which includes a general bibliography on Cretan emigration to the Ionian Islands; cf. Maltezou, "Eptanissa," 11:212.

50. See A. Miliarakis, *Geografia politiki nea kai archaia tou nomou Argolidos kai Korinthias* (Athens, 1886), p. 267.

51. G. Pojago, *Le leggi municipali delle isole ionie,* vol. 2 (Corfu, 1848), p. 38; cf. Chryssa Maltezou, "Kritokythiraika: I kritiki oikogeneia Kladouri kai to symvoulio ton eugenon sta Kythira," *Thesaurismata* 12 (1975): 257-8.

52. See for instance the applications submitted by Cretan refugees at the end of the seventeenth century to the authorities of Kythira for recognition of their nobility and entrance in the local council (Maltezou, "Kritokythiraika," pp. 258 ff., and idem, "I simassia tou Istorikou Archeiou Kythiron").

53. The strife between the *cittadini* and the poorer classes and the oppression of the latter by the *cittadini* resulted in uprisings of the *popolani* against the magistrates soon after the end of the Venetian occupation (see Petrocheilos, *Istoria tis nissou Kythiron,* pp. 53–60).

54. Sathas, *Documents,* 6:289.

55. Ibid., pp. 303–305.

56. On Petros Kastrophylakas and his manuscript, see Chryssa Maltezou, "Neo agnosto cheirografo tis "Perigrafis tis Kritis" tou Petrou Kastrophylaka (1583) kai to provlima tis kritikis ekdosseos tis," in *Proceedings of the Third International Cretological Congress,* vol. 2 (Athens, 1974), pp. 176 ff., where the previous bibliography may be found.

57. Biblioteca Marciana (Venice), *Cod. Marc. It.,* VII, 1190, coll. 8880, fol. 303.

58. The place names in italics indicate that identification has not been possible. In some censuses, the same village is listed sometimes under one and sometimes under another district. In these cases I have implicitly registered the name of the village concerned in one district. The accompanying map (Figure 3) contains only the identified place names and not the various neighborhoods and sites (e.g., Yiofýri, Sfakianá). It is based on a map of the Army Map Service (Series M708, 1:50,000).

59. The basic bibliography concerning the medieval monuments of Kythira is the following: G. Sotiriou, "Messaionika mnimeia Kythiron," *Kythiraiki Epitheorissis,* 1 (1923): 313–332; A. Xyngopoulos, "Fresques de style monastique en Grèce," in *Proceedings of the Ninth International Congress of Byzantine Studies* (Thessalonica), vol. 1 (Athens, 1955), pp. 510–516; A. Orlandos, "Sphendonion," *EEBS* 28 (1958): 401–405; P. Lazaridis,

"Messaionika kai Vyzantina mnimeia Kythiron," *Archaiologikon Deltion* 20 (1965): B$_1$, 183–199; M. Chatzidakis, ibid. 21 (1966): B$_1$, 22–25, 22 (1967): B$_1$, 17–18; Lazaridis, ibid. 22 (1967): B$_1$, 204–205; Oikonomidis, "Vios tou ayiou Theodorou," pp. 267, 271, 279–280, 288–289; G. Daux, "Chronique des fouilles 1967," *BCH* 92 (1968): 968–972; Lazaridis, in *Archaiologikon Deltion* 24 (1969): B$_1$, 166–168; A. Orlandos, ibid., p. 14; P. Vokotopoulos, "I Vyzantini Techni sta Eptanissa," *Kerkyraika Chronika* 15 (1970): 163–177. See also the two recent papers about the churches of Kythira given at the *First International Congress of Peloponnesian Studies* (Sparta, 1975) by P. Theodorakakou-Varelidou ("Yposkafoi metavyzantinoi naoi ton Kythiron"), and at the *Fifteenth International Congress of Byzantine Studies* (Athens, 1976), by M. Georgopoulou-Meladini ("Le décor absidal des églises byzantines à Cythères, 1100–1257"); cf. also the *Catalogue of the Exhibition of Byzantine Murals and Icons Organized at Athens on the Occasion of the 15th International Congress of Byzantine Studies* (Athens, 1976), p. 72, nos. 76–78.

60. It must be held in mind that the lists of churches have been based on the data given by the censuses. Therefore, they do not include all the churches of the island, only those of populated parishes. Thus, a number of already known churches, mostly Byzantine, like those of Paliochora, are not mentioned here because the whole area was deserted after the invasion led by Barbarossa.

61. Because it is quite common in the censuses to register a parish sometimes in one village and sometimes in another, an effort was made to identify the church when it is evident that since the villages adjoin each other we are faced with one and the same parish (e.g., Santa Croce in Pitsiniánika = Keramotó). Where identification was difficult, differentiation of the church names was preferred. Because of similar difficulties, and in order to avoid serious mistakes, the asterisk was used only where the identification of village and church is absolutely certain. The only exception has been made in the case of the church of the Madonna Messochoritissa, identified with that of the Madonna Messosporitissa (inasmuch as both are situated in the castello of Mylopotamos).

On a recent visit to Kythira, I was informed by the priest of Chora that most of these churches survive and services are being held in them even today. The following eight churches, however, remain unidentified: San Salvatore in Fortezza (district of Fortezza and Borgo), Santa Croce a Lourandiánika, San Giovanni a Kyriakádhika, Madonna a Karbonádhes, San Zorzi a Káto Chorió (district of Livadhi), Santa Trinità a Yiorgádhika (district of Potamos), San Giovanni Battista a Koroniánika, San Zorzi a Fardhouliánika (district of Potamos).

62. See Anonymous, Τὰ Μυρτίδια, ἢ ὁ ἐν Κυθήροις Ναὸς τῆς Θεοτόκου, and Ὁ Ἅγιος Ἰωάννης εἰς τὸν ἐκκρημνόν, ἢ τὸ σπήλαιον, εἰς ὃ ἐνεπνεύσθη τὴν ἀποκάλυφίν του ὁ Θεολόγος (Athens, 1857), pp. 12–16. On the monastery of San Giovanni alla Grotta, see also Coronelli, *Isolario*, p. 190.

63. See local historical archives of Kythira, Inventario ecclesiastico, register of the seventeenth century, where an inventory of the movables and the real property of these monasteries can be found.

Chapter 10

The Properties of the Deblitzenoi in the Fourteenth and Fifteenth Centuries

Nicolas Oikonomidès, *University of Montréal*

This is the story of a piece of land in Chalkidike, which changed hands several times during the fourteenth century and ended up as the property of the monastery of Docheiariou on Mount Athos. It is one case among many many others, but it has the advantage of being rather well documented in the monastic archives and thus allows us to follow the procedure by which monastic landed property expanded in these troubled times at the expense of the decadent empire and of its lay aristocracy.

The basic documents I have used are all preserved in the archives of the Athonite monastery of Docheiariou. Except for the first one, they are all unpublished.[1]

A. Chrysobullos Logos of the emperor John VI Cantacuzenus in favor of Demetrios Deblitzenos. Original. October, indiction 3, A.M. 6858 = 1349.[2]

B. Agreement (*eggrafon*) between Manuel Doblytzenos and the monastery of Docheiariou. Original. The lower part of the document being torn away and lost, its exact date is unknown; from other evidence, we can assume with certainty that it was issued between 1381 and 1384, almost certainly in the autumn of 1381.[3]

C. Decision (*sēmeioma*) of an ecclesiastical tribunal of Thessalonica, in favor of Maria Doblytzene, widow of Manuel. Certified copy, made around December 1419.[4] August, indiction 7, A.M. 6892 = 1384.

D. Agreement (*gramma*) between Maria Doblytzene and the monastery of Docheiariou. Original. January, indiction 12 [1389].[5]

E. Decision (*sekretikon gramma*) of the imperial tribunal of Thessalonica in favor of Maria Doblytzene. Original. October, indiction 13, A.M. 6913 = 1404.

F. Agreement (*gramma*) between Docheiariou and Theodora,

176

daughter of Dobletzenos and wife of Bartholomaios Komes. Original. December [indiction 13], A.M. 6928 = 1419.

G. Confirmation (*gramma*) of the above agreement by the metropolitan of Thessalonica [Symeon]. Original. December, indiction 13 [1419].

The land we are concerned with was situated in Hermeleia (today: Hormylia), a village to the southeast of Polygyros in Chalkidike, at the foot of the peninsula of Sithonia.[6] Many Athonite monasteries had properties around this village, including Docheiariou, which by the mid-1350s was a well established landowner of Hermeleia.

The lay heroes of our story are all members of one family, the Deblitzenoi or Doblytzenoi, who lived in Thessalonica throughout the fourteenth century and were mostly of the military. The documents are not coherent as to the spelling of this family name (Δεβλιτζηνός,[7] Δεβλητζηνός,[8] Δεβλυτζηνός,[9] Δευλιτζηνός,[10] Δελβιτζηνός,[11] Δοβελτζηνός,[12] Δοβλετζινός,[13] Δοβλητζηνός,[14] Δοβλυτζηνός[15]), but there is no doubt that this is only one name, attested in different forms that alternate even when it is a question of the same person.[16] This uncertainty as to the form is already an indication that the name was not Greek, the more so because one Deblitzenos is expressly called "the Serbian." We know, though, that they were all loyal to the Byzantine emperor.

Our story begins with Demetrios Deblitzenos. He was probably one of the sons of Manuel Deblitzenos, the *tzaousios* of the cavalry corps (*mega allagion*) of Thessalonica in 1301, who died before 1317.[17] In 1311, Demetrios is a witness to a document written in Thessalonica; he is called *basilikos stratiōtēs*, that is, a soldier-holder of a *pronoia*; it seems that, in 1321, he already possessed land property in Hermeleia.[18] By 1349, his personal situation had greatly improved: he had become an *oikeios* of the emperor John VI Cantacuzenus and held an *oikonomia* that gave him the handsome yearly income (*posotēs*) of 400 *hyperpyra* (document A, line 2) and placed him among the elite of his time. We may assume that, in exchange for this revenue, he was expected to serve the state, most probably as a high-ranking member of the military.[19]

In 1349, he asked the emperor John VI Cantacuzenus that a yearly income (*posotēs*) be granted to him as if it were his hereditary property (*kata logon gonikotētos*), preferably taken from that which he received from Hermeleia. The emperor agreed, issued a *prostagma* for this purpose (now lost: see document A, line 1) after which he issued a chrysobull in October 1349, which is preserved (our document A) and tells us the whole story.

It is not difficult to guess the reasons for which Deblitzenos was granted this privilege: he may well have been one of those nobles and military men who left Thessalonica during the revolt of the Zealots and joined the cause of the usurper John Cantacuzenus in the civil war of the years 1341–1347. In 1349, while his hometown was still under the Zealots's revolutionary regime, he was with the victorious John VI, presumably in Constantinople, and obviously on good terms with him; moreover, the donation that he obtained was very much in keeping with that granted during the civil war and afterward by both sides in need of supporters.

But what exactly was the object of this imperial donation? We know of several contemporary cases where an emperor, in order to gratify a faithful subject—more often a faithful noble—transformed part of his *pronoia* into hereditary property. So, in order to better understand this, we must keep in mind exactly what the object was of the *pronoia* in the first place.[20]

In return for services offered by an individual to the state (mainly military service), he was granted, instead of a salary, a yearly revenue made up of taxes, or duties, or rents, that he received directly from the contributors, as long as he continued in service. The amount of his revenue, called *posotēs,* was fixed in advance and was equal to the revenue that the state would receive from the same properties, if they were not granted as a *pronoia.* These rights were not necessarily bound to the ownership of the land or other commodity that produced the income. They consisted mainly of taxes that the *pronoiarios,* instead of the tax collector, received. Thus, the main differences between a *pronoia* and a tax exemption (*exkousseia,* as the ones granted to the monasteries) would be: (1) that the former was bound to the condition of performing a service whereas the latter was not, and (2) that the former was often granted in favor of a third person, other than the owner of the taxable property, whereas the tax exemption was always granted to the owner of the property.

Consequently, when an emperor granted to a *pronoiarios* hereditary rights on a part of his *pronoia,* these rights concerned only the revenue that belonged to the emperor and that was granted as a *pronoia* in the first place, not the allodial ownership of the taxable property, which could well belong—and continued to belong—to anyone. Otherwise, the emperor would be giving away something to which he had no right.[21]

I think that the allodial owner of the taxable property could also be the *pronoiarios* himself, and I shall try to demonstrate this in the case of Deblitzenos. Our document A speaks only of a *posotēs* of 100 *hyperpyra* that came from certain properties in Hermeleia. On the other hand, we know that Deblitzenos was already a land-owner in Hermeleia in 1321; we also know that the Hermeleia properties had belonged to the Deblitzenos family for a long time, certainly before 1349, and that they were these same prop-erties for which·our document A was issued because this docu-ment remained with the properties and is now in the archives at Docheiariou. Consequently, I tend to reconstitute the whole procedure as follows: (1) Deblitzenos owns landed property in Hermeleia and is supposed to pay taxes for it. (2) Having entered the imperial service, he is entitled to a reward and is granted a *posotēs* taken, at least partly, from the taxes that he has to pay to the state; in other words, he receives a tax exemption, but this revenue is, in fact, a reward for services and as such is classified as an *oikonomia*. (3) In 1349, he obtains from John VI Cantacuzenus the favor that this *posotēs* be granted to him on an hereditary basis, but nowhere in the document is it said that he has the right to alienate (e.g., sell) this right.[22] Consequently what was origi-nally a personal reward became a family privilege.

It is very doubtful whether Demetrios Deblitzenos enjoyed for long—if at all—the idea that he and his children would take plea-sure in their properties in Hermeleia without paying taxes. Already in 1345 Serres, the most important town of eastern Macedonia, fell into the hands of the Serbian czar Stephen Dušan, together with the eastern part of Chalkidike, including Mount Athos. It is not impossible that Hermeleia remained for some time in Byzan-tine hands; but, if so, she was on the frontier and eventually fell to the Serbs.[23] Deblitzenos, who, unlike others, chose to remain on the Byzantine side, had no more access to his property. But he kept our document A in his personal archives in the hope that times would change and that he might return, although it appeared then that the Serbs were there to stay. He never returned. Instead, he finished his days as a monk, dying on a 26 September (see n. 41), having taken the monastic name of Daniel; his wife also took the veil, adopting the name of Eugenia (document B, lines 36–37).

Their son, Manuel Deblitzenos, was also a military man and an *oikeios* of the emperor (document C, line 1). He lived in Thessa-lonica, where he was witness to a deed on 27 October 1381.[24] Long before that date, he had married a widow, who already had at least one son from her first marriage.[25] After her death, he married again, and very successfully, in high society: a young, rich girl, who was going to outlive him by some thirty-five years. She was named Maria and, although illiterate (she signs with a *signon* our document D), she belonged to the distinguished Thessalonian family of the Angeloi.[26] She brought to him an important dowry worth more than 1,610 *hyperpyra*, to which, later on, were added some houses in Thessalonica as well as movable goods worth another 80 *hyperpyra* that she inherited from her grandfather Choneiates.[27] This was added to Manuel's personal property, which, at the time of his marriage, included real estate in Thessalonica, other movable goods, and according to the document that he made on this occasion (*propittakon*), 3,500 *modioi* of arable land around Thessalonica, plus his paternal (*egonika*) domain of Hermeleia; the extent of the latter was not indicated in the *propittakon* (document C, lines 38–40), presumably because, at the time of his second marriage, this domain was still under Serbian occupation, and there was no recent and reliable *praktikon* in the hands of the Deblitzenoi.

This couple, members of high society, who joined lives and fortunes sometime before 1371, had more than one child,[28] but only their daughter Theodora, who was illiterate like her mother,[29] lived long enough to be known to us. She also received an important dowry (document G, lines 33–34) when she married a man of her class, Bartholomaios Komes, some time before 1404,[30] probably after her father was killed in 1384 (see below). When her mother, Maria, died in May 1419 (document F, line 8), Theodora remained the only survivor of the Deblitzenoi.[31]

The Byzantines returned to Hermeleia in the last months of 1371, after the Serbian Despot of Serres, John Uglješa, was defeated by the Turks at the Marica River (26 September 1371); in November of that year, Manuel Palaeologus entered Serres and restored the Byzantine rule over eastern Macedonia. But the general situation was no longer rosy, for a new and more dreadful enemy, the Ottomans, now became a major power in the Balkans. In spring 1372, the Turks launched several important though unsuccessful attacks, one of which reached Thessalonica itself,[32] while they also prepared a fleet and menaced Mount Athos.[33] Unable to resist, the Byzantines signed a humiliating peace agreement with the sultan Murad I in 1373.[34] Thus, their newly recovered territories were left in precarious—and often interrupted—peace. The Turkish danger was so obvious that the Byzantine government secularized half of the *metochia* of the Athonite and Thessalonian monasteries and turned them into *pronoiai* in order to reinforce its own armed forces and be able to face the raids of the irregular ghazis.[35] But this did not change much of the general situation, for the raids continued; more important, it was obvious that a regular Turkish conquest of the countryside of eastern Macedonia was only a matter of time. So, many monasteries came to terms with their prospective conqueror: while still being under Byzantine rule, they asked and obtained sultanic firmans confirming their properties and granting them protection. This anticipated submission to the Turks was more than a simple guarantee of what the monasteries possessed; it also turned them into institutions that were secure, because they were protected by both sides, and consequently allowed them to launch into considerable business activities and increase their property at the expense of the lay Byzantines.[36]

During the Serbian rule, Deblitzenos's domain of Hermeleia, being very valuable, was taken over and exploited by others. The Byzantine administration, when it returned in 1371, showed no eagerness to expel them from there in order to restore the lands to their previous lawful owners. We may assume that Deblitzenos complained bitterly about this situation, the more so because this Hermeleia domain had belonged to his family for a long time (ἐκ πολλῶν χρόνων) and he could prove it by producing many valid titles of ownership; in any case he thought that the situation was so intolerable that he calls it a "tyranny" (τυραννὶς) that continued even during the first years of the Byzantine domination. But eventually things were arranged in his favor: the emperor first issued a chrysobull permitting all lawful allodial owners to recover their properties; then, he issued a *prostagma* in favor of Manuel Deblitzenos, granting him personally the right to recover his own paternal domain.[37] When at last he recovered his land, he decided to use it to benefit the souls of his parents, and for his own benefit: he made an agreement and donated almost the whole domain to the monastery of Docheiariou[38] that possessed property in the immediate neighborhood (ἀνακεκοινωμένως καὶ ἀναμὶξ) five years before our document B was issued, while Ioannikios was *higoumenos*. But the monks failed to observe all the clauses of this agreement, and Manuel was forced to take back his land and to obtain a letter from the metropolitan of Thessalonica declaring that he was correct in so doing. Moreover, he took an oath forbidding himself any further discussion with Docheiariou on this matter. The monks regretted that because of their own negligence, they had deprived themselves of such a domain and of such a friend (τοιοῦδε κτήματος καὶ φίλου στέρησιν). They went to the metropolitan, who arranged matters. First, he blamed them for breaking their agreement and for pushing Deblitzenos into taking an oath, which in itself is a sin.[39] Then he reconciled Manuel with the monks and absolved him from the sin (πταίσματος) of the oath (and from the obligations that he had undertaken in swearing it). Last, after long discussions and much advice (πολλαῖς διδασκαλίαις καὶ παραινέσεσι), he convinced Manuel to restore his donation to Docheiariou:

Manuel gives to Docheiariou (*higoumenos* Jonas) almost the whole of his domain of Hermeleia,[40] which includes arable land (unspecified quantity), a water mill, rights of *ampelopakton*, fruit trees, and *paroikoi* (unspecified numbers); he gives them everything that he possesses there, together with all his titles of ownership.

In return, the monks undertake (1) to commemorate forever Manuel's parents in every vespers and matins and in every Saturday mass and to hold a special commemoration service (μνημόσυνον) for them every 26 September;[41] (2) to deliver every year to Manuel, inside their *metochion* of Thessalonica, the food corresponding to three *adelphata*, that is, the following goods and quantities, that Manuel undertakes not to contest: 24 *tagaria adelphatarika* of wheat, which make three *kartai*; 4 *tagaria* of dry vegetables (ὀσπρίων); instead of the statutory wine, another 16 *tagaria* of wheat; 2 *tetartia* of olive oil; and fifty *litrai* of cheese. Manuel and, after him, a second person that he will designate, will receive for life the *adelphata*, no matter what happens to the Hermeleia domain. After their deaths, the *adelphata* will stop, and their names will be inscribed in the *brebion* of Docheiariou [for eternal commemoration, cf. document G, line 14].

As already pointed out, the end of our document B, from which we learn the above story, is now missing. But we know that the lost part contained mainly penal clauses stipulating that, if the monks did not keep the agreement, they should receive a spiritual punishment according to canon law (εὐθύνεσθαι κανονικῶς) and they should return gratis the whole estate in the same condition as it was when they took it over, as well as give to the Deblitzenoi everything that they owed them for the time that they kept it.[42] In order to add to the solemnity of the whole agreement, four imperial officials, including the *kastrophylax* of Thessalonica Demetrios Talapas, signed on the verso.

The information contained in our document B is partly confirmed by a deed of August 1375, preserved in the archives of
Saint Panteleimon.[43] We learn that the emperor John V Palaeologus
had issued an *horismos* ordering the restitution to the lawful
owners of all the land that had been taken away from them by
force, provided they could show their valid titles of ownership to
this land. A Byzantine noble, Alexius Palaeologus, tried to recover his paternal property, which he had abandoned during the
Serbian occupation; but he realized that the Serbs had given it to
the monastery of Saint Panteleimon and that the monks had already obtained a chrysobull from John V confirming the holdings
of all their properties, including his own. As he himself had been a
prisoner of the Turks and had lost all his titles to ownership, he
solemnly renounces any revindication, provided the monks guarantee that, when he goes to the monastery, he will receive an *adelphaton.*

It is not difficult to see what happened in eastern Macedonia
after 1371. During the first phase, the Byzantine government very
cautiously avoided any radical change of the status quo established by the Serbs: the Turkish menace was an obvious reason
dictating that the Byzantines should not displease their newly
recovered subjects.[44] But Constantinople, pressured by influential people like Deblitzenos, changed its attitude when the peace
of 1373 with the Ottomans was signed. John V issued, probably
already in 1373, a chrysobull ordering the restitution to the lawful
owners of any piece of property that had been taken from them
illegally.[45]

When this happened, Alexius Palaeologus no longer had his
titles of ownership, while his formidable opponents, the monks
of Saint Panteleimon already had a chrysobull in their hands. He
had no chance, so he settled for an *adelphaton.* In other words,
he obtained the guarantee that, whatever happened, he would
not be found without bed and food. On the contrary, Manuel
Deblitzenos had many titles of ownership (our document A was
one of them), obtained an imperial *prostagma* for himself, and
recovered his domain. But then, after trying to develop it himself, he preferred, curiously enough, to make an agreement with
Docheiariou and give his land to the monastery. This took place,
in all likelihood, in 1376.[46]

We do not know what the terms were of this first agreement;
but it is certain that it contained financial clauses that the monks
did not observe and that caused the quarrel. When the quarrel

ended by the intervention of the metropolitan, who did his best
to arrange matters according to the wishes of the monks, the
parties reached a new agreement, which was undoubtedly very
similar to the first one.

In order to understand better the substance of this agreement,
one must bear in mind that an *adelphaton*, which, initially, meant
the food and clothing that every monastery gave to the member
of the brotherhood (*adelphos*) as long as he lived, was also conceived as a lifelong revenue, always in kind, granted or sold by
the monastery to an individual who was in need or who paid the
price.[47] In the second half of the fourteenth century, and also in
the fifteenth century, the normal price for one *adelphaton* was
100 *hyperpyra*, but the interested individual could substitute for
cash a donation of land. In the case of Deblitzenos, we know
that, in 1349, his estate in Hermeleia was taxed to an amount
that would be equal to 100 *hyperpyra* and, consequently, that it
was worth several times the 300 *hyperpyra* in cash that Deblitzenos would have needed in order to buy his three *adelphata*.

Moreover, if one examines the quantities of food that are promised to Deblitzenos and compares them to other *adelphata*, one
realizes that, here again, the monastery is unfair to Deblitzenos.[48]
Table 1 compares what he received to that promised to Theodore
Anatavlas by the monastery of Esphigmenou in 1388 or 1403.[49]
This comparison shows clearly that what Deblitzenos received
corresponded to two *adelphata* equal to the one of Anatavlas—and
this, in spite of the fact that our document B, and several others,
speak always of three *adelphata*. One may assume that the quarrels and the bargaining between our man and the monastery were
concerned mainly with these quantities that were obviously lower
than normal, and that finally Deblitzenos accepted and agreed
in advance not to contest the matter.

An *oikeios* of the emperor, a member of the Thessalonian high
class, gives away a valuable estate and accepts in return, after
quarrels and bargaining, a revenue of three *adelphata* that, in
reality, corresponds to only two: this case needs an explanation,
above and beyond Manuel's piety and the pressures of his metropolitan. It is obvious that the Hermeleia estate, the land of which
remained intact, had lost much of its productivity and value between 1349 and the early 1380s. We also know of the estate of
Anna Palaeologina at Mariana (to the southwest of Hermeleia),
which, in 1373, was left without any *paroikoi*. Although the wife
of the grand domesticus, she did not have the means to put it

Table 1. **Comparison of** *Adelphata* **Promised to Deblitzenos and Anatavlas**

	Deblitzenos, 3 *adelphata*	Anatavlas, 1 *adelphaton*
Wheat	24 *tagaria*[a]	12 *tagaria*
Dry vegetables	4 *tagaria*	2 *tagaria*
Wine	instead of wine, wheat: 16 *tagaria*	24 *metra*
Olive oil	2 *tetartia*[b]	6 *metra*
Cheese	·50 *litrai*	30 *litrai*

[a]In order to convert from the Byzantine to our measures, one should use the equivalents established by E. Schilbach, *Byzantinische Metrologie* (Munich, 1970). This is an arduous task because our knowledge of the value of Byzantine weights and measures is far from being certain. For example, our document allows us to establish that, in 1384, 24 *tagaria adelphatarika* were the equivalent of three *kartai*; but this was no longer true in 1419 (doc. G, line 10: κάρτας τρεῖς τοῦ τότε καιροῦ), and none of the values established by Schilbach for *tagarion* and for *karta* confirms what is said in our document. Further research in this direction is needed; but for the time being, we may bypass this difficulty for the purposes of our comparison, because fortunately, the same Byzantine measures are mostly used in both documents.

[b]If one applies here the equivalents established by Schilbach, pp. 115–120, for the *tetartion* and the *metron* of oil, Deblitzenos would be receiving, for three *adelphata*, 4.26 l., while the one *adelphaton* of Anatavlas would give him twenty-four times this quantity. This difference is absurd and is probably due to our ignorance of the real value of these measures.

into production again and so decided to sell it, at a very low price, to a monastery.[50] We may assume also that the Turkish raids in eastern Macedonia, particularly that of 1372, but also subsequent ones, were responsible for this situation. Insecurity, lack of labor force, and as a result, lack of prospective buyers, explain why the lay aristocrats were led to renounce their estates and give them away for next to nothing to the Athonite monks. Most probably, the latter were confident that their separate contacts with the sultan would allow them to exploit these new domains without hindrance from the Ottoman ghazis, and by selling *adelphata*, they disposed of the surplus of their agricultural production while substantially increasing their property.

Things were not always as easy as that. It is probable that when, after their first agreement with Deblitzenos, the monks took possession of his estate in Hermeleia in 1376/1377, they found it as desolate as Anna Palaeologina found hers; this they knew, because they were neighbors; but they may also have realized that they could not put it into production, as they wished, because of scarcity of manpower. So they refused or "neglected" to deliver to Deblitzenos what they owed him and thus provoked the quarrel. But with time, and the relative peace that prevailed, conditions improved and they tried, once again, to renew their very profitable agreement. Pressured by the metropolitan, by his inability to properly exploit or sell his domain, and by the fact that hostilities with the Turks were about to start again,[51] Deblitzenos returned to the bargaining table in 1381: it is probable that he lessened his demands; and the monks took the formal engagement to give him what was agreed upon, "no matter what happens" (εἴ τι ἄρα καὶ συμβῇ) to the Hermeleia domain. In any case, after this agreement, Deblitzenos started receiving the *adelphata* (document D, line 4).

We know what happened next from our document G that contains a detailed summary of the whole affair. Some time after the second agreement, Deblitzenos received an order from the emperor Manuel II to go and fight the Turks at Chortaïtes, and he was killed there. At the immediate request of his widow, church officials made a general evaluation of her property in order to make sure that she received all she was entitled to as compensation for her dowry. They attributed to her, among others, the Hermeleia estate, without having proceeded with a regular evaluation, which was then impossible because of the blockade of Thessalonica,[52] and issued for this purpose our document C, in August 1384.

Chortaïtes is a village and a mountain with a famous monastery some 10 kilometers east of Thessalonica. That a battle with the Turks was fought there, in which the Byzantines were defeated, we already know from a letter of Cydones, who places the event after the fall of Serres to the Turks (19 September 1383).[53] Our document C allows us to say now that the Chortaïtes battle was fought in summer 1384, shortly before the document C was issued, and to propose a slightly different chronology of the events of 1383/1384:

After the capture of Serres, the Ottomans sent an ultimatum to Thessalonica, asking a heavy tribute and, in case of refusal, menacing with military action. This ultimatum arrived in Thessalonica before 26 October 1383 and is mentioned in the homilies of the metropolitan Isidore; Manuel II convened an assembly of the Thessalonians and read there an "advisory discourse," suggesting, in substance, a rejection of the ultimatum and proposing to send an embassy to the Turkish camp to discuss peace.[54] These discussions certainly took time; winter had started; and consequently, one would not expect the Turks to begin major operations at that time of the year. Because no agreement was reached, they moved in 1384, crushed the Byzantine army at Chortaïtes, and commenced their blockade of Thessalonica that was to last until April 1387.[55]

There is no doubt that the news of her husband's death reached Maria Deblitzene very soon. Her reaction was the one of a widow who intended to keep absolute control over her family or, maybe, who tried to avoid paying any debts of her husband's: as soon as she put on her black dress of mourning, she went to the metropolis and requested the authorities to make a census of the properties of her husband and herself and reserve to her all that she was entitled to because of her dowry, all according to the law.[56] A commission first examined the agreement before her marriage (σύμφωνον) and discovered that her dowry was then evaluated at 22 *litrai*, that is 1,584 *hyperpyra*, to which they added, according to the law, one third of them, that is, another 528 *hyperpyra*, for a total of 2,112 *hyperpyra*. Then, they evaluated that which was still in her possession, subtracted it from the above sum, and declared that the sum of 1,107 *hyperpyra* was due to Deblitzene. To this they added 26 *hyperpyra* that was missing from her additional dowry (ἐπανοπροίκων), 62 *hyperpyra* that were missing from the inheritance that she received from her grandfather Choneiates, and 50 *hyperprya* of expenses for her mourning clothes and for her food during the current year and arrived at a grand total of 1,245 *hyperpyra* due to Deblitzene. They then evaluated her husband's real estate and movable property in Thessalonica and found it worth 374 *hyperpyra*, plus the inheritance that he received from his stepson, which amounted to something between 90 and 99 *hyperpyra*.[57] Deblitzene took all this, but she was still lacking approximately 780 *hyperpyra*. So the commission granted her all the estates that her husband possessed outside Thessalonica (3,500 *modioi* of land) plus the Hermeleia estate, without proceeding to an evaluation; gave her the right to receive any revenue that she might get therefrom; and declared that, when peace prevailed again, an evaluation would be made and she would receive, according to the law, what was due to her. The remaining should be kept for Manuel's children.[59]

By menacing Maria with excommunication, the commission

made sure that she did not hide anything from them, although, strangely enough, she did not declare any cash in her possession. But even if we also believe her declaration, we realize that by 1384 the Deblitzenos's property had diminished by 202 *hyperpyra*, compared to what it had been at the time of their marriage and what they subsequently inherited. If one takes into consideration the suspicious absence of any cash and the fact that this decrease is partly due to the wear and tear of dresses (41 *hyperpyra*) and partly to the devaluation of a vineyard situated near Thessalonica (50 *hyperpyra*),[60] and if one also points out that they still possessed considerable jewelry, icons, and precious utensils and that Deblitzenos, who undoubtedly went to war on horseback, had two more horses in his stable (lines 34–35, ἀλόγου . . . παρίππιν), then one comes to the conclusion that their financial situation was still healthy because they had started very well. But they obviously did not manage to increase their property, not even to replace all things that were worn out. In normal times, this might well be due to a certain style of life; but in the context of the year 1384, this economic stagnation may well be the result of the general situation that pushed Manuel Deblitzenos into giving his Hermeleia estate to Docheiariou: their regular revenues from their estates in the countryside had dramatically decreased in the years that preceded 1384. Has it not been pointed out that, after the middle of the fourteenth century, even some Palaeologi had started having financial difficulties?[61]

The Turkish blockade of Thessalonica lasted until the city surrendered in April 1387. It is almost certain that during the blockade Deblitzene did not receive any *adelphata* from Docheiariou, or its domains, which were mostly in the countryside held by the Turks. Also, as the metropolitan Symeon puts it in 1419, when the city gates were opened, most of the estates that were reserved (by the commission as a compensation) for her dowry were now occupied by the Turks, who also took the city. After the capture, however, the widow contacted the monks and again received from them all that her late husband had arranged.[62] This arrangement is the only object of our document D, of January 1389, in which Maria, who inherited the three *adelphata* from her husband and thus became the "second person" entitled to them, declares that, according to the initial agreement, she recognizes the monastery's right to stop completely these *adelphata* after her own death. It is clear that, while the other estates of Deblitzenos were taken over by the Turks, Hermeleia was not touched, obviously because it belonged to Docheiariou, which still possessed it in 1404 (see below), 1409,[63] and 1419 (see below). One has the impression that the monks were not at all affected by the Turkish domination.

Thessalonica and Chalkidike returned to Byzantine rule in late 1403 or at the beginning of 1404.[64] Once again, the monks of Docheiariou tried to stop the *adelphata*. But now Deblitzene was assisted by her son-in-law, Bartholomaios Komes, whom she authorized to take the affair to the imperial court of the city. The court—composed of the *doulos* of the emperor Constantine Ivangos;[65] of the *sakelliou* of the metropolis, Nicholas Prevezianos; and most conveniently for the case of Deblitzene, of another Komes, named George—examined the titles of Deblitzene and heard futile explanations from the monks, who said that certain difficulties that occured at that time (καιρικὴν περίστασιν) gave them the impression that they had the right to stop the *adelphata*. In October 1404 the decision was published ordering the monks to forget any pretext for not doing so, to continue delivering the *adelphata* to Deblitzene as long as she lived, and to stop them only after her death. This decision is our document E.

We do not know what the pretext of the monks was. The expression καιρικὴν περίστασιν used in our document points to something that affected the monastic revenues before, or during, 1404. We do know that when the Byzantines returned to Thessalonica and eastern Macedonia, the Athonite monasteries faced important financial problems: following the policy that he had himself inaugurated shortly after 1371, Manuel II Palaeologus took away "temporarily" half of their *metochia*, in order to transform them into *pronoiai*, and added new taxes to the remaining half. In October 1404, and again in December 1408, pressured by the monks, he was forced to take new measures in order to alleviate the fiscal burden of the monasteries.[66] In this context, especially during the first year of Byzantine rule (1403/1404) when conditions were not yet settled and regularized, we can understand why the monks of Docheiariou, whose properties diminished and whose taxes climbed, thought that they were authorized to ignore certain obligations that they had previously undertaken. But the tribunal of Thessalonica believed the emperor's declarations, considered that these exactions were temporary (καιρικὴν), and obliged them to respect their engagements toward Maria Deblitzene.

Maria received the three *adelphata* until her death, in May 1419.

The monastery had thus fulfilled its engagement and could now keep the Hermeleia estate without any obligation. But Bartholomaios Komes and his wife Theodora, born Deblitzene, thought otherwise: they went to the metropolitan of Thessalonica, Symeon, and declared that they were ready to go to court and contest the rights of Docheiariou to the estate. Their arguments were that the Hermeleia estate belonged to Theodora's father (true),[67] that it was given to her mother without being properly evaluated (true), and that, consequently, Theodora, as her father's successor, had certain rights over it, the more so inasmuch as she had in her possession some more titles of ownership concerning the estate. The metropolitan examined the agreements and realized that the monks had fulfilled their engagements. Moreover, he questioned Theodora's silence all this time, when, being adult, she saw her mother receiving the *adelphata*; and he remarked that the whole fortune of Maria went, in fact, to her only child, Theodora, either as dowry, or as inheritance. So, he discouraged the couple from going to court with such a weak case and proposed an arrangement: the couple would solemnly renounce any claim over this estate and hand over to the monks any relevant title of ownership that they possessed; the couple would receive in return, once and for all, the three *adelphata* of the current year (1419/1420) and the lump sum of 12 *hyperpyra*. This was a small compensation for the couple, who faced financial difficulties. The monks reluctantly accepted the arrangement, and the whole affair ended in December 1419, when Theodora received the promised food and money and signed a deed renouncing any claim to the estate. This is our document F; it was immediately confirmed by the metropolitan, Symeon, who issued our document G to this effect.

This was a case study, showing some general aspects of Byzantium in decline: the state alienated its revenues to the benefit of lay aristocrats; the latter lost some of their sources of income because of the Serbian and Turkish wars and were faced, first with economic stagnation, then with financial problems; the monastery increased its landed property on the most profitable terms, simply by promising to give, in exchange, yearly *adelphata* in kind; it kept and developed this property in spite of the Turkish menace and, later, the Turkish domination, which does not seem to have affected it. On the contrary, it faced financial difficulties only after its return to Byzantine rule, at a moment when the government of Constantinople, in its desperate effort to stop the Ottoman advance by creating an efficient army, took measures favorable to its own lay aristocracy, and detrimental to the monastic properties.

The preoccupations of the church were somehow different and, by far, more realistic. Everyone knew what had happened to the ecclesiastical institutions of Asia Minor during the Turkish conquest; everyone knew how difficult it was for such institutions to survive under Latin domination. The monks of Macedonia obviously preferred to be on the safe side: by coming to terms with their prospective conqueror, the Ottoman sultan, not only did they avoid disaster but they also became the only stable institutions in the general uncertainty of the times and drew all the economic advantages that such a reputation might offer them. In this context, it is not surprising that "the monasteries with their huge properties survived the [Byzantine] state."[68]

Notes

1. Only three of these documents (A, E, and G) are mentioned (as numbers 1Δ´, KH´, and M´) in the catalogue of the Archives of Docheiariou, compiled by C. Ktenas, "Ta keimēliarcheia tēs en Hagiō Orei Athō hieras, basilikēs, patriarchikēs kai stauropēgiakēs monēs tou Docheiariou," *EEBS* 7 (1930): 108, 110, 112.

2. Document published by C. Ktenas, "Chrysoboulloi logoi tēs en Athō hieras basilikēs, patriarchikēs kai stauropēgiakēs monēs tou Docheiariou," *EEBS* 4 (1927): 291–292, no. 4; F. Dölger, *Aus den Schatzkammern des heiligen Berges* (Munich, 1948), no. 10. Cf. F. Dölger and P. Wirth, *Regesten der Kaiserurkunden des Oströmischen Reiches*, vol. 5 (Munich and Berlin, 1965), no. 2954.

3. This document was issued before August 1384 (the date of our doc. C), while the metropolitan of Thessalonica Isidoros Glabas was in the city. We know that Isidoros was consecrated on 25 May 1380, that he was still in Constantinople in June of the same year, and that he reached Thessalonica shortly afterward. On the other hand, we also know that he left his see for Constantinople in the spring or summer of 1384. Because he participated personally in several phases of the quarrels that ended with our document (cf. lines 19 ff.), the latter cannot belong to the very beginning of his stay in Thessalonica and has to be dated between the beginning of 1381 and spring 1384. For Isidoros's moves, see G. T. Dennis, *The Reign of Manuel II Palaeologus in Thessalonica, 1382–1387* (Rome, 1960), pp. 16–17, 91–92. A more precise dating, autumn 1381, is proposed inf., note 46. The other persons mentioned in our document fit well with this dating. Jonas, *higoumenos* of Docheiariou, is also mentioned in an unpublished document of 27 October 1381. The *doulos* of the emperor George Doukas Tzykandeles, who signs

with other officials on the *verso*, is known as a Thessalonian justice, from
an unpublished document of Docheiariou of February 1373, and from a decision of June 1375: G. Theocharides, *Mia dikē kai mia diathēkē byzantinē*
(Thessalonica, 1962), p. 49.

4. The copy is certified by two officials of the metropolis of Thessalonica:
the [great *oikonomos*] George Senacherim, who was a priest, and the great
chartophylax [Nicholas] Prevezianos, who was a deacon (line 48). Both
sign, with the same titles, an unpublished document of Xenophon of December 1419 (no. 34 in Laurent's forthcoming edition). The latter was the *sakelliou* of the metropolis in 1404 (he signs our doc. E, line 31); but in February
1414, still a deacon, he already was great chartophylax (unpublished document of Docheiariou) and kept the same position at least until 14 April
1421 (Dölger, *Schatzkammern*, no. 102, line 85). It is obvious that the present copy was made during the quarrels that ended with our documents F
and G, both of December 1419.

5. The present document was issued certainly after 1384 (doc. C) and before May 1419 (death of Maria Doblytzene, see p. 189). In this span of time,
the twelfth indiction occurs in 1389, 1404, and 1419. This last year has to
be excluded since our document was issued shortly after Maria was entitled
to receive for herself the three *adelphata* ("*τῶν ἀδελφάτων εἰς ἐμὲ ἐλϑόντων,
ἐζήτησεν ἡ μονὴ ὡς ἂν ποιήσω γράμμα πρὸς αὐτήν*," lines 7-8; cf. sup., p.
188). The year 1404 also, should, most probably, be excluded, because, if
the present document really belonged to January of this year, there would
be no point in going to the imperial tribunal that issued our document E
nine months later, in October 1414. The only remaining date is 1389, when
Thessalonica was, for two years, under Turkish rule. In this context, one
understands better how it happened that, although five witnesses sign this
deed, none of them is called a *doulos* or *oikeios* of the emperor, in spite of
the high social standing of Doblytzene. This is even more significant when
one thinks that among these witnesses we find Maria's own brother John
Angelos, and a certain Andronicus Chalazas, who may have had a personal
relationship with the emperor Manuel II around 1383: cf. Démétrius Cydonès,
Correspondance, vol. 2, ed. R.-J. Loenertz, Studi e Testi 208 (Vatican, 1960),
p. 256, no. 326, line 25.

6. See G. Theocharides, *Katepanikia tēs Makedonias* (Thessalonica, 1954),
pp. 75-76. Hermeleia also gave its name to a whole *katepanikion*, but our
documents indicate clearly that the property was situated near the village,
not somewhere in the *katepanikion*.

7. (a) V. Mošin, "Akti iz svetogorskih arhiva," *Spomenik*, Académie Serbe
91 (1939), p. 207, of 1300 (Manuel; see also n. 7, prosopographical indications); (b) unpublished document of Docheiariou, 28 December 1311, lines
5-6 (Demetrios); (c) F. Dölger, *Sechs byzantinische Praktika des 14. Jh. für
das Athoskloster Iberon* (Munich, 1949), K, line 595 of 1317 and P, line 582
of 1321 (no first name); (d) P. Lemerle, A. Guillou, N. Svoronos, and Denise
Papachryssanthou, eds., *Actes de Lavra*, vol. 2 (Paris, 1977), no. 108, lines
559, 571 of 1321 (no first name); (e) our document A of 1349 (Demetrios);

(f) W. Regel, E. Kurtz, and B. Korablev, eds., *Actes de Zographou, Viz. Vre.* 13 (1907), Prilož?enie, no. 27, lines 30, 51 of March 1328; cf. Dölger and Wirth, *Regesten*, no. 2704 (no first name); cf. also the falsified documents recorded in ibid., nos. 2874, 2875.

8. Unpublished document of Docheiariou of 27 October 1381, line 20 (Manuel).

9. Regel, Kurtz, and Korablev, *Zographou*, no. 24, line 7, 17 August 1296 or, more probably, 1311 (Philip); for the date, see Dölger and Wirth, *Regesten*, no. 2194.

10. F. Miklosich and J. Müller, *Acta et diplomata graeca*, vol. 1 (Vienna, 1860), pp. 283–284.

11. (a) L. Petit and B. Korablev, eds., *Actes de Chilandar, Viz. Vre.* 17 (1911), Prilož?enie, no. 130, line 16 of May 1339 (Theodore); (b) P. Schreiner, "Zwei unedierte Praktika aus der zweiten Hälfte des 14. Jh.," *Jahrbuch der Österreichischen Byzantinistik* 19 (1970): p. 34, line 5 (Λυκόπουλος Δελβι-τζηνὸς ὁ Σέρβος).

12. Dölger, *Praktika*, A, lines 452–453 of March 1301 (Manuel).

13. *Viz. Vre.* 9 (1902), p. 133 of 1341 (Constantine).

14. Our documents F and G (both of 1419).

15. Our documents B (ante 1384); C (1384); D (1389); E (1404); Dölger, *Schatzkammern*, no. 63, line 25 of May 1409 (Manuel).

16. Manuel Dobeltzenos (sup., n. 12) is probably identical to the Deblit-zenos mentioned in note 7a and is certainly identical to the one in note 7c; Delbitzenos of note 11a is probably identical to the Deblitzenos of note 7f; Debletzenos of note 8 is certainly identical to Doblytzenos, or Dobletzenos of notes 14 and 15, and probably identical to Deulitzenos of note 10 (cf. inf., n. 25). In the following pages I use only the form Deblitzenos, for all members of the family.

17. Texts quoted sup., notes 7a, 7c, and 12. This hypothesis is supported by the fact that Demetrios's son was also called Manuel, after his grand-father.

18. Texts quoted sup., note 7b and d.

19. This income is certainly much superior to the one that then was given to the rank and file of the Thessalonian cavalry, which normally amounted to 70–80 *hyperpyra* per year (N. Oikonomidès, "Notes sur un praktikon de pronoiaire," *Travaux et Mémoires* 5 (1973): 340, n. 13); Deblitzenos's *pronoia* can be compared to the one of Alexios Soultanos Palaiologos (380 *hyperpyra*: Dölger and Wirth, *Regesten*, no. 2896).

20. Beside the basic book of G. Ostrogorsky, *Pour l'histoire de la féodalité byzantine* (Brussels, 1954), one should also see: Hélène Glykatzi-Ahrweiler, "La concession des droits incorporels: Donations conditionnelles," *Actes du XIIe Congrès International des Etudes Byzantines*, vol. 2 (Belgrade, 1964), esp. pp. 100 ff.; K. V. Hvostova, *Osobennosti agrarnopravovyh otnoz?enij v pozdnej Vizantii XIV–XV vv.* (Moskow, 1968), pp. 205 ff.; E. P. Naumov, "K istorii vizantijskoj i serbskoj pronii," *Viz. Vre.* 34 (1973): 22–31; and M. V. Bibikov, "Svedenija o pronii v pis'mah Grigorija Kiprskogo i 'Istorii'

Georgija Pachimera," *ZRVI* 17 (1976): 93-99 (with previous bibliography).

21. Except if this particular property belonged to the crown, or if the previous owner was expropriated. But if either was the case, it could not but be clearly mentioned in the imperial charter of donation, which should also serve as a title of ownership. On the problem of allodial ownership and state rights on land, see M. J. Sjuzjumov, "Suverenitet, nalog i zemeljnaja renta v Vizantii," *Antičnaja Drevnost' i Srednie Veka*, vol. 9 (Sverdlovsk, 1973), pp. 57-65.

22. Similar formulas are to be found in John VI Cantacuzenus's chrysobull of 1347 in favor of Demetrios Kabasilas: N. Oikonomidès, ed., *Actes de Dionysiou* (Paris, 1968), no. 2. It seems to me that the phrases of the chrysobulls referring to "hereditary rights" but with no indication of the other undeniable rights of an allodial owner—such as to sell, donate, etc.—show clearly that the object of the donation had nothing to do with the ownership of the land and that it concerned only its fiscal revenue.

23. The evidence, concerning the fate of western Chalkidike in the late 1340s and the 1350s, is contradictory: see G. Ostrogorski, *Serska oblast posle Dušanove smrti* (Belgrade, 1965), pp. 38 ff., and E. P. Naumov, "K istorii serbo-vizantijskoj granicy vo vtoroj polovine XIV v.," *Viz. Vre.* 25 (1964): 231-234. Hermyleia was taken by the Serbs before July 1349: *Actes de Xéropotamou*, J. Bompaire, ed. (Paris, 1964), no. 26, lines 78, 83.

24. Unpublished document of Docheiariou, line 20.

25. Document D, line 1: κατὰ δευτέρους γάμους (the expression κατὰ πρῶτον συνοικέσιον in our document C, line 1, refers to Maria's marriage, which was in fact the first and only one for her). A clear reference to Manuel's first wife and his stepson is to be found in our document C, lines 45-47, where it is said that Deblitzenos inherited certain properties from his stepson (προγόνου), who, consequently, must have died before him. It seems that Manuel did not have any children of his own from this first marriage. All this resembles very much what we learn from a patriarchal document of December 1348 (Miklosich and Müller, *Acta et diplomata* 1: 283-284): "A Thessalonian girl, Anna Sarantene Indanina, after losing her first husband who had given her two boys and one girl, married another Thessalonian called Deblitzenos; she later died, without having any more children. Deblitzenos hurriedly took for himself all her properties, but, at the request of her sister, the Patriarch intervenes and orders that, if Anna has not left a will, the law should be followed in distributing her property, of which her children should get their rightful part." Here, again, we have a Deblitzenos who married in Thessalonica a widow with children; his wife did not give him any more children and died before him. It seems to me that there is a very good chance that this Deblitzenos was our Manuel. If this is the case, he must have been a fairly young man when he lost his first wife in, or shortly before, 1348, because we know that he died some thirty-six years later, in 1384, while fighting the Turks.

26. Doc. D, lines 17-18: τοῦ αὐθέντου μου τοῦ ἀδελφοῦ μου τοῦ Ἀγγέλου κῦρ Ἰωάννου. There is no need to insist upon the importance of the Angeloi

family in Byzantium during the fourteenth century: cf. *Prosopographisches Lexikon der Palaiologenzeit*, vol. 1 (Vienna, 1976), pp. 12–21; see also the following note.

27. Doc. C, lines 4–21. The family of Choniates is well attested in Thessalonica. In October 1361, we hear about a Thessalonian *archōn* Symeon Choniates, who possibly could be Maria's grandfather (unpublished document of Docheiariou of October 1361). The phrases in our document C, lines 18–21, concerning the inheritance from Choniates, repeatedly state that Maria received one third of the properties. We may assume that the second third went to her brother, John Angelos. And one may wonder whether a certain George Angelos, who witnesses the unpublished deed of Docheiariou of 27 October 1381 (line 21) together with Manuel Deblitzenos, was not the third brother who received the rest of the inheritance.

28. Doc. C, line 47: παίδων αὐτῆς (i.e., of Maria Deblitzene) in 1384.

29. Doc. F, line 26: she signs with a *signon*.

30. Doc. E, line 3; doc. F, line 1 (Bartholomaios Komes is called an ἄρχων); doc. G, line 22. It is worth remembering here that a certain George Komes, *doulos* of the emperor, signs, as a member of the imperial tribunal of Thessalonica, our document E, line 32, in 1404.

31. Doc. G, line 34: παιδὸς ἄλλου μὴ προσόντος ἐκείνῃ.

32. G. T. Dennis, *The Reign of Manuel II*, p. 33.

33. N. Oikonomidès, "Monastères et moines lors de la conquête ottomane," *Südost-Forschungen* 35 (1976): 3, and n. 6. This operation may have taken place in 1372 or in 1373, but the former date seems more probable.

34. Dölger and Wirth, *Regesten*, no. 3136.

35. Mošin, "Akti," pp. 165–166. Cf. Ostrogorsky, *Féodalité*, p. 161 ff.

36. Oikonomidès, "Monastères," pp. 1–8.

37. Doc. B, lines 7–10: "ὁ . . . βασιλεὺς ἐχορήγησε καὶ εὐηργέτησε κοινῶς μὲν ἅπασι τὴν τῶν ἰδίων γονικῶν κτημάτων ἐλευθερίαν διὰ . . . χρυσοβούλλου, ἰδίως δ᾽ ἐμοὶ διὰ . . . προστάγματος τὴν τοῦ εἰρημένου γονικοῦ μου κτήματος ἐλευθερίαν τε καὶ ἀνάληψιν."

38. With the exception of the land that was around the tower, belonging to another monastery, Vatopedi (doc. B, line 12). In fact, Vatopedi possessed a tower in Hermeleia before 1356: M. Goudas, "Byzantiaka eggrapha tēs en Athō hieras monēs tou Batopediou," *EEBS* 4 (1927): 239.

39. Cf. Matt. 5:34; can. 25 of the Holy Apostles.

40. With the same exception mentioned sup., note 38.

41. One may assume that the choice of this specific date was motivated by the fact that it was the anniversary of the death of one of his parents, most probably that of his father.

42. This lost part of our document is summarized in our document E, lines 19–22.

43. *Akty russkago na svjatom Afone monastyrja sv. Panteleimona* (Kiev, 1873), no. 23, pp. 184–186.

44. The more so, since these new users of the land were, in good part at least, *pronoiarioi*: e.g., Theocharides, *Mia dikē*, p. 43.

45. There is no doubt in my mind that the chrysobull mentioned in our document B (sup., n. 37) and the *horismos* mentioned in the deed of Saint Panteleimon are one and the same document—a *chrysoboullos horismos?* (cf. F. Dölger and J. Karayannopulos, *Byzantinische Urkundenlehre* [Munich, 1968], pp. 127-128). I also think that it should have been issued in 1373 because: (a) When the document of Saint Panteleimon was written, in August 1375, the imperial *horismos* had existed for some time already, during which Alexius Palaeologus made his futile efforts to recover his property. (b) In August 1373, Anna Palaeologina sells her allodial estate of Mariana, which was occupied by the Serbs, given to be cultivated by others, then returned to the Byzantines, and finally, restored to her (Ktenas, "Chrysoboulloi logoi," p. 301). So, at least some of the lands were returned to their lawful owners before August 1373. In the same line, the Greek protos of Mount Athos, received the order to take back all the monastic *kellia* that his Serbian predecessors had distributed: cf. Oikonomidès, *Dionysiou*, p. 70.

46. The fact that Manuel Deblitzenos signs, as a witness, an unpublished deed of Docheiariou on 27 October 1381 (*higoumenos* Jonas), shows that our man had by then good personal relations with the monastery; but we do not know whether this deed was drafted before their quarrel or after their reconciliation. It seems to me almost certain that we must retain this second possibility, for we know that, after his second agreement, Deblitzenos received more than once the *adelphata* (doc. D., line 4: καὶ ἐλάμβανε ταῦτα: the form ἐλάμβανε—and not ἔλαβε—shows that this action was repeated). As Deblitzenos died in summer 1384, before that year's harvest, one has to assume that he actually received his *adelphata* at least for the years 1382 and 1383. So, he must have made his second agreement in 1381 (cf. sup., n. 3), when Jonas was, in fact, the *higoumenos* of Docheiariou; and we can deduce that his first agreement with the *higoumenos* Ioannikios was made in 1376.

47. Miriana Živojinović, "Adelfati u Vizantii i srednevekovnoj Srbiji," *ZRVI* 11 (1968): 241-270; idem, "Monaški adelfati na Svetoj Gore," *Zbornik Filozofskog Fakulteta* of the University of Belgrade 12, no. 1 (1974): 291-303; Oikonomidès, "Monastères," pp. 6 ff.

48. Examples in Živojinović, "Adelfati," pp. 257 ff.

49. J. Lefort, ed., *Actes d'Esphigménou* (Paris, 1973), no. 29; for the date see Oikonomidès, "Monastères," p. 4, n. 11.

50. Ktenas, "Chrysoboulloi logoi," no. 8.

51. Manuel Palaeologus made a successful campaign in 1382 and relieved Serres from the Turkish menace: Dennis, *The Reign of Manuel II*, pp. 61 ff.

52. Doc. G, lines 14-19: "ὁ Δοβλητζηνός, μετὰ καιρὸν ἀπελθὼν ἐν τῇ μάχῃ τῶν Τούρκων εἰς τὸν Χορταΐτην, ἐτελεύτησεν ἐκεῖ. Καὶ εὐθὺς ἐξήτησεν ἡ ἐκείνου σύζυγος ἐνταῦθα εἰς τὴν ἐκκλησίαν καὶ γέγονε καταγραφὴ καὶ ἔλαβε τὸ δηλωθὲν κτῆμα . . . εἰς ἱκάνωσιν . . . τῆς προικὸς καὶ τοῦ τρίτου αὐτῆς · πλὴν οὐ διετιμήθησαν διὰ τὸν ἀποκλεισμόν. . . ."

53. Dennis, *The Reign of Manuel II*, pp. 75-76.

54. Dennis, *The Reign of Manuel II*, pp. 78-85.

55. There is some contradiction in the sources concerning how long the

siege of Thessalonica by the Turks lasted: a chronological note says that it lasted four years (Dennis, *The Reign of Manuel II*, p. 8), whereas in the Life of Saint Athanasius of Meteora it is said that it was to last three years (ibid., p. 155, n. 11). Dennis, who thought that the siege started late in 1383, has suggested (ibid., p. 76, n. 66) that "these are round numbers and if the siege lasted three and a half years, both could be correct." I think that in fact the siege lasted three years or even less but that this span of time covered part of four indictional years, which start in September (first year: from the battle of Chortaïtes to 31 August 1384; second year: 1 September 1384 to 31 August 1385; third year: 1 September 1385 to 31 August 1386; fourth year: 1 September 1386 to the capture of the city in April 1387).

56. Byzantine law has always protected a woman's dowry by guaranteeing that, in case of the death of the husband, the widow was the first in line to receive back the whole of her dowry (provided that its exact value in money was established from the beginning) and by replacing whatever was missing from her husband's property. She was also entitled to increase it by one third (such was the fourteenth-century *hypobolon*). See Constantini Harmenopuli, *Manuale Legum sive Hexabiblos*, ed. G. E. Heimbach (Leipzig, 1851), pp. 534 ff., 566 ff. (Lib. IV, tit. 10, 11, 12, 13). Cf. N. Matses, *To oikogeneiakon dikaion kata tēn nomologian tou patriarcheiou Kōnstantinoupoleōs tōn etōn 1315-1401* (Athens, 1962), pp. 157-163.

57. The line 46 of our document C is destroyed, so all we know about this inheritance is that it was also evaluated by the church in *hyperpyra*, the number of which started with the letters ἐνε-, that is ἐνε[νήκοντα], or any number up to ἐνε[νήκοντα ἐννέα].

58. In our document G, line 17, instead of this sum we find a round number, 800 *hyperpyra*.

59. Doc. C, line 43: "*ἵνα ἵσταται λόγῳ τῶν παίδων τοῦ ἀνδρός.*" One should stress here that this phrase should not be understood as an indication that Manuel had children from a previous marriage. It means that, if Maria remarried and had more children, these would be debarred from making any claim to Manuel's property, which is reserved for his own offspring.

60. This vineyard of 14 *modioi*, situated in the region of Kontorryakion, was evaluated at the time of the marriage at 2 *litrai* (144 *hyperpyra*), including the value of its grapes that were ready to be picked (τρύγης). In 1384, the commission evaluated it (ἀρτίως) at 94 *hyperpyra* because by then it was deserted (δι' ἣν ὑπέστη ἐρήμωσιν) and did not bear any grapes. It seems to me that the vineyard was abandoned and destroyed as a result of the Turkish blockade of the city; but the Thessalonian commission still had access to it and managed to proceed with its evaluation because it was situated near the city walls. One has to bear in mind that in 1384 the Ottomans did not undertake a regular siege of Thessalonica; they just blockaded it by cutting off all access to it by land, hoping to starve it into submission. So the immediate vicinity of the city was not necessarily occupied by the Turkish troops, but their raids discouraged any permanent installation outside the city walls.

61. B. Ferjančić, "Posedi pripadnika roda Paleologa," *ZRVI* 17 (1976): 127-164.

62. Doc. G, lines 19-21: "Μετὰ δὲ τὴν ὑπάνοιξιν τῆς πόρτης, τὰ μὲν πλείω τῶν τοιούτων χωραφίων παρὰ τῶν ἀσεβῶν κατείχοντο, ὡς καὶ τῆς πόλεως κατασχεθείσης παραχωρήσει Θεοῦ, περὶ δὲ τοῦ εἰρημένου κτήματος τῆς Ἑρμιλείας συνεβιβάσθη ἡ σύζυγος τῷ Δοβλητζηνῷ μετὰ τῶν ἐν τῇ εἰρημένῃ μονῇ μοναχῶν καὶ ἐλάμβανεν ὑπὲρ τῶν ἀδελφάτων ὅσα κατ᾽ ἀρχὰς ὁ ἀνὴρ αὐτῆς συνεφώνησεν."

63. In the *praktikon* that the Thessalonian officials Paul Gazes and George Prinkips issued to Docheiariou in May 1409, the estate of Deblitzenos (παλαιοχώριον τὸν Ἅγιον Νικόλαον, called such probably because of a church that existed therein) is mentioned among the other properties of the monastery: Dölger, *Schatzkammern*, no. 63, lines 24-26. The term παλαιοχώριον seems to indicate an abandoned village, but this does not mean that the lands were not cultivated by the *paroikoi* of Docheiariou, who lived on the monastery's old Hermeleia estate.

64. G. Dennis, "The Byzantine-Turkish Treaty of 1403," *Orientalia Christiana Periodica* 33 (1967): 72-88; cf. N. Oikonomidès, "John VII Palaeologus and the Ivory Pyxis of Dumbarton Oaks," *Dumbarton Oaks Papers* 31 (1977): 335 n. 43.

65. On Constantine Ivangos, see G. T. Dennis, *The Letters of Manuel II Palaeologus*, Dumbarton Oaks Texts, 4 (Washington, D.C., 1977), p. xlvi.

66. For the fiscal policy of Manuel II in the region of Thessalonica and Mount Athos, see: Mošin, "Akti" (as in n. 7 sup.), pp. 165-167 = Dölger and Wirth, *Regesten*, no. 3321 and the commentary by Ostrogorsky, *Féodalité*, pp. 161 ff.; *Grēgorios ho Palamas* 2 (1918): 449-452 = Dölger and Wirth, *Regesten*, no. 3301 and my commentary in: "Le haradj dans l'empire byzantin du XVe s.," *Actes du Ier Congrès International des Etudes Balkaniques et Sud-Est Européennes*, vol. 3 (Sofia, 1969), pp. 682 ff.

67. Doc. F, lines 10-11; doc. G, line 23. In document F, we find the detail that Manuel had received this estate by imperial chrysobull: it seems to me that there is confusion here between the chrysobull of 1373, which ordered the restitution to their lawful owners of all the estates taken over by the Serbs, and the *prostagma* in favor of Deblitzenos specifically concerning the Hermeleia estate. See sup., note 45. This could also be a reference to our document A.

68. P. Charanis, "The Monastic Properties and the State in the Byzantine Empire," *Dumbarton Oaks Papers* 4 (1948): 118.

Chapter 11

The Anconitan Colony in Constantinople and the Report of Its Consul, Benvenuto, on the Fall of the City

Agostino Pertusi, *late of Fondazione Cini, and Catholic University*
translated by Anthony Di Candia

It is known that Ancona enters into the more direct orbit of Byzantine interests during the first half of the twelfth century when Byzantium, in order to oppose the intentions of the Normans of Sicily, on the one hand, and the influence of the German Empire on the other, as well as the Venetian desire for hegemony in the Adriatic, decided to establish on the Adriatic Coast, and specifically at Ancona, a diplomatic and military foothold.[1]

In spite of the many failures of Byzantine-Anconitan diplomacy between 1149 and 1171,[2] failures that caused Ancona to submit twice (1158 and 1167) to Frederick I Barbarossa, it seems that the Byzantines did not fail to express their gratitude to the Anconitans for the services rendered for the benefit of the Eastern Empire. Thus, immediately after the liberation of the city of Ancona by the armies of Guglielmo Marcheselli of Ferrara and those of Aldruda Frangipane of Bertinoro from the terrible siege undertaken by Christian of Buch, bishop of Magonza and chancellor of the German Empire in 1173–1174, it seems that Manuel I Comnenus, "εὐρανθεὶς τούς τε Ἀγκωνίτας ἐπαίνοις τῶν γεγονότων ἀμείβεται καὶ τοῖς ἰσοπολίταις τῷ γένει Ῥωμαίων ἐγκρίνας ἅπαντα ὑπισχνεῖται παρέξειν ὅσα οἱ ἀμεμῆ τε καὶ δυνατὰ κἀκείνους δέον αἰτεῖν."[3] It is possible that Nicetas Choniates here refers to a chrysobull released to the Anconitans upon such an occasion,[4] with which the emperor, pleased at the loyal behavior of the citizens, conceded them equal rights with the Romans and promised them to fulfill whatever honest and feasible requests they might have. Among the requests of the Anconitans, was there also one asking for a territorial zone, in Constantinople? The possibility should not be excluded; as a matter of fact, judging from the documents, it seems that they did obtain a zone, most probably located on the Golden Horn, similar to those zones already in the possession of the other Italian republics such as Venice, Pisa, and Genoa. Because of a lack of precise information in the sources, however, it is not possible to determine where the Anconitan colony was located in Constantinople, although it is certain that it existed from the end of the twelfth century.

A document dated 11 February, 1199 shows that the church of Saint Stephen was in existence; its prior, Dominick, undersigned a protocol on a matter regarding Benenato, prior of the church of Saints Peter and Nicholas of the Pisans.[5] The church of Saint Stephen must still have existed in the fourteenth and fifteenth centuries because an appendix of an Anconitan portolan mentions "del datio che se de' pagare de quelli che vai in Costantinopoli per la chexa de Sancto Stephano de Chonstantinopoli . . . Tutti li merchadanti che naviga in Chostantinopoli sia tenuti e debia pagare per ciaschedune cento de ciascheduna mercantia 3 carati per cento de perpari per la chexa de Santo Stefano, la qual stai nella detta ciptà di Costantinopoli e per l'opera de concime (= reparation) de questa chiexa. . . ."[6]

Therefore, without a doubt, the Anconitans already possessed a territorial concession at the end of the twelfth century, with warehouses and a church dedicated to Saint Stephen. The Anconitan merchants had established themselves in Constantinople before 1173, as attested by Buoncompagno da Signa, who, speaking about the siege of Ancona in 1173–1174, states that many citizens were away from their country because "causa negotiandi erant in Alexandria, in urbe Constantinopolitana et Romania."[7]

If the presence of the Anconitan prior in a matter regarding the Pisan prior has any significance, it could be that the territorial concession of the Anconitans was quite close to that of the Pisans, that is, near the "Porta Veteris Rectoris," on the Golden Horn, between the Pisan and the Genoese possessions.[8]

Unfortunately, even the chrysobull released to the Anconitan ambassadors Florio Stefano di Tarveli and Antonio di Bartolomeo in July 1308 by the emperor Andronicus II Palaeologus does not help us to define precisely the location of the Anconitan land concession. This document confirms a previous, lost chrysobull, to which it specifically refers, according to which the Commune of Ancona is given the privilege of paying a 2 percent tax on goods entering and leaving the port of Constantinople, just as the Genoese and the Venetians already did.[9]

In the year 1322, two Anconitans made a commenda contract for goods shipped on the boat of a certain Rosso di Vagile of Fermo, who was to transport them to Constantinople and to sell them there.[10]

The documents that have survived, known or published, regarding the history of the Anconitan community in Constantinople are few, but it is possible that others exist, buried in the state archives of Ancona, Pisa, or Florence. It would, in any case, be desirable to study systematically the *Consiliorum Libri* and the *Fragmenta Consiliorum* in the archives of Ancona, in a more detailed and more trustworthy manner than did Makušev. Here follows a brief summary of the documents already known:

17 August 1380. The Consilium Generale of the commune of Ancona orders that the cost of the transport of wheat by ship to Ancona "de partibus Turchie et Romanie" be kept reasonable so that the commune would not suffer any damage.[11]

30 September 1380. The Consilium Generale elects as "Consul in partibus Romanie" Giovanni Angeli di Michele, an Anconitan citizen. Furthermore, as a result of a request of the Anconitan citizens of Constantinople, who had been harmed by the Byzantine emperor (John V Palaeologus), the Consilium Generale decides to send a ship with many Anconitan citizens and two ambassadors, Giovanni Angeli, consul elect, and Nicola Deoli, to provide for the protection of the rights of the citizens oppressed by the emperor.[12]

1389. The Consilium Generale deliberates on the sum of monies necessary for the reparation of the church (of Saint Stephen) and of the Loggia, that is, of the palace of the merchants in Constantinople.[13]

29 July 1392. The Consilium Generale decides to send the nobleman Ciuccio de Arduinis with a ship "ad partes Romanie" to congratulate the Byzantine emperor (Manuel II Palaeologus) "de suo felici statu" and to beseech him to preserve the Anconitan merchants resident in Constantinople "in eorum gratiis, privilegiis et honoribus"; also, to present to him the apologies of the Commune of Ancona for the "gesta et operata" of Nicola Gherarducci of Ancona, "in displicentiam imperatorie majestatis," and to bring him a gift, paid by the resident Anconitan merchants, valued at 25 or 30 ducats.[14]

8 April 1419. The Consilium Generale deliberates on a response to the Byzantine emperor (Manuel II Palaeologus) "in forma

placida" that it is happy with the election of Filippo de Alfer-
iis as "Consul Anconitanorum in Constantinopoli et partibus
Romanie."[15]

20 April 1430. At the meeting of the Assembly of the Commune of Ancona, it is decided that, when the ambassadors of
the Byzantine emperor (John VIII Palaeologus) arrive in
Ancona on their way to the pope (Martin V), they will be
received with every honor and will be housed in the "Palazzo
della farina," so that afterward they might give good reports
to the emperor about the treatment received from the Anconitans, "et nos conservemur in bona gratia et benevolentia illius
imperii." The commune will also undertake as its own responsibility the provisioning of the members of embassy.[16]

21 April 1440. The Consilium Generale deliberates that the
consules of the Anconitan community in Constantinople, who
hold the post for 3 years, receive "pro eorum provisione," a
quarter of a ducat for every "*centenario*" (that is, for every
100 librae) of merchandise that arrives "ad ipsorum consola-
gium."[17]

9 May 1440. Nicola Francisci di Giovanni of Ancona is elected
consul of the Anconitan community in Constantinople.[18]

Hence, the Anconitan community in Constantinople not only
had continued to exist, but it certainly had a territorial concession
in the Byzantine capital, because we now find in the documents
mention either of the church of Saint Stephen or of the Loggia,
that is the palace of the merchants, the probable seat of the Consul Anconitanorum. Such a consul, appointed by the mother
country, remained in charge for a three-year period and was assisted
by a "Collegium mercatorum in Romania existentium."[19] The
kind of government, therefore, was entirely similar to that of the
other Latin communities, such as those of the Venetians who had
their *baiulus*, and those of the Genoese who were ruled by their
potestas. "Consul" was the title given not only to the leader of the
Anconitan community but also to the leaders of the Pisan and
Catalan communities.[20] It is certain that the Anconitan consul
already in the fourteenth century held a position of prestige in the
hierarchy of foreign dignitaries present in the Byzantine capital.[21]
At the time of the Turkish siege of 1453, the Anconitans participated in the defense of Constantinople.[22]

As is known, the Anconitans had commercial wharves not only
in Constantinople but also in Alexandria in Egypt, and in the Near

East. We have knowledge of one wharf in particular, that of Gallipoli (Gelibolu), through the story told by an interesting Anconitan
personality, a certain Lillo Ferducci. This port had been an important naval base and a strong arsenal for the Byzantines; it was later
conquered by the Venetians in 1204 and retaken from them by
the emperors of Nicea in 1234-1235; it afterwards fell into Catalan hands and finally was occupied in 1354 by the Ottomans, who
took advantage of an earthquake that devastated the coast of Asia
Minor. In the fifteenth century, it must have been also a commercial port.[23]

Lillo Ferducci, an Anconitan merchant and important shipowner,
settled there during the 1420s. Writes his son Othman Lillo in the
letter of dedication to Mehmed II of the poem *Amyris*,[24] which he
commissioned Gian Mario Filelfo to write:

> Lillus Ferduccius, pater meus integerrimus, apud Amorattim
> clarissimum patrem tuum incredibili valuit et auctoritate et
> gratia. Fuit enim ab ineuntibus suis, ut ita dixerim, annis
> Callipoli ea cum omnium procerum benevolentia, merca-
> torum fide, principis aequissimi favore, ut in hunc usque
> diem [ca. 1471-1476] nulla rubigo vetustatis e Callipolita-
> norum mentibus deleverit eius nomen. Egit autem in regno
> [sc. Amorattis] maxima cum omnium laude annos circiter
> quatuor et viginti.

Hence, Lillo Ferducci, still very young, had gone to the Orient
to be a merchant and had based himself precisely at Gallipoli
during the reign of Murâd II (1421-1451). It seems that the sultan
had entrusted him with "multas et amplas causas," and that he
placed in him great faith because of his integrity and intelligence.
He was also much esteemed by "Saragia," that is by Sarudja Paŝa,
one of the three viziers of the time,[25] who was described by
Othman Lillo as *praeses provinciae* of Gallipoli. He became very
rich through the protection of the sultan; it seems that he ransomed those Turks who had been taken captive and who had been
put up for sale as slaves, for which reason he was considered an
enemy of the Christians—or so states Othman Lillo. It is more
realistic to believe that his father practiced the commerce of slaves
and paid a tax to the Ottoman government in order to ransom
those of Turkish origin and to donate them to the sultan. Having,
then, become rich, he had bought a house, sometimes called
"peregregia" and sometimes "amplissima et paene regia,"[26] in

Gallipoli itself, planning to spend the rest of his life there. Having been called back to his country by his relatives, he requested permission to leave from Murâd II; and Murâd tried to dissuade him, "verum etiam Anconam prohibitus regredi," because he liked him and held him in high esteem. Ultimately, under the pressure of Lillo's relatives, the sultan allowed him to return to Ancona, and Lillo promised him to return again to Gallipoli and to name his firstborn son Othman. Having entrusted his house and all his possessions to a Greek he trusted, a certain Theodore, Lillo returned to Ancona, where he married and had a number of children; to the firstborn he gave the name Othman Lillo.[27] Not being able to return to Gallipoli, he sent a certain Lorenzo Ferducci—probably a relative of his—to administer his estate, but Lorenzo, instead of preserving and enlarging Lillo's patrimony, "arbitratus se commodius rem nostram [that is to say, of the Ferducci's] agere," he proceeded to sell the house to the Greek, Theodore, much to the disappointment of the proprietor. A little later, Murâd II died (3 February 1451), and almost at the same time, it seems, died Lillo Ferducci, without having realized his dream of returning to Gallipoli.[28]

His son, Othman Lillo, decided to follow in his father's footsteps, that is to say, to establish himself at Gallipoli in order to engage in trade there, but he could not do so because of the financial state of the family. The father, who had bought some *praedia* for 25,000 *nummi aurei* (ducats), had then been compelled to contract loans for 10,000 *aurei*, following many reversals of fortune, and furthermore the patrimony had been divided among the dowries of the daughters who had married. Hence Othman Lillo's difficulties in resuming the road toward the East, although he never abandoned the idea. His desire was reinforced by a fact that gave him proof of the fame left by his father among the Turks and of the benevolence demonstrated by the new sultan Mehmed II immediately after the fall of Constantinople; at that time, Mehmed had liberated his brother-in-law Angelo Boldoni and returned the ship full of merchandise that the Turks had taken away from him in the port of Constantinople: "Angelus enim Boldonus," writes Othman Lillo, "cui soror mea iam nupserat cuique navis esset suis et nostris onusta rebus et pulcherrima et opulentissima, in Constantinopolitano excidio captivus factus est et statim, quod Lilli diceretur fuisse gener, tua munificentia et libertate donatus est et rebus omnibus quae sibi fuissent communes cum nostris."[29]

The same story is told by the chronicler Lazzaro de Bernabei of Ancona in his *Chroniche anconitane* of 1492:

> La città de Ancona etiam partecipò de tal ruina, per che tra li altri morti et presi Angelo Boldone patrone de una sua nave fo preso con tutta la sua compagnia de la nave. Ma tra molti tremori, paventi et periculi et desenestri, habbe assai bona fortuna ne la fine, per che andando li homini per el filo de le spade et le femine col le altre robbe ad saccomanno, esso fo recognosciuto dal Gran Turcho essendoli restituita la nave con tutte le mercantie se retrovonno in essa. Li fonno etiam renduti li suoi homini.[30]

Lazzaro de Bernabei suggests, though, that the *cagione* ("reason") for this generous act on the part of Mehmed II was not the high esteem in which the sultans held the Ferducci family, as Othman Lillo says. Rather, it was the fact that Boldoni, some years earlier at Gallipoli, had made a gift of an armed ship to the very young Mehmed Čelebi, who had expressed his admiration for the beauty and the state of the ship. The story is also repeated by other chroniclers later on, for instance by Lando Ferretti, and by Guilelmo Saracini, who copies Ferretti.[31] Nevertheless, while Othman Lillo and Lazzaro de Bernabei speak of Boldoni solely as an owner of ships and a merchant, and relative of the Ferducci's, not only do Ferretti and Saracini speak of him as "a great merchant from Ancona and a *consul* of his city in Constantinople,"[32] but they also say that the intermediary to Mehmed II for his release had been a certain unspecified man who had been housed by Boldoni in Ancona and with whom he had earlier become friends in Constantinople. If truly there was an intermediary involved in the liberation of Boldoni, and if this intermediary, as the two most recent chroniclers say, "was very dear to the Great Lord Mohammed," it is possible that this was Ciriaco of Pizzicolli, who in 1453–1454 was with Mehmed II as counselor and man of culture.[33]

But this is only a hypothesis, which would need further documentation to assume the appearance of historical truth. Rather, the identification of Angelo Boldoni with the "consul of the Anconitans" present at Constantinople at the time of her fall, is to be abandoned by now, even though it has been repeated recently by Natalucci,[34] not only because it is totally hypothetical, but because it is refuted by a document that we have discovered in a codex of Wolfenbüttel.

Codex Guelferbytanus lat. 42. 3 Aug. 2°, no. 2505 Heinemann,[35] is a paper manuscript of the fifteenth century, 23¼ by 20¼ centimeters, of 315 folios, written by different hands, miscellaneous, which, according to Heinemann who described it, contains the following in folios 290r-292v:

Tres epistolae de destructione et captivitate Constantinopolis et de factis Turcorum. *Ep. 1. Inc.* "Benevenutus civis Anchonitanus, in Constantinopoli consul, dicit se omnia infra scripta vidisse preter articulum de morte inperatoris et provisorum." *Expl.* "Datum in meo ducali palatio die ultima julii Indictione prima MCCCCLIII Franciscus Foscari Venetorum dux." *Ep. 2. Inc.* "Diu pater beatissime cogitavi crebriusque mente revolvi." *Ep. 3 inscriptio est sic:* "Infra scripta est copia cuiusdam littere fratris Pe(tri) de Alliaco catholici capellani mercatorum in civitate Adrianopoli, ubi est sedes regis Turcorum, scripte ad fratrem B. Tholomensem de Jano, virum ordinis minorum in partibus Constantinopolitanis."

Having undertaken elsewhere the study and edition of the last two letters, which refer to another very important historical event,[36] but certainly not to the fall of Constantinople, let us limit ourselves to the observation that the so-called *Ep. 1* is, in reality, composed of two letters:[37] the first one, which begins with "Benevenutus, civis Anchonitanus, in Constantinopoli consul, etc." and stops on the same folio 290r with the following words: "solus evasit quia manserunt pedestres in platea. . . ," and the second one, which begins: "Sanctissimo ac reverendissimo in Christo patri et domino domino Nicolao divina providencia pape quinto ac sacrosancte Romane ecclesie summo Pontifici, devota pedum oscula beatorum. Quamquam existimamus, b[eatissime] p[ater], tam literis r[everendi] p[atris] d[omini] archiepi[scopi] Ragusini, legati apostolici hic existentis, etc.," at the end of the same folio 290r, and which stops towards the end of folio 290v with the words: "Datum in meo ducali palatio, etc." This last letter is one of the few exact copies of the original letter sent by the doge of Venice, Francesco Foscari, to Pope Nicholas V on 30 June 1453, announcing the fall of the Byzantine capital, of which letter a rough copy is also preserved in *Sen. Secr.* 19, fol. 202r.[38]

Let us now read the document of Benvenuto, "consul of the Anconitans," which narrates the fall of Constantinople into the hands of the Turks:

> Benevenutus, civis Anchonitanus, in Constantinopoli con-
> sul, dicit se omnia infra scripta vidisse preter articulum de
> morte inperatoris et provisorum. In primus, quod quarta
> die Aprilis inperator Turcorum venit cum exercitu suo
> 5 noctis tempore ante civitatem Constantinopolis et die se-
> quente complete fuit exercitus per terram et mare colloca-
> tus. Item quod fuerunt pavlioni 60.000 per terram, idest
> sexaginta milia. Item quod fuerunt inter galeas et fustes
> per mare 300 ⟨per⟩ tria milia. Item quod inter omnes erant
> 10 homines per terram 300.00 ⟨idest⟩ tercenta milia homi-
> num. Item quod fuerunt per mare homines 36.000, ⟨idest⟩
> triginta sex milia. Item quod era una bomberda que simul
> emittebat tres lapidus inequales: item quod lapis maior
> erat ponderis 1300 librarum; item quod lapides alii duo
> 15 erant ponderis 600 librarum pro quolibet 300 librarum.
> Item quod stetit campus eius sive exercitus ante dictam
> civitatem a dicta die quarta Aprilis usque ad XXIX Maii,
> et sunt dies 56 inclusive. Item quod die qualibet ter da-
> bat bellum per terram in diversis locis cum bomberdis,
> 20 sagittis et scobetis [scoletis]. Item quod, donec Jus-
> tinianus Longus, custodiens simul cum inperatore Con-
> stantinopolitanam et suis nobilibus locum fractum per
> bomberdas, affugit cum 360 hominibus civitatis, egregie
> fuit civitas per inexistentes defensata ad modum ut ex
> 25 custodientibus civitatem solum 40 persone interfecte
> fuerunt et ex Turcis ultra 7000. Item quod XXVIII Maii
> de nocte incepit bellum per mare et per terram circum-
> circa civitatem, et resistebant optime inexistentes ipsi
> Turco, sed pos⟨t⟩quam dictus Justinianus affugit ad-
> 30 veniente die XXIX Maii media hora die⟨i⟩ capta fuit
> civitas Constantinopolitana. Item quod audivit ab uno
> trumpeta quod inperator Grecorum fuit interfectus et
> eius caput super lancea Turcorum domino presentatum.
> Item quod de reverendissimo domino cardinali nichil
> 35 scit det⟨er⟩minate, nisi quod stabat super murum ad cus-
> todiam; vidit tamen multos eici mortuos et vivos de
> muris. Item quod, duobus diebus antequam daret bellum,
> emissum fuit a Turcorum inperatore bannum seu edic-
> tum, et quisque christianus libere exire possit per viam

40 Pere, alias quicumque repertus fuerit in civitate postea, si
   eum capi contigerit, ab annis octo supra, morti sine
   venia daretur. Item quod per duos dies dedit civitatem et
   singula ad predam sakmannis. Item quod erant menie ad
   custodiendum 11.000 ⟨passuum⟩. Item quod erant tan-
45 tum homines ad custodiendum menias cum reverendissimo domino cardinali 7000. Item quod provisores solum
   per terram erant 300, quorum caput erat baiulus Venetorum; predictus Benevenutus, consul, Anchonitanus civis
   et magnus dux baro inperatoris ⟨ . . . ⟩. Item quod predicti
50 omnes provisores, ut credit, interfecti erant ipseque solus
   evasit, quia manserunt pedestres in platea ⟨ . . . ⟩

---

inscr. deest   9 per *addidi*   10, 11 idest *addidi*   20 scoletis *seclusi*
29 postquam *scripsi*: pusquam *cod.*   30 diei *dub. correxi*   35 determinate *correxi*: detminate *cod.*   42 daretur *vel* daret *cod.*   43 sakmannis, sic *cod.*, i.e. *saccomannis*   44 passuum (*vel* milium) *supplen-
dum esse videtur*   49 *post* inperatoris *lacunam conieci*   51 *post*
platea *desunt quae sequebantur in archetypo*

This new document, unfortunately not complete, fills a fairly
serious gap in our information concerning the "consul of the
Anconitans" and his presence at the fall of Constantinople. Unfortunately, we do not have the heading, that is, the address which
must have specified to whom the letter should have been sent.
Given the form in which it is compiled, however, that is, the form
of an "account" or "information," or "message," one will not be
far from the truth if one supposes that it must have been sent to
the authorities of the Commune of Ancona. It was, therefore,
something similar to the account that Jacopo Loredan, "capitano
generale da mar," sent to Venice from Nigroponte, where the fleet
that was sent to help Constantinople was still anchored, on the 2
or 3 of June 1453, entrusting it to the three galleys from Romania,
which, having escaped capture, were about to return to Venice
under the command of Alvise Diedo. Diedo, having reached
Venice on 4 July, was invited to give a report on the events that
same day in front of both the Council of Ten and the Senate.[39]

The extremely unadorned style, and the dryness with which the
events are listed, introduced repeatedly by the chancery term
item, cause us to believe the document to be absolutely authentic,
written a little after the catastrophe. A similar document, but
differently written because sent to his brother, is the document

by Angelo Giovanni Lomellino, *podestà* of Pera, who, for one reason or another, as it is said at the end of the letter, had not the courage to write an official account to the doge, Pietro di Campofregoso.[40]

The document is of singular importance, not only because it gives us the name of the "consul of the Anconitans"—although it is difficult to say who this Benvenuto was. Perhaps he was Benvenuto di Candrio, known through the Anconitan chronicles since 1428; he was sent in that year by the council of the city to the deputy of the Marca of Ancona because the council wanted the repeal of the prohibition imposed on the Commune of Ancona against minting silver coins, as would happen later.[41] The document is also important because it is full of information, which, compared to other documents and accounts of the time, confirms certain facts of great importance for the history of the siege and the fall of Constantinople.

Benvenuto's account appears to be very reliable, especially in regard to some numerical facts. For example, the figure of 300,000 men in the Turkish army is largely confirmed by trustworthy sources such as Kritoboulos; Isidore of Kiev; Leonardo of Chios; Enrico of Soemmern; Nicola of Foligno; and the Anonymous Venetian, author of the *Lamento di Constantinopoli*, whereas other sources vary from 160,000 to 400,000 and even to 700,000.[42] If the *pavliones*, that is, the military tents all around the city were 60,000, it is also clear that each tent contained an average of five soldiers, a credible figure. Thus also, the number of 300 Turkish ships (counting small and large ones) is, I believe, close to reality. It is the same number given by Ducas, whereas Kritoboulos gives the number 350, and Sphrantzès, on the other hand, agreeing with the Turkish sources (Nešri, Qyvâmi, Ibn Kemal), mention 400.[43] Other sources vary from 250 to a little more than 100; but perhaps these sources do not count accurately the small ships. The number of 36,000 men on board, giving an average of 120 men per ship, seems to include not only the sailors, but also the soldiers; this figure is absolutely new, not given by any other source. As for the numbers of the defenders of the city, the figure of 7,000 is in accordance with what was already known from other sources. I have already observed that the figure given by Sphrantzès (4,773 Byzantines and 200 foreigners = 4,973) is not acceptable because it is certainly low regarding the number of foreigners, that is, of Latins (Venetians, Genoese, Catalans, Anconitans, people from Candia, etc.). Benvenuto's figure is closer to

that given by Tedaldi (7,000–8,000), by Della Tuccia and by
Leonardo of Chios (6,000 Greeks and 3,000 Latins).[44] As for the
number of *provisores*, or even better, the "commanders" for the
defense of land and sea walls, 300 seems to be a somewhat exaggerated figure. It is possible to recover from the sources about
forty names, including Byzantines, Venetians, Catalans, and
Genoese;[45] but it is possible that there are gaps in the sources. It
is not even exact that the *baiulus* of the Venetians, the well-
known Girolamo Minotto, was at the head of the *provisores*.
Certainly, it is possible that he had a more responsible role from
the time when he was put in charge of the defense of the imperial
palace of Blachernae (after 6 April), replacing the emperor Constantine XII, who had placed himself at the side of the Genoese
condottiere Giovanni Giustiniani Longo, named *protostrator* of
the defense of the land walls between the Gate of Saint Romanos
and the Charisios Gate. However, it must be remembered that not
even Barbaro, who tends to exalt the actions of the Venetians
beyond measure, gives any more precise indication.

Unfortunately, there are some gaps in the part of the text where
Benvenuto talks about himself. Thus, the role he played in the
defense of the city is not specified, nor is it stated in which part
he fought, while we read that he had received a courtly title:
"magnus dux baro inperatoris," something fairly common in
those days for the leaders of foreign communities in Constantinople.

Although he is very exact with regard to the duration of the
siege (from 4 April to 29 May, that is, 55 days); the proclamation
of Mehmed II before the final attack; and other particulars, such
as the use of *scobeti*, that is, arquebuses, by the Turkish troops—
in particular, it appears, by the janissaries—he is less exact with
regard to the use of cannon. He writes that Mehmed had "una
bomberda que simul emittebat tres lapides inequales," that is of
1,300, 600, and 300 librae (= 423.9, 195.6, and 97.8 kilograms).
The information is not exact, although it does contain some truth.
The weight of the *lapides*, that is, of the stone projectiles, corresponds to the weight given by other sources, more or less; but they
were fired by cannon of different caliber, and not by a single
one.[46] Still, it is appropriate to recall that, according to the essentially similar testimony of Chalkokondyles and Qyvâmi,[47] Mehmed's largest cannon, which shot projectiles of almost 400–450
kilograms, had two smaller cannons on the sides of the gun carriage.
These served, very probably, for adjusting the firing (the Turks, in
fact, called the cannon "Eniklu ayu," that is, "Bear with cubs").

Hence Benvenuto's error in believing that all the projectiles of various sizes that fell on the city were thrown by only one cannon.

Finally, the fact that he does not appear to be well informed on the fate of the emperor Constantine XII and of Cardinal Isidore of Kiev does not speak against the truthfulness of the document; it indicates only that the document was drafted quickly, a few hours after the catastrophe, when there was still great confusion and it was not possible to check the news that was circulating. After all, he tells only what was told him by a *trumpeta* about the end of the emperor, while for the fate of Cardinal Isidore he only says "nichil scit determinate, nisi quod stabat super murum ad custodiam," but that "vidit . . . multos eici mortuos et vivos de muris."[48] What is not clear, however, is the last sentence, in which he says that "ut credit," all the *provisores* fell fighting, "quia manserunt pedestres in platea," while he "solus evasit." The sentence would allow it to be believed that at a certain point the surviving leaders met together in a square (in the Forum Constantini or in the Augusteon in front of Saint Sofia?) and there they faced, on foot and with their arms, the Turkish troops spread throughout the city. Does this mean that if they had been on horseback they could have saved themselves?

One notes, after all, what Benvenuto says about the Genoese captain Giovanni Giustiniani Longo. It does not seem to me that here the consul of the Anconitans shows any animosity toward Longo, as does, for example, Barbaro, but he lets one believe that the Genoese captain "affugit"—and the verb is repeated a good two times—together with his fellow soldiers from Chios, who were only 360 men. The figure is close to those sources that speak of 400 men, whereas others mention 700. But leaving that aside, it is interesting to note that Benvenuto does not make the least reference to the reason for Giustiniani's abandonment of the defense posts, that is, of the injury or injuries incurred in the last battle in front of the Gate of Saint Romanos. It is true that the writers of memoirs and the chroniclers are anything but in agreement on the matter of Giustiniani's injuries—and somebody even says that "he feigned injury"—but, in general, they admit that he had been hit either by an arrow or the bullet of an arquebus.[49] Following a rumor that perhaps was spread precisely by the Venetians, Benvenuto also places in a cause-and-effect relationship the abandonment of the front by Giustiniani and his men, and the collapse of the defense at daybreak on 29 May ("adveniente die"). Certainly, the abandonment of the defense by Giustiniani greatly weakened the action at a particularly delicate point of the land walls, but we must not forget that almost at the same time that the defenses were breached at the Gate of Saint Romanos by Mehmed II's select troops, they were also breached at two other places at least, that is, in the environs of the so-called *Kerkoporta* of the imperial palace of Blachernae, and in the environs of the Charisios Gate.[50] After all, Cardinal Isidore was right when, in his letter to Duke Philip of Burgundy, he did not deny the responsibility of Giustiniani but considered it the same as that of all the others who fought too weakly at such an already precarious point.[51]

Unfortunately, the document, lacking the final part, has deprived us of perhaps other news of great importance, but even as it is, in its simplicity and straightforward style, it is of primary importance for the history of the fall of Constantinople and of the presence of the Anconitans in the last act of the drama that marked a turn in the history of the eastern Mediterranean.

Notes

1. On the general situation between the Byzantine Empire and Italy between 1149 and 1173-1174, cf. F. Chalandon, *Histoire de la domination normande en Italie et en Sicile*, vol. 2 (Paris, 1907), pp. 135 ff.; idem, *Les Comnène, II, Jean II Comnène et Manuel I Comnène* (Paris, 1912), pp. 317 ff.; E. Caspar, *Roger II (1101-1154) und die Gründung der normannisch-sicilischen Monarchie* (Innsbruck, 1904), pp. 370 ff.; P. Rassow, "Zum byzantinisch-normannischen Krieg 1147-1149." *Mitteilungen des Instituts für österreichische Geschichtsforschung* (1954):213-219; P. Lamma, *Comneni e Staufer: Ricerche sui rapporti fra Bisanzio e l'Occidente nel secolo XII*, vol. 1 (Rome, 1955), pp. 99 ff., and vol. 2 (Rome, 1957), pp. 1 ff.; L. Bréhier, *Vie et mort de Byzance*, 2d ed. (Paris, 1969), pp. 271 ff.; G. Ostrogorsky, *Storia dell'impero bizantino* (Torino, 1968), pp. 348 ff.

2. Cf. M. Natalucci, *Ancona attraverso i secoli*, vol. 1, *Dalle origini alla fine del Quattrocento* (Città di Castello, 1961), pp. 243-270.

3. Nicetae Choniatae, *Historia*, ed. I. A. van Dieten, vol. 1 (Berolini et Novi Eboraci, 1975) (= *Corpus fontium historiae Byzantinae* XI/1), p. 202, lines 40-43.

4. It is surprising that F. Dölger, in *Regesten der Kaiserurkunden des Oströmischen Reiches von 565-1453*, vol. 2, *Regesten von 1025-1204* (Munich and Berlin, 1925), p. 85, while he registers the embassy of Constantine with a large sum of money to help beseiged Ancona (no. 1515), does not register privileges on the basis of Nicetas Choniates. But the text of Choniates leaves no doubt that a "promise" was officially made.

5. Cf. G. Müller, *Documenti sulle relazioni delle città toscane coll'Oriente cristiano e coi Turchi fino all'anno 1531, raccolte e annotate* (Florence, 1879), p. 82; W. Heyd and F. Raynaud, *Histoire du commerce du Levant au moyen-âge*, vol 1 (Leipzig, 1885), p. 262, n. 3. It is not the document of 12 December 1199, in G. L. F. Tafel and G. M. Thomas, *Urkunden zur älteren Handels- und Staatsgeschichte der Republik Venedig*, vol. 1 *(814-1205)* (Vienna, 1856), ("Fontes Rerum Austriacarum," II: 12), pp. 280-281, and then in L. Lanfranchi, *S. Giorgio Maggiore*, vol. 3, *Documenti 1160-1199 e notizie di documenti* (Venice, 1968), ("Fonti per la storia di Venezia," Sez. II), pp. 451-452, of different content, to which R. Janin refers repeatedly in *Constantinople byzantine: Développement urbain et répertoire topographique*, 2d ed. (Paris, 1964), p. 254, n. 2, and *La géographie ecclésiastique de l'Empire Byzantin*, vol. 1, pt. 3, *Les églises et les monastères*, 2d ed. (Paris, 1969), p. 575, n. 3. According to the above-cited document, Benenato, "ecclesiarum sanctorum Petri et Nicolai Pisanorum Constantinopoleos prior," proves with the testimony of different people that his predecessor, Peter, owing to a privilege given by Pope Alexander III, confirmed children, blessed chalices, and carried "*insignia pontificalia*." The document, drawn up in Constantinople, "*in domo diaconi Leonis*," is drawn up "in presentia Iohannis Robici et *presbyteri Dominici prioris Anconitanorum* et presbyteri Boneiunte, convocatorum testium" (Müller, *Documenti*, p. 82).

6. N. Jorga, *Notes et extraits pour servir à l'histoire des Croisades au XVᵉ siècle*, vol. 4 (Paris, 1915), pp. 24–25.

7. Boncompagni, *Liber de obsidione Ancone*, ed. G. C. Zimolo, in *RIS*, 2d ed., 6/3 (Bologna, 1937), p. 17.

8. On the location of the two territorial possessions of the Pisans and of the Genoese, cf. Janin, *Constantinople*, pp. 249–251.

9. F. Miklosich and I. Müller, *Acta et diplomata graeca medii aevi sacra et prophana*, vol. 3, *Acta . . . res graecas italasque illustiantia* (Vienna, 1865; anastatic ed., Athens, n.d.), pp. xvi–xix, and in Italian, V. Makušev, *Monumenta historica Slavorum meridionalium vicinorumque populorum*, vol. 1, pt. 1 (Warsaw, 1874), pp. 156–158; Dölger, *Regesten der Kaiserurkunden*, vol. 4 (Munich and Berlin, 1960), p. 52, nos. 2314–2315; Heyd and Raynaud, *Histoire du commerce*, vol. 1, p. 474. It is a bit strange that in this document no mention is made of the Anconitan territorial zone in Constantinople, nor their warehouses, nor the church of Saint Stephen of the Anconitans; but the omission occurs because the privileges granted were strictly fiscal.

10. R. Marcucci, ed., "Un contratto di commenda in Ancona 1322," in *Atti e memorie della R. Deputazione di storia patria per le Marche*, ser. 4, vol. 1, fasc. 2 (Ancona, 1924), pp. 247–252. It is a notarial document by which Alberto di Andrea Guerra receives "in recommandicium ad quartam partem lucri" from Franceschino di Guido Talento a sum invested in some goods. The contracting party pledges to sell such goods "et pretium quod inde perceperit investire et renvestire," with all the risks and dangers "maris et gentis" on Franceschino's shoulders. At the end of this one-year contract, Alberto promises to return the accounts to Franceschino or to his heirs and to give back or insure the restitution of the capital given to him, with three parts of the profit, keeping for himself the remaining fourth part as payment.

11. Makušev, *Monumenta*, I, 1. 161.

12. Ibid., p. 161. It is not clear, judging from the decision, whether the damage is fiscal or material. It is possible that such a damage ("*aliqua noxia*") should be connected with the rebellion of Andronicus, John V's first son, who had been excluded from the succession to the crown and who, upon returning to Constantinople, after having been prisoner in Lemnos, went against his father and the Venetians who supported him (1376–1379). Perhaps the Anconitans had sided with John V and suffered the consequences.

13. Natalucci, *Ancona*, vol. 1, p. 409.

14. Makušev, *Monumenta*, I, 1. 161–162. The dispatching of a special ambassador is to be related to the coronation of Manuel II Palaeologus, which occurred a little after 16 February 1391. It is not known what Nicola Gherarducci had exactly done "in displicentiam" of the imperial majesty.

15. Ibid., p. 162.

16. Ibid., pp. 162–163. The embassy here alluded to, which was headed by Marcos Iagaris, "*grande stratopedarca*," and by Macarios Macros, abbot of the monastery of Pantokrator, left Constantinople at the beginning of 1430 and arrived in Venice: cf. J. Gill, *Il Concilio di Firenze* (Florence, 1967), pp. 50–53; V. Laurent, *Les "Mémoires" du Grand Ecclésiarque*

de l'Eglise de Constantinople Sylvestre Syropulos sur le Concile de Florence (1438-1439) (Paris, 1971), p. 118, notes 1-7. In reality it appears that the Byzantine embassy stopped at Ancona not on the way to Rome but upon returning from Rome. Always with regard to the negotiations for the unionist council, it should be remembered that the Anconitans were also called with the Genoese, the Venetians, and the Catalans to the church of Anastasis in order to listen to the reading of the preamble to the decree *Sicut pia mater* issued by the Council of Basel, appropriately corrected by the Latin delegates to mitigate certain phrases that the Greeks had considered offensive: cf. Gill, *Il Concilio*, p. 77; Laurent, *Les "Mémoires,"* p. 158.

17. Makušev, *Monumenta*, I, 1. 163-164. It is not clear which *centenario* it is, the Byzantine one (equal to 32.61 kilograms), the Genoese (34.84 kilograms) or the Venetian (47.69 kilograms).

18. Ibid., p. 164. The deliberation states: "9 Maii electus fuit Nicolaus Francisci Iohannis de Ancona"; therefore it is not altogether clear if it is about a new consul.

19. Ibid., p. 162.

20. Regarding the Catalan consul, cf. A. Pertusi, *La caduta di Costantinopoli*, vol. 1, *Le testimonianze dei contemporanei* (Milan, 1976), p. 370, n. 185, and p. 400, n. 39; S. Cirac Estopañan, *Byzancio y España: La caida del imperio byzantino y los Españoles* (Barcelona, 1954), pp. 58-59.

21. Cf. Pseudo-Kodinos, *Traité des offices*, ed. and trans. J. Verpeaux (Paris, 1966), 209. 19-20. The Anconitan consul followed the Genoese *podestà* of Pera and the Pisan consul during imperial ceremonies.

22. Nicolò Barbaro refers to the Anconitans present at the fall of Constantinople in two places in his *Giornale*; the first time, when he points out that a ship belonging to the Anconitans, of 1,000 *botte*, was used with other merchant ships to protect the defense of the chain that blocked the entrance to the Golden Horn; the second time, when he states that "dentro dal porto ne romaxe nave quindexe de Zenovexi e del imperador e de Ancontani" (cf. Pertusi, *La caduta*, vol. 1: 37 and 368, n. 179). Jacopo Tedaldi, instead, in his *Informations*, discusses only the damage suffered by the Anconitans upon the fall of the city, and he estimates it at 15,000 ducats (ibid., 1:186 and 413-414, n. 33).

23. For the history of this port cf. H. Ahrweiler, *Byzance et la mer* (Paris, 1966), pp. 318-325, 380, 405, 427, 438. Fra Bartolomeo di Giano, OFM, who was in Constantinople between 1435 and 1442, writing a letter titled "De crudelitate Turcarum" to brother Alberto of Sarteano in Venice on 12 December 1438, states that through the port of Gallipoli passed goods very much sought by the Turks, such as steel, sold by the Italian merchants to the Hebrew and Greek merchants and by these to the Turks. He also says that this port was a transit point for ships transporting slaves; it appears that the city of Corinth alone paid "millia et millia ducatorum" every year for the "pedagium captivorum de Gallipoli in Turchiam transeuntium." (*PG* 158. 1058a, 1063d).

24. G. Favre, ed., *Mélanges d'histoire littéraire . . . recueillis par sa famille et publiés par J. Adert*, vol. 1 (Geneva, 1856), pp. 182-188 and particularly p. 182. The letter had already been published by C. Hopf and P. A. Dethier, in *Monumenta Hungariae Historica*, XXI, 1. 263 ff. (but this edition is very rare because volume XXII, 1-2, was not accepted by the Hungarian Academy, and the few copies printed have almost all been destroyed). Cf. Pertusi, *La caduta*, vol. 1:lvi. As for the Ferducci (or Freducci) family of which the letter speaks, it seems that it was one of the richest families in Ancona during the fifteenth century, but little is known of its history and of its members. Notwithstanding the misfortunes and the expansion of the family through marriage, about which Othman Lillo speaks (cf. n. 29), it is certain that this family still had a notable estate around the years 1471-1476, when Othman Lillo commissioned to Gian Mario Filelfo the poem celebrating Mehmed II. A son of Othman Lillo was the "Conte de Hectomanno Freducci de Anchona." who drafted and signed a nautical chart around the years 1514-1515, illustrated extensively by E. Casanova, *La carta nautica di Conte di Ottomanno Freducci d'Ancona* (Florence, 1894); a man of great activities and knowledge, he also drafted ten other maps and atlases between 1497 and 1539 (cf. ibid., p. 9). Angelo Freducci also was perhaps either a nephew or a relative of Othman Lillo; he was also a cartographer and published an atlas in 1556 (cf. G. Uzielli and P. Amat di S. Filippo, *Studi biografici e bibliografici sulla storia della geografia in Italia*, vol. 2, *Mappamondi, Carte nautiche, Portolani* (Rome, 1882), pp. 94, 110-111, 114-115, 117, 119, 129. The Freducci continued the Anconitan tradition initiated by Grazioso Benincasa, author of a portolan chart in 1435, and by Andrea Benincasa, both designers of nautical charts of much value (cf. ibid., pp. 66, 76-84, 92, 99, 100, 106); M. Emiliani, *Le carte nautiche dei Benincasa, cartografi anconetani* (Rome, 1936); E. Spadolini, *Il portolano di Grazioso Benincasa* (Florence, 1907); Natalucci, *Ancona*, vol. 2, *Dall'inizio del Cinquecento alla fine del Settecento* (Città di Castello, 1960, p. 113). It appears that the Ferducci family became extinct in its main branch by the year 1537 (cf. Natalucci, *Ancona*, vol. 2, p. 246). A brief mention about Lillo and Othman Ferducci is made in F. Babinger's "Mehmed II. der Erober, und Italien," in *Aufsätze und Abhandlungen zur Geschichte Südosteuropas und der Levante*, vol. 1 (Munich, 1962), p. 174.

25. About him, cf. F. Babinger, *Maometto il conquistatore e il suo tempo* (Turin, 1967), Italian trans. by E. Polacco, pp. 49-50, 61, 66, 82, 121.

26. Here is the text by Othman Lillo from Favre, *Mélanges*, p. 187: "Quotiens Lillus pater meus observantissimus tuae laudis redimebat ex diversis nationibus Turcos tibi subditos per id temporis, quo fruebatur hac luce praestantissimus Amorattis pater tuus felicissimus, eosque Anconitanis cum navibus in tuam ditionem remittebat? Nam qui ab Hunnis Pannonibusque captivi vendebantur, quos servire sciret audiretve Lillus, eos continuo servitutis jugo sua vel grandi cum pecunia liberabat libertateque donatos in patriam suo sumptu non parvaque impensa remitti reducique procurabat, nec prius ea in re mens eius quiescebat, quam suo nomine Amoratti regi designatos et condonatos certo accepisset. Nec id semel aut rursus factum est, sed

tam quidem saepe, ut nonnunquam sine maximo discrimine fieri non posset a Lillo, quippe qui ab invidis malevolisque accusabatur Christianorum hostes, a quo qui poterant facillime Christiani perfici, reducerentur ad Turcos."

27. Favre, *Mélanges*, pp. 182, 183.

28. Ibid., pp. 182–183.

29. Ibid., p. 184.

30. Lazzaro de Bernabei Anconitano, "Chroniche anconitane," in *Collezioni di documenti storici antichi inediti ed editi rari delle città e terre marchigiane*, ed. C. Ciaverini, vol. 1 (Ancona, 1870), pp. 176–178.

31. Lando Ferretti, *L'Historia della città d'Ancona . . . nella quale non pur si veggono l'origine, i fatti et le fortune . . .* , MS. Vat. Chig. lat. H. III., 70, sec. XVI, fols. 290v–291r (autograph); Guil. Saracini, *Notizie historiche della città d'Ancona* (Rome, 1675), pp. 265–266.

32. Babinger, *Mehmed II. der Erober*, p. 174, and Natalucci, *Ancona*, 1:469, have recently repeated the same thing that was previously stated by G. Gariboldi, *Angelo Boldoni, Racconto storico offerto al sign. dott. A. Ambrosi* (Ancona, 1879), pp. 11–15, a pamphlet of little value.

33. On the relations between Ciriaco d'Ancona, Murâd II, and then Mehmed II, cf. F. Pall, "Ciriaco d'Ancona e la crociata contro i Turchi," *Bulletin historique de l'Académie Roumaine* 20 (1937): 16 ff.; E. Jacobs, "Cyriacus von Ancona und Mehemmed II," *BZ* 30 (1929–1930): 197–202; E. W. Bodnar, *Cyriacus of Ancona and Athens* (Brussels and Berchem, 1960), (= *Latomus*, 36), pp. 54, 64–68; F. Babinger, "Notes on Cyriac of Ancona and Some of His Friends," *Journal of the Warburg and Courtauld Institutes* 25 (196?): 321–323; idem, *Mehmed II. der Erober*, pp. 175–178; idem, "Vom Amurath zu Amurath," *Aufsätze und Abhandlungen* 1:131–133; idem, "Maometto il Conquistatore e gli umanisti d' Italia," in *Venezia e l'Oriente fra tardo Medioevo e Rinascimento*, ed. A. Pertusi (Florence, 1966), pp. 441–445; R. Weiss, "Ciriaco d'Ancona in Oriente," in Pertusi, *Venezia e l'Oriente*, p. 328; Babinger, *Maometto*, pp. 30–33, 47–48, 81, 89, 118, 124, 541–543; P. Mastrodimitri, *Kyriakos ho ex Ankonos eis Euboian* (Athens, 1966); C. G. Patrinelis, "Kyriakos ho Ankonites: He dethen hyperesia tou eis ten aulen tou soultanou Moameth tou Porthetou kai ho chronos tou thanatou tou," *EEBS* 16 (1968): 152–162, the last of whom advises us not to confuse Ciriaco d'Ancona with Demetrio Apocauco Kiritzis, also a secretary at the court of Mehmed II between 1446 and 1453/1454; A. Pertusi, "Le epistole storiche di Lauro Quirini sulla caduta di Costantinopoli e la potenza dei Turchi," in K. Krautter, P. O. Kristeller, A. Pertusi, G. Ravegnani, H. Roob, C. Seno, *Lauro Quirini umanista* (Florence, 1977), p. 196.

34. Cf. sup., n. 32.

35. Cf. O. von Heinemann, *Kataloge der Herzog-August-Bibliothek Wolfenbüttel*, 2 Abt. [vol. 6], *Die Augusteischen Handschriften*, 3d ed. (Wolfenbüttel, 1898; anastatic ed., Frankfurt am Main, 1966), pp. 229–233.

36. Cf. A. Pertusi, "La situazione dell' Europa orientale dopo la caduta di Smederevo (1439) in una lettera inedita di fra Bartolomeo di Giano," in *Mélanges Ivan Dujčev* (Paris, 1979), pp. 157–192.

37. The same error, incurred by Heinemann, is repeated in W. Röll, "Ein zweiter Brief Isidors von Kiew über die Eroberung Konstantinopels," *BZ* 69 (1976):13, n. 5, and by me, *La caduta*, 2:499, nos. 24-26, before I had seen the codex.

38. Cf. Pertusi, *La caduta*, 2:18-23.

39. Ibid., 1:347-348, n. 29.

40. Ibid., 1:39-51.

41. Natalucci, *Ancona*, 1:507.

42. Pertusi, *La caduta*, 1:lxxiii.

43. Ibid., 1:lxxvi.

44. Ibid., 1:lxxii.

45. Ibid., 1:lxxi-lxxii.

46. Ibid., 1:lxxiv-lxxv.

47. Ibid., 2:458, n. 13.

48. On the end of Emperor Constantine XII, cf. Pertusi, *La caduta*, 1: lxxxv; 364-365, n. 159; 463-465, n. 59. On the misfortunes of Cardinal Isidore of Kiev, cf. ibid., 1:52-53, and 2:92-95.

49. Pertusi, *La caduta*, 1:362-363, n. 141.

50. Ibid., 1:lxxxv.

51. Ibid., 1:106-109.

Chapter 12

The Country and Suburban Palaces of the Emperors

Steven Runciman, *British Academy*

It was never wise for the ruler of the Eastern Roman Empire to absent himself for long from the neighborhood of Constantinople. Theodosius the Great was the last emperor to travel widely round his vast dominions until the Palaeologans, who moved about through their shrinking lands and even visited the West in search of aid. From the beginning of the fifth century until 1204, the only ruler to make a long peaceful tour in the empire was Irene the Athenian, who, when regent, progressed in state along the Bulgarian frontier as far as western Macedonia.[1] It was safe for a warrior-emperor to leave the capital on a campaign, if he had the imperial army with him. No one then was likely to plan a palace revolution, unless the emperor, as in the case of Romanus IV Diogenes, was routed in battle and taken prisoner by the enemy.

This does not however mean that the imperial family spent all its days within the Great Palace. The emperor had to be there for much of his time. It was the seat of the administration, and most of the ceremonies that showed the holiness of the imperial office started out from there. But the Byzantine civil service was well trained and capable. It was well able to carry on the daily administration while an emperor was away at the wars. Indeed, the empire was never more efficiently run than under the two greatest warrior-emperors, Constantine V and Basil II. There was often a co-emperor who was glad to take over ceremonial duties, as did Constantine VIII when his brother Basil II was campaigning. Moreover, although if we study the works of Constantine Porphyrogenitus we might suppose that imperial life was one unending ceremony, his program was probably ideal rather than actual; and even so it only occupied some seventy days in the year. In fact, the emperors must have enjoyed many moments of relaxation, and the proof of it lies in the number of suburban and country palaces that they maintained and enjoyed. The imperial family liked to spend the summer months outside of the city, and there would be hunting expeditions in the winter. Palaces and villas were built to satisfy these needs.

The oldest suburban palace seems, however, to have been built for ceremonial rather than recreational purposes. At Hebdomon, 7 miles west of the city on the shore of the Marmora, was the camp where the imperial army assembled for a campaign in Europe. A palace was built there for the convenience of the emperor. It was called the Magnaura. We first hear of it in the reign of Valens, but it had probably been erected previously, perhaps by Constantius. Theodosius I added a church, dedicated to Saint John the Baptist, to which the court would go in pilgrimage. The emperors Marcian, Valens, Arcadius, Theodosius II, and Leo I were all proclaimed by the army at Hebdomon.[2] Justinian I built a new palace there, called the Jucundiana, on a peninsula, with a fine view along the coast to east and to west. He used it for pleasure rather than for ceremony. Tiberius retired to it when he fell ill in the summer of 582 and had his successor, Maurice, proclaimed there. It is doubtful if any later emperor lived in the Jucundiana, but the palace survived to be destroyed by the Bulgarian Khan Krum, in 813. Hebdomon continued to be of ceremonial importance, as the starting point for a triumphal procession into the city of a commander who had been victorious on a campaign in Europe. There must therefore always have been some sort of ceremonial pavilion there.[3] Justinian also built a palace at Pege, close to the shrine of Our Lady of the Source, for the use of the imperial family when it visited the church. This was probably a pavilion rather than a residence.[4]

Most emperors had a favorite resort. Arcadius, who otherwise never left the city, liked to go in the summer, so the Latin poet Claudian tells us, to Ankyra. But it is improbable that he should have chosen to face the torrid heat of the Anatolian tableland. Claudian must have mistaken Ankyra for Ankyro (or Ankyrona), an imperial villa on the sea near Nicomedia, the villa in which Constantine the Great had died.[5] Theodosius II remained closer to the capital. He had a summer villa at Chalcedon, the modern Kadiköy; and in his younger days he would visit his sisters at the Palace of Rufinus, which had been confiscated from the minister whom their father Arcadius had disgraced and executed.[6] It was situated on the Asiatic coast of the Marmora, probably at the modern Caddebostan, some 5 miles southeast of Kadiköy. This palace was later given to Belisarius and his wife Antonina.[7]

Leo I, in 469, after a great fire in the city had done some damage to the Great Palace, built himself a palace at Saint Mamas, the present Beşiktaş, on the Bosporus, and spent six months there. It had its own harbor, its own hippodrome, and a fine portico.[8]

Justinian liked to visit his palace at Hebdomon; but Theodora insisted on spending the summer months at Hieria on a peninsula, now called Fenerbahçe, jutting out into the Marmora, a little beyond Kadiköy. Justinian built her a large palace there, with baths and a small harbor, adding a public park and a church dedicated to Our Lady. The courtiers, so Procopius tells us, hated to have to go there, as the journey was always made by sea, and they were frightened of seasickness and of the great whale that for about fifty years used to attack small boats as they sailed along the coast. Indeed, it must have been irritating for aspiring politicians, who knew that Theodora's goodwill was just as important as Justinian's, to have to hurry to and fro between Hieria and Constantinople or even Hebdomon.[9] Justin II built a palace on the Asiatic side of the Bosporus, facing Constantinople. He called it the Sophianae, after his wife. It was begun in 568, and a second building connected with it was built the following year.[10] He also built a palace on Prinkipo, the largest of the Prince's Islands, but we hear no more of it. When Alexius I's wife Irene Ducaena stayed on the island in 1115, she seems to have been lodged in its celebrated convent, founded by Irene the Athenian.[11] Tiberius built a small palace at Bryas, on the Marmora coast about 20 miles beyond Kadiköy, but his favorite palace was built at Damatrys, some 12 miles inland from Bryas, in good hunting country. Both buildings were, it seems, completed by Maurice.[12]

The emperors thus had many country homes from which to choose. It is not surprising that, until the reign of Theophilus, no more, as far as we know, were built, except for a palace built at Chalcedon by Constantine III in about 680, to which he retired in the hope that the fresher air would restore his failing health.[13] In the seventh and eighth centuries, the most popular country palaces were Hieria and Saint Mamas. Heraclius I preferred Hieria; he spent the first summer of his reign there. It was there that he met the senate and the high officials of the empire when he returned in triumph from the Persian war, bringing with him the Holy Cross.[14] Indeed, Hieria became the Asiatic equivalent of Hebdomon for such occasions. In 838 Theophilus similarly received the senate there at the start of a triumphal procession

celebrating a moderately successful campaign in the East. Basil I
copied his example in 875.[15] Heraclius spent the last years of his
life at Hieria, when a sort of hydrophobia made him refuse to
cross any piece of water.[16] The Isaurians made use of it. Constantine V summoned his Iconoclastic Council to meet there in
753.[17] In 768, Leo IV's bride, Irene, was lodged there for some
months after her arrival from Athens, while she learned the eti-
quette of the imperial court, and as empress she often revisited
the palace.[18] Basil I, who paid it many visits, repaired the structure and added an oratory in honor of Saint Elias. Constantine
Porphyrogenitus admired the freshness of its air; and in his time
the yearly procession in honor of the vintage set out from Hieria.[19]
Nicephorus Phocas paused there in 963 while preparing for his
coronation as emperor and his marriage to the empress-mother
Theophano.[20] Romanus IV joined the imperial army there on his
way to the disaster at Manzikert. The Comnenian emperors,
however, let it fall into ruins.

We hear nothing of the palace of Saint Mamas from Leo I's
time until we come to the regency of Irene. She and her son
Constantine VI went to live there in February 782, when a severe earthquake had damaged the Great Palace. Constantine liked
the palace. He was there when he ordered the blinding of his
uncles in 785; and in 795 he celebrated there, with forty days of
festivities, his marriage to his mistress Theodote.[21] The buildings
were destroyed by Khan Krum in 813 but were rebuilt soon afterward, probably by Theophilus. It was the favorite residence of
Michael III, who particularly liked to use the private hippodrome
for chariot racing. It was at a dinner party there that he was murdered by Basil the Macedonian.[22] After his death, the palace
seems to have been left empty and gradually fell into ruins. No
doubt Basil's descendents did not like to be reminded of the circumstances in which he obtained the throne.[23]

The inland palace at Damatrys enjoyed a certain popularity.
It was at Damatrys that Justinian II was captured by rebel troops
and put to death in September 711. But it was used as a hunting
box rather than a summer resort. Leo VI paid it at least one visit.
Its chief patron was Manuel I Comnenus, who liked to go there in
the winter months. It was there that he slew a beast that seemed
to be half a lion and half a leopard.[24] Michael VIII Palaeologus
sometimes hunted there. In June 1296, when Constantinople and
the suburbs were devastated by a series of earthquakes, Andronicus II and the court retired there for several weeks, living not in

the palace but in tents. A few years later, the territory was occupied by the Ottoman Turks.[25]

The Sophianae Palace was in use till the later eighth century. Heraclius's eldest son, Constantine III, was born there in May 612. Constantine V stayed there for a time in 773 and celebrated a victory over the Arabs in the course of his visit. It is not mentioned again.[26]

Of the later country palaces, the most splendid was that built by Theophilus at Bryas, where Tiberius had had a house long ago. The new palace was Arab in style, following plans brought to the emperor by John the Syncellus, who had been his ambassador in Bagdad. The actual architect was called Patricius. Much of the material came from a ruined temple at Satyron, a few miles away. The only parts of the complex of buildings that were not in the Arab style were an oratory dedicated to the Mother of God and a large church dedicated to Saint Michael. The palace was finished in 832, and thenceforward Theophilus spent most of the summer there. None of his successors, however, lived there. Possibly it was thought to be a little too far from the capital. Possibly it was damaged by earthquake or by fire and would have been expensive to repair.[27]

More continuously popular was a palace built as a hunting lodge at Philopation, not far from the land walls of Constantinople. This too was probably built by Theophilus. It is first mentioned in Michael III's reign; and Theophilus's widow, the prudent regent Theodora, was too economically minded to indulge in building programs. Its exact location is uncertain. We are told that it was visible from the towers of the Blachernae Palace, at the north end of the land walls. It must have been on fairly level ground, as there was a racecourse attached to it. It was in wild country where game of all sorts abounded, and streams and lakes provided good fishing.[28] In Michael III's time, the future emperor Basil I slew an enormous wolf nearby. A little later, a certain Jacovitzes, who had helped Basil to murder Michael, was killed in a hunting accident there.[29] Constantine IX Monomachus, who liked to go there for the Ascension Day festival, called in gypsies to clear the area of savage beasts.[30] Alexius I liked to retire there for the hunting.[31] His son, John II, was living there soon after his succession, when his sister Anna attempted a coup against him.[32] In the course of the Second Crusade, Manuel I housed Conrad of Germany in Philopation. The German troops did endless damage to the grounds, and Conrad made off with any article of furniture that took his fancy: so we are told by Eudes of Deuil. But the palace was in good enough condition to house Eudes' master, Louis VII of France, quite comfortably a few months later.[33] It was the favorite residence of Andronicus I, who, like Constantine IX, used to celebrate the Ascension Day service in the palace chapel. It was also used by Alexius III Angelus.[34] After 1204 it seems to have been abandoned.

Basil I built a palace at Pegae, (not to be confused with Pege) on the further side of the Golden Horn, at the modern Kasimpaşa. It had four chapels and two oratories attached to it. He liked to spend the summer there, as did his son Leo VI.[35] The palace was burned by Symeon of Bulgaria in 921 but was later rebuilt, as Nicephorus Phocas spent three weeks there in the summer of 968.[36] Leo VI also had a villa at Damianou on the Bosporus, the modern Ortaköy, to which he would retire with his mistress, Zoe, daughter of Zautzes. Her brother planned to murder him there; but Zoe heard noises in the night, and she and the emperor escaped through the darkness to Pegae.[37]

Romanus Diogenes built a group of houses as a summer resort at a spot called Aretae, on a bleak and windy but well-watered slope some 2 miles inland from Hebdomon. It is doubtful if the court ever visited it after his time, but the Comneni used it as their base when they attacked the city walls in 1081.[38]

Manuel I's favorite palace was the Scoutarion, at Üsküdar. He probably built it himself, and it was there that he spent the last 2 months of his life. It was occupied by the Crusaders in 1203 and was thereafter abandoned.[39] Andronicus I in his short reign seems to have built two suburban palaces, one, at the source of the little river Hydralis in the forest of Belgrade, intended as a summer resort, and one at Meloudion, on the Asian side of the Bosporus, probably at the modern Beylerbey, which he liked because of the good hunting in the wooded hills behind the palace.[40]

The Palaeologan emperors do not seem to have built any new suburban palaces. We hear of them staying at Pege. John V was there in 1375 when his son Andronicus brought off a successful coup against him. The palace must have undergone many repairs and alterations since it had been built by Justinian.[41]

Other suburban palaces are mentioned by the chroniclers, but without any indication of who built them or who resided in them. There was an early palace on the Asian shore of the Bosporus that Theodora, Justinian's wife, converted into the Convent of Metanoia, or Penitence, for prostitutes who had been unwillingly rescued from their old profession.[42] There was a palace of Saint Theodora at the head of the Golden Horn, which was raided by the Bulgarians in 922,[43] and a palace of Argyrolimne, the Silver Lake, apparently on the Golden Horn not far from the city walls, which was sacked by the soldiers of the First Crusade.[44] There was also a palace at Therapia, on the Bosporus, where Irene for a time kept her brothers-in-law, the younger sons of Constantine V, under house arrest.[45]

Some emperors and empresses varied their routine by going to take the waters at the hot springs in Bithynia. Constantine the Great visited the baths at Pythia, the modern Yalova. Theodora found them especially beneficial. She paid her first visit there in 529, with an escort of four thousand attendants. Justinian found it necessary to build her a palace there, and he made many improvements to the baths themselves. Further baths were added by Justin II and Sophia, who were equally fond of the spa.[46] The baths at Pythia were still in operation at the end of the twelfth century, when Alexius III Angelus paid them a visit.[47] Irene preferred to take the waters at Brusa, to which she paid several visits. In 796 she was there with her son, Constantine VI, and most of her ministers. It is doubtful whether she had a residence there. More probably, buildings were requisitioned to house her and the court.[48] Constantine VII visited the baths at Brusa when on his pilgrimage to the monasteries of Bithynian Olympus.[49]

The existence of so many palaces outside the walls of the city shows that the emperors by no means spent all their days occupied by administrative and ritual duties within the Great Palace. It is true that their country houses were all within a reasonable distance of the capital, so that it was not too difficult for ministers to wait on them and keep them informed of the affairs of state. Even when they were in the city, they did not always reside in the Great Palace. Blachernae was often used as a residence long before it became the official palace under the Comnenian emperors. Irene, whose constitutional position was an empress-regnant, preferred to live in her House of Eleutherios, some 2 miles from the palace.[50] The lives of the emperors were much more informal than accounts of the imperial ritual would suggest. The emperors were very lightly guarded. Would-be assassins had easy access to their private rooms, even into the empress's quarters. Byzantium liked its emperors and empresses to be persons of dignified but affable demeanor and outwardly respectable behavior; those that fell short of the desired standard did so at their peril. But they had many moments when formality could be forgotten, moments of relaxation and pleasure in the parks and gardens that surrounded the incomparable city of Constantinople.

Notes

In writing this essay I have been enormously indebted to R. Janin, *Constantinople Byzantine* (Paris, 1950), for his complete list of the suburban palaces, pp. 137–153, and his identification of their sites, which I accept, except where I have stated otherwise.

1. For Irene's journey, see Theophanes, *Chronographia*, ed. C. de Boor (Leipzig, 1883), 1:457. Constantine VII shortly before his death made a pilgrimage as far as the monasteries on Bithynian Olympus: *Theophanes Continuatus* (Bonn, 1938), pp. 464–465.

2. For the site and early history of Hebdomon, see Janin, *Constantinople*, pp. 137–138.

3. Procopius, *De aedificiis*, ed. H. B. Dewing, Loeb Classical Library (London and Cambridge, Mass., 1960), p. 92; Theophanes, *Chronographia*, 1:231; *Chronicon Paschale* (Bonn, 1832), 1:571. Gregory the Great *Epistulae* 11. 11, calls the palace "Secundianus." For Tiberius at Hebdomon, see Theophylact Simocatta, ed. C. de Boor (Leipzig, 1887), p. 218. For its destruction by Krum, Symeon Magister, Bonn ed., p. 614. Hebdomon is frequently mentioned in Constantine VII's *De cerimoniis*, when describing Imperial triumphs.

4. Procopius, *De aedificiis*, p. 40. According to *De cerimoniis* (Bonn, 1829), 1:113, the court went to Pege for the Ascension Day services.

5. Claudian, *In Eutropium* 2, line 98. Jerome S. *Eusebii Hieronymi chronicon, PL* 27. 679–680, says that Constantine died *in Ancyrone publica villa juxta Nicomediam*. Claudian, who though born in Alexandria, lived all his adult life in Italy, could easily have mistaken Ankyro for the celebrated city Ankyra.

6. Theophanes, *Chronographia*, 1:98; Socrates *Historia ecclesiastica, PGL* 67. 1560; Theodoret Cyrensis *Epistulae, PGL* 83. 1464.

7. Procopius, *De bello Persico* (Bonn, 1833), 1:133–134.

8. *Chronicon Paschale*, 1:598.

9. Procopius, *De aedificiis*, pp. 92–93, and *Anecdota (historia arcana)*, ed. H. B. Dewing, Loeb Classical Library (London and Cambridge, Mass., 1935), p. 186.

10. Theophanes, *Chronographia*, 1:243; Marianus Scholasticus, *Palatine Anthology*, 9:657.

11. Theophanes, *Chronographia*, 1:243. For Irene Ducaena's visit, cf. Anna Comnena, *Aléxiade*, ed. B. Leib (Paris, 1945), 3:190. For the convent on Prinkipo founded by Irene the Athenian, see Theophanes, *Chronographia*, 1:478.

12. T. Preger, *Scriptores Originum Constantinopolitarum* (Leipzig, 1901–1907), 3:268–269.

13. Nicephorus Patriarcha, *Epitome Historiarum*, ed. C. de Boor, p. 28.

14. *Chronicon Paschale*, p. 702; Theophanes, *Chronographia*, 1:328; Nicephorus Patriarcha, *Epitome*, p. 25.

15. *De cerimoniis, Appendix ad I* (Bonn, 1830), p. 504; *Theophanes Continuatus*, p. 307.

16. Nicephorus Patriarcha, *Epitome*, p. 25.

17. Theophanes, *Chronographia*, 1:247.

18. Ibid., 1:444, 474.

19. *Theophanes Continuatus*, pp. 337, 451.

20. Leo Diaconus (Bonn, 1828), p. 46; Atteliates (Bonn, 1853), pp. 142-143.

21. Theophanes, *Chronographia*, 1:464, 470. Janin, *Constantinople*, p. 140, refers in error to Constantine's marriage to Maria, in 788.

22. Theophanes, *Chronographia*, 1:503; *Theophanes Continuatus*, p. 254.

23. The palace was still standing in the tenth century: Preger, *Scriptores*, 3:266.

24. Nicephorus Patriarcha, *Epitome*, p. 47; *Theophanes Continuatus*, p. 369; I. Cinnamus, *Epitome rerum ab Ioanne et Alexio Comnenis gestarum*, ed. A. Meineke (Bonn, 1836), p. 266.

25. Pachymer, vol. 1 (Bonn, 1835), pp. 945-954; vol. 2 (Bonn, 1835), p. 233.

26. *Chronicon Paschale*, 1:702; Theophanes, *Chronographia*, 1:451.

27. *Theophanes Continuatus*, pp. 98-99; Georgius Monachus, *Chronicon* (Bonn, 1838), additions by Symeon, p. 798.

28. After discussing the opinions of other scholars, Janin, *Constantinople*, pp. 143-144, places the palace opposite to the Gate of Saint Romanos. The site seems now a little bleak for so luxuriant a park, but the area was probably well-wooded in Byzantine times, and the river Lycus could have provided water for the lakes and canals described by Eudes of Deuil, *De Ludovici VII itinere*, ed. H. Waquet (Paris, 1949), p. 39. Eudes does not name the palace, which is identified by Cinnamus, *Epitome*, pp. 74, 83. Nicetas Choniates (Bonn, 1835), p. 529, says that the palace could be seen from Blachernae. There was also a Philopation palace within the city: see Janin, *Constantinople*, p. 132.

29. *Theophanes Continuatus*, p. 231; Georgius Monachus, *Chronicon*, p. 839.

30. *Vita S. Georgii Hagioritae*, in *Analecta Bollandiana* 36 (1917): 102-103, 140.

31. Zonaras (Bonn, 1897), 3:753.

32. Nicetas Choniates, p. 15.

33. Eudes of Deuil, *De Ludovici VII*, p. 39; Cinnamus, *Epitome*, pp. 74, 83.

34. Nicetas Choniates, pp. 380, 492, 529.

35. *Theophanes Continuatus*, p. 337.

36. Ibid., pp. 401-402.

37. Cedrenus, 2:257.

38. Anna Comnena, *Aléxiade*, 1:90.

39. Nicetas Choniates, p. 260; Geoffroi de Villehardouin, *La Conquête de Constantinople*, ed. N. de Wailly (Paris, 1872), p. 76.

40. Nicetas Choniates, pp. 428, 448.

41. Sphrantzes, *Cronica majora*, ed. V. Grecu (Bucharest, 1966), p. 196.

42. Procopius, *De aedificiis*, pp. 74–75.

43. *Theophanes Continuatus*, p. 402.

44. Anna Comnena, *Aléxiade*, 2:221.

45. Theophanes, *Chronographia*, 1:473.

46. John Malalas (Bonn, 1831), p. 441; Procopius, *De aedificiis*, pp. 328–330. For an account of Justin II's buildings there, see E. Mamboury, *Istanbul touristique* (Istanbul, 1951), pp. 600–601.

47. Nicetas Choniates, p. 601.

48. Theophanes, *Chronographia*, 1:471.

49. *Theophanes Continuatus*, p. 465.

50. Theophanes, *Chronographia*, 1:467, 472, 476, 478.

Chapter 13

The Naval Engagement at Phoenix

Andreas N. Stratos, *Athens*

•

One of the most perplexing episodes in the history of seventh-century Byzantium is the celebrated naval engagement that took place at Phoenix between the imperial and Arab fleets. Not only are the details of the battle obscure, but the major facts such as the date, the composition of the respective armadas, the reasons leading to the clash, and the results of the battle are difficult to unravel. Regarding the details of the latter, all chroniclers, irrespective of ethnic origin, are in complete agreement, as are almost all contemporary historians. But the results of the battle appear to conflict with these conclusions. Many contemporary historians have described the naval engagement, but most have confined themselves to generalizations. Famous historians have based their narrative of the events exlusively on the chroniclers, without in any way attempting to draw rational deductions.

To find the answers to the various questions that arise, the battle should be examined within the framework of conditions existing at the time of the engagement. The reliability of the different chroniclers must be analyzed; then the causes leading to the clash must be studied in connection with the subsequent sequence of events. Moreover, the results of the battle must then be determined with logical conclusions.

* * *

Greek, Arab, Syrian, and Armenian chroniclers have all dealt with the naval battle, but none, with the exception of Sébèos, was contemporary with the event. Of the Byzantine chroniclers, nearest to the date of the battle were Theophanes and George the Monk, known as Harmatolus.[1] The former wrote between A.D. 810 and 815; the latter, about the year 850. Consequently, both historians wrote in their distant monastic retreats about events that had occurred some 150 to 200 years before their time. It is cer-

tain that they used various sources or traditions contemporary
with the events, but unfortunately without any critical investigation and often with a lack of continuity and reason as regards
the sequence of events. Both were distinguished for their hostility
toward the emperor Constantine III (Constans II).[2] This hatred
was a result of the emperor's support of the Monothelite dogma
of his grandfather Heraclius, although in actual fact Constantine
was not one to get involved in religious controversy. It is unfor-
tunate that the patriarch Nicephorus, the most serious and reliable
of chroniclers of that period, has entirely omitted events covering the reign of Constantine III. Other chroniclers such as Leo
Grammaticus, Zonaras, and Cedrenus flourished at a much later
date and used as their sources, for the most part, Theophanes and
George Monachus.

Not a single Arab chronicler is contemporary with the battle of
Phoenix, nor did any write reasonably near the time of the engagement. All Arabs wrote of the events centuries afterward and
relied exclusively upon the oral traditions, inasmuch as contemporary written accounts did not exist. Precisely because of this
fact, they used sources that were passed on orally from generation
to generation, with the result that there was a lack of continuity
in the sequence of events and an inevitable accretion of much
phantasy.

Of the Armenian chroniclers, Bishop Sébèos's narrative is contemporary with the events; yet here again the text does not
appear to have survived intact in its original form, but as the
chronicle of a certain Xoszov or Xoszovik who used the Armenian
bishop's history as a source.[3] This source, which is unusually
reliable for events that took place in Armenia, tends to become
highly imaginative and inconsistent in the chronology. Other historians or chroniclers who are not contemporary with the events
rely mostly on Sébèos, and indeed several actually copy him verbatim. All without exception are highly fanciful and replete with
irrational statements.

The same holds true in the case of the Syrian chronicles. Some
were composed at the time of the events, especially certain monastic chronicles, which, however, were usually closely interrelated.
Several later chronicles supply significant information, but again
they are highly imaginative and fanciful and tend to the super-
natural; many also display animosity for the Greeks, and especially
for the Greek Church.

Such are the sources from which we must draw to relate and
portray the celebrated naval battle of Phoenix.

* * *

To obtain some kind of clear picture of the events, the framework within which these events occurred must be described. At that particular point in history, the Byzantines had somehow managed to arrest the irresistible advance of the Arabs. It is true that after the expiration of the truce in the late spring or early summer of 653, the Arabs resumed their incursions, soon after subduing the formerly Persian Armenia with the acquiescence of a large part of the Armenian nation. The Arabs habitually undertook two invasions (razzias) into imperial territory yearly, but in no instance did they succeed in permanently occupying these territories. The greatest threat to the Byzantine Empire, however, was the establishment and strengthening of an Arab naval force that was destined to become an ever-growing menace to the Greeks, in view of the extensive coastlines of the Empire and the innumerable islands in its domain.

Soon after assuming power in Syria and Palestine, Muawiyah realized that without a strong fleet he could never seriously challenge the power of Byzantium. He therefore sought the blessing of the caliph Umar for the founding of a fleet, but the latter, in view of his intense dislike of the sea, refused the request in no uncertain terms.[4] But following Umar's decease, Muawiyah again asked for the building of a fleet, but this time from the new caliph, Uthman, who finally yielded to his pleas.[5] His initial expedition was against Cyprus, which he plundered in 649 but soon abandoned upon learning of the impending arrival of the imperial fleet. In 651 a truce[6] of two or three years' duration was drawn up, but this expired in 653. The Byzantines agreed to pay a yearly tribute (*pacta*) to the Arabs, the amount of which is unknown.

Taking advantage of the truce and the *pacta* that he collected, Muawiyah increased the number of ships in his fleet. It is certainly true that it was not an easy task to build a fleet powerful enough to seriously challenge Byzantine control of the Mediterranean. The shipbuilding yards in Arab territories were few in number. Egypt possessed only two naval arsenals,[7] one each at Alexandria and Klysma (near the present-day Suez). In Syria, naval yards existed at Beirut, Tripoli, and possibly Palestinian Caesareia.[8] Muawiyah hastened to multiply the number of naval yards in Syria and reached an agreement with the Egyptian military governor Abd Allah ibn Sad ben Abi Sath to increase the

number of naval yards in Egypt. The major problems confronting
the Arabs were the supply of suitable timber and the manning of
the ships.

The most important raw material for shipbuilding at the time
was timber. For centuries the forests in the areas under Arab control—where these existed—were cut down to supply the yards of
their regions with timber. Forests existed in the hinterland as well,
but the transportation of lumber from distant forests was problematical if not impossible. Rich woodlands also existed in the
islands of the Aegean, in Cyprus, and especially along the coast of
Asia Minor. As regards shipbuilders and naval architects, there
was a great shortage, and on this account Muawiyah was forced
to bring carpenters and shipwrights from the Persian Gulf[9] to help
construct the first vessels. In time he drafted numerous shipwrights from other regions that had fallen within the power of
the Arabs.

The problem of crews was not difficult to solve. It is true that
the Arabs were not sailors, with the exception of a certain number
from the coastlands of the Arabian peninsula. Even these had little
maritime experience, and their naval tradition was very limited.[10]
On the other hand, the Syrians, the Egyptians, and particularly the
inhabitants of ancient Phoenicia were exceptionally fine sailors
with a centuries-old naval tradition. This fact greatly facilitated
the task of the Arabs, for they could draw upon these peoples to
man their ships with numerous and experienced crews who were
skilled seamen and were familiar with the seas in which they oper-
ated. The papyruses of Egypt inform us that the crews were distinguished between warriors and ordinary seamen. The former,
who comprised the military faction, were all ethnic Arabs or
Egyptian converts to Islam. The sailors, on the other hand, were
for the most part Christian and often had no relationship with
the Moslem soldiery.[11] An almost identical system existed also in
Syria, although the Moslems there were far more numerous on
account of the many Arab tribes that readily converted to Islam
to avoid the payment of taxes and because numerous Arab migrants had flocked hither from the Arabian peninsula. Officers
and sailors, who were Christian for the most part, were the first
mentors of the Arabs in maritime matters.[12]

* * *

Yet the launching of a powerful fleet was not the only problem

Muawiyah overcame to obtain naval supremacy. The crews had to be properly trained and drilled, and the naval bases of the Byzantines that were near the coasts of Syria and from which the movements of the Moslem fleet could be detected had to be neutralized. As soon as the preparations were completed or the truce was denounced and he had acquired a respectable number of warships, Muawiyah began to undertake raids against the islands of the Aegean to train his crews further and to destroy any Greek naval bases that existed there.

At the close of 653 or in early 654 (in the fifty-third year of the Hegira), a powerful armada led by Abu'l Awar, one of the more distinguished military leaders of Muawiyah who had taken part in the battle of Yarmuk in 636, again plundered Cyprus and installed in the island a garrison as well as a naval arsenal.[13] Soon thereafter Muawiyah himself led a strong force against Rhodes, which he plundered.[14] It is reputed that in the same year Abu'l Awar raided the island of Cos and the northeastern coast of Crete.[15]

The object of all these raids was not only the collection of booty but also the acquisition of timber supplies for their shipyards, especially the cypress wood of which the Moslems had much need for the masts of their vessels.[16] For this reason, they established many naval yards near forests that they could surreptitiously use. In this manner, they would repair their ships at the same site from which they obtained the raw material for their yards.

* * *

The straits of the Byzantines compounded with the successes of Muawiyah, the collapse of Persia, and the murder of the last Sassanid king, Yazdagerd III, whetted Muawiyah's appetite for even more success. Precisely when he first conceived the idea of attacking and capturing Constantinople is unknown. This information is given only by the Byzantine and Syrian chroniclers. The Armenians confuse it with the attack of 675 in the reign of Constantine IV. On the other hand, the Arab chroniclers make no mention of Muawiyah's preparations for an assault against Constantinople. Precisely because of this conflict in the sources, it becomes impossible to verify whether Muawiyah in fact did plan an attack against the imperial capital. At all events, after his initial naval successes, preparations for the further strengthening of the fleet were accelerated. According to Armenian and several Byzantine chroniclers, a major effort was made to improve the organization of the army that would take part in this grand assault, in view of the fact that Muawiyah intended, as the chroniclers record, to approach Constantinople by the overland route also.

The Greeks were greatly alarmed by the continual naval raids of the Moslems, and it is quite probable that they had received intelligence of the major naval and military preparations being undertaken by them. As a result, so it is reputed, they equipped a strong fleet. It is true that the Byzantines had not yet established their "thematic fleet"; yet the imperial one had always been powerful. Whenever more vessels were required, either they simply, when time permitted, launched more boats in the various shipyards at their disposal or they armed merchant ships, which they then used for their naval operations. Both methods were used in the age of Justinian I as well as in the age of Heraclius I.[17] The emperor Constantine III himself commanded the fleet, and it is reputed that he was accompanied by his younger brother Theodosius.[18]

A remarkable incident then took place, which is recorded by all the Greek and Syrian sources. Theophanes reports that the greatest activity in the preparation of the Arab fleet took place at Tripoli in Phoenicia. Why Tripoli should be the great center, in view of the fact that vessels were being launched at all seaports where shipyards existed, I cannot understand. It is possible that the concentration of the flotilla took place here.

In this city there were two Christian brothers, "the sons of Vucinator," as all the sources record. It appears that they were in the service of the Arabs,[19] but being "smitten by a Godly zeal," they, in concert with others, rushed to the prison of the city where many "Roman" prisoners were confined, broke open the doors, and freed the captives. They all thereupon armed themselves and attacked the governor's residence, where they slew the *"ameer"* (presumably the emir or governor of the city) and those "with him" (probably the garrison). Afterward they set fire to "all the stores" (?). Elie Bar Sinaya writes the "ships," whereas Anastasius Bibliothecarius, who translated Theophanes into Latin, records "the preparations." They succeeded in escaping to Romania by ship, according to Agapius, or in a small boat, according to Michael the Syrian.[20]

The narrative leaves many questions unanswered. Inasmuch as Tripoli was the harbor in which the Arab fleet was assembled, there would be numerous soldiers and seamen present in addition to the garrison. The liberated prisoners would have to be a goodly number to be able to eliminate the guards of the governor's residence and to neutralize any countermeasures on the part of the army and the populace of Tripoli. Another question that arises is the number of vessels that were destroyed and the extent of the damage done to the Arab fleet. There is also the question of how many of those who took part in the break succeeded finally in escaping. We do know, at all events, that one of the sons of Vucinator did make good his escape, for he took part in the subsequent naval engagement. Regarding the remaining escapees, there is no mention whatsoever in the sources. Finally, there is the matter of the dating of the incident, which is most perplexing. The chroniclers give different dates varying from 653 to 656. It is noteworthy that the Armenian and Moslem chroniclers give no hint whatsoever of the affair. Taking into consideration all the sources and in view of the fact that, soon after the escape, there took place the naval battle of Phoenix in which at least one of the sons of Vucinator participated, I would conclude that the escape occurred in 655 and that such a date is the most probable if we are to accept the incident as historical fact.[21]

Such are the framework and the conditions within which the naval engagement of Phoenix must be set.

* * *

The description of the naval battle between the imperial and Arab armadas as recorded by the chroniclers is a mixture of fact and fancy, replete with Byzantine prophetic utterances, on account of (1) the deep hatred of the Greeks for Constantine III; (2) the exaggerations of the Moslems, who relate the sequence of events in an entirely different order; and (3) the bizarre exaggerations, surpassing all reason, of the Armenian chroniclers. Thus, a welter of questions is left unanswered. Under the circumstances, an attempt must be made to unravel the mystery and to find some sensible explanation for the chain of events. These explanations must somehow agree with the events as they unfolded during and after the naval engagement. It is odd indeed that, although all chroniclers without exception agree regarding the outcome of the battle, the repercussions are in fact quite the opposite of their conclusions. Although there is some doubt concerning the actual date of the battle, it appears that most historians agree that the probable year in which it took place was 655.[22]

Another difficulty concerns the size of the respective forces that took part in the clash.[23] I would dismiss without further ado the fanciful and absurd figure of Sébèos, which is repeated by Acoghig de Daron and Vardan,[24] who state that all the Arab armies were assembled from as far apart as India and Egypt and that three hundred large ships as well as five thousand smaller ones were gathered. Each of the large vessels carried 1,000 troops, whereas the small ships each held 100 soldiers. It appears that Sébèos did not bother to complete his calculations, for 300 times 1,000 would give the absurd figure of 300,000 men, and 5,000 multiplied by 100 would give another 500,000, or all told, an army of 800,000 men, not including the crews—an incredibly fanciful figure.

The number of imperial ships is also certainly exaggerated. The Greeks could not have possessed such a large fleet of warships in view of the fact that transports are not included in the number, and the vessels were exclusively warcraft. It would perhaps be worth noting at this point that, in the reign of Justinian I, when Belisarius sailed against the Vandals in North Africa, his transports consisted of five hundred units carrying eighteen thousand men, escorted by a flotilla of 92 *dromons*.[25] This was then considered a very large fleet. In the light of these facts, the Byzantines probably had no more than 200 or 250 *dromons* all told.

Even more difficult to estimate is the size of the Moslem armada. The difficulty is compounded by the fact that the Egyptian armada under the Egyptian leader Abd Allah ibn Sad and the Syrian fleet led by Abu'l Awar both took part in the engagement. All Arab and Syrian sources record as fact that both fleets participated in the battle.[26] As a result, contemporary historians have been more confused, some contending that Abd Allah commanded the Moslem fleet and others claiming that Abu'l Awar led the armada.

It is my impression that the Egyptian fleet numbered no more than two hundred units. I would not attempt to guess how many of these were transports and how many, warships. The Syrian armada consisted exclusively of fighting units. After the destruction at Tripoli, I do not believe they could have possessed more than one hundred ships. The fact that the Egyptian fleet included merchant ships emerges from a subsequent paragraph where the reasons for the naval clash are described.

Let us first proceed with the details of the battle as these are recorded by the various sources, including the mythical or divinely inspired interventions of which the chroniclers are so fond; and then attempt to explain or to point out certain episodes that are reputed to have taken place, leaving it to the judgment of the reader to draw his own conclusions. Afterward, I give my version of the story.

* * *

Before relating the details of the battle as they are described in the sources, let us deal briefly with the mythical element that the chroniclers interweave in their narrative. The Arabs record that, on the night of the battle, the Moslems devoted themselves to prayer whereas the Greeks tolled their bells.[27] There is no explanation as to where the Greeks, who had not disembarked, found these bells. Could they have been placed on the ships? Moreover, the crews serving in the Moslem armada were for the most part Christians. To which God did they pray? At all events, the information provided to the effect that an evening elapsed before the decisive action was fought is significant.

The Byzantine chroniclers on the other hand, whose narrative is repeated by the Syrians,[28] state that, on the eve before the battle, the emperor had a dream in which he was in Thessaloniki. When he awoke, he related this vision to the dream interpreter, who answered that it would have been better had he not slept, for the significance of Thessaloniki in the dream was that "victory would not be his," that is, that God would give victory to his foes.[29]

There exist other traditions relating to the battle. The Arabs maintain that the ships were lashed one next to the other in order to give battle as though on land.[30] According to Wakidi, the vessels were bound together after an agreement between the opposing forces, that is to say, one Arab ship tied to a Byzantine ship (in which case, the respective fleets were equal in number). Another tradition relates that the Arabs proposed to the Greeks that they fight on the shore, but the latter rejected the suggestion.[31] Numerous other traditions exist that merely make the story more confusing.

Now let us attempt to describe the battle by unraveling and rearranging the variant narratives of the Byzantine chroniclers. In the year A.M. 6146, 654/655 of the Hegira, Muawiyah armed a large fleet with which he planned to sail to Constantinople (sec.

Theophanes, Zonaras, George the Monk, and Cedrenus), and he put in command of the armada "Abulathar" (Abu'l Awar). The latter proceeded to Phoenix in Lycia, where the Byzantine fleet was under the command of the emperor "Constans" (Constantine III) and a naval battle took place.[32] The emperor went down to the Lycian shipyard where the fleet of the Agars had arrived and where a battle was to take place (sec. Zonaras). While preparing for the naval clash on the morrow, the emperor (sec. Theophanes, Zonaras, and Cedrenus), that evening (sec. George the Monk), had a dream (or on the evening before the battle: Cedrenus). At this point, all the chroniclers relate an identical story as cited above. At daybreak (sec. George the Monk), the naval engagement took place. The Romans were defeated, and the sea turned red from the blood of the Romans (sec. Theophanes, the Monk, and Cedrenus). A plot was reported to the emperor (another version says the emperor was informed of a plot against him) by one of his loyal subjects and friends (sec. George the Monk). The emperor changed clothes with another man (sec. Theophanes, George the Monk, Zonaras, and Cedrenus), and the son of Vucinator leapt into the royal galley and, seizing the emperor, led him on to another ship and in this way saved him "unexpectedly" (sec. Theophanes and Cedrenus). The emperor then took a small ship with "a few men" and sailed off at night for Constantinople "having been saved unexpectedly" (sec. George the Monk). On the following day, the person who donned the royal robes went on to the imperial galley and gave battle (sec. George the Monk); and he [the son of Vucinator] climbed on to the royal galley, fought bravely, slew many, and gave his life for the emperor (sec. Theophanes and Cedrenus). The enemy (?) surrounded him, believing him to be the emperor. He slew numerous men until finally the enemy (?) killed him along with the man "who wore the royal garments."

Such are the details given by the Byzantine chroniclers of the naval battle. Michael the Syrian and the *Anonymous Chronicle of 1234* record more or less the same, but add that the emperor barely escaped being caught by his enemies (?). Agapius reports that the emperor was nearly drowned. Tabari, who has an entirely different story, writes that the emperor was wounded by an arrow.

If we reconstruct the battle using other sources, expecially the Arab ones, the naval engagement takes on another form.[33] The Egyptians had installed a shipyard at the foot of Phoenix in Lycia where timber was available, particularly cypress forests, of which they had need for the masts of the vessels they built. As already pointed out, Egypt had no timber, whereas the coasts of Isauria and Lycia were densely forested. To protect this operation, Abd Allah ibn Sad, military governor of Egypt, was put in charge of two hundred ships. How many of these were warships or transports is unknown. In any case, this naval clash was known by the Arabs as *Dzat or Ghazwah al-Sawari*, that is, "the operation of the 'masts.'" But no reason is given for the participation of the Syrian flotilla under Abu'l Awar.

The Arabs state that the Byzantines opened the attack, whereas the latter say the Arabs had the initiative.[34] At all events, all sources are agreed that the naval battle was a disaster of the first magnitude for the Greeks. The Syrians record that twenty thousand Byzantines perished.[35] It is reputed that two hundred Arab ships were destroyed.

* * *

Before drawing my personal conclusions, I should point out and discuss certain matters that arise in the description of the battle as presented by Byzantine chroniclers. Among the various Greek chroniclers there exist variant narratives as well as certain strange excerpts that of necessity give rise to many doubts.

One chronicler records that, when the emperor learned of the intentions of Muawiyah, he prepared a fleet and proceeded to the "shipyard" of Lycia known as Phoenix.[36] This is substantiated by a Syrian chronicler.[37] Because both writers are later chroniclers, it is certain that they based their history on earlier texts, and the question well arises as to how the Greeks knew that there existed an Arab "shipyard" at the foot of Mount Phoenix within Byzantine territory.

To judge by the various narratives, two naval clashes probably took place. Theophanes writes, "[Abu'l Awar] who arrived at the place . . . gave battle with them." Then follows the story concerning the dream. George the Monk records that the battle was to take place the following day. It would appear therefore that two separate engagements occurred and that the dream was seen by the emperor in the intervening evening.

George the Monk gives another version; he says that a loyal friend of the emperor informed him of a plot against his life. But who plotted against him? Could it possibly have been the Arabs? Yet this could not be, as they were enemies in any case.

It is certainly possible that the Arabs had wished to slay the leader
of their enemies to obtain an early victory, but this would not be
in the nature of a plot. What members of the royal circle had
conspired against Constantine?

George the Monk then proceeds to relate that after the emperor
was advised of the conspiracy by his friend, the latter donned the
imperial garments. That he traded his robes with another person
is verified by Theophanes, Zonaras, and Cedrenus as well as by
several Syrian chroniclers, yet none of these make any mention of
an intrigue. According to George the Monk, the emperor went on
board a small (?) ship with a few companions and sailed in the
night for Constantinople. In other words, the emperor fled in the
night before the final battle. But in that event, when was Constantine wounded? Probably in the first engagement, in which case,
two battles took place.

The odd remark made by all the chroniclers is that the flight of
the emperor resulted in his "unexpected salvation." Theophanes
gives another version, although he also remarks that the emperor
gave his robes to another and was "unexpectedly preserved."
According to his story, the son of Vucinator leaped on to the
royal galley and seized the emperor to carry him to another ship.
Cedrenus gives the same version, as do Michael the Syrian and the
Anonymous Chronicle of 1234. But irrespective of whether the
emperor fled in the night or was saved by the son of Vucinator,
the strange fact is that all the chroniclers are surprised by the escape of the emperor, as though each had expected him to die. At
all events, one thing is certain. Constantine was a brave and com-
petent soldier. He showed this quality throughout his life. Constantine may not have possessed the military genius of his grandfather Heraclius I, but he never shrank from leading his armed
forces against the enemy of his empire. The fact that he abandoned his fleet and his men on the eve of the battle would indicate
that the conspiracy was serious and that in all probability the
plotters were not the Moslem enemies of Byzantium against whom
he was accustomed to fight.

Had his ship been captured by the Arabs and his life endangered,
would it not be an easy matter to abandon it for another vessel to
continue fighting, or if necessary, be covered by other imperial
ships to make good his escape? It is difficult to understand why he
would waste precious time to give his robes to another person.
How would the Arabs know who the emperor was? And why
should he flee in a small boat (sec. George the Monk)?

The chroniclers go on to relate that the hero, that is, the son of Vucinator, returned to the royal galley after having slain many, "sacrificing his life for the emperor" (sec. Theophanes and Cedrenus). Theophanes then continues: "having surrounded him . . . and believing him to be the emperor, they slew him together with the person who had donned the imperial robes." A very odd statement to make indeed. They killed the person wearing the royal garments. Why should they believe that the son of Vucinator was the emperor when it was a different person who wore the robes? Why should the son of Vucinator return to the imperial galley? George the Monk gives another version. According to this, the person who donned the royal robes boarded the imperial galley and began to give battle. The enemy (?) surrounded him, believing him to be the emperor. After having slain many, he was mortally wounded and thus gave his life for his friend. In other words, George the Monk entirely ignores the intervention of Vucinator's son and relates that the friend of the emperor who donned the imperial robes boarded the royal galley.

The question now arises as to why the son of Vucinator should return to the imperial galley or why the person who donned the royal robes should do this. Could it be that in this way they wished to facilitate the escape of the emperor? To give him ample time to flee? But from whom? Again the question arises as to how the Arabs knew that the emperor was present. All such narratives are certainly not based on common sense, and one may well ask whether they had been fabricated to camouflage or silence certain traitorous actions that were not very flattering to the Byzantines. This may well explain the divergencies and garbled versions in the narratives. Having been presented with the various elements of the celebrated naval battle of Phoenix and with the strange and inexplicable events as related by the different chroniclers, the reader may draw his own conclusions as to what actually took place.

*   *   *

Before presenting my version of the story, it would perhaps be useful to dwell briefly on events after the naval engagement. All chroniclers without exception, including Byzantine, Syrian, and Arab, record that the imperial fleet was completely destroyed, and Theophanes in fact equates the defeat with the catastrophe the Byzantines suffered at Yarmuk.[38] Contemporary historians accept these views of the Greek and other chroniclers,[39] but they also agree that the Arabs suffered serious losses, which, on the basis of Moslem sources, are estimated at two hundred ships.

Another doubt immediately arises, however. If the Byzantine fleet was destroyed and in fact, according to Theophanes, this destruction was total and complete, whereas the Arab fleet suffered only partial loss, how was it possible for the imperial navy to emerge again so soon after the battle in Mediterranean waters, while the Moslem fleet returned to the scene years later? The Egyptian flotilla makes its appearance again as late as in 664/665,[40] and the Syrian fleet, in 665/666.[41] It is indeed paradoxical that, although the Arabs plundered the islands of the Aegean, Cyprus, Rhodes, Crete, and so on, despite the existence of the imperial fleet, and are reputed to have planned at the same time an operation against Constantinople, the Moslem fleet appears to have disappeared from the eastern Mediterranean after the destruction of the Byzantine armada. It is contended that Muawiyah ceased further operations on account of his dispute with the new caliph, Ali. Yet the caliph Uthman was murdered in the summer of 656, a year after the naval battle, after which Ali was chosen as the new caliph.[42] Soon after, the rivalry between the Moslem leaders reached a climax, in 657, with Muawiyah's expedition in which the major operations were in what is now Iraq. Indeed, what role could the fleet have played in this episode? Under these circumstances, to argue, on the one hand, that the Byzantine fleet was destroyed whereas in fact it continued to operate, and on the other hand, that the Moslem fleet suffered some losses whereas in actual fact it disappeared from the Mediterranean for ten years, would not, I believe, hold water.

* * *

At this point, I give my own version of the events, but I must point out that this version is not based on any extant source. I should again mention the basic fact that the Greek chroniclers displayed undisguised hostility to Constantine and indeed, one could say, a deep hatred for him. This was on account of his support for the Monothelite heresy; they regarded him as no less than a heretic. But this was a mistaken notion, for Constantine in fact shied away from all religious controversy. Understandably, he could not easily renounce the policies of his grandfather, Heraclius I, which some of his subjects, particularly the westerners, desired he should do. On this account, he had forbidden any discussion of religious dogma until a more appropriate time when an ecumenical council, which was the singular body that could resolve the thorny problem, could be summoned.

The Egyptians had installed a naval arsenal at the foot of Mount Phoenix near the promontory in Lycia known as Chelidonia. Egyptian vessels called there to load supplies of timber from the cypress forests in the vicinity essential for the construction of ship masts.[43] They were protected by warships commanded by Abd Allah ibn Sad, the military governor of Egypt. The actual number of merchant ships and warships respectively is not known. Disturbed by the continual raids against the islands of the southern Aegean, the Byzantines decided to take countermeasures. The imperial armada, led by the emperor Constantine, sailed into southern waters; and it was then, in all probability, that they received intelligence of the establishment of a naval yard and the timber operation.

The size of the Byzantine armada is not known. It should be borne in mind that the *dromon*, the crack fighting ship of the imperial fleet at the time, was of 100 tons displacement and usually carried 80 to 100 sailors and oarsmen and a complement of 30 soldiers.[44] Thus a fleet of 500 to 1000 ships would require some 60 to 130,000 men to man and to be fully armed. On this account, I believe that the reputed figure of 200 to 250 vessels to be nearer the truth.

Having then perhaps encountered the refugees from Syria and learning of the destruction suffered by the Moslems at Tripoli, they believed they had nothing to fear from the Syrian armada and therefore launched an attack against the Egyptians, who sustained considerable losses. In the course of the engagement, the emperor was wounded (I assume only superficially). The Egyptians had suffered such great losses that their fleet did not appear on the scene for some ten years thereafter.

That same evening, the emperor was informed of a conspiracy against him. Obviously, the Moslems of the Egyptian armada could not have been involved in the plot. First, they had been defeated, and second, the idea of a conspiracy against the emperor on the part of the enemy is far-fetched. The plot was apparently organized by people in the Byzantine ranks. This is a tenable supposition in view of the fact that there was a faction within the Greek camp that had wished to eliminate Constantine and to replace him with his brother Theodosius. In this way, the religious policy would be placed in alignment with that of the West. Moreover, the animosity of Constantine for his brother began at this time and ended soon after with the latter's death on the orders of the emperor.

Apparently fearing that the conspiracy had assumed major proportions and that he could not hope to crush it at Phoenix, the emperor took the advice of a loyal subject and changed his robes with a friend, then with a few followers boarded another ship and made good his escape in the night to Constantinople, thus unexpectedly saving his life. The next morning, the conspirators, who believed they had nothing to fear, attacked the royal galley and the fratricidal struggle began, with the result that the individual who had donned the imperial robes was slain. As a consequence, the effectiveness of the Byzantine fleet was further weakened, inasmuch as it had already suffered losses in the previous day's clash with the Egyptians.

Quite probably, soon after this episode, a small squadron of the Syrian fleet loomed into view. It had been pursuing the refugees from Tripoli or had come to reinforce the Egyptian fleet. It fell upon the flanks of the Greek ships warring among themselves. Under the circumstances, the defeat of the imperial fleet, which was large, experienced, and possessed of a long naval tradition, is not surprising, preoccupied as it was with fratricidal warfare.

Such is my interpretation of the chain of events that took place immediately before, during, and after the naval engagement at Phoenix. To make this interpretation, I did to some extent use the existing sources, but my attention and suspicions were aroused particularly by the paradoxical phrase "was unexpectedly preserved," as though the event were quite out of the ordinary. At all events, the entire episode should be carefully reexamined, and the conclusions drawn from the battle of Phoenix should in future be based on more irrefutable argument.

Notes

1. Theophanes, *Chronographia*, ed. C. de Boor (Leipzig, 1883); George the Monk, *Chronicle*, ed. C. de Boor (Leipzig, 1904).

2. It should be pointed out that all contemporary historians refer to him as Constans II (although there never was a Byzantine emperor with such a name). He was baptized with the name of Heraclius and was renamed Constantine in 641, when co-emperor, because the reigning monarch was then his uncle Heraclius II, and both rulers could not use the same name.

3. G. Abgarian, "Remarques sur l'histoire de Sébèos," *Revue des Etudes Arméniennes* 1 (1964): 203-215.

4. Baladhuri, *Kitab Futuh Al-Buldan*, ed. Ph. Hitti (Beirut, 1916; repr. 1966), p. 196; Tabari, *Annales*, ed. M. de Goeje (Leiden, 1879-1901), 3: 562.

5. Baladhuri, *Kitab*, p. 196. L. Caetani, *Annali dell Islam* (Rome, 1905-1926), 7:40.

6. Theophanes, *Chronographia*, p. 344; Sébèos, *Histoire d' Héraclius*, ed. F. Macler (Paris, 1904), p. 111.

7. M. Lombard, "Arsénaux et bois de marine dans la Méditérranée musulmane," in *Le navire et l'économie du Moyen Age* (Paris, 1958).

8. S. Runciman, "Byzantine Trade," in *Cambridge Economic History*, 2: 89.

9. *Al-Yakubi . . . Ibn Wadhi, qui decidur . . . Historiae*, ed. G. Wiet (Cairo, 1937), p. 178.

10. Ibn Khaldoun, *Les Prolégomènes*, ed. and trans. Macguckin de Slane (Paris, 1936), 2:39.

11. F. G. Kenyon and H. Bell, *Greek Papyri in the British Museum* (London, 1898-1907), 4:92 ff. Fahmy Ali, *Muslim Sea Power in the Eastern Mediterranean* (London, 1950), p. 104.

12. A. Vasiliev, *Byzance et les Arabes* (Brussels, 1935), 1:218.

13. P. Van den Ven, *La légende de St. Spyridion* (Louvain, 1945), p. 145; G. Hill, *A History of Cyprus* (Cambridge, 1949), 1:285; A. Dikigoropoulos, "A Contribution to the Chronology of Events in Cyprus," in *Proceedings of the 9th Congress of Byzantine Studies* (Athens, 1956), 2:366; A. Papageorgiou, "Les premières incursions arabes en Chypre," in *Afieroma Spyridakis* (Athens, 1964).

14. Theophanes, *Chronographia*, p. 345. Zonaras, *Epitome Historiarum*, ed. I. Dindorf (Leipzig, 1868-1872), 3:314 ff. Michael the Syrian, *Chronique*, ed J. B. Chabot (Paris, 1899-1904), 2:442.

15. Neither Byzantine nor Arab chroniclers mention these raids. Michael the Syrian is the single source.

16. M. Lombard, "Le bois dans la Méditerranée musulmane," in *Annales*, vol. 14 (Paris, 1959).

17. A. Stratos, *Byzantium in the Seventh Century* (Amsterdam, 1975), 3:229 ff.

18. Michael the Syrian, *Chronique*, 2:445. J. B. Chabot, ed., *Chronicon Anonymum ad A.D. 1234*, in *CSCO* (Louvain, 1965), p. 214.

19. Agapius de Menbidj, *Kitab al-Unvan*, ed. A. Vasiliev, in *Patrologia Orientalis*, vols. 5, 7, 8, 9, p. 224. Elie Bar Sinaya, *La Chronologie*, ed. Delaporte (Paris, 1910), pp. 86-87, writes that there were involved two young men who had been imprisoned but succeeded in inspiring confidence.

20. Theophanes, *Chronographia*, p. 345. Cedrenus, ed. I. Bekker, vol. 1 (Bonn, 1838), p. 755. Agapius, *Kitab*, pp. 223-224. Michael the Syrian, *Chronique*, 2:445. Elie Bar Sinaya, *Chronologie*, pp. 86-89. Chabot, *Chronicon Anonymum ad A.D. 1234*, p. 214. A. Baethgen, "Fragmente syrischer und

arabischer historicker," in *Abhandlungen für die Kunde des Morgenlandes* (repr. Leipzig, 1917), 8, pt. 3, p. 113.

21. E. W. Brooks, "The Chronology of Theophanes," in *BZ* 8 (1899). E. Dulaurier, *Recherches sur la Chronologie Arménienne* (Paris, 1859), pp. 234-235.

22. The dates as recorded by the different chroniclers are as follows: Theophanes, A.M. 6146 (A.D. 655). Other Byzantine chroniclers support the same date. Michael the Syrian, *Chronique*, 2:445, the year 966 (A.D. 655), the thirty-fifth year of the Hegira, 655/656. Abu Faraj Bar Hebraeus records the year 966 (655) and the thirty-seventh year of the Hegira (657/658), whereas Elie Bar Sinaya says the year 965 (654) and the thirty-fourth of the Hegira (654/655). The Chabot, *Anonymous Chronicle of 1234* records the year 966 (655) and the thirty-seventh of the Hegira (657/658). Of the Arabs, Makrizi, *Description historique et topographique de l'Egypte*, ed. and trans. P. Casanova, in *Mémoires des membres de l'Institut français d' archéologie orientale du Caire*, vol. 3 (Cairo, 1906), pp. 157 ff., gives the thirty-fourth year (654/655); Al-Kindi agrees with the thirty-fourth year; whereas Tabari, *Annales*,1:2,865, 2,927, records two dates: (a) on the basis of Wakidi, the thirty-first of the Hegira; (b) on the basis of Abou Masar, the thirty-fourth year of the Hegira. Al Athir, *Chronicon*, ed. C. Tornberg (Leiden, 1867–1876), also reports the two dates, whereas Huwaraismi [Baethgen, "Fragmente," 7, no. 3 (1884): 113] records the thirty-fourth year. From this list of the most important chronicles, it would appear that the majority agree with the year 655, or the thirty-fourth Arab year (22 July 654/10 July 655). Under the circumstances, the date should be placed before July 655, when the thirty-fourth year of the Arabs ends and the two dates coincide, i.e., 655 and the thirty-fourth year of the Hegira. The naval battle probably took place at the end of June 655.

23. The Chabot *Anonymous Chronicle of 1234* reports a large number of ships in the Byzantine fleet. Agapius, *Kitab*, p. 224, records likewise. Makrizi, *Egypte*, 3:157 ff., writes that the Byzantines had seven hundred ships; another source says one thousand; whereas the Arabs, under Abd Allah ibn Sad, had only two hundred units. Tabari says the imperial fleet consisted of five hundred vessels and the Arab one of a mere forty, with thirty-thousand men. One might well ask how such a large number could be accommodated in only forty ships, but the question would go begging.

24. Sébèos, *Héraclius*, pp. 139-140. Stephanos von Taron, *Armenische Geschichte*, ed. H. Gelzer (Leipzig, 1907), p. 152; Vardan, *Histoire Universelle*, ed. J. Muyldermans (Paris, 1927), pp. 140-142.

25. Procopius *De Bello Vandalico* 1. 11, ed. J. Haury, p. 362. E. Stein, *Historie du Bas Empire* (Paris, 1949), 2:312-313.

26. See all sources cited in Caetani, *Chronographia Islamica*, 2:360.

27. Tabari, *Annales*, 1:2,687 ff.

28. Theophanes, *Chronographia*, p. 346. George the Monk, *Chronicle*, p. 716. Zonaras, *Epitome*, 3:314. Cedrenus, p. 756. Leo Grammaticus, *Chronographia*, ed. I. Bekker (Bonn, 1842), p. 108. Michael the Syrian,

Chronique, 2:445. Chabot, *Anonymous Chronicle of 1234*, p. 214.

29. It is rather odd that a monk should believe in magicians and dream interpreters and accept such beliefs as natural and not sinful.

30. Ibn Al-Hakam, *Futuh Misr*, ed. Torrey (New Haven, 1922), French trans., "La conquête de l'Afrique du Nord," in *Revue Tunisienne* (1931): 233-260, and (1932):71-78.

31. See a list of all the traditions in Tabari, *Annales*, 1:2,868 ff.

32. Lycia was a province in the southwest corner of Asia Minor. Phoenix was a mountain near the sea, covered with cypress forests. The battle took place at the promontory of Chelidonia, at the foot of Mount Phoenix.

33. L. Caetani, *Annali*, 8:92 ff.; Lombard, "Arsénaux," passim. See also Tabari, *Annales*, 1:2,865, 2,967. Caetani in fact states that the information given is not sufficient to reconstruct this episode.

34. Mirkhond, *Rusat-us-Safa*, ed. F. F. Arbuthnot and E. Rehatsek (London, 1894), 5:152 ff.; Tabari, *Annales*, 1:2,867.

35. Michael the Syrian, *Chronique*, 2:445-446.

36. Zonaras, *Epitome*, 3:314.

37. Agapius, *Kitab*, pp. 223 ff.

38. Yarmuk was a river in Palestine where the Byzantines were routed in 636 by the Arabs. The great advance of the Arabs began in that year. Theophanes records on p. 332 of *Chronographia* that the Byzantine emperors were defeated because of their impiety, then refers to the various battles, and goes on to say "the destruction of the Roman army and fleet at Phoenix was complete. . . ." Oddly enough, there was a Byzantine fleet but no army at Phoenix.

39. M. Canard, "Les expéditions des Arabes contre Constantinople," *Journal Asiatique* 208 (1926):61-121. J. Wellhausen, "Die Kämpfe der Araber," in *Nachrichten von der Kön. Gesellschaft den Wiss. zu Göttingen* (1901): 419. E. W. Brooks, in *Cambridge Medieval History*, 3:393.

40. The expedition of the army of Egypt led by Muawiyah ibn Hudayg al-Kindi against North Africa. A military engagement with the *patricius* and *strategos* Nicephorus, who finally embarked on the imperial fleet that the Arabs were unable to confront.

41. Busr's expedition (Busr Ben Abi Artah) to reinforce the army of Abd al Rahman, which had penetrated Asia Minor.

42. 17 June 656.

43. Tabari, *Annales*, 1:2,865-2,927; Zonaras, *Epitome*, 3:314; Caetani, *Annali*, 8:92; Lombard, "Arsénaux."

44. L. Bréhier, "La Marine de Byzance," in *Byzantion* 19 (1949):11.

Chapter 14

The Case of Bishop Guichard of Troyes

Joseph R. Strayer, *Princeton University*

The case of Bishop Guichard of Troyes has little to do with Byzantium, though Guichard was briefly, and unhappily, a bishop in Bosnia.[1] It does suggest that so-called Byzantine intrigue was not unknown in the court of France and that a French king like Philip the Fair could manipulate the French church about as successfully as a Byzantine emperor could manipulate the Greek church. It is an intensely personal story, and it throws some light on the characters of Philip, his wife, and his advisers. No great principles were involved, though they could have been if Pope Clement V had wanted to make an issue of Guichard's treatment. Philip violated clerical privileges in arresting and imprisoning Guichard, but both he and the pope were already deeply involved in trying to decide what to do with the charges against the memory of Boniface VIII and with the prosecution of the Templars. Guichard represented no particular cause; he held no dangerous opinions; he was not the leader of a faction. He stood alone, a disagreeable man perhaps, but not important enough to justify adding a new complication to the already strained relations between king and pope.

Guichard had risen rapidly in the Church—prior of Saint-Ayoul of Provins by 1273 when he was still a young man, abbot of Montier-la-Celle in 1284, bishop of Troyes in 1298—and it seems fairly certain that he owed these promotions to Blanche of Artois, dowager queen of Navarre and countess of Champagne and to her daughter, Jeanne, who married Philip the Fair in 1284. Guichard was present at the christening of Charles, Jeanne's third son, in 1294 and may have been one of the child's godfathers.[2] The depositions collected during the investigation of the charges against him stress his close ties with the two queens and the favor that they showed him. But Guichard was not just a courtier; in fact, in his later years he was anything but courtly. He was a first-rate businessman; he enriched his monastery[3] and, probably, himself during the years of his abbacy. He certainly had an important

voice in the administration of Champagne during the years of
transition to royal control that followed Jeanne's marriage, and he
also gained the confidence of Philip the Fair. Rigault may have
exaggerated a little in calling him the king's delegate in Champagne,[4] but he certainly fulfilled this function when he acted as
one of the two collectors of the subsidy of 1300 in Champagne.[5]
The other collector was Guillaume de la Chapelle, a not-very-
important king's clerk; Guichard was clearly the senior member of
the team. The appointment is another indication of Guichard's
reputation for financial expertise. Guichard also sat in the Grands
Jours of Troyes (the high court of Champagne) from 1296 to
1299, and he was named in an ordinance of 1296 as one of those
who could enter the Chamber of Pleas of the Parlement of Paris
when he wished. He was too busy with his financial and judicial
work in Champagne to make much use of this privilege, but he did
take part in a case that involved a rent on the fairs of Troyes.[6]
He would have known more about this problem than most of his
colleagues.

By 1300 Guichard was a fairly important man, not yet one of
the inner circle of royal officials, but with some prospect of reach-
ing that level. His career was ruined by the very thing that had
brought him to the attention of Jeanne and Philip: his involvement in the financial administration of Champagne. Blanche, the
dowager queen of Navarre, was very careful to protect her financial interests. She became suspicious of Jean de Calais, canon of
Troyes, who had been treasurer for her second husband, Edmund
of Lancaster, and then administrator of her dower lands. Rightly
or wrongly, Blanche believed that Jean had cheated her;[7] she had
him arrested and asked Guichard to guard him in the episcopal
prison at Troyes. Jean escaped and fled to Italy; Guichard was
accused of taking an enormous bribe to let Jean go. The accusation was not completely implausible. Guichard could not have
carried out his administrative duties in Champagne without know-
ing Jean, and his own concessions to his cathedral chapter in 1304
show that he had been rather unscrupulous in building up his
income.[8] On the other hand, no direct evidence against Guichard
has survived;[9] he was never convicted of the offense, and it seems
unlikely that a man who knew Blanche so well would have risked
an act that he knew would infuriate her. The two chief accusers of
the bishop were Jean of Calais himself and a certain Noffo Dei
(Arnoldo Deghi), a banker whose firm had had some dealings with
the treasurers of Champagne.[10] Neither man had a very good

character; in fact some writers later confused or connected Noffo with Esquinus de Floyrano, who denounced the Templars to James of Aragon and to Philip the Fair.[11] Both Noffo and Jean retracted their accusations, Jean on his deathbed, in letters that seem sincere. Rigault suggested that both Jean and Noffo (who was also in prison at the time) were allowed to flee France in return for incriminating Guichard.[12]

This explanation solves some problems but raises others: who hated Guichard so much that they were willing to procure false testimony and spend several years in seeking his condemnation? The most likely answer is a group clustered around Simon Festu, archdeacon of Vendôme. Simon, like Guichard, was a financial expert, collector of tenths and annates in the province of Bordeaux and parts of the provinces of Toulouse at various times from 1291 to 1299, and a collector of subsidies in Poitou and Limousin, 1299–1300.[13] He may have been jealous of Guichard, who had gained his reputation while staying quietly at home; Simon, a native of Fontainebleau, had had to spend years roaming the Southwest. He may have been annoyed by the fact that Guichard was already a bishop; Simon had to wait until 1308 before becoming bishop of Meaux. He may have seen Guichard as a rival for high office; Simon became treasurer in 1307, a post that Guichard might well have hoped to fill. It also seems very likely that the two men were competing for the favor of Queen Jeanne; one witness later called Simon a clerk of the queen and he was one of her executors when she died in 1305.[14] If there was such competition, Simon had already won the contest by 1300; in spite of all his efforts, Guichard never regained the confidence of the queen.

The greatest men of the Council did not become involved in the process against Guichard; they had Boniface and the Flemings on their minds. But the commission that was eventually appointed to investigate the charges included some of the ablest servants of the king. Four of them later became bishops, Raoul Grosparmi (Orléans, 1308), Robert de Fouilloy (Amiens, 1308), Richard Leneveu (Béziers, 1305), and Pierre de Grès (Auxerre, 1308, also chancellor of the young Louis of Navarre). The others were Guillaume de Plaisians (not very active), André Porcheron, and Hélie de Maumont, all three legal experts.[15] There must have been considerable pressure on the king to name such a distinguished group. Probably the pressure came from the queen, but it is not impossible that some of these men were friends of Simon Festu, or at least that they shared his dislike of Guichard.

The death of the dowager queen in 1302 did not help Guichard; it simply started a new rumor that he had poisoned her. This report was not taken too seriously at the time, but it was revived later. Meanwhile Queen Jeanne proved just as hostile to Guichard as her mother had been. Guichard made a great effort to clear himself in 1303, but he had little support at court. Jean de Montrolles, bishop of Meaux, gave him some help, but while Jean had had a respectable career in the Parlement,[16] he was not a very influential member of the government. In any case, he was frightened off, and Guichard's agents were accused of procuring false testimony.[17] Usually Jeanne was not so vindictive, but this case touched her personally. Her mother had been wronged; her income from her own county of Champagne had been reduced by fraud; one of her own protégés had betrayed her. It clearly was not wise to give Guichard any assistance.

Nevertheless, it was hard to proceed with the case after the deathbed letters of Jean de Calais (17 April 1304) in which he denied that Guichard had helped him to escape.[18] Jeanne had to be satisfied with regaining her losses at the expense of the bishop. She had already taken over his temporalities, and according to Guichard, had deprived him of 40,000 l. t.[19] Even allowing for the fact that she had cut down his timber trees, a very profitable operation, the sum seems exaggerated, but it could not have been completely false. Guichard had obviously been a very wealthy man. Now the queen demanded that the bishop promise to pay her 40,000 l. t.[20] This was a huge sum; even in the inflated currency of 1304 it was worth over 12,000 l. t. of "good" money. It was as large as the amounts collected from the *bailliages* of Bourges, Tours, and the *sénéschaussée* of Poitou for the very heavy tax of 1304,[21] also paid in inflated money. When, how, and if Guichard raised the money is unknown. Perhaps the sums already taken by the queen were credited against the debt.

Jeanne died in 1305 and Guichard had a brief respite from his troubles. He had not been officially acquitted, but nothing more was done about the accusations of Jean de Calais, and Clement V clearly believed that the bishop had been the victim of jealous rivals.[22] It was obvious that Guichard would never regain his position in the royal government, but he could have expected a peaceful and fairly comfortable existence as bishop of Troyes.

All these hopes were blasted by a new set of accusations that were made in 1308. Guichard was charged with killing Queen Jeanne by sorcery (the old story of the waxen image pierced by a

pin) and of trying to poison Charles of Valois and Louis of Navarre. This accusation was taken seriously by Guillaume de Hangest
the younger, *bailli* of Sens, who reported it to the king early in
1308.[23] The problem of the Templars caused some delay, but
Philip eventually asked the pope to investigate the charges and
threatened to judge the bishop himself if the pope did not act. On
9 August 1308, Clement V ordered the archbishop of Sens, the
bishop of Orléans (Raoul Grosparmi) and the bishop-elect of
Auxerre (Pierre de Grès) to begin an inquiry.[24] Both Raoul and
Pierre had been members of the earlier commission of investigation in 1302–1303. They certainly were not favorable to Guichard,
and the illness and then the death of the archbishop of Sens gave
them full control of the proceedings.

Guichard was arrested and placed in the prison of the archbishop
of Sens but soon transferred to the Louvre. This was clearly a
breach of clerical privilege, but Clement did not protest and
appearances were saved to some degree by establishing Denis, dean
of Sens, as guard of the prisoner. Denis was a respectable ecclesias-
tic, a career civil servant, a frequent attendant at the Parlement.[25]
The imprisonment was not very harsh. Guichard continued to
issue letters as bishop of Troyes,[26] for although his temporals had
been seized, he had not been suspended from his ecclesiastical
functions. He also seems to have been able to speak freely with
his lawyers.[27]

The first set of charges was soon supplemented by another group
that revived all the old stories about cheating the king and the
queens, conniving in the escape of Jean de Calais, and causing the
death of Blanche of Champagne and that added some details
about Guichard's abuse of power. The first draft of these accusations was prepared by Noffo Dei (who had not died when he
thought he was mortally ill) and were submitted to Nogaret,
keeper of the seals. It is doubtful if Nogaret did more than glance
at them and touch them up a little. The second version of these
accusations has an addition that is typical of Nogaret: the bishop
was a heretic and only pretended to take communion.[28] But
Nogaret was a busy man, occupied with the affair of the Temple
and the process against Boniface. He seems to have lost interest at
this point; the new charges, as submitted to the bishops of Orléans
and Auxerre,[29] do not read like a work of Nogaret's. They add
many details about Guichard's relations with imps and devils, and
about his violent and oppressive behavior as abbot and bishop, but
they have little of the picturesque detail and stinging phrases that

can be found in Nogaret's attacks on Boniface. Moreover, Nogaret had no reason to attack Guichard. The two men had never been rivals; they had worked in quite different fields (Nogaret was no financier), and a man who had just been made keeper of the seals did not have to worry about a bishop who had lost all influence in the government. It was obviously sensible for Guichard's enemies to keep Nogaret informed about the case inasmuch as he was one of the leading members of the Council and the Parlement. They may have asked his advice about the second set of charges because he was an expert in drawing up criminal accusations. He may also have helped to organize a public meeting on the Ile de la Cité where the charges against Guichard were explained to the people— this technique, used against Boniface and the Templars, was also a specialty of Nogaret's.[30]

If not Nogaret, then who was responsible for the renewed attack on Guichard? Rigault's answer is basically that it was the old gang, Simon Festu and his friends.[31] But Simon and his friends are scarcely mentioned in the accusations, nor were they of any importance as witnesses. Doubtless Simon had been annoyed by the fact that the first investigation of Guichard's conduct had not resulted in a conviction, but he had gained his chief objectives. Guichard had been driven from court; Simon was now treasurer and about to become bishop of Meaux. What good could it do him to start a new process that probably would (and did) last for several years and distract him from his official duties?

It is possible, of course, that there was such deep personal resentment between the two men that Simon could not rest until Guichard had been utterly ruined. The best evidence to support this view is that Simon had probably been associated with Noffo Dei at the time of the first accusations and that Noffo appeared again as an accuser in 1308. But Noffo came into the case only after the bishop had already been accused of sorcery and poisoning; he added some useful details, but the charges were already grave enough to have convinced both Philip and Clement that an investigation was necessary. The first official accusation was made by Guillaume de Hangest the younger, *bailli* of Sens, on the basis of a story told by a poor hermit;[32] Noffo had nothing to do with this. Noffo probably had his own reasons for disliking Guichard; as a "Lombard," he or his associates must have had dealings with the bishop during the period when Guichard helped manage the finances of Champagne.[33] The bankers could always be accused of usury and were frequently forced to pay large sums to the king.[34] Guichard may have squeezed them, too, for his own advantage or that of Blanche and Jeanne, and Noffo may have been one of those who suffered. In any case, Noffo Dei was not a very reliable accomplice; he failed to pay his creditors at the fairs of Champagne and was hanged in Paris in 1313 for this or for some other crime.[35] If Simon Festu wanted to destroy Guichard, more credible witnesses were available, but no connection has yet been established between Simon and those who gave the most damaging testimony.

A case could be made that there was collusion between Simon Festu and the younger Guillaume de Hangest. Why did the *bailli* take the hermit's story so seriously? Such rumors were common whenever a great person died; for example at the time of the death of Philip the Fair's elder brother. Simon Festu must have known the Hangest family well; the elder Guillaume was a fellow treasurer, and the two men had had dealings with each other in the 1290s when Guillaume was already a treasurer and Simon was a very active collector of tenths and subsidies. But there was no very good reason for a Hangest to oblige a Festu. Guillaume the elder was far more influential at court than Simon; he had reached high position much earlier; he had already established his son in a successful administrative career. There was nothing to be gained and much to be lost by becoming involved in an intrigue against an unimportant bishop.

Nogaret, Festu, Noffo Dei, and Guillaume de Hangest all played some role in the process against Guichard, but none of them was the chief promotor of the case. This leaves only one possible candidate, the king himself. We do not know how Philip felt about his mother-in-law; we do know that he was deeply attached to Jeanne. The mere suspicion, never proved, that Guichard had cheated the queen had been enough to make him drive the bishop from his court and to establish a very powerful commission to investigate the charges. Jeanne's untimely death shocked him; he remained faithful to her memory for the rest of his life. The worst possible crime, in his eyes, would have been to encompass the death of the queen. Anyone who tried to hush up such a crime, even if the evidence was flimsy, would have incurred Philip's wrath. If the hermit's story had reached Philip's ears before Guillaume de Hangest had reported it, the Hangest family would have been ruined. Therefore the *bailli* acted promptly to start the investigation; therefore Nogaret helped to strengthen the case by endorsing the dubious evidence of Noffo Dei and perhaps by arranging a public meeting to hear the charges; therefore Raoul Grosparmi and Pierre de Grès made a tremendous effort to find witnesses who would support the accusations. Even when Guichard had, in effect, been cleared, Philip would not let him return to his diocese; he could not believe that the bishop was completely innocent.

This explanation is consistent with all that we know of Philip's character. His narrow piety and his high standard of morality in his private life made him very credulous in cases involving heresy and immorality. He certainly believed the charges of adultery against his daughters-in-law though to believe them went against his interests. He almost certainly believed the charges against the Temple and against Boniface VIII; he profited from both actions, but profit was not his only motive. There is no reason why he should not have believed the charges against Guichard; in this case the profit was psychic, not financial or political. An explanation of her death would help assuage his grief; vengeance on her murderer would be the last and most fitting tribute he could pay to her memory.

Other people were not so credulous. The depositions of the witnesses against Guichard are not very convincing.[36] Curiously enough, the stories about the construction and piercing of the wax doll and the preparations of the poison for Valois and the king's sons are full of lifelike detail, whereas the evidence about Guichard's dishonesty and oppressive behavior as an abbot and as a bishop is thin and perfunctory. Yet Guichard probably did take advantage of his office to build a fortune, and in his compromise with his chapter he admitted that he had abused his power,[37] while he certainly did not attempt the poisoning and almost certainly did not practice sorcery. The two bishops, Raoul Grosparmi and Pierre de Grès, must have known Guichard very well by the time they had completed their investigation; after all, they had spent at least a year on the affair of Jean de Calais and two years on the charges of sorcery and poisoning. They clearly did not think that they had a good case. Perhaps they were too sophisticated to believe in the wax-doll technique and too knowledgeable to believe that Guichard had found scorpions (one ingredient of the poison)[38] in Champagne. In any event, they came to no conclusion and did not protest when Guichard continued to exercise his episcopal functions. If they had been convinced of Guichard's guilt, they would have asked the pope to suspend him, and they could easily have cut his communications with his diocese.

The two bishops, in fact, were in an unenviable position. On the one hand, Philip was pressing for an unfavorable report; on the other hand the pope was asking impatiently for the results of their investigation.[39] They stalled as long as they could but finally sent in all the pieces of the process on 1 April 1311. It is probable that Guichard was released from the Louvre and sent to Avignon at the same time; he was certainly in Avignon early in 1313.[40]

Clement had reserved judgment to himself and hoped to settle the affair at the Council of Vienne, but the case never came up. It is doubtful if Clement had ever been convinced of Guichard's guilt, and he became even more sceptical after the bishop reached the papal court.[41] The final blow to the accusation came, fittingly enough, from Noffo Dei. As he was about to be hanged "pro suo crimine" at Paris in 1313, he confessed that Guichard was innocent.[41] The prosecution was dropped.

Contemporary chroniclers and later fourteenth-century writers were convinced that Guichard was innocent.[43] Philip the Fair was not. He had driven Guichard from court in 1300; he now wanted to drive him from France. Guichard could not return to his diocese; he remained in Avignon. Finally, in 1314, Enguerran de Marigny, by now the king's chief minister, found a solution that was much more pleasing to Philip than to Guichard. Clement V translated the bishop to the see of Diakovar, (or Djakovo), which was almost *in partibus infidelium*. The bishop of Diakovar was titular bishop of Bosnia, but there were few Catholics in Bosnia and many heretics and schismatics. Diakovar was not even in Bosnia (it would now be considered in Croatia); it had become the seat of the bishop early in 1252 or 1253 when it became impossible for him to remain in his diocese. Diakovar was poorly endowed and on an endangered frontier of the Roman Church;[44] it must have been one of the least desirable bishoprics that the pope had at his disposal.

Rigault thought that this appointment was due to the fact that Marigny had always been hostile to Guichard, but Favier has shown that there was no real evidence to support this theory.[45] Marigny was simply doing his usual job of smoothing out difficulties between king and pope, and Clement, as usual, was willing to go more than half way to satisfy the king. Jean d'Auxy, one of Philip's most reliable clerks, long active as a collector of revenues, as an *enquêteur*, and as a member of Parlement was named to Guichard's old see.[46] At last the king had a bishop of Troyes whom he could trust.

As for Guichard, it is doubtful if he ever went to Bosnia. In any case, he resigned early in the pontificate of John XXII and died soon after in January 1317.[47] He left a rent to the church of Troyes and his executors gave an additional 100 l. t. The fact that he was mentioned in the necrology and in the memorials of the cathedral suggests that the report that he was buried there is true.[48] Philip the Fair was dead; Guichard could at last rest in peace in his old home.

Notes

1. The fundamental work on Guichard is Abel Rigault, *Le Procès de Guichard, Évêque de Troyes* (Paris, 1896). Rigault published or summarized all the basic documents on the case; nothing of any great importance has been discovered since his time. It is possible to differ with him on some points, but his work is reliable, his interpretations of the facts are reasonable, and this is largely a commentary on his book.

2. Rigault, *Le Procès*, pp. 11, 14.

3. Ibid., p. 9

4. Ibid., p. 10. The evidence comes from witnesses who were questioned much later (1309 or 1310) when he was on trial. They said he was "mestres en Champagne," "sire en Champagne pour le roi." They had some reason to exaggerate; the more he had been trusted, the blacker his crimes.

5. Robert Mignon, *Inventaire d'anciens comptes royaux*, pub. by Ch. V. Langlois (Paris, 1899), no. 1324; Jules Viard, *Les journaux du Trésor de Philippe le Bel* (Paris, 1940), no. 5290.

6. John F. Benton, "Philip the Fair and the Jours of Troyes," *Studies in Medieval and Renaissance History* 6 (1969), pp. 334–335; Ch. V. Langlois, *Textes relatifs à l'histoire du Parlement* (Paris, 1888), pp. 161, 164 (Langlois was not sure about the traditional date of 1296, but Renaud Barbou, who is on the list, was dead early in 1298, and Guichard, who appears as abbot of Montier-la-Celle, was elect of Troyes in the same year). Cf. Beugnot, *Les Olim* (Paris, 1842), 2:423.

7. Rigault, *Le Procès*, pp. 21–22. Rigault says, p. 25, that Blanche was "non sans âpreté, soucieuse de ses intérêts."

8. Ibid., pp. 261–265 (pièce justificative, no. 7).

9. Again, almost all the stories about this affair come long after the event, in the investigation of 1309–1310, see p. 255.

10. Rigault, *Le Procès*, pp. 23–24. Noffo was at one time connected with Cepperello Diotaiuti, who had collected revenues in Champagne in 1295.

11. Villani began this confusion: see H. Finke, *Papsttum und Untergang des Templerordens* (Münster, 1907), 1:113–114.

12. Rigault, *Le Procès*, pp. 41–42.

13. Viard, *Journaux*, nos. 3384, 4224; Mignon, *Inventaire*, nos. 524, 752, 754, 1206, 1331.

14. Rigault, *Le Procès*, pp. 23, 38; *Gallia Christiana* 8. 1633.

15. Rigault, *Le Procès*, pp. 16, 161. Rigault became a little confused as to which commissioners were named by the archbishop of Sens and which by the king, but as the text he printed on p. 161 shows, André Porcheron and Pierre de Grès, while technically the archbishop's men, were, like the others, appointed "de mandato regis." Pierre de Grès, cantor of Paris, had been a negotiator for the king in Flanders in 1298 and had worked in the Parlement of 1300-1301 (Viard, *Journaux*, nos. 2382, 4664). He had good connections; he advised Charles of Valois on several occasions [J. Petit, *Charles de Valois* (Paris, 1900), p. 343] and his brother Jean was a marshal of France. Richard Leneveu, archdeacon of Auge, was one of the king's most trusted servants. He worked in the Parlement of 1298-1299 (Viard, *Journaux*, no. 3182) and was used frequently as an investigator in the South (Viard, *Journaux*, no. 2029; *Histoire générale de Languedoc*, vol. 11, pp. 242, 253, 257, 259), most notably in looking into the charges against Bernard Saisset, bishop of Pamiers [P. Dupuy, *Histoire du differend* (Paris, 1655), *preuves*, pp. 628-632]. André Porcheron, canon of Paris and of Arras, was associated with the Parlement for at least twenty years, from 1295 to 1314 (Beugnot, *Olim*, 2:370; 3:49; Langlois, *Textes*, p. 178; AN, K38, no. 9[2] and JJ50, no. 52). Hélie de Maumont was connected with a powerful family of the Limousin. His uncle, Gérard, was prominent in the king's service, and both uncle and nephew served in the Parlement of 1299 (Viard, *Journaux*, no. 2434). Raoul Grosparmi was a king's clerk and well versed in both laws (*Gallia Christiana* 8. 1471.) Robert de Fouilloy, like André Porcheron, was active in the Parlement for many years, from 1302 to his death in 1321 (Langlois, *Textes*, pp. 178, 205; Beugnot, *Olim*, 3:157; Bibliothèque Nationale, MS lat. 4763, fol. 65, MS Moreau 218, fol. 253; AN, JJ40, no. 156; *Gallia Christiana* 10. 1190-1191.

16. Jean de Montrolles (the name is spelled in many ways), cantor of Bayeux and then bishop of Meaux, served in the Parlements of 1290, 1291, 1296, and 1298 [L. Tanon, *Histoire des justices . . . de Paris* (Paris, 1883), p. 351; Langlois, *Textes*, pp. 157, 163; Beugnot, *Olim*, 2:423]. He was Master at the Grands Jours of Troyes, 1296-1298, where he worked with Guichard (Benton, "Philip the Fair and the Jours of Troyes," pp. 334-335). He had enough standing to be a member of the Council that imposed a subsidy in October 1303 [*Ordonnances des roys de France* (Paris, 1725), t. I, p. 408], but he died soon thereafter.

17. Rigault, *Le Procès*, pp. 30-33.

18. Ibid., pp. 37-39 (with facsimile). Guichard's enemies of course claimed that the letters were forgeries, but if they were it is hard to see why the case was dropped. Moreover, Noffo Dei, when he thought that he was dying in August 1306, also admitted that he had falsely accused Guichard.

19. Ibid., pp. 28-29; Jean Favier, *Enguerran de Marigny* (Paris, 1963), p. 58. Enguerran, as *panetier* of the queen, was said to have made an inventory of Guichard's goods in 1303. If he found 40,000 l. t. for her, this might explain his rapid rise to power in the following years.

20. Rigault, *Le Procès*, p. 263 (pièce just., no. 7). Guichard promised his chapter on 15 May 1304 that they would not be held liable for the "obligatione quadraginta millium librarum turonensium et earum solutione quas fecimus in manu domine regine."

21. Mignon, *Inventaire*, nos. 1478 (Bourges, 35,095 l. t., not all paid), 1487 (Tours, 45,895 l. t., not all paid), 1540 (Poitou, 39,458 l. t., not all paid).

22. Rigault, *Le Procès*, p. 268. Guichard had been cited to Rome by Benedict XI. Clement excused him, saying that "quedam sinistra de te per nonullos emulos tuos false fuerint insinuatione suggesta" but that some cardinals speak for him and want the truth to shine again through the clouds of calumny, 3 June 1307.

23. Ibid., pp. 55–57, 60–65.

24. Ibid., pp. 57–59 and *pièces just.*, nos. 12, 13.

25. Ibid., pp. 60, 103 (n. 1), and for Denis de Sens see p. 215. Denis was one of the most regular attendants at the Parlement from 1299 to 1316 when he sat in the Grand' Chambre (Viard, *Journaux*, nos. 2530, 5998; Beugnot, *Olim*, 3:72, 89, 97; Langlois, *Textes*, p. 178; AN, JJ57, fol. 64v). He collected subsidies in 1300 and 1303 (Mignon, *Inventaire*, nos. 1296, 1429). He was used to collect adhesions to the appeal against Boniface VIII throughout the South [Georges Picot, *Documents relatifs aux Etats Généraux* (Paris, 1901), pp. 101, 261, 265, 269, 279, 287, 321, 323, 482, 483], and he was especially harsh to the Dominicans of Montpellier (ibid., pp. xxv–xxx). He took declarations of fidelity from the citizens of Lyons in 1311 (Bonnassieux, *De la réunion de Lyon à la France*, p. 135). He was an executor of the will of Philip the Fair (*Gallia Christiana* 12. 111).

26. Rigault, *Le Procès, pièces just.*, no. 19, and pp. 215–216. He was allowed to use his seal.

27. Ibid., pp. 104–109.

28. Ibid., pp. 95–99 (the first draft), 100–101 (the draft after Nogaret had been consulted).

29. Ibid., pp. 110–115.

30. Ibid., p. 65. The meeting was held the day before the bishops opened their inquest, obviously to put pressure on them.

31. Ibid., pp. 101–102. "C'étaient donc les vieux ennemis de Guichard . . . qui dirigeaient encore ce nouveau procès . . . c'étaient les vielles haines . . . qui se ranimaient contre l'évêque."

32. Ibid., pp. 60–65.

33. Ibid., pp. 23–24.

34. J. R. Strayer and Charles Taylor, *Studies in Early French Taxation* (Cambridge, Mass., 1939), p. 17; Mignon, *Inventaire*, nos. 2073, 2076, the Lombards paid a large sum (at least 152,000 l. t. and perhaps, or in addition, 221,000 l. t.) in 1293 when Guichard had a prominent role in the finances of Champagne.

35. Rigault, *Le Procès*, p. 219.

36. Ibid., pp. 209–212; Rigault points out that, although over two hundred witnesses were produced, most of them knew little about the case and that

those who gave the most damaging testimony were suspect for various reasons.

37. Ibid., *pièces just.*, nos. 6, 7.

38. Ibid., p. 82.

39. Rigault, *Le Procès*, pp. 216-217. Clement asked for a report on 18 June 1310 and repeated his demand on 9 February 1311.

40. Ibid., p. 218. The records of the investigation were sent to Clement on 1 April 1311. Pp. 219-220, Guichard was at Avignon by 19 April 1313.

41. Ibid., pp. 219, 233-234.

42. Ibid., p. 219, citing Guillaume de Nangis (HF, 20:608).

43. Rigault, *Le Procès*, p. 219 and the section "Le procès de Guichard de Troyes et l'opinion," pp. 227-236.

44. H. Heberg, *Taxae pro Communibus Servitiis* (Vatican, Studi e Testi, 144), pp. 23, 122. Throughout the fourteenth century, Diakovar paid only 200 florins; Troyes paid 600 florins in 1314 and 2,500 florins thereafter.

45. Rigault, *Le Procès*, pp. 223-224; Favier, *Marigny*, pp. 132-133. Both Rigault and Favier thought that it was impossible for Guichard to return to Troyes, but bishop Bernard Saisset, accused of treason, heresy, and defaming the king, was allowed to return to Pamiers. The evidence against Saisset was rather better than the evidence against Guichard; Saisset had probably made some indiscreet remarks about Philip. Once more, it seems that the king was personally involved in the Guichard affair; he would not let the bishop go unpunished.

46. Jean d'Auxy, king's clerk, was in the Parlements of 1296, 1299, 1300, 1302, 1307, and 1309 (Langlois, *Textes*, pp. 161-167; Beugnot, *Olim*, 2: 436, 3:76, 307, 309, 312; Viard, *Journaux*, nos. 4762, 5888); he was a collector of subventions in 1300 (Mignon, *Inventaire*, no. 1343); he was in charge of payments from the Jews in 1301; (Viard, *Journaux*, no. 5659); he secured adhesions to the appeal to the council against Boniface VIII in the central provinces in 1303 (Picot, *Documents*, pp. xxi, 334, 355, 370, 392, 450, 459); he summoned southern lords to the army in 1304 (AN, JJ36, fol. 73v, nos. 172, 173); he was sent to the South with sweeping powers as an *enquêteur* in 1305-1306 [HL, 9, pp. 282-283, 290; 10, pp. 436, 447; see also entries under his name in Robert Fawtier, *Registres du régne de Philippe le Bel* (Paris, 1958)] ; he was an *enquêteur* again in 1311 and in 1313 [Beugnot, *Olim*, 3:520, and Ch. V. Langlois, "Doléances recueillies par les enquêteurs," *Revue historique* 100 (1909):54].

47. Rigault, *Le Procès*, pp. 225-226. John was elected on 7 August 1316; Guichard must have resigned very soon thereafter.

48. Ibid., pp. 226-234. Ironically enough, Jean d'Auxy, Guichard's successor, died in the same month of 1317, and perhaps in the same week.

Chapter 15

Albanian Settlements in Medieval Greece: Some Venetian Testimonies

Peter Topping, *Dumbarton Oaks*

My purpose is to analyze some of the Venetian evidence that pertains to the settlement of Albanians in the Greek peninsula and islands in the late-fourteenth and fifteenth centuries. It has long been recognized that the immigration into Greece of this pastoral, equestrian, and martial people had important consequences, affecting the population, society, and economy of the country. The subject deserves a comprehensive treatise.[1] In this article, I have chosen to analyze in some detail a limited number of documents, some of whose texts have been available for nearly a century in the editions of Sathas. I have to cite several documents in the form of summaries published by Iorga and Thiriet. Through my analysis, I illustrate more precisely than has yet been done the character of the agreements between Venetian authorities and groups of Albanians whereby the intruders were allowed to settle in various districts of Greece.

On Sunday, 3 June 1397, a Turkish army of six or seven thousand men captured Argos and enslaved most of its inhabitants.[2] The Venetian government acted promptly, after the withdrawal of the Turks, to repeople its strategic colony of Nauplia-Argos by authorizing the *podestà* there to settle Albanians in the town and territory of Argos.[3] The Albanians were not, however, to be allowed into the famous Larissa of Argos. It is likely that these Albanians included women and children and were a sizable band of pastoralists. They probably had moved very recently with their flocks from central Greece through the Isthmus of Corinth into the Peloponnesos.[4] By admitting these settlers, the Venetian authorities were pursuing a policy closely parallel with that of Theodore I Palaeologus, the Despot of Mistra, who a few years earlier had accepted about ten thousand Albanians as colonists in his lands, following negotiations with their chieftains at the isthmus.[5]

From a senate document of 31 December 1404[6] we learn that the Venetians were continuing their efforts to repopulate and strengthen their Argolic colony.[7] The *podestà* was instructed to make grants of uncultivated arable soil and of vineyards to foreigners (*forinseci*) willing to settle in Nauplia, Argos, and their territories. The extent of the grants was to vary in accordance with the social position and rank (*condicio et qualitas*) of the immigrants. Appropriate charters would record the grants and reserve the commune's superior rights (*iurisditio*). In recognition of these rights, the tenant would pay a due (*recognitio*). Otherwise the recipients were exempt from all service and payments. The subjects of the Serenissima Republic from other colonies were expressly forbidden to settle in Nauplia-Argos. Those inhabitants who had left the colony because of Turkish attacks could, however, return and receive their former possessions, even if these had to be taken back from new settlers. The latter were to be compensated by grants from the commune's uncultivated lands.

Although there is no mention of Albanians in the document of 31 December 1404, it is highly probable that they were among the foreigners, along with Greeks of the despotate, whom the Venetians were trying to attract.[8] The presence of Albanians in some numbers in the plain of Nauplia a few years later is attested in a letter of the *podestà* Marco Baffo addressed to the duke of Crete, dated 16 February 1411.[9] Again, Turks were raiding the colony, this time together with men of Antonio I Acciaiuoli, lord of Thebes and duke of Athens. The raiders carried off a large booty in animals, besides about twenty-five persons who were Venetian subjects and a few Albanians. The Albanians are described as possessing an "infinite multitude" of animals of all kinds.

Albanian families continued to arrive in the Nauplia-Argos colony in the first half of the fifteenth century. We learn of this and of the precise terms of their settlement from a senate document of 26 July 1451 addressed to the community of Argos.[10] The senate was responding to certain petitions and complaints of the Argives, who had begun by recalling the capture and burning of their city in 1397 and the enslavement of fourteen thousand of its inhabitants. The Argives had referred to the policy of inviting many foreigners, especially Albanians, to repopulate the colony, and they had complained that the immigrants were favored over the natives.[11] At least 115 families had been received on the following terms: in return for dues of only 4 *hyperpyra* a year, each immigrant family was granted 40 *stremmata* of "dry and uncultivated" plowland belonging to the commune, 4 *stremmata* of unused vineland, and half-burned stone houses.[12] The newcomers, it is stated, repaired the houses and restored the vineyards. The senate instructed the *podestà* of Nauplia and the rector of Argos to respect the privileges of the Argives: they could purchase land freely, and they could recover plots that had been bought cheaply by the Albanians and later abandoned. The officials were to keep a close watch on the Albanians, whose hostile feelings toward both the natives and the Venetian authorities are remarked.

In treating of the Albanians in Venetian-held Argolis, we must take notice of acts of interference there by the Byzantine government of Mistra, and of temporary movements in the region by transhumant Albanians who were subjects of the despot. On the same day that the senate addressed the Argives, it responded also to petitions presented by the community of Nauplia.[13] The senate noted the efforts of the despot's agents to exact personal services from the Albanians who were settled in the Venetian colony; the authorities there were to request the despot to cease this usurpation. Other trespasses were even more damaging to the colony's economy. Albanian subjects of the despot were helping themselves to salt from the salines beneath the castle of Thermísi in southern Argolis.[14] Moreover, shepherds from Byzantine Morea, both Albanians and Greeks, who every winter descended with their flocks to grazing lands in the colony, paid a pasture tax (*herbadigo*) to the despot's agents rather than to the Venetians.[15]

One of the jewels of Venice's maritime empire was the fertile island of Negroponte (Euboea). As the Turkish power waxed in the fourteenth century in the Balkan and Aegean world, the defense and the welfare of this possession were a constant preoccupation of the Venetian Senate. The Black Death and subsequent outbreaks of the plague, together with the slave-taking raids of Turkish and Catalan pirates, had diminished its population. The Albanians had become nearly ubiquitous in continental Greece in the course of the fourteenth century. Thus, "to supply our island of Negroponte with inhabitants," the senate on 20 April 1402 ordered the colony's administration to proclaim that

> any Albanians or other folk not our subjects who with horses should wish to settle in the island of Negroponte within the next two years, shall be admitted and be free in perpetuity of all forced service real and personal; and to them shall be given uncultivated lands of the Commune still fit to be tilled; on condition nevertheless that the said Albanians or other equestrian race shall be held to keep as many horses as there

are heads of families; nor shall they leave the island without permission but shall be held as often as needed to ride to its defense. And after their death the said lands shall be of their heirs with the aforesaid service; if heirs are lacking, they shall revert to the Commune.

The island's officials were to make the grants of land "according to the rank of the persons and the size and circumstances of the family."[16]

We do not know the number or immediate place of origin of the settlers of 1402. Some years later, on 22 May 1425, the senate ordered the colonial officials of Euboea to admit three hundred Albanian families who had already arrived in the island from the duchy of Athens and "diverse districts." The Venetian community in the capital town of Negroponte (today's Chalkis) reportedly was very pleased to have the newcomers on the island. The terms of acceptance of the three hundred families and of "other Albanians" who might come later do not include any details concerning concessions of land and service for it. For reasons of security, the immigrants must not be permitted to reside in any fortresses; they could only visit them a few persons at a time. They must not injure any Venetian subjects, and they must swear an oath of loyalty to Venice. The island regime should see to it that the coming of the Albanians was turned to the advantage of the Venetian dominion and its faithful subjects. As for the protest that had been voiced by the "magnificent" Antonio Acciaiuoli, duke of Athens, concerning the migration of the three hundred families, if he complained again, the officials were to make excuses "with the best words and manner" possible.[17]

Evidently Acciaiuoli renewed his protest and was not put off by the Negropontine officials' best excuses. We infer this from the senate response of 6 November 1425 to the envoy whom the duke had sent to Venice to negotiate over several questions. One of these concerned the Albanian families who had recently entered Euboea. The senate disingenuously stated that it lacked information on this and would reply as soon as it heard from Negroponte.[18] In the end, Acciaiuoli obtained satisfaction, for we learn from a senate decree of 21 January 1427[19] addressed to the colonial administration that the Albanian families claimed by the duke should be allowed to return to his realm accompanied by all of their animals, both large and small cattle, and without paying any tax on these. Other Albanian families, however, who had come from the regions of Levadia and Vlachia (Thessaly) and whom the island's officials considered to be "useful and obedient," were to be provided with public lands and other necessaries for their sustenance (but with as little cost to the commune as could be managed). The senators even expressed their regrets to Acciaiuoli, their "most excellent friend."

Since 1206 the Venetians had held the ports of Modon (Methone) and Coron (Korone) at the southwestern tip of the Peloponnesos. These important way stations on the sea route to the Levant were aptly called the "chief eyes of the Republic." Here, too, at about the beginning of the fifteenth century, we find Venetian authorities negotiating with Albanians, as in Nauplia-Argos, and for the same reason—the Turkish menace. On 16 February 1402 the senate instructed the castellans of the two ports to hire twelve Albanians, "or other men who are fearless horsemen," who possessed good mounts and the customary arms, for the substantial wage of 15-20 *hyperpyra* a month for each, the better to enable them to perform their duties. These consisted, first, of watching passes to ascertain quickly the approach and design of the Turks or other enemies who might injure the Venetian colony, and second, of escorting peasants of the colony to fortified places in times of pressing danger. The families of the hired scouts were to be allowed to settle within Venetian territory.[20]

The handful of Albanians employed by Venice in 1402 were harbingers of their much more numerous compatriots who served in the forces of the principality of Achaia and the despotate of Mistra. The Albanian mercenaries, especially mounted men, employed by the despots, enabled the Byzantines to complete the absorption of the Latin state by 1430. Whether as mercenaries or as migrant clans with their horses and flocks, the Albanians were a difficult folk to deal with and to try to control. Often playing the role of mediator among the petty warring states of Morea (including the Tocchi of Cephalonia-Leukas established for a time in Elis), the signoria took advantage of their conflicts to expand its Messenian colony in the 1420s. This expansion reached the celebrated bay of Navarino, which was dominated by the fortress that the Franks had erected at its northern end in the 1280s.

It was in order to strengthen their hold on Navarino and three neighboring fortresses that the Venetians admitted two companies (*comitive*) of Albanian horsemen into their enlarged colony in 1425. One band consisted of five thousand horse, the other of five hundred, each under its own chieftain. The date of the relevant

decree is 22 May 1425, the same as that admitting the three hundred Albanian families in Euboea. The senators obviously had to
give much attention to Greco-Albanian matters on that day. The
two documents bear resemblances. In the case of the Messenian
colony, the committee of senators acted with great dispatch, for
the letters received from the castellans of Modon and Coron were
dated 4 May. The Albanian chiefs were seeking land to occupy
permanently. They wanted plains and meadowlands on which to
live with their horses, herds, and flocks, "as is their custom."[21]
The castellans were instructed to provide the needed lands in the
rural districts that were controlled from four fortresses: Zonclum
(i.e., Navarino), Sancta Elia (Hagios Elias), Molendini ("The
Mills"), and Nichlina (Niklaina).[22] As was the case in Euboea, the
Albanians were not to be admitted within any fortresses except
for a few individuals at a time. The two companies were also to
receive an annual subsidy (*provisio*) not to exceed 400 ducats a
year. In recognition of the Venetian dominion, the Albanians must
pay a hearth tax of one ducat per household; the families unable
to make this payment were permitted to substitute grain or other
produce. Most importantly, the Albanians were obligated to help
in the defense of the Messenian colony against the Turks and "all
others" (meaning, principally, the Greeks of Mistra).

We would wish to know other terms of the settlement of this
large group of Albanians in the newly acquired frontier zone of
the colony of Modon and Coron. How much land and pasture did
each family receive? Such details, however, were usually left to the
local officials to determine. The essential condition was to obtain
the military service of the Albanians, especially in the form of
cavalry, in view of the serious Turkish danger. Only two years
earlier (1423), the Turks had again made a devastating sweep
through Morea; it was marked, among other disasters to the population, by the massacre of some eight hundred Albanians at Daviá
near Tripolitzá (today's Tripolis). All of the "seven peoples" of the
Peloponnesos,[23] now including the Albanians, were living under
the same threat. No wonder that the two Albanian chiefs are
described as making their request to enter Venetian territory "very
persistently" (*cum maxima instantia*).

Another document—the last—on which I comment, shows
Venice in the role of an intermediary and sponsor helping to bring
about the settlement of Albanians on the island of Zante, a few
years before she herself took permanent possession of the "flower
of the Levant" (1485–1797). This migration was an episode of the

"long war" (1463–1479) between the Serenissima and the Ottoman Porte and was one of many upheavals caused by that conflict. We learn from an account dated 8 June 1473 that about ten thousand Greeks and Albanians had moved from their villages in Elis to Zante "under the protection of the most illustrious signoria and as her subjects."[24] The Turks had completed the conquest of Morea in 1460. These ten thousand Moreotes (*Moraiti*) (we do not know the proportions of Greeks and Albanians) had declared for Venice at some point after war began in 1463. Venice's commander in Elis was the Albanian Michali Ralli, a renowned captain of soldiery. It proved difficult, however, for Ralli to shield this part of the population against Turkish attacks. Arrangements were then made for the short sea crossing to Zante. As an ally of Venice's, Leonard III Tocco, the count of Cephalonia, gave his consent to the migration.

On Zante the migrants received "uncultivated, barren and wild" tracts that through great exertions they soon transformed into productive fields. Giacomo Loredan, the captain-general of the Venetian forces, had appointed as their leader (*governatore*) a certain Martino da Drin, with the title of *consolo*. The latter's surname indicates he was of Albanian birth or descent.[25] Dissension broke out when the bishop of Zante and certain landlords and citizens of the island tried to exploit the immigrants as if they were their own serfs.[26] It was at this juncture that Giacomo Marcello, former Venetian proveditor in Morea, mediated the following articles of agreement between the two sides:[27]

1. The Moreotes would pay a tithe of the produce of their lands and animals.
2. They would pay a due (*recognitio*) to the lords who had, it seems, or were asserting, rights to the lands the Moreotes were cultivating.
3. They were subject to a duty (*dazio*) on the animals that they sold to butchers.
4. In civil lawsuits, the captain of Zante would be the judge when a Moreote was the plaintiff, whereas the consul would decide when a Zantiote brought charges.
5. In criminal cases, the consul was judge over the Moreotes, using the "arm" of the captain of Zante when needed to enforce sentences.

The foregoing articles were in conformity, our informant concludes, with "ancient customs" applicable to subjects of the signoria. It is clear that the ten thousand Moreotes formed a community of their own, distinguished by certain rights and privileges from the mass of the Greek peasants of Zante at the time.

The invasion and migrations of the Albanians in Greek lands in the fourteenth and fifteenth centuries conformed to an age-old pattern of the movements of tribes in the Balkan and Greek peninsulas. Like so many intruders in this region before them, the Albanians were a nomadic and pastoral people who sought and received lands and pastures from rulers of sedentary populations whose territories were often depopulated and in need of colonists. Although they tended to remain a mountain-dwelling, transhumant people living to a large extent from their flocks, the newcomers also showed an aptitude for working the soil of vacant lands formerly under cultivation, or even for clearing virgin tracts. Not least, they were also sought after as soldiers. Having a warlike disposition and being horse breeders possessing excellent mounts, they often agreed to provide specified military service in return for lands or hired themselves out as mercenaries. They specialized also in guarding defiles for Venetian and Turkish authorities.[28]

As alien and refractory tribesmen, the Albanians were bound to clash with the native Greek population and its rulers, whether Byzantine despots, Frankish princes, Venetian colonial officials, or Ottoman Turks. Collisions were the more likely in the turbulent and sometimes anarchic conditions that marked the Greek provinces in the Palaeologan centuries. There is abundant evidence in Venetian sources on the bad relations of the Albanians with Greeks, Venetians, and others.[29] Eventually, of course, the Albanians of Greece—better, the "Arvanítes," the Greeks of Albanian ancestry—were to make an enormous contribution to their new fatherland in a social and national (or patriotic) sense; but this involved a process of symbiosis and Hellenization that required a number of generations to work its effects fully.

Notes

1. The article of T. Jochalas, "Über die Einwanderung der Albaner in Griechenland," *Dissertationes Albanicae* 13 (1971):89–106, is a valuable survey; that of A. Ducellier, "Les Albanais dans les colonies vénitiennes au XVe siècle," *Studi Veneziani* 10 (1968):47–64, is instructive for Venetian policy and attitudes toward the Albanians, and it has observations on their social organization and way of life.

2. *Short Chronicle* no. 33, in P. Schreiner, *Die byzantinischen Kleinchroniken*, vol. 1 (Vienna, 1975), p. 245. Cf. Chronicle no. 32, ibid., p. 234.

3. F. Thiriet, *Régestes des délibérations du Sénat de Venise concernant la Romanie*, vol. 1 (Paris and The Hague, 1958), no. 950, p. 221, summary of document of 7 September 1398.

4. It is also possible that Albanians already in the Peloponnesos in Achaia or Arcadia now entered the Argolid from those districts; they might have crossed into the peninsula from continental Greece at the western end of the Gulf of Corinth, toward the end of the fourteenth century.

5. Cf. D. A. Zakythinos, *Le Despotat grec de Morée*, vol. 2 (Athens, 1953; repr. and rev. London, 1975), p. 32.

6. Text in C. N. Sathas, ed., *Documents inédits relatifs à l'histoire de la Grèce au Moyen Âge*, vol. 2 (Paris, 1881), pp. 123-124. Cf. summary in Thiriet, *Régestes*, vol. 2 (1959), no. 1172, p. 49.

7. These efforts included the senate's invitation, of 27 July 1399, to inhabitants of Argos who had fled in 1397, to return and receive lands and houses free of any service for five years except for watch duty on the city's walls. Summary of this document in Thiriet, *Régestes*, vol. 1, no. 967, p. 224. Cf. K. M. Setton in *A History of the Crusades*, vol. 3, *The Fourteenth and Fifteenth Centuries* (Madison, Wis., 1975), p. 261, n. 120.

8. Cf. Ducellier, "Les Albanais," p. 58.

9. N. Iorga, "Notes et extraits pour servir à l'histoire des croisades au XVe siècle," in *Revue de l'orient latin*, vol. 4 (Paris, 1896), pp. 504-506.

10. Thiriet, *Régestes*, vol. 3 (1961), no. 2865, pp. 168-169. Summarized also by Iorga, "Notes et extraits," *Revue de l'orient latin*, vol. 8 (1900-1901), p. 79.

11. In 1450 the *podestà* of Nauplia reported declining revenues because Albanians and other foreigners had received the best lands and were defaulting in their dues (Thiriet, *Régestes*, vol. 3, no. 2841, p. 161, of 27 October 1450).

12. Iorga quotes the passage with these terms from the original in the Venetian dialect. He then gives these figures for the immigrant families: 18 came first, from Morea (i.e., the Greek despotate of Mistra); 7 families followed these; finally, the migrants numbered 115 families, "without counting the new arrivals." The date of arrival of the 115 families is unfortunately not indicated by Iorga; perhaps it was well before 1451. (The eighteen families, Iorga notes, made up a *scuvyna*. Perhaps this word is related to Serbo-Croatian *skupina*, "group," "batch," "assembly," etc. Was the *scuvyna* a group or clan of related families?)

13. Thiriet, *Régestes*, vol. 3, no. 2866, of 26 July 1451, pp. 169-170. Iorga's summary of this document ("Notes et extraits," p. 79, last 6 lines) is very incomplete.

14. The senate document calls the Thermísi salt pond the finest in the Levant, "a fount of gold" (*un pozo d'oro*) that could supply all of Morea (Thiriet, *Régestes*, vol. 3, p. 169n.).

15. The winter pastures in question were no doubt on the south shores of Argolis and in the Kranídi peninsula. Some of the pastures could well have been the lands in this district that, according to the response to the Naupliotes

(Thiriet, *Régestes*, vol. 3, no. 2866, par. 3), the despot and his *archontes* and subjects had encroached upon. D. Jacoby has had occasion, in another connection, to cite the relevant passage from the original register of the series *Senato, Mar*, in his *La Féodalité en Grèce médiévale* . . . (Paris and The Hague, 1971), p. 122 n. 1: "*lo territorio de Sancta Marina del Didimo et castri et altre asai campagne et territorii, i qual luogi era sempre soto la jurisdiction vestra* [i.e., of Venice] *da Napoli et Argos.*" I take *castri* to be Kastrí, the present-day Ermióni (Hermione), a village with a rather fertile territory including good grazing land. The church of Ayía Marína is still standing and in use, in the southeastern part of the basin of Didyma (Dídimo): the Hellenized Albanians (Arvanítes) of this village have been important herdsmen and stock raisers for several centuries. Cf. H. A. Koster and J. B. Koster, "Competition or Symbiosis? Pastoral Adaptive Strategies in the Southern Argolid," *Regional Variation in Modern Greece and Cyprus* . . . , Annals of the New York Academy of Sciences, vol. 268 (New York, 1976), pp. 275–285.

16. *secundum qualitatem personarum, et quantitatem ac conditionem familie.* The text of this document is in Sathas, *Documents inédits*, vol. 2 (Paris, 1881), pp. 79–80; summary in Thiriet, *Régestes*, vol. 2, no. 1051, p. 26. Jochalas ("Einwanderung," pp. 97–98), reprints the text from Sathas.

17. Sathas, *Documents inédits*, vol. 3 (Paris, 1882), pp. 287–288; text reprinted in Jochalas, "Einwanderung," p. 98. Cf. Thiriet, *Régestes*, vol. 2, no. 1985, p. 227.

18. Sathas, *Documents inédits*, vol. 1 (Paris, 1880), p. 178; cf. Thiriet, *Régestes*, vol. 2, no. 2007, p. 232.

19. Text in Sathas, *Documents inédits*, 3:319–320, where the date is given as 21 January 1426, *more veneto*; cf. Thiriet, *Régestes*, vol. 1, no. 2045, p. 241.

20. Text in Sathas, *Documents inédits*, 2:65–66, dated 16 February 1401, *more veneto*.

21. "*locis nostris campestribus et pratis ut possent permanere et vivere cum eorum animalibus ut est moris eorum.*" Sathas, *Documents inédits*, 1:176; full text of decree on this page; summary in Thiriet, *Régestes*, vol. 2, no. 1985, p. 227.

22. On the recent acquisition of these places by Venice, and on the problem of their identification, see A. Bon, *La Morée franque: Recherches historiques* . . ., text ed. (Paris, 1969), pp. 284–290, 431–436, and Jacoby, *Féodalité en Grèce médiévale*, pp. 231–232.

23. Herodotus, VIII, 73 (cf. *Herodotus the Histories*, trans A. de Sélincourt, Penguin Classics, p. 522). For the ethnic situation at this time, see the striking passage by the Byzantine satirist, Mazaris, in *Mazaris' Journey to Hades* . . . , *Greek Text with Translation* . . ., Seminar Classics 609 (Buffalo: State University of New York at Buffalo, 1975), pp. 76 ff., and pp. xii and 118 for notes and references.

24. Text in Sathas, *Documents inédits*, 1:269–271. We can assume that the Venetians provided the transports for the crossing from the Elian coast. Three

villages are named: Vomero (= Voúmero, officialy Goúmero), Olena, the old episcopal see, and Chilidoni (= Chelidóni); all three exist today.

25. Drin, the river flowing out of Lake Ohrid through east and north Albania to the Adriatic.

26. Sathas, *Documents inédits*, 1:269–271, *parchi e villani* (p. 269, line 29); and *parchi* (p. 270, line 5), i.e. *paroikoi*, "serfs," on Byzantine estates.

27. The document we are analyzing is the testimony (*depositio*) that Marcello drew up at the request of envoys of King Ferdinand I (Don Ferrante) of Naples, who was the suzerain of Leonardo III Tocco. He set down the articles from memory, not having before him, he remarks, their original text bearing his seal that his Greek chancellor had composed; this remained in the island.

28. Cf. the expression *expensa custodia Seraley* in Sathas, *Documents inédits*, 1:118, line 17. It is found in the senate's instructions to Dolfin Venier for his important embassy to the Greek despot in 1422 (cf. Bon, *Morée franque*, pp. 298–299), in a passage concerning the prospect of Venier subsidizing Albanian chiefs. Sathas printed "Seraley" as if it were a place-name, but it must be the common noun *serale, serrale*, "defile" (cf. Ducange, *Glossarium*, s.v., and Italian *serra*, "ravine," "narrow valley").

29. I cite certain incidents from Sathas, *Documents inédits*: vol. 4 (1882), p. 136, lines 1–19 (doc. dated 14 February 1416, i.e., 1417), p. 143, lines 23 ff. (19 May 1420), and p. 149, lines 32 ff. (10 August 1432); especially 3:175, line 16 to p. 176, line 12, and p. 177, lines 24 ff. (doc. dated 11 June 1418: cf. Thiriet, *Régestes*, vol. 2, no. 1697, pp. 164–165). See also my summary of a document of 30 August 1410, in W. A. McDonald and G. R. Rapp, Jr., eds., *The Minnesota Messenia Expedition . . .* (Minneapolis, 1972), p. 69, col. B.

Chapter 16

The Flight of the Inhabitants of Greece to the Aegean Islands, Crete, and Mane, during the Turkish Invasions (Fourteenth and Fifteenth Centuries)

Apostolos E. Vacalopoulos,
University of Thessalonica, Emeritus,
translated by George Pilitsis

After the landing of the Turks on the peninsula of Gallipoli in 1354, a tragic historical period began for the Greeks, as well as for the other peoples of the Balkans. When the Turks had advanced toward the western regions of Asia Minor, flocks of refugees had fled toward the European shores or toward the isles of the Dodecannes, a movement we will not examine here. Similarly, after the landing at Gallipoli, many of the inhabitants of Thrace, Macedonia, and other Greek areas, especially from the large cities of Constantinople and Thessaloniki (for these at least we have explicit evidence), fled to the southern parts of Greece, as far as the Peloponnesos, and most of all, to the Aegean Isles, which were under Frankish domination, and which by their nature provided greater security. Crete in particular, lying isolated in the middle of the eastern Mediterranean, was a secure castle, a true floating fort.

The subject of the flight of the people for almost a century, from 1354 to 1453, constitutes a great problem for which no systematic study has been made as yet. Such a study constitutes a scholarly desideratum. In my *History of Modern Hellenism*, I tried to touch upon various points of the problem, to appropriately stress its significance, and to arrive at certain conclusions. Here, I gather certain attestations and discuss certain views concerning the flight of the Greek population to Mane and to the Aegean Isles only, with the hope that some young scholar, having more time available to him, will take it upon himself to study in a broader and more systematic manner this sociopolitical subject, which has many interesting aspects.

Tzympe, on the peninsula of Gallipoli, captured in 1352,[1] and Gallipoli itself, seized in 1354, constituted the solid bridgeheads of the Turks. There followed the conquest of Thrace, Macedonia, Epirus, and the southern areas of Greece, attended by plunder and destruction that brought disorder and misery to the inhabitants and resulted in the general retrogression of civilization. As a result, the Greeks from the north began to flee to the Aegean Islands, in the hope of escaping the sufferings of slavery. They first fled to those islands that lay near the Thracian and Macedonian shores, especially to Thasos, and to the isle of Euboea, in which some people settled permanently, and to places even further south.

Although the relevant information is lacking, the science of linguistics can be very useful. Thus, in the more southern islands of Tenos, Andros, Myconos, and Syra, I. K. Voyatzides locates settlements of northern Greeks from the area of Chalkidike by observing the relationship of their dialect with the corresponding one of specific locations of the above-mentioned islands, that is, mutation and change of the unaccented *e* and *o* to *i* and *ou* (a phenomenon of northern vowelization). He dates these settlements exactly in the period under discussion, that is, between 1364 and 1413.[2]

The evacuation of the capital, as well as, undoubtedly, of other cities (even though we do not have information about them) occurred at a rapid pace from the end of the fourteenth century, mainly during the long-lasting siege of Constantinople from 1391 to 1398.[3] The effects of this flight of the inhabitants became evident soon after the siege of the city: economic decay; and the ruin of palaces, buildings, churches, and monasteries, which the Spaniard Clavijo witnessed in 1403.[4] People fled on boats to the isles beyond the Propontis and the Hellespont, mainly to the Venetian-held island of Crete. But life there was very difficult for the refugees.[5] Crete had for decades been a well-known place of refuge, known even to faraway Pontos: thus, in 1363 the Venetians had agreed to the settlement of Armenian families in Crete and even in Methone;[6] and in 1414 another eighty families from Trebizond, Sivas, and other places were settled in Crete or Euboea.[7] This, I think, explains the similarities between the dress of the people of the Pontic shores and of the interior (e.g., the area of Amaseia) to the Cretan dress.

Important for my topic is the campaign of Musa, son of Bayezid, in Macedonia and Thrace, and his sieges of Thessaloniki and Constantinople in the years 1411–1413. At this time, Musa was trying to prevail over his brothers, Suleiman and Mehmet, in order to take over the throne.[8] During these campaigns, many people had fled to different areas of Greece that were under Venetian rule. Musa, pursuing Orchan, the young son of Suleiman, whom he captured and blinded, reached the outskirts of Thessaloniki but was not able to conquer it. He only destroyed the suburb Hortiatis, which lies outside the city.[9] When, with the victory of Mehmet I (1413-1421) in the civil war, peace was restored in the Near East, the Greek refugees (we do not know whether a few or many) asked the Venetian authorities for permission to repatriate. The Venetian Senate granted them the permission in October 1415.[10] It seems, however, that certain families delayed their return for several months, because we see that, on 12 January 1417, the Venetian Senate granted permission to certain families from Thessaloniki to return from Euboea to their country, from which they had fled during the time of Musa's hostilities.[11]

From the middle of the fourteenth century, as we see, there was a flocking of Greek and Armenian populations mainly to Crete, to such villages as Armenoi, outside Chania—preserved to the present day. There was, at the same time, direct communication with Constantinople, installation of teachers and scribes (like the monk, Athanasios,[12] and Ioannis Symeonakis),[13] and a transfusion of educational and artistic currents that exercised a great influence on the later development of the island.

With Murad II's accession to the throne, and after the sieges of Thessaloniki and Constantinople by the Turkish armies, these cities continued to be evacuated by the terrified inhabitants. The Greek population fled to the still-free regions or to those under Frankish rule, mainly to the islands of the Aegean. Ioannis Anagnostis,[14] the historian of Thessaloniki's fall (1430), makes reference to the desertion of the city by her inhabitants, as does a request that the people of Thessaloniki submitted to Venice through their representatives in 1429. In this, they observed that

many leave Thessaloniki, forced by the absence of means of preservation. Because of the long-lasting war, that is seven years, they have decided to sell all their belongings, and after having exhausted everything, they depart, as if condemned, and with tears in their eyes, in search of means of existence, and in order to live through this until the Lord our God will consent to change the situation. They all depart with the hope that they will return to their homes. But unfortunately, after their departure, their houses are seized and demolished, as also their trees and other possessions are being destroyed, which is a great injustice. Similar acts force those who leave to lose every hope of returning one day to their homes. That is why we beg of Your Lordship to provide accordingly.[15]

Unfortunately, the documents do not mention the places of destination of the refugees; however, this is easy to guess. The first island stop would, of course, have been the Northern Sporades (to these islands, refugees from Chalkidike and the area around Olympus fled during the Greek revolution of 1821).[16] But at that time these islands, despite being under Byzantine sovereignty, were pirates' nests and essentially ungoverned, and thus unsuitable for refuge.[17] Consequently, the fleeing Thessalonians would have headed toward Euboea, as they had in the past. After all, there was in Euboea a central government, a strong base, and a naval squadron.[18] A number of Thessalonians surely must have returned to their city after its fall, obeying the decree of Murad II that recalled them, with the promise that he would give them "everything, buildings and property, churches and monasteries and the sources of their revenues," because he wished to resettle the city.[19] But most of them regretted it, especially after the sultan's decision (after July 1432) to seize the churches and monasteries with their revenues, to make records of the homes of the present and absent inhabitants, and then to grant the most beautiful buildings to his family members and officers, as well as to a thousand Turkish settlers who had come from Genitsa.[20]

As the fall of Constantinople came closer, the noose around the city became tighter, and the flow of her people to more secure places continued, with the consequence of economic decay.[21] Many post-Byzantine legends talk about the flight of prominent families to the large islands of the Aegean.[22] Long before their flight, several homonymous families (i.e., families that shared the cognomen of the great Byzantine families of Komnenos, Palaiologos, etc., and that may have had a distant or even close relationship with them) surely must have been residing in these islands.[23] Other families—for instance, Palaiologoi, Komnenoi, and Phocades in Syra—arrived on the island in the end of the sixteenth and the beginning of the seventeenth century, perhaps like others with the same cognomen who arrived in Andros and perhaps in various other islands of the then-duchy of the Aegean. They came at the time Ioannis Komnenos, an Athenian Catholic, governed those islands, or rather functioned as a tax farmer for the Sublime Porte.[24] The traveler Dallaway, certainly echoing a local tradition, reports that, in 1452, many Greeks, considering the fall of Constantinople imminent, withdrew to Mytilene and from there they scattered to the Peloponnesos and afterward to other islands.[25]

The oral tradition of Thasos preserves the information that many inhabitants of Constantinople (in my opinion many years before the fall and perhaps even during the siege) found protection in this island. They built there two neighboring settlements, namely the Ano Polites and the Kato Polites, in a location three-quarters of an hour distant from the village of Theologos. They also built the churches of Saint Constantine and Saint Charalampos in the two settlements, respectively. The inhabitants still show the few remaining ruins of these settlements. In this island, one comes across family names such as Laskaris, Komnenos, Skleros, Gavras, Vranas, Palaiologos, Lovoulos (from the Byzantine Olovolos), and others. Several feminine proper names also have a Byzantine origin, for example, Pokaukina (from the masculine Apokaukos), Skamandriani, Louvolina, Doukaina.[26] How and when did these settlements disappear? I think that their abandonment and destruction must have been the result of the raids of pirates who ravaged the Aegean during the first centuries of the Turkish domination. The people must have fled to the village of Theologos, which is the farthest removed from the shore.

The people of the islands near the Dardanelles, such as Thasos, Lemnos, Imbros, equally panic stricken because of the imminence of the fall, contemplated flight, and some of them, certainly the wealthiest, carried it out. Thus, about two hundred of them with their women and children left, some for Crete, others for Chios, and others for Euboea.[27] The Chiot historian Aimilia Sarou-Zolota writes about the flight of the Constantinopolitans to Chios:

> Then countless Byzantines, almost all of whose last names can be found in the archives [of the Latin bishopric of Chios] took refuge in Chios, then under Genoese domination. The swarming of people, who took refuge in Chios at the time of the Fall was such, that serious epidemic diseases broke out there, as we are informed by the Genoese documents of those years, when Galeazzo Longo was governor, or *potestas*, of the island. He was a man of action, and also a brother of Giovanni Longo Giustiniani, the defender of the City. Galeazzo showed great concern for the noble refugees.[28]

Perhaps in the future new evidence may be found in the Genoese archives that will broaden our knowledge regarding this interesting topic.

An official document has survived, providing the information that, during the ill-omened day of the fall, many Greek families, mainly nobles—Komnenoi, Lascarids, Palaiologoi, Notarades, Bardas, Metaxas, and others—fled on the galley of the Genoese Zorzi Doria, first to Chios and from there to Chania in Crete. From there, some of the families scattered in Crete; others went to the Peloponnesos, and others to Zacynthus, Cephallonia, and Corfu. Their descendants have survived to this day in some of these places.[29]

From Chios, it also seems that some crossed over to the more isolated and secure island of Ikaria. They hid themselves in the woods, where they lived isolated from the outside world because of the pirate raids of the Turks from the shores of Asia Minor during the fifteenth and sixteenth centuries.[30] The Jesuit, P. Sauger, who knew the Aegean Islands at the end of the seventeenth century, reported that most of the inhabitants who had such famous names as Palaiologos, Komnenos, Kantakouzenos, and others were the impoverished descendants of Byzantine exiles who had become charcoal makers and woodcutters.[31] His view is certainly not correct. Perhaps these were the descendants of refugees. Although the isolated inhabitants, few in number, were in a miserable state economically, the traveler, Sandwich, half a century later, that is during the middle of the eighteenth century, reports:

> they are endowed with a greater share of pride than any people throughout the whole Levant; since esteeming themselves descendants of the royal family of the Porphyrogeniti, upon account of their nobility they refuse all intermarriages and alliances with those of the adjacent islands, deeming them a people far beneath them in point of rank and quality. Throughout the whole island there are about five villages, none of which contain above one hundred houses; the inhabitants whereof, notwithstanding their royal blood, have very great difficulty to support themselves out of the products of their country.[32]

After the conquest of the Peloponnesos by Mehmet II in 1460, some refugees fled to Crete. Many of them had originated from

Constantinople and now had become refugees twice within seven years. These nobles, clergymen, intellectuals, and such were the uprooted, the restless, unable to forget the splendor of Byzantium, and they aroused the suspicions of the Venetian government. Among them was someone by the name of Ioannis Argyropoulos from Constantinople, perhaps the well-known great scholar *"habitator ville de Zechari tractat contra statum nostrum."* The Council of Ten ordered, on 19 June 1461, information to be collected about this individual and also "to watch carefully over the Greeks who would be coming from Constantinople and the Peloponnese, as well as over all the priests and monks."[33]

Because of the revolutionary proclamations against the Venetian government that were scattered in public places and in the houses of Rhethymno and the surrounding villages, the refugees were regarded as participating in a conspiracy. For this reason, the Council of Ten ordered, on 22 June 1461, the most suspicious to be arrested and banished. Specifically, the refugee monks and priests were to be exiled to Corfu and the surrounding areas.[34]

The refugee clergymen from Constantinople and the Peloponnesos were in ferment not only in Crete but also in Corfu, where they formed an organization (*collegium*) consisting of twelve members. The Council of Ten learned about it. Having in mind the revolt of 28 August 1458 in Crete, and because it was informed that the priests "commit unheard of felonies, that the administration takes no measures for the suppression of the disturbances," and that the archbishop does not get involved any more without the council's permission, on 21 July the council informed the governor of Corfu not to permit any longer the existence of this organization, or any kind of meeting.[35]

The Constantinopolitan nobles, seeing from Corfu that the hopes they had placed upon the crusading activities of the Despot of the Peloponnesos, Thomas Palaiologos, in Italy were in vain, slowly began to scatter here and there, lamenting their fate.[36] Some of them settled permanently in Corfu. Among them was George Sphrantzes, the former *protovestiarios* of the last tragic emperor, Constantine XI Palaiologos; in 1486, under the constant exhortations of the noble Corfiots and of his compatriots, Sphrantzes began to record his memoires of the tragic events of the fall of the Byzantine Empire.[37]

Eight years after the fall of Constantinople, in 1461, Trebizond was conquered by the Turks. The historian of this city, Savvas Ioannides, wrote, based on surviving oral tradition, that the nobles of Trebizond scattered in the islands of the Aegean, in the Peloponnesos, in Italy, and elsewhere.[38] This tradition can not be considered totally untenable if one remembers that, about one hundred years earlier, Armenian families (Greeks, I suspect, from Pontos) had asked to settle in Crete and that the Venetians had their own representatives in Trebizond.[39] What prevents us then from accepting the possibility that, several years before the fall of Trebizond (1461) and even after, the inhabitants left for the Aegean and particularly for Venetian-ruled Crete and Messenia? For some of the refugees, it was not at all difficult to go from the latter region to Mane. However, the tradition that a certain Stephanos, son of Alexios I Komnenos (1081–1118), supposedly fled to Mane because of a murder and then became the ancestor of the family of Stephanopouloi, is certainly a product of the imagination of that family.[40] Furthermore, the documents that Demetrios Stephanopoulos, a French officer of Greek descent, presented to the king of France, Louis XVI, were probably forged and fake. These documents, which were accepted as genuine after being examined by his archivist, Cherin (reasons of friendship made him be agreeable to the family of Stephanopoulos), prove that the Stephanopouloi of Mane descend from Nikephoros, the only son of David Komnenos to survive the general massacre of his family in Constantinople on 1 November 1463.[41] Nevertheless, we do not reject as totally untrustworthy the tradition that people from Trebizond sought refuge in the Peloponnesos and, ultimately, in Mane.

Already in 1782, the Count de Choiseul-Gouffier, having perhaps in mind the above-mentioned documents and the matter of the nobility of Demetrios Stephanopoulos, mentions for the first time, in the prologue of his book *Voyage pittoresque*, the flight of the Komnenoi, Palaiologoi, Phocades, and Lascarids to Mane.[42] This is also cited in 1790, in the book of the abbot Della Rocca, general vicar of Syra, *Traité complet sur les abeilles*.[43] Surely with de Choiseul-Gouffier's book in mind, he talks about the arrival of the Komnenoi, Lascarids, Phocades, and Kantakouzenoi in Mane, and also about their descendants, who were still living there. He himself accepts and supports the view that the last one to take refuge there was Nikephoros Komnenos, who was even called "Protogeros," or as he says, first senator, or as we would rather say, the president or the head man of the district of Mane. Della Rocca also regards the document, which had been brought to King Louis, as authentic.

The tradition of their descent from the Komnenoi was also

preserved by the family of the Gregorakides of Mane, as Anastasios N. Goudas mentions. It is alleged that a member of this family escaped from Constantinople and found refuge there. Goudas himself, however, regards as probable the tradition that the family was a native one.[44]

More clear is the problem of the flight of Byzantine families to Mane from the Byzantine mainland of the Peloponnesos during the first campaign of Mehmet II in the Peloponnesos (1458)[45] and also at the time of the destruction of the despotate of the Morea (1460). Even greater was the flight after the outbreak of the Venetian-Turkish war of 1463-1479. It is clearly testified that many inhabitants of Mistra had taken refuge in the surrounding natural strongholds—*catafigi*, as they are called in the Venetian texts of that period. It seems that crowds of refugees accumulated in mountainous Tsakonia, as well as in the inhospitable and isolated peninsula of Mane, upsetting the natural distribution of the population.

This disorder, the resistance of the Peloponnesians and the Albanians who were being guided and helped in their operations by the Venetians, as well as the anarchy that reigned in this important region of the Ottoman Empire, disturbed the Turks greatly. Thus, the sultan again sent there the vizier Mahmout, who knew the people and the affairs of the area. Along with Omer, son of Turahan the governor of Thessaly, Mahmout invaded the Peloponnesos in October 1465. He employed Asanes Matthaios, brother in-law of Demetrios Palaiologos, to persuade those who fled to the various castles to return to the city. Moreover, Asanes sent envoys to Mane and Tsakonia and tried to blame the Venetians for being the cause of future misfortunes. He tried to persuade the inhabitants to return to their homes without any fear, because, according to the decrees of the sultan, no one was to harm them. Some were, in fact, convinced by his words and secretly returned home, while others were afraid and hesitated. They were expecting to hear some good news regarding the advance of the Hungarians to the south. The Venetians were comforting them and encouraging them by circulating the information that the Hungarians would soon cross the Danube and spread over the enslaved Balkan countries, while they themselves would advance from the Isthmus to the Hellespont. It seems that those who hesitated to leave their shelters settled in them permanently, throughout the period of the Turkish occupation.[46]

Even later, after the surrender of Nauplia by the Venetians to the Turks in 1540, it is not surprising to see that members of the De Medici family of this city sought refuge in Prasto of Kynuria and from there in Oetylo in Mane. They appeared in Mane in the beginning of the seventeenth century.[47] Also, the Atzagioles (Acciaiuoli) appeared in Messenia. We see, for example, the poet Ioannis Atzagiolis, descendant of the old Frankish dynasties of Corinth and Athens, who was, in all probability, the governor of Korone in 1532.[48]

Notes

1. See H. Inalcik, "Gelibolu," in the *Encyclopedia of Islam*, new ed. (1954).

2. See I. K. Voyiatzides, "Glossa kai laographia tes nesou Androu," *Andriaka Chronika* 4 (1949):51-56.

3. See A. E. Vacalopoulos, *Origins of the Greek Nation, the Byzantine Period 1204-1461* (New Brunswick, N.J., 1970), pp. 79, 302-303, with relevant bibliography, Cf. idem, *Historia tou Neou Hellenismou*, 2d ed. (Thessalonica, 1974), 1:151.

4. Clavijo, *Embassy to Tamerlane, 1403-1406*, trans. Guy Le Strange (London, 1928), p. 88.

5. R.-J. Loenertz, *Correspondance de Manuel Calécas* (Rome, 1950), pp. 264-265.

6. Freddy Thiriet, *Régestes des délibérations du Sénat de Venise concernant la Romanie*, vol. 1, *1329-1399* (Paris, 1958), nos. 1329-1399, pp. 105, 107.

7. Ibid., 1:120.

8. See "Musa Celebi" in *Enzyklopaedie des Islam* (1936) 3:799; Max Braun, *Lebensbeschreibung des Despoten Stefan Lazarević von Konstantin dem Philosophen* (Wiesbaden, 1956), pp. 31 ff.

9. Braun, *Lebensbeschreibung*, pp. 50-51.

10. N. Jorga, *Notes et extraits pour servir à l'histoire des croisades au XV siècle*, 1st s., vol. 1 (Paris, 1889), p. 240.

11. Ibid., p. 259.

12. R.-J. Loenertz, *Démétrius Cydonès, Correspondance*, (Vatican, 1947), p. 364.

13. S. G. Mercati, "Di Giovani Simeonakis, Protopapa di Candia," *Miscellanea G. Mercati* 3 (1946):312-314. Cf. B. Laourdas, "Kretika Palaiografica," *Kretika Chronika* 2 (1948):539-545, with bibliography.

14. I. Anagnostes, ed. I. Bekker (Bonn, 1838), pp. 526-527; idem, *Narration on the Last Fall of Thessaloniki* (in Greek), ed. G. Tsaras (Thessalonica, 1958), p. 67.

15. C. D. Mertzios, *Monuments of Macedonian History* (in Greek) (Thessalonica, 1947), pp. 78-79.

16. A. E. Vacalopoulos, *Refugees and the Refugee Problem during the Greek Revolution of 1821* (in Greek) (Thessalonica, 1939), pp. 21-27.

17. A. E. Bacalopulos, "Les limites de l'empire byzantin depuis la fin du XIV siècle jusqu'à sa chute (1453)," *BZ*, 55 (1962):56-65 with bibliography.

18. Freddy Thiriet, *La Romanie Vénitienne au Moyen Age*, (Paris, 1959), pp. 210-211, 363 ff.

19. Anagnostes, Bonn ed., p. 521; idem, *Fall of Thessaloniki*, p. 54.

20. A. E. Vacalopoulos, "Symbole eis ten historian tes Thessalonikes mikron meta ten halosin autes tou 1430 hypo tōn Tourkōn," *Gregorios Palamas* 20 (1936):7-15.

21. Pero Tafur, *Travels and Adventures 1435-1439*, trans. and ed. with an introduction by Malcolm Letts (New York and London, 1926), pp. 145-146.

22. O. Dapper, *Description exacte des îsles de l'Archipel* (Amsterdam, 1703), p. 17.

23. See I. Bekker, ed., *Laonici Chalcocondylae historiarum libri decem* (Bonn, 1843), pp. 564-565; E. Darkó, ed., *Laonici Chalcocandylae historiarum demonstrationes*, vol. 2 (Budapest, 1923), pp. 306-307; cf. K. Sathas, ed., *Documents inédits relatifs à l'histoire de la Grèce au Moyen Age*, vol. 6 (Paris, 1884), p. 23; cf. also the word *Comino*, on p. 52.

24. Vacalopoulos, *Historia tou Neou Hellenismou* (Thessalonica, 1968), 3:287-288, with bibliography. On the Palaiologoi and Chalcocondyles of Athens, cf. ibid., 2d ed. (1974), 2:364, with bibliography.

25. Jacques Dallaway, *Constantinople ancienne et moderne et description des côtes et Isles de L'Archipel et de la Troade* (Paris, year vii = 1798-1799), 2:139.

26. A. E. Vacalopoulos, *Thasos, son histoire, son administration de 1453 à 1912* (Paris, 1953), p. 16.

27. Critoboulos, in C. Müller, *Fragmenta historicorum graecorum*, I, 75, 2.

28. Aimilia Sarou-Zolota, "To archeion tes Latinikes episkopes Chiou," *Byzantinisch-Neugriechische Jahrbücher* 14 (1937/1938):425-426. Cf. G. Zolotas, *Historia tes Chiou* (Athens, 1924), 2:560.

29. K. D. Mertzios, "Peri Palaiologōn kai allōn eugenōn Konstantinoupolitōn," in *Geras Keramopoulou* (Athens, 1953), pp. 359-361. Cf. Vacalopoulos, *Origins of the Greek Nation*, pp. 215, 351, with bibliography.

30. Ioannis Melas, *The history of the Island of Ikaria* (in Greek) (Athens, 1955), 1:147, 159-160.

31. P. Sauger, *Historia tōn archaeōn doukōn kai loipōn hegemonōn tou Aegeou pelagous . . .*, trans. Alex M. Karalis (Hermoupolis, 1878), ("He parousa katastasis," p. 15).

32. Earl of Sandwich, *A Voyage round the Mediterranean in the Years 1738 and 1739* (London, 1799), p. 322.

33. See V. Lamansky, *Secrets d'état de Venise* (Saint Petersburg, 1884), pp. 045-047.

34. Lamansky, ibid., pp. 047 ff. Cf. also M. I. Manousakas, *The Conspiracy*

of Sephes Vlastos in Crete (1453-1454) and the New Conspiracy Plot of 1460-1462 (in Greek) (Athens, 1960), pp. 71-156 passim.

35. Lamansky, ibid., p. 049.

36. Georgius Phrantzes, *Chronicon*, ed. I. Bekker (Bonn, 1838), p. 412.

37. Ibid., pp. 425-453.

38. Savvas Ioannides, *Historia kai statistike Trapezountos kai tes peri tauten horas, hos kai ta peri tes entaftha hellenikes glosses* (Constantinople, 1870), p. 119.

39. Thiriet, *Régestes*, 1:25.

40. Cf. G. C. Pappadopoulos, *Chronographia peri tes katagoges ton en te Mane Stephanopoulaion* (Athens, 1865), p. 11, 5-9.

41. Pappadopoulos, *Chronographia*, pp. 12-14. William Miller, *Trebizond, 1204-1461*, anastatic ed. (Chicago, 1969), pp. 113-114. Cf. also Patrice Stephanopolis, *Histoire des Grecs en Corse* (Paris, 1900), pp. 147 ff., 181, 206, which rejects the authenticity of the titles. Cf. Vacalopoulos, *Origins of the Greek Nation*, p. 227.

42. *Voyage pittoresque dans l'empire Ottoman*, 2d ed. (Paris, 1842), 1:l.

43. *Traité complet sur les abeilles* (Paris, 1790), 1:150-154.

44. For these legends see A. N. Goudas, *Vioi paralleloi* (Athens, 1876), 8:1-3.

45. F. Miklosich and J. Müller, *Acta et diplomata Graeca Medii aevi sacra et profana* (Vienna, 1865), 3:290.

46. Vacalopoulos, *Historia tou Neou Hellenismou* (1968), 3:33-34, with bibliography.

47. M. G. Lamprynides, "Hoi Medikoi en Helladi," in *Ethnikon Hemerologion*, Const. Ph. Skokos 15 (1900), p. 362.

48. See George T. Zoras, *Ioannou Axagiolou diegesis synoptike Karolou tou V* (Athens, 1964), pp. 31-34, with bibliography. Cf. also Vacalopoulos, *Historia tou Neou Hellenismou* (1974), 1:344.

Chapter 17

Travelers as a Source for the Societies of the Middle East: 900–1600

Speros Vryonis, Jr., *University of California at Los Angeles and University of Athens*

It is perhaps redundant for me to commence my talk with remarks specifically relevant to this occasion, redundant, for the man we are honoring on this occasion is well known to all of you. As I gaze upon the audience my eye alights upon members of his family, upon his colleagues, upon his many students and friends. All of you have known Professor Charanis well, and in many cases far longer than I and so whatever I might say at this moment would do nothing more than confirm what you already know by immediate and long experience. Therefore the few words that I shall address to you in this respect will only serve to confirm what Professor Charanis's family, colleagues, and students already know well.

It is difficult for me to express the honor, the pleasure, and the gratitude I feel in accepting Professor Schlatter's invitation to participate in today's ceremony. I did not have the privilege of being Professor Charanis's student at Rutgers, nor have I ever been his colleague in this great institution. Nevertheless, in another sense I have been his student ever since I began to read his contributions to the field of Byzantine studies and have always felt that I was a colleague, privileged to share discussions and opinions with him. In all of this I always came away enriched and pleased with what Professor Charanis managed to impart to me. Indeed this has been an experience shared by many other scholars in the field, all of whom have derived intellectual stimulation and encouragement from the written and spoken words of Professor Charanis.

As I first became initiated into the field of Byzantine scholarship I naturally encountered the written word of Professor Charanis and found this to be a sure guide to my own understanding of scholarly learning and research. Some years later I actually met Professor Charanis at his home, in the company of the late George

Soulis, and from that time I began to know the person, not only the scholarly research and publications, and found therein a great force of personality. The two personal traits that characterize the man and that reverberate throughout all his scholarly being are truth and passion. Truth is the essence of all scholarship, and passion is the essence of humanity. I have known scholars who, while exemplary in their scholarly objectivity, have perpetrated the unforgivable sin of carrying this passionless outlook into their lives as human beings. Contrarywise, the passionate human being who is not able to shed his passions when he enters the field of scholarship is, for me, an equal disaster. Professor Charanis has remained a paragon of the type of objective scholar–passionate human. It is perhaps banal for me to have stated this, but if so, it is none the less true that it is precisely for this reason that I esteem and honor Professor Charanis as a scholar who pursues the truth relentlessly and who remains a human being of great warmth and feelings. These are the marks of a great teacher and scholar.

It remains, perhaps, for me to say a word by way of justifying the choice of the topic, travelers as a source for the societies of the Middle East, 900–1600. Before the Renaissance and early modern era, the historian has a very meager body of source materials on the basis of which to reconstruct the history and societies of the Middle East during these earlier periods. Archival materials have largely disappeared, and for the time before the appearance of the vast Ottoman and Venetian archives in the fifteenth and sixteenth centuries, the historian has to piece things together on the basis of what little has accidentally survived. Thus the body of travel literature assumes a disproportionate importance for the period prior to the emergence of the vast state archives, and even afterward this body of material retains a substantial and supplementary importance. The topic is, therefore, justified by the overall importance of the material as a historical source; but there is a second aspect of the subject that, it seems to me, justifies its treatment on this occasion. The travelers were enterprising spirits who dared to go forth into the unknown or to brave dangers of great proportions. It is they who charted (for their own societies) the unknown of other societies and the geographic regions little or completely unknown. They represent one of the most attractive traits of the human mind: restless curiosity. In this respect I think that Professor Charanis will feel at home with the subject and will recognize in Marco Polo, Ibn Battuta, and other travelers kindred spirits. For he too has been a pioneer; has helped to chart the waters of Byzantine scholarship; has plumbed the depths of Byzantine ethnography, society, and economics; has trained a group of excellent students who in turn have pushed forward on the frontiers of Byzantine knowledge; and has made of Rutgers University one of the important centers of Byzantine studies. When Professor Charanis undertook all this, Byzantine studies were in their infancy, virtually unknown in the United States. Today they are an established part of the American university curriculum and of American scholarly life.

Is the subject of travelers and travel accounts a serious subject that merits intensive research? When we think of travelers today, we think of hotels, guides, tourist offices, for long trips to foreign lands are considered quite ordinary and are accessible to large numbers of individuals who manage to accumulate sufficient savings from their salaries to take these trips. This is especially true with the rise in the standard of living in the world after 1945. Further, contemporary travel books do not have any substantial historical value. Popular books such as Henry Miller's *Colossus of Maroussi* and Patrick Lee Fermour's books on Greece are chiefly enjoyable for their descriptive and literary character, not for historical and sociological data. Indeed historical information about most countries is readily available in scholarly works, the informative content of which far surpasses that to be found in contemporary travel accounts. Although mass travel is a relatively modern phenomenon, even the most cursory acquaintance with ancient and medieval history will indicate that ancient and medieval man did undertake long and difficult journeys. The accounts of Herodotus, as indeed of other ancients, derive much of their charm from travel observations made by the authors, or by their informants, as for instance among the nomadic Scythians and the Egyptians.[1] Rudenko's remarkable excavations at Pazaryk have provided striking confirmation of the reliability of the observations made by Herodotus or by his informants in regard to the funeral rites of the Scythians.[2] Pausanias's travel account of the monuments of the ancient world was so accurate that modern archaeologists have utilized his account to locate such monuments.

The basic causes for travel in the Middle Ages were religious, economic, and political, but by the Renaissance the rise of humanism had variegated the causes by instilling new interests, in historical and archaeological monuments; in the study of flora and fauna; and in the collecting of manuscripts, inscriptions, coins, and works of art.[3] Travel at all times remained an arduous undertaking because of the underdeveloped nature of the technology of transportation, because of the difficulties of climate and geography, because of bandits and pirates, because of plague, because of nomadism, and finally, because of religious animosity. Yet, aside from the dynamics of commerce, politics, and religion, which made of travel a necessity, there were certain times and conditions that greatly facilitated travel. Political unification of large areas provided maximum security for travelers, upkeep for roads, and political stability. Thus the creation of the great Islamic Empire, the enforcement of the Pax Mongolica in the latter half of the thirteenth century, and the emergence of the powerful Ottoman Empire in the late-fifteenth and early-sixteenth centuries provided conditions felicitous for intensive travel activity in the Middle East. Muslim and Christian states built caravansaries, xenodochia, *fondachi*;[4] they regulated maritime and land travel; and they often tried to protect merchants, ambassadors, and religious officials who traveled through their realms.

The travel literature that deals with the Middle East between 900 and 1600 is largely, though not exclusively, Muslim, up to the time of the crusades, and thereafter an increasingly large travel literature appears in the West. Let me first say a few words about these two bodies of travel literature, single out a few of the most interesting and the most characteristic travel accounts, and demonstrate the rich variety and interest of this material.

It is noteworthy that, although both Islamic and Western civilization produced substantial and important travel literature, the genre is largely absent from Byzantine literature, a fact that is somewhat puzzling inasmuch as we know that the Byzantine state kept extensive diplomatic archives from the various missions of its legates and ambassadors to foreign courts. It is equally striking that, whereas the ancient Greek geographers are fundamental in the development of that discipline, the Byzantines largely abandoned the geographic genre for a thousand years. The first real break in this Byzantine tradition, in the tradition that ignores geography and travel literature, comes at the end of the empire in the history of Chalcocondyles.[5] This historian, a close imitator of Herodotus and Thucydides, includes long excurses on the ethnography, history, and institutions of the Russians, South Slavs, Arabs and Turks, Roumanians, Italians, French, Germans, and English. His interest in all these non-Greek peoples is startling given the complete lack of interest the majority of Byzantine authors had previously shown, and it indicates that he had abandoned the traditional Byzantine literary attitude toward such subjects.

It was the Arabs, not the Byzantines, who fell heirs to the classical geographic and ethnographic traditions and who pursued this double genre with a certain freshness and a very observing and discerning eye. A sampling of this literature at once reflects the poverty of Byzantine geographic and travel literature and the immature and simplistic nature of the earlier Western equivalent literature. There are three basic phases in the emergence of this important literature in the Islamic world. First was the rapid expansion of the Arabs in the seventh century and the foundation of the Umayyad Empire, which brought the Arabs into contact with India, Iran, Syria, Africa, and Spain, all lands new and largely unknown to them. Prior to this expansion, Arab geographic lore was primitive and limited to the narrow world of the Arabian peninsula, where it was concerned only with local toponymy. The basic sources for this geographic lore were the Koran and pre-Islamic poetry. With the astonishing conquests of the seventh century, the Arabs had to become acquainted with new worlds, peoples, climates, institutions; and a certain basic geographic knowledge was necessary for the successful administration and economic exploitation of their new empire. Thus the first reason for the emergence of this literature was essentially administrative and practical.

As this data began to accumulate, it was necessary to codify it within a scientific or theoretical structure. This occurred with the great work of translations from Sanscrit, probably from Persian, and certainly from Greek, which so vitalized Islamic society and civilization from the ninth through the eleventh centuries. With the foundation of the *bayt al-hikma* in Baghdad and the fervid translation activities from Greek into Arabic, the works of the Greek geographers, astronomers, mathematicians, and philosophers were rendered into Arabic; and so Arab intellectuals were provided with the necessary theoretical framework to codify Arabic geography, *djughrafiya*, into a scientific discipline.[6] This is the second phase in the development of this literature.

The third and final phase was the branching off of travel literature from *djughrafiya* and its extensive development from the twelfth century onward. This was closely tied first to the *hadj*, or pilgrimage to the holy cities of Arabia, a trip enjoined upon all the faithful; then to the widespread commercial activities of Muslim merchants; but also to the ease with which Muslims, no matter of what ethnic background, were free to travel from Spain to India and yet still remain within Islamic civilization; and to the increasing diplomatic and missionary activities of various Muslim states. Thus we see that intellectual and political conditions were fundamental in the creation of a rich geographic and travel literature in the Islamic Middle Ages.

Though not the most spectacular of these Arab travelers, Ibn Hawkal of Nisibis in Mesopotamia is in many ways typical.[7] He was at one and the same time a merchant, a religious missionary, and as a result of his many voyages, a geographer. His accounts are based primarily on personal observations, *iyan.* His trips, beginning in 943, continued at least until 973, during which time he traversed North Africa, Spain, the Sahara, Egypt, Armenia, Azerbaijan, Iraq, Khuzistan, Fars, Khwarezm, Transoxiana, and Sicily. Of his two works, only the "Kitab masalik wa'l mamalik" ("Book of Roads and Kingdoms") has survived; it was dedicated to Sayf ad-Dawla and went through three editions by the end of the tenth century. Aside from the importance of Ibn Hawkal as typifying the essence of the Arab travel accounts, his work extended Islamic geographic interest to non-Muslim peoples such as the inhabitants of South Italy and the Turks, Chazar, Sudanese, and Nubians.

Spectacular is the case of the Islamic genius al-Biruni, undoubtedly one of the greatest minds of the Middle Ages, both in terms of the range of his knowledge and in terms of the objectivity and freedom of spirit of inquiry.[8] A profound and original thinker, this Persian Muslim had mastered mathematics, astronomy physical sciences, history, philosophy, and of course, geography. In the last-named discipline, Biruni, as master of the Greek, Sanscritic, and Persian elements, composed the definitive, critical summation of Islamic geography. But more remarkable was his "Tarih al-Hind," "History of India."[9] Having been taken captive by the victorious Gaznevid armies, he was brought to their capital of Gazna in Afghanistan in the year 1017, and thence he accompanied the sultan Mahmoud on his great conquests in India. There he availed himself of the opportunity to study Sanscrit and the Hindu religion at the feet of Hindu scholars, and in exchange he taught them the Greek sciences. His education, experience, and observations in India were incorporated into the extraordinary "Tarih al-Hind," composed in 1030.

The "Tarih al-Hind" constitutes a unique and original book for the Middle Ages, and if one were to read it without any previous knowledge of the author and his times (and of course ignoring certain internal indications that are clearly Muslim), one might well imagine the book to be the writings of a modern philologist, sociologist, or historian. In this work, al-Biruni has undertaken, successfully, the analysis of a foreign civilization, the civilization of India. His undertaking is austerely objective, when we consider the fact that the Hindus were considered to be enemies and idolators, and when in addition we call to mind the hatred, prejudice, and ignorance with which medieval Muslims, Christians, Jews, and Hindus often wrote about each other's religions. This objectivity, so deeply rooted in the psychosynthesis of al-Biruni, was not enough in and of itself to assure the work great importance. What strikes the modern scholar is the fact that, when al-Biruni decided to describe the society of the Hindus, a society completely foreign and repulsive to Islam because of its caste system, he nonetheless proceeded to a calm, systematic analysis. Realizing that he must analyze the basic texts, he began to learn Sanscrit, and then he read the basic Sanscrit texts with his Hindu teachers. As a third task, he undertook to study the contemporary status of the society and the castes. In this manner, he analyzed and described an entire civilization, giving his description both a historical and a sociological dimension, and his work remains not only a monument to the genius of al-Biruni but an invaluable and authoritative description of the society at that time. One would look in vain for anything comparable in the literature of the contemporary Latin and Byzantine worlds.

In the latter years of the existence of the Abbasid caliphate, the Turks, a central-Asiatic people, came to play an increasingly important, and finally a dominant, role in the history of the Middle East. Muslim travel literature, and afterward, Western travel accounts, concerned themselves rather extensively with the history and culture of these new Islamic people. Fundamental in the description of their early history and society are two works in Arabic by Ibn Fadlan and Muhammud al-Kashgari.

The Abbasid caliph al-Muktadir sent Ibn Fadlan on an important diplomatic mission to the king of the Bulgars, a Turkic people whose kingdom was located astride the Volga River.[10] Ibn Fadlan brought with him an official letter from the caliph and gifts for the king and his entourage; and he was to build a mosque for the propagation of the faith, to supervise the Muslim jurists and teachers that the caliph had sent to the king, and to build a wall around the city of the Bulgar khan. The caliph was interested in aligning the pagan Turks politically against the various heretical sects and Iranian nationalists. The description of this journey, the "Rihla," is a historical document of the first order of importance for the description of Turkic society on the eve of its Islamization, for it is the most important historical source for the society of the Turkic nomads in central Asia since the Orhon inscriptions of the eighth century. It also covers a great gap in the history of this district on the northeast borders of the Islamic world between the time of the Scythians and that of the Mongols in the thirteenth century. Ibn Fadlan informs us in the introduction that he will recount all that he saw in the lands of the Turks, Chazar, Russians, Slavs, and Bashkir, in regard to their religions, their kings, and generally in regard to their customs and way of life.

Of particular interest is the description of the organization of travel and commerce in these regions, for it was through central Asia that the merchants reached the commercial emporia of China. First, Ibn Fadlan informs us that the caravan consisted of some three thousand animals and five thousand men, a vast enterprise that called for complicated organization on the part of the merchants.[11] Second, as they were traveling vast distances through sparsely settled regions that were covered with deep snows in the winter and roasted by fierce heat in the summer, the merchants had to accommodate themselves to these inclement climatic conditions by arrangements with the local inhabitants, and so Ibn Fadlan gives an account of the interesting symbiosis between the caravan merchants of the Muslim world and the Turkic nomads of the central-Asiatic steppes. No Muslim, says Ibn Fadlan, can set foot in the land of the Turks if he does not first come into contact with a Turk and establish a formal bond of friendship with him. The merchant accomplished this by making gifts of clothing for the Turk's wife, and gifts of pepper and spice as well. In return, the Turk prepares for the merchant a tent and supplies him with sheep for his table. When the Muslim merchant wishes to travel beyond, and if his camels and horses are exhausted, he leaves these with his Turkic host and borrows from him other animals and money as well. When the Muslim returns from his trip, he returns the money and the animals. If, however, the Muslim should die before returning, the Turkic host can obtain the return of animals and money from the leader of the caravan. Conversely, if the dead Muslim had owed money to the caravan, the Turkish host is expected to pay it.

If the Turkic host should go to the Muslim city of Gurganiya, then he is the guest of his Muslim friend and enjoys rights and privileges comparable to those that his Muslim friend enjoys in the steppe lands of the Turks. There is one rather bizarre difference. If the Turk should die in Gurganiya, his Muslim host, should he ever return to the land of the Turks, is then killed by the Turks (possibly a shamanistic practice).[12] In this simple description, Ibn Fadlan has outlined the basic symbiosis of merchant and nomad and the institutions that made possible Muslim contact not only with central Asia but with the rich emporium of China, an emporium that played such an important role in the commerce and material culture of the Middle East.

Of equal fascination is Ibn Fadlan's description of travel in the central Asiatic winter; he remarks that when the caravan reached the river Gaihun they found it frozen to a depth of 7 cubits, with the result that the entire caravan of three thousand animals and five thousand men was able to pass over it with all its baggage and carts. He states that it remains frozen for three months, and he notes, "We perceived that we had reached the gates of a cold hell."[13] In this icy land of the Khwarezmians, the beggars have the legal right to come inside a man's dwelling, to remain one hour by the fire, and then to ask for a piece of bread. Ibn Fadlan's caravan remained in Gurganiya from November to February because of the great cold, during which stay he relates the misadventure of two members of the caravan. These two merchants had gone out with twelve camels to gather wood for their fire, but the camels died from the cold, for the merchants had forgotten to take their flints for the lighting of the fire. The streets and market place of the town were empty of people, and Ibn Fadlan tells us that when he came out of the *hamam* his beard froze into one solid icicle. The intensity of the cold split the earth and boughs of all the trees, as well as the water fountains. After three months in Gurganiya the worst part of the winter was over, or so they thought, and the members of the caravan set out once more. Ibn Fadlan describes the veritable mountain of clothing that each merchant wore:

> Each one of us wore a qurtaq [waist coat], and on top of the qurtaq a khaftan [clothing of cotton, or camel or sheep wool], then on top of that a bustin [sheep pelt] which was covered with a kepenek [felt mantel]. Over all this we wore a skin through which only our two eyes were visible and also a simple undertrouser and a lined one. Over this were outer trousers, house boots of granulated leather and over them

another pair of boots. We were so heavily garbed that whenever we dismounted from our camels we could not budge an inch.[14]

From Gurganiya they took a Turkic guide and proceeded toward the land of the Turks. On 3 March 922 so much snow fell that the camels were sinking in it up to their knees, so that the journey halted for two days. For the next ten days they traveled without encountering a soul, only cold and more snow. It was so cold that the winter months spent at Gurganiya now appeared to the merchants to have been more like summer. In fifteen days they encountered their first Turks, and at this point Ibn Fadlan begins to describe their nomadic way of life, their customs, and their code of morality.

It is obvious that different groups of Turks have different practices and beliefs, and Ibn Fadlan so differentiates. He is, as a good Muslim, very much concerned with religion and ethics and drops the following facts about these phenomena among the nomads. They are not connected to a belief in God by any known religion. It is true that on occasion they recite the Muslim credo, but they do this only to please the anxious Muslim merchants. They do not practice religious or ethical ablutions; for instance, they do not wash themselves after sexual intercourse, or after excretion and urination. They have nothing to do with water during the winter and avoid it carefully. Ibn Fadlan warns the reader that should he find himself in such lands he must be careful of this taboo. For, he says, when a Muslim engages in sexual intercourse with a local woman and then seeks to cleanse himself with water, he must wait until nightfall so that the Turks may not see him washing himself. Should they see him, the Turks will punish him, as they believe that such a practice will hex their tribe. As to their religious beliefs, Ibn Fadlan describes phallus worship and totemism throughout the central-Asiatic steppe, facts reflecting upon a primitive state of social and religious development. His description of personal and sexual morality among the Turks is somewhat contradictory. He relates, on the one hand, that nomadic women do not hide any part of their body from men, nor do they wear a veil, as was the custom in Islam. He relates that on one occasion the wife of their Turkish host accidentally revealed her private parts, and when the Muslims displayed their embarrassment, the host related to them that the local women were moral and continent. Further, Ibn Fadlan relates, the Turks punished homosexual behavior by rending in half each of the guilty parties. Yet, from the earlier incident wherein Ibn Fadlan warned the merchants not to wash after intercourse, it is obvious that there must have been several levels of sexual behavior in nomadic society. Marriage is concluded by the paying of the bride price to the father of the bride. Once this is paid, the groom can come into the house and seize his bride whenever he so desires. On the death of the head of a household, his son inherits and marries all his wives, save for his own mother.

I have given only a brief sampling of the variety and richness of Ibn Fadlan's "Rihla," so important for the society and culture of the Turks before their Islamization and for the ties and relations that they began to experience with the Muslim world in the tenth century.

The second author, who also deals with the Turks, Muhammud al-Kashgari, is one of the most important observers to have traveled the regions of Persia, Iraq, and western portions of central Asia in the eleventh century.[15] Kashgari represents two different worlds: As a Muslim he is well versed in, and a part of, Islamic civilization, and his book, which was written in 1075, is written in Arabic and dedicated to the caliph al-Muktadir. At the same time, he is a Turk, a member of the royal family of the Karahanids (the first dynasty of Turkic nomads to found an Islamic kingdom). As a Karahanid Turk and as a Muslim, Kashgari bridges two worlds at the most crucial moment in the historical evolution of the Middle East in the later Middle Ages. It is the moment at which the political authority of the caliphate is passing from the hands of the older Muslim peoples (Arabs and Persians) into the hands of the newly arrived and recently Islamized Turks. Kashgari represents both of these worlds.

Though he was fully bilingual, in Arabic and Turkish, it is significant that he wrote his opus in Arabic and not in Turkish. He wrote his "Kitab diwan lugat at-Turk" ("Book of Collection of the Dictionary of the Turks") in Arabic because it was intended for the caliphal court and had as its object to describe for them the language, the customs, and the culture of the Turks, knowledge of which was an absolute necessity, for the Turkish conquerors were now the new masters of Islam. Consequently the older ruling class had to reorient itself to the new political circumstances. Kashgari informs the reader that he has traveled throughout central Asia, both in the steppes, where most of the Turks dwell, and in their few cities: "I travelled through all the steppes and the cities of the Turks, studying their dialects and poetry."[16] The "Kitab diwan lugat at-Turk" constitutes one of the two most important philological monuments in the history of the Turkic languages in the Middle Ages and is fundamental, along with the Orhon inscriptions, for the philological study of these languages. In explaining different words, Kashgari refers to more extensive Turkic texts, usually in proverb or poetical form, from the popular tradition. Thus scholars, in studying his dictionary, are able to cull important information on the geography, customs, popular beliefs, and basic social organizations of the Turks.

These two Arabic texts, the "Rihla" of Ibn Fadlan and the "Kitab diwan lugat at-Turk," are the compositions and observations of intelligent travelers, and without them the medieval world of the Turks in the crucial period of the tenth–eleventh centuries would have remained a closed book for us.

The last Muslim traveler-author whom I wish to mention is the renowned Moroccan Ibn Battuta, born in 1304 in Tangier, died in Morocco either in 1368 or 1377.[17] From June 1325, at the age of twenty-one when he set out on his first trip, until his death some forty-three or fifty-two years later, Ibn Battuta traveled incessantly over the continents of Europe, Asia, and Africa, and over the Mediterranean, Red, and Persian seas and the waters of China and the East Indies. The length, as well as the number, of his journeys is prodigious even in our own day, but in the fourteenth century when one had to travel by camel and sail, his accomplishments seem incredible. Let us look briefly at the schedule of some of his many journeys.

1. In June 1325 Ibn Battuta set out on his first trip, from Tangiers to Mecca, via North Africa, Egypt, and Syria, arriving in Mecca in the month of September 1326.
2. Less than two months later, November 1326, he departed from the holy Muslim city on his second trip, which took him to Iraq, Khuzistan, Fars, Djibal, Tabriz, Baghdad, Samara, Mosul, Baghdad, and back to Mecca in 1327, where he remained until 1330.
3. His third trip, largely maritime, took him over the Red Sea to Yemen, Aden, the trading ports of east Africa, and the Persian Gulf, where he joined a pilgrimage and returned to Mecca in 1332.
4. The fourth trip was even more spectacular, going from Egypt and Syria to Asia Minor, Constantinople, the lands of

the Golden Horde, Transoxiana, Afghanistan, and thence through the Indus Valley to Delhi, where he arrived in September 1333 and where he remained for the next decade.

5. In 1342 he set out for China by way of the Maldive Islands, Ceylon, Bengal, Assam, and Sumatra, finally arriving at the Chinese port of Zaytun (Ts'uan-chou).

6. In 1347 Ibn Battuta began his return via Sumatra and Malabar, then up the Persian Gulf, to Baghdad, Syria, and Egypt, and tying into a pilgrimage caravan, made his way to Mecca once more.

7. His seventh trip brought him to Egypt, where from Alexandria he set sail for Tunis in 1349, then for Sardinia on a Catalan ship, then returned to Fez by Algiers, and then visited the Christian land of Granada.

8. In 1353 he left Sidjilmasa in North Africa, crossed the Sahara, and visited the valley of the Niger, and then returned to Sidjilmasa.

Though his trips continued long after this date, it is obvious from this brief perusal of his earlier itineraries that Ibn Battuta lived most of his life traveling from one foreign land to another. How could he have lived his life thus? Again the narrative of his "Rihla" tells us something about travel and Muslim society at the same time. First, Ibn Battuta was a qadi, that is to say a Muslim judge, a learned man who knew the Koran and Islamic law. The existence of Islamic states and a relatively unified civilization from Spain to India meant that as a qadi Ibn Battuta could find, not only respect wherever he went, but also profitable employment and the patronage of the mighty. Indeed he had set out on his first trip in order to study in the schools of the most learned qadis of Mecca, but once he tasted the pleasures of travel, study of the law became secondary and travel primary. Before his first trip had ended, Ibn Battuta had decided upon the one rule that was to be his sole guide throughout life: Never travel the same road twice. He stayed in Mecca less than two months and began his series of long travels over the known world. Thereafter he utilized his professional skill in order to accommodate his passion for travel, always making it a point to ingratiate himself with, and to attach himself to, princes and governors. By his third trip he had become famous as a judge and was able to exploit his professional standing from that time on.

But this only accounts for the aspect of economic security in his life. What of family life? Again we catch a glimpse of this aspect of the society of travelers from his "Rihla." Islamic society, in contrast to Christian, did not glorify asceticism (at least not to the same degree), and indeed the physical pleasures are promised the faithful in the Koran itself when the prophet apostrophizes: "Houri and ghilman will gladden the hearts of the faithful in paradise." During the first trip, which was a hajj to the holy places, Ibn Battuta married a local beauty from Tripoli, and she and her father accompanied Ibn Battuta on the pilgrimage. So we see that long trips did not disrupt the more usual aspects of social relations.

At some point during the trip, however, it seems that the young groom and his father-in-law had differences, with the result that Ibn Battuta promptly and easily divorced his wife, and without so much as losing a breath, married the daughter of the qadi of Fez, who was also on pilgrimage. At this point Ibn Battuta halted the caravan in order to celebrate his marriage and to invite his fellow travelers to dinner and to other festivities. Throughout his travels he records the purchase of concubines and the death of his children and wives, as well as their burials, all as if this were a most natural part of travel.

In many ways his description of India and China form the most spectacular part of the work. He comments on the fact that Chinese Muslims eat not only the flesh of swine but also of dogs, that the Chinese store their gold above the sills of their house doors, and most interestingly, that whenever a foreigner enters a province he must report to the government authorities, who then have his portrait painted and copies sent throughout the province with the necessary identification of the foreigner.[18]

But in many ways the most important historical document in Ibn Battuta's "Rihla" is the description of his trip through Asia Minor in 1333.[19] It depicts Anatolian society some sixty years after the decline of the Seljuk sultanate of Rum from the attacks and conquests of the Turkish nomads, and at a time when the new nomadic emirates were just beginning to become sedentarized. Anatolia then consisted of some twenty-five or more petty Turkmen principalities, all at war with one another, and the land was only just beginning to recover from the uncontrolled nomadism that had destroyed the sultanate of Konya. Though we have another source for this period, that of the Arab geographer al-Umari, the latter was an armchair geographer who had never left his comfortable domicile in the large and distant city of Cairo.[20] He

derived his information from others and restricted his account to a
colorless recitation of the names of the Turkmen principalities,
the size of their armies, and the principal agricultural products of
their domains. Ibn Battuta traveled extensively in Asia Minor, was
the honored guest of many of the emirs, and above all observed
the basic sociocultural and economic institutions of the time. Thus
he supplements Ibn Fadlan and al-Kashgari in describing the
societies of the Turkic peoples. His visit to Anatolia brought him
to many of the most important towns and through much of the
intervening countryside, with the result that he reports on the
courts of various emirs, the economic particulars of their domains,
religious life, the various social and religious groups. He is particularly informative as to the effects of nomadism. But he is an
almost unique source for the existence of the socioreligioeconomic
institution of the *akhi*, which played such an important role in the
society and history of thirteenth- and fourteenth-century Anatolia.
These were organizations of young men in the towns, usually
artisans, often armed, and under the leadership of a religious man,
frequently a dervish. Ibn Battuta says of them:

> Account of the Young Akhis. The singular of akhiyya is akhi,
> pronounced like the word akh (brother) with the possessive
> pronoun of the first person singular. They exist in all the
> lands of the Turkmens of al-Rum, in every district, city, and
> village. Nowhere in the world are there to be found any to
> compare with them in solicitude for strangers, and in ardour
> to serve food and satisfy wants, to restrain the hands of the
> tyrannous, and to kill the agents of police and those ruffians
> who join with them. An Akhi, in their idiom, is a man whom
> the assembled members of his trade, together with others of
> the young unmarried men and those who have adopted the
> celibate life, choose to be their leader. That is (what is called)
> al-futuwwa also. The Akhi builds a hospice and furnishes it
> with rugs, lamps, and what other equipment it requires. His
> associates work during the day to gain their livelihood, and
> after the afternoon prayer they bring him their collective
> earnings; with this they buy fruit, food, and other things
> needed for consumption of the hospice. If, during that day, a
> traveller alights at the town, they give him lodging with them;
> what they have purchased serves for their hospitality to him
> and he remains with them until his departure. If no new-
> comer arrives, they assemble themselves to partake of the

food, and after eating they sing and dance. On the morrow they disperse to their occupations, and after the afternoon prayer they bring their collective earning to their leader. The members are called fityan, and their leader, as we have said, is the Akhi. Nowhere in the world have I seen men more chivalrous in conduct than they are. The people of Shiraz and of Isfahan can compare with them in their conduct, but these are more affectionate to the wayfarer and show him more honor and kindness.[21]

When Ibn Battuta journeyed through Anatolia, he found free and generous hospitality at these *akhi* convents throughout the length and breath of the peninsula, and it is obvious from this alone that the akhi brotherhood was at the height of its political and economic existence.

The last three travelers we have considered, Ibn Fadlan, al-Kashgari, and Ibn Battuta, are bound together by at least one common element. They relate to us aspects in the development of the societies of the Turks at three different places and times of their history: in central Asia, when they were still pagan nomads; in the Muslim world when they have been converted to Islam and have taken over the political fortunes of the caliphate; and in Anatolia where they have begun to sedentarize, to inhabit towns, practice crafts, and to absorb the Greek and Armenian elements of Anatolia. All three stages were vital in the historical evolution of the Turks, and without the accounts of our three travelers, the societies of the Rum Seljuks and the early Ottomans would have been far less comprehensible than they now are.

The early European travel accounts come largely from pilgrims to the holy land and from diplomats. The accounts of pilgrims tend to be rather naïve, credulous, and lacking in historical content and analytical insight. Typical are the accounts of Saewulf, of the Russian monk Daniel (eleventh–twelfth century), and above all, of the Scandinavian pilgrim-mercenaries who left northern Europe in large numbers to seek service in Byzantium and to visit the holy land during the eleventh and twelfth centuries. One need only read, at random, in the "Heimskringla" of Snorri Sturlouson to grasp the semilegendary and unsophisticated character of much of this early literature, a literature often more revealing as to the state and nature of Scandinavian society than it is of the regions of Byzantium and the Levant, a society for which the *jorsalafarin* (Jerusalem journey) represents the high point of a king's accomplishments.

The lively and colorful account of Liudprand's stay in Constantinople under the somewhat less than generous circumstances provided by Nicephorus Phocas must be considered an exception to the low historical level of this early European travel literature.[22]

Western travel literature begins to mature with the crusading movement and the intensification of Western contacts with the East at several different levels: political, economic, religious, and scientific. To cite but two examples, William of Tyre has left us a detailed and important account of the history and society of the Near East based on personal observation and on the fact that he was himself an active participant in these events; De Joinville, in chronicling the crusade of his monarch to the Near East, has left us a perceptive analysis of the Mameluk state and its peculiar institutions, of the state of the Assassins, of Muslim military technology, and some considerations of the Nile that recall Herodotus.[23]

A second step in the widening contact of the West with the East, and in the accumulation of knowledge, coincides with the Pax Mongolica and the expansion of papal missionary activities in the East as a result of Mongol religious tolerance. Such missionaries as William of Rubruque, John of Pian Carpini, Orderic of Pordenone have left us invaluable descriptions of the societies of the Middle East and central Asia, particularly important for the comprehension of the organization and institutions of the greater and lesser nomadic political entities.[24] Though commercial interest in the Middle East had long existed in the Italian city-state of the late Middle Ages, the first important travel account from the class of Western merchants comes from the Mongol period; it is the account of Marco Polo.[25] Indicative of this intensification of contact is the journey of the Italian monk Ricoldo da Monte Croce, to Mongol Baghdad, where he remained for a number of years studying Arabic and Islamic law and theology, his intent having been to master Arabic so that he might translate the Koran into Latin.[26] Baghdad during the early decades of Mongol rule was, religiously, an open city, and the Mongols, with their official religious toleration, provided the conditions within which open religious discussions and debate took place among Christians, Muslims, and Jews, much to the horror of the former Muslim masters of the caliphal city. Ricoldo took part in these debates, and though there is no indication that he ever did translate the Koran into Latin, he composed a religious polemic against Islam that came to be the single most important source of accurate knowledge of the Muslim religion in the Christian West and Byzantium. It was translated into Greek in the fourteenth century and was printed in Latin in early sixteenth-century Spain, where it was used as a handbook in combating the Muslim religion.

Western travel literature reached a certain fullness of development in the Renaissance, by which time there is a steady outpouring of travel literature, not only from diplomats, merchants, pilgrims, and missionaries, but also from humanists, bankers, musicians, and prisoners of war. Though the older tastes for religious monuments and shrines persisted, our traveling observers are by now possessed of keener analytical eyes, and their observations on society are much more refined. Their descriptions of economic life, both as to products and technology, are much more detailed. Their view of Middle East society has been expanded to include not only the basic political facts but also the gradations of society according to class; vocation; ethnic and religious affiliation; the physical framework of the society, that is to say, physical geography; the flora; the fauna; and finally, quantitative descriptions of many of these aspects. Western society had begun to study the Middle East in a scientific and systematic way. In this light I wish to say a word or two about three travelers in particular: The Burgundian courtier Bertrandon de la Brocquière, the Genoese merchant Jacopo de Promontorio, and the German monk and pilgrim Felix Fabri.

Bertrandon de la Brocquière was sent on a mission to the Levant by Philip the Good of Burgundy in 1432, and his return took him from the city of Antioch, via southern and western Anatolia, Constantinople, and Adrianople, back to Western Europe.[27] Of particular importance is his account of that portion of the trip that took him through the Turkmen nomadic settlements between Antioch and western Asia Minor. Here he traveled with nomads, lived among them, and became conversant with their society. Now it is obvious, from the remarks I have made on Ibn Fadlan, al-Kashgari, and Ibn Battuta, that nomadism was, and remained, an extremely important phenomenon in Turkish society, even in early Ottoman times; and it is equally true that Ottoman sources from this period give us no satisfactory description or analysis of this phenomenon. To the members of Turkish society, nomadism was a phenomenon so well known that it needed neither description nor analysis to make it comprehensible. It was simply the old, ancestral way of life. It remained for a Western observer, to whom nomadism was something novel and strange, to give us a detailed

account of the phenomenon. Bertrandon tells us about their political and military organization; their numbers; their military movements, weapons, and tactics; a little about their political thought
and action; a great deal about nomad economy; something of their
religion and poetry; much about their domiciles, diet, clothing,
and physiognomy; how they settled on the land; and their impact
on the sedentary population. In short, he is the best observer of
Turkish nomadism who has left us an account of his personal
observations. I shall simply quote one passage from his narrative
that will give us something of the color and detail of his perception:[28]

> At the foot of the mountains, near the road and close to the
> seashore, are the ruins of a strong castle, defended on the
> land side by a marsh, so that it could only be approached by
> sea, or by a narrow causeway across the marsh. It was [for-
> merly] inhabited, but the Turcomans had posted themselves
> hard by. They occupied one hundred and twenty tents, some
> of felt, others of white and blue cotton, all very handsome,
> and capable of containing, with ease, from fifteen to sixteen
> persons. These are their houses, and, as we do in ours, they
> perform in them all their household business, except making
> fires. We halted among them; they placed before us one of
> the table-cloths before mentioned, in which there remained
> fragments of bread, cheese, and grapes. They then brought us
> a dozen thin cakes of bread, with a large jug of curdled milk,
> called by them yogurt. The cakes are a foot broad, round, and
> thinner than wafers; they fold them up as grocers do their
> papers for spices, and eat them filled with the curdled milk.[29]

Then he describes how the nomads make their bread:

> That day, accompanied by the Armenian, we once more
> lodged with the Turcomans, who again served us with milk. It
> was here I saw women make those thin cakes [of bread] I
> spoke of. This is their manner of making them; they have a
> small round table, very smooth, on which they throw some
> flour, and mix it with water to a paste, softer than that for
> bread. This paste they divide into round pieces, which they
> flatten as much as possible, with a wooden roller of a smaller
> diameter than an egg, until they make them as thin as I have
> mentioned. During this operation they have a convex plate of

iron placed on a tripod, and heated by a gentle fire under-
neath, on which they spread the cake and instantly turn it, so
that they make two of their cakes sooner than a waferman
can make a wafer.[30]

Bertrandon has casually described the essence of nomadic life
and cuisine; their homes and cooking apparatus were all mobile,
and so their bread was not baked in an oven and was not leavened.
They inhabit, in their tents, the ruins of former sedentary habitation that they themselves have ruined, and they have replaced the
sedentary populace. Not only does our traveler describe in detail
the nomads and their life styles, but he makes of them the noble
savages of later and earlier European literature.

In many ways, one of the most remarkable accounts of the
Middle East and its societies is the "Recollecta" of the Genoese
merchant Jacopo di Promontorio, who spent a number of years at
the court of the Ottoman sultan Muhammad II and who has
described the political, military, and religious institutions of the
Ottomans, as well as the financial organization and incomes of the
empire.[31] This is the single most important source for Ottoman
institutional history in its formative stage, that is, in the fifteenth
century. The Turkish documents of the period are important, but
incomplete, and in no case do they attempt to give an overall
picture of Ottoman institutional life. Jacopo stands in the tradition of the Italian merchants who, since Marco Polo, began to
assay Middle Eastern society with an increasingly quantitative eye.
Already the Italian merchant Badoer had traveled through the
Balkans and Anatolia recording the prices and quality of the
various goods he bought and sold there.[32] It is precisely from this
vantage point that Jacopo analyzed Ottoman society; that is to
say, he placed a dollar, or ducat, sign by each institution. His
arrangement of the material follows the classical outlines of the
Ottoman administrative structure. He lists the *sancak begs* of
Europe under the *beglerbeg* of Turchia, furnishing the cash income
of each officer. He describes the central administrative institutions
of the sultan in Istanbul and the manning and organization of the
palace, always giving the size of the various bodies and the financial outlay. Equally imposing is his enumeration of the sultan's
income from the empire at large, and Table 1 is his entry delineat-
ing his income from the European provinces.[33] Jacopo then proceeds to list similar incomes from the provinces of Asia Minor and
presents us with the totals in Table 2.

Table 1. **Income from All Graecia**

	Ducats
1. Charadj from non-Muslims	850,000
2. Galipoli-Istanbul, passage of slaves, men	50,000
3. Commercium of Istanbul	70,000
4. Commercium of Galipoli	9,000
5. Saltworks from all Rumeli	92,000
6. Minting of aspers	120,000
7. Minting of Venetian ducats	3,000
8. Mines	120,000
9. Commercium of Ainos	11,000
10. Commercium of Saloniki	2,500
11. Commercium of Negroponte	12,250
12. Commercium of Morea	10,500
13. Fishing, Valona	1,500
14. (Not clear)	20,000
15. Commercium of Sofia	1,000
16. Commercium of Adrianople (on slaves)	12,000
17. Commercium of Cingali	9,000
18. Baths of the sultan	8,000
19. Rice works and cultivation	15,000
20. Commercium on pasturage	10,000
21. Tribute of Wallachia	10,000
22. Tribute of Venetians	10,000
23. Tribute of Chios	12,000
24. Tribute of Ragusa	20,000
Total income	1,478,750

Table 2. **Income Totals from the Provinces**

	Ducats
Charadj from Europe	850,000
Income from Europe	628,750
Income from Asia Minor	331,000
Total income	1,809,750

The change in the mentality and outlook of the Western traveler is clearly evident from this brief sampling of the "Recollecta" of this late fifteenth-century Italian merchant. The observations of other travelers are no less informative and precise, and here I shall refer to one more example, that of the German monk Felix Fabri, who made two pilgrimages to the holy land in the last half of the fifteenth century and described them in a four-volume work. It is significant that his account of the first pilgrimage took only some fifty pages, whereas the second account took up most of four volumes. The reasons for this are of interest in that they differentiate between the mentalities of the Middle Ages and the Renaissance, and Felix embodied elements of both. He writes:

> At the end of the first trip I was not at all satisfied with the first pilgrimage, for the trip had been rushed, and I had visited the holy places too quickly without understanding or perceiving anything. . . . After my return to Ulm I began to reminisce about the Holy Sepulcher . . . about the holy city . . . and about other monuments, only to discover that their shape, appearance, and arrangement had now escaped me, and it seemed to me that I knew less about the holy land than I did before my trip to Jerusalem. . . . This greatly saddened me because I suffered much on the trip, I spent much time and money, and all this without any corresponding recompense . . . and without having acquired knowledge. . . . So I decided to revisit the Holy Land.[34]

It is of interest to note how he went about preparing himself for the second trip: "In the meanwhile . . . I read all the books on the subject . . . and brought together all the accounts of the pilgrimages of the Crusaders, the compositions of the pilgrims, the descriptions of the Holy Sepulcher, and I read them carefully. The more I read the more I was troubled for . . . I realized how superficial, incomplete, confused had been my own pilgrimage."[35] This passage illumines for us the mind and thought of Felix and shows us its power of reflection, analysis, and self-criticism. We are dealing not with a simple medieval monk, but with the type of German religious from whom came Martin Luther. The account of his second pilgrimage is a classic and provides us with one of the best descriptions of maritime life in the eastern Mediterranean before the modern era. First, he writes on the various types of sea and winds and on their dangers. Second, he describes the trireme and its construction and parts. Finally, he analyzes the order and manner of life on a trireme and offers advice to passengers.[36]

I shall restrict myself to certain aspects of the third category, which deals with the polity and institutions that prevail on board ship. Felix begins by paraphrasing Aristotle, who says that there exist three basic relations in the society of the household: There is the bond of (1) husband and wife, (2) master and slave, and (3) father and son. The maritime society on the ship, says Felix, contains the latter two relations, for there is the captain and those who serve him, and second, he is the father and protector of the pilgrims on board. The major difference between the household society that Aristotle describes and the society on board ship, says Felix, is that, in the former, the society has as its goal the continuation of the society, whereas, in the maritime household, the members of the society have as their goal the dissolution of their society at the termination of the voyage. The captain is both monarch and governor on the ship; all obey him; and in this manner the ship reaches its destination. All show him extreme respect, and it is he who dissolves all differences. He is usually an aristocrat and is accompanied and advised by aristocrats.[37] Other officials who assist him are the security officer (who is a soldier and who arms the ship with weapons), the steward (who is responsible for provisions and for the meals), the caliph (responsible for repairing the ship), the pilot (who sits at the rudder and is assisted by men experienced in reading the stars; by others, in reading the seas and winds; and by the movement of fish, and who is furnished with a compass and maps).

At a slightly lower level in this maritime society is the *comes*, who is in charge of the rowers and who takes directives and information from the pilot and thus regulates the movement of the ship. He regulates this by blowing on a silver whistle that hangs about his neck and that serves as a signal to the rowers, who, upon hearing the signal, run to their oars whistling in return the appropriate signals. The rowers fear the *comes* as if he were the devil himself, for he disciplines and punishes them in a most inhumane manner. The *comes* is assisted by the baron, who is stationed under the main mast, whence he relays the signals of the *comes* to all of the rowers. They are assisted by the six *compani*, or companions, "men who know how to run about the ropes like cats, who ascend the shrouds very swiftly up to the cap, run along the yard standing upright even in the fiercest storms, who weigh up the anchors diving deep into water if they stick fast, and who do all the most dangerous work on board. They are in general very active young men, who are quite reckless of their lives, and are also bold and powerful in the galley like a baron's armed followers."[38]

Subordinate to the *compani* are the *marini*, whose duty it is to sing when the others are pulling at the oars, for, says Felix, "the maritime life is very hard. The man who supervises the rowers sings out his commands and these *marini*, who are older men, sing in response to the commands and in this manner the tempo of the rowing is regulated (to the sounds of their song)."[39]

At the bottom of the social scale of the naval society are the rowers. Felix relates:

> They are many and all of them are large and well built, but their work is more fitting for donkeys than for men for they curse and beat them in order to get them to work. Just as they whip a horse which is straining to ascend a hill, just so are these pitiful creatures flogged as they pull hardest at their oars. As I write this I shudder at the thought of the tortures and punishments which these rowers suffer. Not even beasts are whipped so mercilessly. They are forced to row with their backs bared, their shoulders and arms exposed, so that they will not be shielded from the blows. Most of these men are slaves bought by the captain, or prisoners of war, or exiles, all men who cannot return to their fatherland. Whenever there is fear that they might attempt to escape they are chained to their benches. Usually these rowers are Macedonians, or from Albania, Achaia, Illyria and Sklavonia. There are, occasionally, Turks and Saracens among them, but they hide their religion. I have never seen German rowers for I imagine that they would never be able to survive such harsh conditions. . . .[40]
>
> They are so accustomed to their misery that they work feebly and to no purpose unless someone stands over them and beats them like asses and curses them. They are fed most wretchedly, and always sleep on the boards of their rowing benches, and both day and night they are always in the open air ready for work, and when there is a storm they stand in the midst of the waves. In general they are thieves and spare nothing that they can find; for which crime they often are most cruelly tortured. When they are not at work they sit and play cards and dice for gold and silver, with execrable oaths and blasphemies. I have never heard such terrible swearing as on board of the aforesaid vessels, for they do nothing, either in jest or in earnest, without the foulest blasphemies of God and the saints. Sometimes there are among them some respectable merchants, who subject themselves to that most grievous servitude in order that they ply their trade in harbors.

Some are mechanics, such as tailors or shoemakers, and in their season of quiet make shoes, trousers, and shirts on board ship; some are washermen, and wash shirts on board for hire.

Indeed in this respect all galley slaves are alike; they are all traders, and everyone of them has something for sale under his bench, which he offers for sale when in harbor, and trading goes on daily among them. Moreover they generally know at least three languages: to wit, Sklavonian, Greek, and Italian, and the greater part of them know Turkish as well.[41]

It is time to draw something of a conclusion from this disparate narrative, and I would propose that the phenomenon of the travelers has a double meaning or importance. First, obviously, it is a phenomenon that has provided the scholar with rich historical materials for the reconstruction of past societies and cultures in the Middle East. Second, it is a phenomenon ultimately linked to man's restlessness and curiosity, in which there is a certain ambiguity as to the purpose of the voyage. This is well illustrated by the symbolism of Ithaca in Kavafis's poem by the same name. Kavafis, in this celebrated poem, exhorts the reader not to hurry his trip to Ithaca. Rather, he says, one should stop and linger at all the mysterious ports, savoring their exotic goods. If at the end of the journey one finds Ithaca poor, rocky, and barren, one should not be disappointed, for Ithaca gave him the adventure. In this respect, our life of intellectual endeavor has the nature of an intellectual odyssey in which the journey is often more exhilarating than the attainment of the goal.

Notes

This paper was originally delivered as a lecture at the retirement ceremony held for Peter Charanis at Rutgers University.

1. Herodotus, IV, 59–76.

2. S. Rudenko, *Frozen Tombs of Siberia: The Pazaryk Burials of Iron-Age Horsemen* (Berkeley and Los Angeles, 1970).

3. For bibliography, consult the following works: G. Atkinson, *La littérature géographique française de la Renaissance, répertoire bibliographique: Description de 524 impressions d'oeuvrages publiées en français avant 1610, et traitants des pays et des peuples non européens, que l'on trouve dans les principales bibliothèques de France et de l'Europe occidentale* (Paris, 1927); E. G. Cox, *A Reference Guide to the Literature of Travel*, 2 vols. (Seattle, 1938); Von Viktor Hantzach, *Deutsche Reisende des sechzehnten Jahr-*

hunderts (Leipzig, 1895); N. Iorga, *Les voyageurs français dans l'ouest euro-péen* (Paris, 1928); Amat de San Filippo, *Biografia dei viaggiatori italiani* (Rome, 1882); K. Simopoulos, *Xenoi Taxidiotes Sten Elladha Demosios kai idiotikos vios, laikos politismos ekklesia kai oikonomike zoe apo ta periege-tika chronika*, vol. 1, *333-1700* (Athens, 1970); and above all, the descriptive catalogue by S. H. Weber of the rich collection in the Gennadeion Library, *Voyages and Travels in Greece, the Near East and Adjacent Regions Made Previous to the Year 1801* (Princeton, 1953).

4. For examples of and references to such buildings, see: K. Erdmann, *Das anatolische Karavansaray des 13. Jahrhunderts*, vols. 1-2 (Berlin, 1961); S. Vryonis, *The Decline of Medieval Hellenism in Asia Minor and the Process of Islamization from the Eleventh through the Fifteenth Century* (London, Los Angeles, and Berkeley, 1971), pp. 30-33, 211.

5. For Chalcocondyles, see: the numerous studies of H. Ditten, who has examined the accuracy of Chalcocondyles as well as the question of later additions to his work; *Der Russland Exkurs des Laonikos Chalkokondyles* (Berlin, 1968); "Laonikos Chalkokondyles und die Sprach der Rümanen," in *Aus der byzantinischen Arbeit der Deutschen Demokratizchen Republik*, ed. J. Irmscher, vol. 1 (1957), pp. 93-105; "Die Korruptel *chōrobion* und die Unechtheit der Trapezunt und Georgien betreffenden Partien in Laonikos Chalkokondyles' Geschichtswerk," *Studia Byzantina* (1966):57-70.

6. See the article "Djughrafiya" in the *Encyclopedia of Islam*, 2d ed.; A. Miquel, *La géographie humaine du monde musulmane jusqu'au milieu du XIe s.* (Paris, 1967).

7. *EI*, s-v. "Ibn Hawkal." The text is edited in M. de Goeje, *Bibliotheca geographorum arabicorum* (Leiden, 1938-1939), 2:1-2.

8. A number of commemorative volumes have appeared in the postwar era: *Al-Biruni Commemorative Volume* (Calcutta, 1951); *Beyrunî'ye armağan* (Ankara, 1974); *Millenary of Abu Raihan al-Biruni* (Karachi, 1973); H. Nasr, *Al-Bîrûnî: An Annotated Bibliography* (Tehran, 1973).

9. *EI*, s.v. "Al-Bīrūnī." For the editions, E. Sachau, ed., *Kitāb Ta'rīkh al-Hind* (London, 1887); *Kitāb fī tahqīq-ī-mā li'l Hind or al-Bīrūnī's India* (Hyderabad, 1958). For the full English translation, E. Sachau, trans., *Alberuni's India: An Account of the Religion, Philosophy, Literature, Geography, Chronology, Astronomy, Customs, Laws and Astrology of India about AD 1030* (London, 1888, 1910).

10. *EI*, s.v. "Ibn Fadlan." M. Canard, "La relation d'Ibn Fadlan chez les Bulgares de la Volga," *Annales de l'Institut d'Études Orientales de la Faculté des Lettres d'Algers* 16 (1958):41-146, repr. in *Miscellanea Orientalia* (London, 1973). D. M. Dunlop, *The History of the Jewish Khazars* (Princeton, 1954), pp. 109-114. R. P. Blake and R. N. Frye, "Notes on the Risala of Ibn Fadlan," *Byzantina-Metabyzantina* 1, pt. 2 (1949):7-38.

11. *Ibn Fadlan's Reisebericht*, in *Abhandlungen für die Kunde des Morgen-landes*, vol. 24, pt. 3, ed. and tr. Z. V. Togan (Leipzig, 1939).

12. For such examples, J-P. Roux, *La Mort chez les peuples altaïques anciens et médiévaux* (Paris, 1963).

13. Ibn Fadlan, pp. 13–15.

14. Ibid., p. 16.

15. *EI*, s.v. "Muhammud al-Kashgari." C. Brockelmann, *Mitteltürkischer Wortschatz nach Mahmud al Kašgaris Divan Lugat At-Turk* (Budapest, 1928). R. Dankoff, "Kašgari on the Tribal and Kinship Organization of the Turks," *Archivium Ottomanicum* 4 (1972):23–43. J. M. Kelly, "Remarks on Kašgari's Phonology," *Ural-Altaïsche Jahrbücher* 44 (1972):179–193.

16. *EI*, s.v. "Muhammud al-Kashgari."

17. *EI*, s.v. "Ibn Battuta"; H. A. R. Gibb, ed., *The Travels of Ibn Battuta* (Cambridge, 1958–), vols. 1–3; C. Defrémery and B. R. Sanguinetti, ed., *Voyages d'Ibn Batoutah* (Paris, 1853–1859), vols. 1–4.

18. Defrémery and Sanguinetti, *Voyages d'Ibn Batoutah*, 3:125 ff.; 4:254 ff.

19. Defrémery and Sanguinetti, *Voyages d'Ibn Batoutah*, vol. 2, pp. 254 ff. For Asia Minor at this time: Vryonis, *Decline of Hellenism, passim*; C. Cahen, *Pre-Ottoman Turkey* (London, 1968); O. Turan, *Selçuklular zamanında Türkiye* (Istanbul, 1971); I. Uzunçarşılı, *Anadolu beylikleri ve Akkoyunlu devletleri* (Ankara, 1937); G. Arnakes, *Oi Protoi Othomanoi* (Athens, 1947).

20. F. Taeschner, *Al-Umari's Bericht über Anatolien in seinem Werke masālik al-absar fī mamālik al-amsār* (Leipzig, 1929). E. Quatremère, "Notices de l'ouvrage qui a pour titre: Mesalek . . . ," in *Notices et extraits des mss. de la bibliothèque du Roi*, vol. 13 (Paris, 1838).

21. Gibb, *Travels of Ibn Battuta*, 2:418–420.

22. *The Travels of Saewulf, AD 1102 and 1103*, in T. Wright, ed., *Early Travels in Palestine* (New York, 1968). Daniel, *Kholozhenie. Abt Daniil Wallfahrsbericht. Mit einer Einleitung und bibliographischen Hinweisen*, ed. K. D. Seemann (Munich, 1970). C. W. Wilson, *The Pilgrimage of the Russian Abbot Daniel in the Holy Land, 1106–1107, AD, PPTS*, 4 (London, 1895). P. Riant, *Expéditions et pélerinages des Scandinaves en Terre Sainte au temps des Croisades* (Paris, 1865). S. Laing and R. Anderson, *The Heimskringla or the Sagas of the Norse Kings from the Islandic of Snorre Sturlason* (London, 1889), vols. 1–4. Liudprand, *Legatio*, in *Die Werke Liudprands von Cremona*, 3d ed., ed. J. Becker, *MGH, SS* (Hannover and Leipzig, 1915).

23. William of Tyre, *A History of Deeds Done beyond the Sea*, tran. and annotated by F. A. Babcock and A. C. Krey (New York, 1943). De Joinville, *Histoire de Saint-Louis*, 2d ed., ed. Natalis de Wailly (Paris, 188?).

24. A. Van den Wyngaert, *Sinica Franciscana* (Florence, 1929), I. C. Dawson, *The Mongol Missions: Narratives and Letters of the Franciscan Missionaries in Mongolia and China in the Thirteenth and Fourteenth Century* (New York, 1955).

25. A. C. Moule and P. Pelliot, *Marco Polo, the Description of the World* (London, 1938), vols. 1–2.

26. Ricoldo de Monte Crucis, in *Peregrinatores medii aevi quatuor*, ed. J. C. M. Laurent (Leipzig, 1873). Ugo Monneret de Villard, *Il libro della peregrinazione nelle parti d'Oriente di Frate Ricoldo da Montecroce* (Rome, 1948).

27. C. Schefer, *Le voyage d'outremer de Bertrandon de la Broquière* (Paris, 1892). An English translation, *The Travels of Bertrandon de la Brocquière, A.D. 1432 and 1433*, appeared in T. Wright, *Early Travels in Palestine* (New York, 1968).

28. For details and background, Vryonis, *Decline of Hellenism*, pp. 258-285.

29. Wright, *Brocquière*, p. 314.

30. Ibid., p. 315.

31. F. Babinger, ed., *Die Aufzeichnungen des Genuesen de Promontorio de Campis über den Osmanenstaat um 1475*, in *Bayerische Akademie der Wissenschaften, Philosophisch-historisch Klasse, Sitzungsberichte, Jahrgang 1956*, no. 8 (1957).

32. Francesco Balduci Pegolotti, *La pratica della mercature*, ed. A. Evans (Cambridge, 1936). Giacomo Badoer, *Il libro dei conti (Constantinopoli 1436-1440)*, ed. U. Dorini and T. Bertelé (Rome, 1956).

33. See Vryonis, "Laonicus Chalcocondyles and the Ottoman Budget," *International Journal of Middle East Studies* 7 (1976):423-432. I had not yet looked at the study of Ditten (see n. 5 sup.) in *Studia Byzantina* and was perhaps incautious in attributing all the sections on Ottoman finance in the "Histories of Chalcocondyles" to Chalcocondyles himself. Ditten has argued that many sections in Chalcocondyles are later additions. Jacopo in Babinger, *Aufzeichnungen*, p. 71, errs in his addition and instead of 1,478,750 ducats (table 1) as the sum of the income from all Graecia, he reports a total of 1,469,000 ducats.

34. On Felix: H. F. M. Prescott, *Friar Felix at Large: A Fifteenth Century Pilgrimage to the Holy Land* (New Haven, 1950); *Jerusalem Journey: Pilgrimage to the Holy Land in the Fifteenth Century* (London, 1954); *Once to Sinai: The Further Pilgrimage of Friar Felix Fabri* (London, 1957). *Fratris Felicis Fabri Evagatorium in Terrae Sanctae, Arabiae et Egypti Peregrinationem*, ed. C. D. Hassler, 3 vols. (Stuttgart, 1843-1849). For an English translation, A. Stewart in *PPTS*, vols. 7-10 (London, 1892-1897); quotation from 7:48 ff.

35. Hassler, *PPTS*, 7:50.

36. Ibid., 7:111.

37. Ibid., 7:132.

38. Ibid., 7:136.

39. Ibid., 7:136.

40. Ibid., 7:137.

41. Ibid., 7:138.

Chapter 18

Two Historical Parallels: The Greek Nation under Roman and Turkish Rule

D. A. Zakythinos, *Academy of Athens*

There have been three major periods in Greek history during which the Greek nation has not been constituted as an independent, autonomous state, or as a number of such states: the periods of Roman, Frankish, and Turkish rule. This is an overschematic generalization, but it is necessary to limit the area of historical inquiry to the three periods in question and ignore a large number of phenomena that, though of intrinsic interest, were of only local importance or of an ephemeral nature and consequently do not form a solid foundation for the construction of general theories.

Of the three periods under consideration, the period of Frankish rule differed from the other two in that it did not present an aspect of unity or universality. Frankish domination was imposed on Greece after the capture of Constantinople by the Latins and the dissolution of the Byzantine state (1204), which was succeeded not by another single empire but by a number of more or less independent states: the Latin Empire of Constantinople, the short-lived kingdom of Thessaloniki, the principality of Achaea, the duchy of Athens, and other, smaller feudal principalities. The Venetians acquired a more lasting control over parts of mainland Greece, and especially over Crete, over the Cyclades, for a short time over Cyprus, and over the Ionian Islands, where the rule of the Serenissima Republic continued until the Treaty of Campoformio in 1797.

The Greek resistance, which manifested itself immediately in a number of areas, crystallized at a very early date around three states, all of them claiming descent from the dismembered Byzantine Empire: the empire of Nicaea, the empire of Trebizond, and the despotate of Epirus. These were later joined by a fourth after the occupation of Lakonia and the establishment there of a strong Greek state, the despotate of the Morea. It is therefore inaccurate to speak of the Greek nation not wielding sovereign power at this time, and it is clear that the period of Frankish rule is morphologically different from the other two in that it failed to create a unified state and also in that the Byzantine Empire continued to exist in a variety of forms, all of them exhibiting a tendency toward unity.

The periods of Roman and Turkish rule are both characterized by greater unity and are much clearer cases.[1] Roman rule was the result of the gradual extension of Roman control in the East. Beginning in the Balkan peninsula, it spread to the islands in the eastern Mediterranean, to all the territories bordering on it, and to the Black Sea and the Red Sea. This policy of conquest was punctuated by a number of major landmarks: the initial intervention of Rome against the Illyrians in 229 B.C.; the battle of Pydna in 168; the destruction of Corinth in 146; the acquisition by Rome of direct control of the kingdom of Pergamum and the formation of the province of Asia in 133–129; the conquest of Syria and Palestine in 63; and finally the conquest of Egypt in 30 B.C. The territories in the northern part of the Balkan peninsula were subjugated and formed the provinces of Illyricum, Upper and Lower Moesia, and Dacia. The whole of the Balkan peninsula, Asia Minor, Syria, Palestine, Egypt, and North Africa were thus united under Roman rule in the two hundred years between the middle of the second century B.C. and the middle of the first century A.D.[2]

The geographic expansion of the Ottoman Empire followed a similar pattern, though in this case the movement was from the east. The Osmanlis were originally an obscure Turkish tribe whose existence is first noted in Bithynia during the last decades of the thirteenth century. They first appeared on the stage of history on 27 July 1302, when they defeated the Byzantine armies at the battle of Bapheus near Nikomedeia, a victory that marked the beginning of the rapid rise of Turkish power, which ended in the founding of the Ottoman Empire. The major landmarks in the conquest of Asia, Europe, and Africa were: the capture of Brusa (6 April 1326); the capture of Nicaea (2 March 1331); the descent on Gallipoli (2 March 1354); the conquest of Adrianople in 1361; the battle of the Maritsa (26 September 1371); the captures of Serres (1383), of Sophia (1393), and of Thessaly (1394); the battle of Nikopolis (25 September 1396); the final subjugation of Thessaloniki (1430) and that of Ioannina (1430), the conquest of Serbia (1439 onward); the battle of Varna (10 November 1444); and the fall of Constantinople and subsequent dismantling of the

Byzantine Empire (29 May 1453). There followed the collapse
of the despotate of the Morea (1460), the empire of Trebizond
(1461), Euboea (1470), Naupactus (1499), Modon and Coron
(1500), Rhodes (1522), Cyprus (1571), and finally Crete (1669).
In the meantime, Ottoman sovereignty had been established in
Egypt in 1517.[3]

Both the Roman and Ottoman Empires were thus formed by
conquest. Chronologically they are separated by an interval of
about fifteen centuries. In geographic terms, the heartland of each
covered much the same territory—an area centering on the eastern
Mediterranean and divided between the continents of Europe,
Asia, and Africa. The Roman Empire, of course, also included the
Italian peninsula and Rome's other European possessions until
395, when it was finally divided into Eastern (*pars Orientis*) and
Western (*pars Occidentis*) sections. The Ionian Islands, under the
control of the Venetians, the Ionian Sea, and the Adriatic con-
stituted the general line of the western border of the Ottoman
Empire.

Typologically, the Roman and Ottoman states were both
empires (*imperia*). According to one recent definition "l'empire
en tant que grande puissance est un État souverain, s'étendant
durant un certain temps sur un vast térritoire, habité par de
multiples groups socio-politiques placés sous l'autorité d'un même
gouvernant ayant une politique tendant à l'hégémonie."[4] The main
features of an empire are thus its great territorial extent, the
exercise of authority by a single agent throughout the entire state,
its continued existence over time, the multiracial composition of
the social groups of which it is comprised, and the tendency
toward absolute rule.

Both empires are secondary, in that they derived from a gradual
process of conquest of great states that had already reached an
advanced stage of political and social decomposition: the Roman
Empire from the disintegration of the empire of Alexander the
Great and the decline of the Hellenistic kingdoms; the Ottoman,
from the decline and disintegration of the Byzantine Empire, the
Byzantine-inspired Balkan states, and, locally, from the dismem-
berment of the Asian state of the Seljuk Turks.

Both empires were multinational states in which the conquerors
formed a minority, the relative size of which varied in different
areas. There was also local variation in religious belief, education,
level of culture, and mentality and intellectual and psychological
make-up of the inhabitants. In their advance eastward, Hellenism
and the Roman Empire had assimilated the religions of Asia and

Egypt alongside the traditional Olympian gods and the Roman Pantheon. The Magna Mater, Isis, Mithra and a host of other gods and goddesses all found their way into the complicated pattern of the Roman Pantheon.[5] Similarly, in addition to Islam and Greek Orthodoxy, the state of the Osmanlis embraced a number of religious beliefs, heterodoxies, and heresies of both these faiths.

Both empires came into contact politically and culturally with Greece and Greek education before they reached the height of their power. The scale of this contact differed considerably, of course, and the influence exercised by it on the two empires was in no way comparable, in terms either of its intensity and depth or of the nature and quality of it. Rome came into contact at a very early date with the flourishing Greek civilization of Magna Graecia, Campania, Lucania, Apulia, and Calabria and Bruttium, and at a later date with that of Greek Sicily after the conquest of that island.[6] Greek influences on Rome are as old as the city itself, and recent writers speak of the Hellenization of religion, art, and literature from as early as the fourth, third, and second centuries B.C.[7] The comment of Henri-Irénée Marrou is representative:

> Cas particulier du fait fondamental qui domine toute l'histoire de la civilisation romaine: une civilisation autonome proprement italienne n'a pas eu le temps de se développer parce que Rome et l'Italie se sont trouvé intégrées dans l'aire de la civilisation grecque; parcourant rapidement les étages qui séparaient leur barbarie rélative du niveau de culture atteint précocement par l'Hellade, elles se sont assimilé avec une remarquable facilité d'adaption, la civilisation hellenistique. . . . S'il demeure légitime de parler d'une culture latine, c'est en tant que facies secondaire, variété particulière de cette civilisation unique.[8]

The origins of the tribe of the Osmanlis before their move to Bithynia are lost in obscurity. For the early period of its history, transitional between a nomadic or seminomadic existence and settlement in a permanent territory, the sources are scanty and confused. A new period in the progress of the Ottomans toward urban life was ushered in by the capture of the great cities of Brusa (1326), Nicaea (1331) and Nikomedeia (1337). The early decades of the fourteenth century thus saw the addition to the original Turkoman and Seljuk substratum of elements deriving from an urban and Greek environment. There are early references

to contacts between Greeks and the newcomers, though religious
and political factors, as well as fundamental differences of outlook,
meant that the influence exercised by the Greeks on the Turkish
conquerors was limited. It occurred mainly in the sphere of institutions and the systems of government and taxation, in the field
of diplomacy, and in the area of land tenure and cultivation. It has
been observed that the mutual influences felt by the two populations belong mainly in the sphere of *Volkskultur*. It should also be
noted, however, that a large number of Byzantine institutions
were handed on to the Ottomans through Seljuk syncretism.

The rise of the Turkish state was accompanied by a corresponding growth of Byzantine influence, which reached its peak a few
decades before and during the first century after the fall of Constantinople. One piece of evidence for this phenomenon is the
wide use of Greek as the language of international relations.[9]
The turning of Turkish attention to Asia Minor and the conquest
of Syria (1516), Egypt (1517), the Persian territories on the
Euphrates (1534), and southern Arabia (1568) had the effect of
weakening the Greek influence on the empire and of intensifying
the Islamic nature of its culture. The Sultans turned once more to
the Greek element in the empire during the seventeenth century,
and particularly after the second attack on Vienna (1638) when
they abandoned their schemes of conquest in favor of European-
style diplomacy.[10]

The dissolution by the Romans of the kingdom of Egypt, the
last of the Hellenistic states, in 30 B.C.; the fall of Constantinople,
and with it the Byzantine Empire, to the Turks on 29 May 1453;
and the capture of the Peloponnesos in 1460 and of Trebizond,
capital of the Greek empire of Pontos, in 1461, were all events
that resulted in an immensely significant change in the history of
the Greek nation. On each occasion, the states that formed the
legally constituted framework through which the Greeks exercised
their political activity were obliterated; in other words, there no
longer existed any independent Greek state. The state is defined
by G. Jellinek as "a people permanently established in a particular
country, organised as a legal body, and possessing political sovereignty," and Nikolaos Saripolos observes that "political sovereignty, or authority in its own right is one of the main hallmarks of
the state, which differs from other legal bodies in that it assumes
the prerogative of the sole exercise of political power, issuing
commands to free individuals and compelling the observation of
them."[11] In the case of both the Hellenistic states and the declining

years of Byzantium, the sovereign authority of the Greeks was fragmented, but this does not conflict with the general rule. Though Hellenism was divided, it constituted an ideal community over and above the boundaries of space and time.

It was precisely through this ideal community, existing without reference to particular events and circumstances, that Hellenism continued to flourish during the long periods of time that it did not constitute an independent sovereign state. In the received historical and sociological terminology, the Roman and Turkish conquests were periods during which the Greeks were deprived of the ability to form a state and merely constituted a nation. According to the definition of R. Johannet, a nation is "the concept of a collective body, which may vary in inspiration, self-consciousness, intensity and size, and which has some relationship with the state either in that it represents a once unified state that no longer exists, or in that it coincides with an existing unified state, or in that it aspires or has the tendency to found a unified state in the future."[12] The first and third parts of this definition are applicable to the periods with which we are concerned.

During the periods of domination by the Romans and the Ottoman Turks, the Greek nation was isolated in the midst of barbarian peoples, geographically fragmented, and torn by civil strife and political dissension. Despite the fact that it had been defeated on the battle field and had been compelled to yield to the superior force of the barbarians, however, it preserved its creativity intact. The path it had to follow was a difficult one, deprived as it was of the power to control its own destiny, but it continued to flourish in terms of its intellectual achievements and influence.

On the eve of the Roman conquest, the Hellenism of Greece proper was manifestly in decline. The center of gravity, however, had long since shifted to the east. This period commenced with the campaigns of Alexander the Great (334-323), which marked a turning point in world history. From that time until the capture of Constantinople by the Turks, the history of the Eurasian and Mediterranean civilizations presents a unified appearance, despite its gaps. Unless this point is fully grasped, it is impossible to arrive at a correct historical interpretation of Greece or Rome, of the spread of Christianity, of Byzantium, or in the final analysis, of the foundations of the European spirit. It has pertinently been observed that Alexander "introduced a new civilisation." Although his empire disintegrated in political terms, its achievements were enduring, for the real significance of his campaign lay in "giving a

vigorous and decisive impetus to a movement that had started
before his time, but which had so far existed only on a limited
scale: the expansion of the Greeks and their culture outside the
bounds of the old Greek world."[13]

With the publication of the first edition of J. G. Droysen's
classic *Geschichte des Hellenismus,*[14] the period of Alexander's
successors and the Hellenistic kingdoms was restored to its rightful place in the history of the Greek nation. Since that time,
research has furnished a wealth of new material, particularly from
epigraphic and papyrological sources. New horizons are being
opened to historians, and it is now seen as one of the great periods
in the history of the Greek spirit. A change of enormous significance took place in the Hellenistic kingdoms between 323 and 30
B.C.: the East was Hellenized and united in the process. "The
destruction of the Persian state and its conquest by Alexander
marked a great change in the fortunes of Greek civilisation." So
said Édouard Will in his recent book. The Greeks

> n'avaient pas vu s'ouvrir à eux une telle possibilité d'expan-
> sion géographique depuis le fin de la "colonisation" archaï-
> que (VIII–VI siècle); encore cette première expansion n'avait
> elle affecté, de façon plus punctuelle que continue, que
> certains régions littorales de la Méditerranée et de ses mers
> bordières, alors que c'est à présent l'immense masse du con-
> tinent asiatique et la vallée du Nil qui s'ouvrent à la présence
> hellénique.[15]

A number of fundamental changes occurred in the political,
social, and economic institutions of the Greek world as a result
of this expansion. But the civilization of the Hellenistic period
(*Hellenismus*) "also (many would say mainly) constitutes a new
chapter, the longest of all, in the history of the Greek spirit."[16]
The Hellenistic period may not have produced immortal monuments comparable with those of the classical period, but the
strength of its spirit and the boldness of its intellectuals were in no
way inferior. It is therefore improper to speak of it in terms of
decline; rather we are dealing with "l'orientation différente de la
puissance créatrice."[17] Art sought new forms; literature showed a
preference for particular genres; the Stoics renewed the foundations of moral philosophy; and most important, the natural and
literary sciences and technology entered a decisive phase of their
development.[18] Hellenistic education is of paramount importance

for the historian who is not content to contemplate intellectual matters merely as creative acts, whether literary, artistic, or scientific, but who perceives them as social phenomena involving the meeting, interacting, and fusion of cultures. One form of the Greek language, the *koine*, became the major international medium for the movement of ideas, and the sole vehicle for international communication and higher education.[19]

A similar outburst of intellectual activity and a comparable increase in international influence accompanied the protracted death throes of the Byzantine Empire. After its spirited resistance to the Latin conquest, and its partial recovery, Byzantine Hellenism struggled to achieve geographic unification. The end of the thirteenth century, however, ushered in a long period of political, military, and economic decline resulting from external pressures and internal dynastic, political, social, and religious cleavages. Nonetheless, the last two centuries of its painful decline were a period of exceptional intellectual and artistic activity.

The Palaeologan Renaissance was achieved amid disaster, conflict, and ruins; yet it was an astonishingly comprehensive revival. Art is the field in which it can best be observed. Constantinople, Thessaloniki, Mystras, Thessaly and Epirus, Thrace, northern Macedonia, the islands, and the distant Slavic centers contain the finest remains. A huge artistic community came into being throughout the whole of the Orthodox world and beyond.

Hellenism was politically in decline, but a vigorous regeneration of thought and literature is observable in a number of areas, such as the capital, which was increasingly deserted with the passage of time; in Thessaloniki, which was shaken by social movements; in Epirus, the Peloponnesos, and Trebizond. Significant contributions were made in every field of letters. Freed from the restraints of the court, an original and flexible popular literature developed. The ancient classics became the subject of philological study. Under the cover of religious strife and heresy was concealed speculation about the major problems of the human spirit. Philosophy was much more open to influences from the current ideas of Western intellectuals; with the passage of time, it gradually freed itself from the heritage of theology and steadily developed its own methods. The Balkans, Eastern Europe, and Italy were all exposed to Greek influence.[20]

The paradox of military and political decay being accompanied by a flourishing of intellectual activity is undoubtedly to be explained in terms of the very close contacts between the Byzantine world and the fecund springs of Hellenism in its birthplace. The revival of Greek patriotism during the last decades of the empire was reflected throughout the entire Christian world. When the final collapse came, a veritable army of intellectuals became part of the diaspora and traveled to the European countries, bringing with them the message of Greeçe.[21] The Greek nation, though entering a new period of its history under foreign suzerainty, was clearly at the height of its intellectual powers, and even in its fall created a new *Hellenismus*, in Droysen's sense of the term, through its international values.[22]

The year 1976 marked the two-hundredth anniversary of the publication of the first volume of one of the most distinguished works of European historiography—the *History of the Decline and Fall of the Roman Empire* (1776-1788), by the British historian Edward Gibbon. The year 1977 was the hundredth anniversary of the appearance of the seven volumes of the *History of Greece from its Conquest by the Romans to the Present Time (146 B.C.-A.D. 1864)*, in which H. F. Tozer gathered together the writings of another British historian, George Finlay, on the history of Greece from 146 B.C. to A.D. 1864. The volume dealing with Greece under Roman rule (146 B.C.-A.D. 716) had appeared separately in 1844. These two works are very different in conception and are written from totally different standpoints, but both have had a profound effect on historiography throughout the world.

We are today in a position to review the period that has elapsed since the publication of these works and to note the enormous changes of interpretation resulting from subsequent scholarship. These derive not only from the discovery of new sources but also from a more general change in the modern historical interpretation of the later Roman Empire, Byzantium, the Turkish and Latin periods, and even the history of modern Greece. A number of special studies published on the occasion of the hundredth anniversary of the publication of Gibbon's History give very lucid accounts of the progress achieved during these two centuries.[23]

It should be noted at this point that modern Greek historians in particular long adopted a negative stance toward the periods of Roman and Turkish domination. Authors writing in the first half of the nineteenth century viewed the battle of Chaeroneia as marking the end of the ancient world and thought of the whole of the subsequent history of Hellenism up to 1821 as a dark period of decadence over which lay the "black mantle of slavery." The pioneering works of Spyridon Zambelios and Konstantinos

Paparrhigopoulos opened the way for a radical revision of their position. Nonetheless, the outmoded interpretations still hover over historical science, perpetuating mistaken views and pervasively affecting the historical education of the Greeks.[24]

The Roman and Turkish dominations of Greece, when evaluated and judged in the light of the present state of our knowledge, were clearly both great periods in the history of Greece, and the lessons to be drawn from the study of them are illuminating and inspire optimism. It should be stated immediately that this is not to underestimate the disasters, the persecutions, the incalculable destruction of human life and material property, the slavery and the bitter humiliation suffered in these periods. But great periods in history are not measured in terms of the sacrifices they entail. Great periods are those that succeed in transforming the disasters and ruins into dynamic forces, into the instruments of regeneration, and into national and international values in which the intellect rules supreme.

Despite the fact that, during both periods under consideration, Hellenism lost its sovereignty and independence, not only did it retain its individual identity as a national, and to some extent an administrative, unit, but it succeeded in accomplishing what it had failed to achieve under more favorable political conditions: under foreign domination, it formed itself into a broad national and moral community. Under the Romans, this community took shape within the small unit of the city, whereas in the Ottoman period the framework was supplied by the wide organizational network of the church.

The city, with its religious, institutional, economic, emotional, and educational structure, was the most important focus on which the activity of the Greeks centered during the Roman period. The policy of founding new cities reached its height under Alexander and his successors, the rulers of the Hellenistic kingdoms. The range of meaningful political activity open to the cities was increasingly restricted, particularly after the Lamian War (323–322) and subsequently under the Romans, but until the end, the Greek cities continued to assimilate from and exercise a civilizing influence on both the peoples of Asia and their conquerors. The creation of the city-state, an institution of purely Greek origin, subsequently adopted by the Romans, was an event of incalculable importance in the history of mankind, for as Oswald Spengler observed, "l'histoire universelle est l'histoire des cités."[25] The Romans, having exploited the network of cities in order to extend and maintain their sovereignty, ultimately fell victim to it. The Roman Empire was "an agglomerate of cities (*civitates-poleis*), self-governing communities."[26]

The activity and influence of the Greeks during the Roman period was multifaceted, aggressive, and ultimately victorious. If Horace had not died in 8 B.C. but had been able to see the founding of Constantinople in A.D. 324, he would surely have felt that his prophetic verses, "Graecia capta ferum victorem cepit et artes / intulit agresti Latio" had been far outstripped by reality. The problem of the relations between the two great peoples of antiquity, the Greeks and the Romans, has been the subject of new research in recent years. A. H. M. Jones, one of the most distinguished Roman historians, has observed that "The most surprising feature of Roman rule in the Greek East is that despite its long duration it had so little effect on the civilisation of the area," and he adds, "The influence was indeed in the other direction."[27]

During the course of their history, the Greeks and the Romans leveled many charges against each other, for all that there was no real conflict of interest between the two peoples.[28] Their exposure to Greek education had prepared the conquerors for their historic change. Beyond the boundaries of the Greco-Roman world, in Asia, in Africa, and in northern Europe, moved the hostile world of the barbarians, organized in some areas, less well organized in others, either free or bearing the yoke of domination with reluctance; and this fact tended to bring the two peoples closer together. The result was that with the passage of time the Greeks became partners in the worldwide empire of Rome, though this occurred tacitly and quietly, without the establishment of an official mechanism or any agreement in principle. Each partner made his own contribution to this curious *condominium* and gained his own successes. Greek writers such as Aelius Aristides in the second century A.D. and Themistius in the fourth, defined the roles of the two peoples. In their view, the dual monarchy was an expression of the universal nature of Roman power on the one hand, and of Greek literature and education on the other.[29]

The dominating position attained by the Greek language under the Roman Empire symbolizes perfectly the degree to which the empire was Hellenized. Roman writers agree. Suetonius (ca. A.D. 75-150) attributes to the emperor Claudius (41-54) the expression *uterque sermo noster*, referring to Latin and Greek; and the Romans frequently used expressions such as *utraque lingua, utraque oratio*, while the Greeks spoke of *hē hekatera glōtta, hē hetera glōtta.* Greek became an official language of administration after the conquest of the eastern provinces, and Greece thereby acquired far-flung linguistic borders to compensate for the loss of her narrow political boundaries. The Roman Empire was bilingual.[30]

Rome's world empire rested on Greek foundations. The Roman state was transformed by the process of conquest. In contrast with its earlier conquests, this one had been preceded by the achievement of a unified civilization, and for this reason its results were more enduring. As Jacques Pirenne has observed, the Roman Empire was, in the final analysis, a Hellenistic state.[31] Consequently "a comprehensive study of Hellenistic civilization or of the Hellenistic world ought to include the study of Roman civilization, at least in the imperial centuries, and not merely in the eastern provinces of the empire. This fact is manifestly a vindication of those historians who extend their analysis of Hellenistic civilization down to Christian times."[32] F. E. Peters has recently gone even further and speaks of "Latin Hellenism" and "Greek Hellenism": "Both branches, the Latin and the Greek, came under the political dominion of the ecumenical Roman Empire, and the European's eyes are naturally directed to the process whereby Hellenism gradually transformed that Roman state and eventually produced the cultures of Europe and America."[33]

The history of the Roman Empire in the East belongs properly and irrevocably within the sphere of Greek history. It was an epoch of great creativity and as such formed an unbroken continuation of the civilizing mission of the period of Alexander and the Hellenistic period, with which it fused to mark a turning point in the history of mankind. Greek Byzantium was nurtured by it, and the syncretism of its education made possible the rapprochement of Hellenism and Christianity.

We saw earlier that religious and political factors combined with fundamental differences of intellectual outlook to inhibit the development of any real communication between Greeks and Ottomans during the Turkish period. The conqueror, for reasons stemming from his own legal system, as well as from more general considerations of political expediency, recognized the religious autonomy of the conquered; the Greek patriarchs were allowed to exercise religious authority over all the Orthodox peoples in the empire. With the passage of time, this developed into a de facto decentralization of religious, legal, and administrative power. This phenomenon played a crucial role in creating the necessary

preconditions for Greek religious, economic, social, and intellectual life.[34]

The Ottoman conqueror, like the Roman governor or emperor
before him, was aware of the superiority of the culture of the conquered and frequently felt an attraction for and was influenced
by their state, political, and intellectual systems. From the seventeenth century onward, the institutions of the grand dragomans,
the dragomans of the fleet, and the rulers of Wallachia and Mol-
davia developed as Greek institutions within the cultural and
administrative framework of Ottoman rule and firmly established
a Greek presence in the state machinery of the empire. This
chapter in Greek history, dealing with the influence exercised by
the Greeks on the general life of the conquerors, remains to be
written.[35]

The presence of Hellenism within the administrative and social
systems of the Ottoman state constituted only one aspect, and
perhaps the least important, of the international influence exercised
by the Greeks. The effects of Hellenism were felt on a very wide
scale, extending to the Christians of the Balkans enslaved by the
Turks, the Orthodox peoples of Eastern Europe, the Christian
minorities of the Near East, and finally to Western Europe itself.
The church was the vehicle through which the ecumenical spirit
of post-Byzantine and modern Hellenism was transmitted. The
Greek churches—the patriarchates of Constantinople, Alexandria,
Antioch and Jerusalem—and the Russian church, which was influenced by the Greek, the patriarchate of Moscow, which was
formed in 1589, were the basis for the creation of a unified culture within a broad nonpolitical society that was firmly Greek
(one might even say Hellenistic) in its origins.

From the very first centuries of the conquest, Byzantine art,
together with its post-Byzantine extensions, was the major graphic
expression of this huge cultural community, constituting at once
a silent language, a canon of faith and belief, and a symbol of self-
assertion and resistance. The other language, spoken and written
Greek, transcended the boundaries of the mainly Greek territories
and became a widely used instrument of communication. The
Humanism of the Renaissance, which flourished in the decline of
Byzantium and was transplanted and cultivated in Western Europe,
was followed by a broad spectrum of other intellectual movements: the religious humanism of the seventeenth and early-eight-
eenth centuries; the Enlightenment of the second half of the
eighteenth and the early-nineteenth centuries, which was nurtured

in the urban centers of Hellenism; and international Hellenism in contact with the literature of antiquity and the modern ideologies of Europe.[36]

There is no need here to examine at length the question of the international values achieved by Hellenism under foreign domination. It need only be stated that, during this great period, Eastern Europe in many ways played a role resembling that of the East in the intellectual life of the Roman imperial period. In both, Greek education was universal and achieved a syncretism of the intellectual tendencies of the Near East under Greek leadership. The bold proposals of Rhigas for unity in the political and social sphere had already been realized in practice in the sphere of the intellect.

This inquiry into these two long periods during which the Greeks did not constitute a sovereign state has not proved vain: though they were separated by many centuries, they exhibited a large number of common features, and this is no coincidence. In the past, and perhaps in some quarters still today, both were believed to be periods of decline and decay—dark and shadowy blemishes on an otherwise brilliant picture. This was not the case. On the contrary, both were great, creative periods—great in terms of the misfortune suffered in them, and great for the Greeks and the peoples of the Balkans and the Near East. The verdict of modern historians on both periods, and especially on the Roman, is unanimous, as some of the remarks quoted above illustrate. The Roman and Turkish periods deserve our particular attention, not only as fields for academic research, but also as crucial subjects in the historical and national education of the Greeks.

The French academic André Siegfried wrote that "in the pyschology of peoples there exists a substructure that can always be traced."[37] This statement springs to mind as one examines these two parallel periods of Greek history. Today we are moving away from the Hegelian concept that there exists in peoples an intellect through which the intellect of the world is revealed; but we can recognize the unity of the intellectual fabric of the Greek conscience. In the psychology of the Greeks, there exists that permanent substructure that can always be traced.

Notes

1. Volumes 6, 10, and 11 of *The History of the Greek Nation* (Ekdotike Athenon) (Athens 1974-1976) are devoted to the Roman and Turkish periods.

2. Andŕe Aymard, *Rome et son empire, histoire générale des nations*, vol. 2 (Paris, 1954). André Piganiol, *La conquête romaine*, 5th ed. (Paris, 1967).

3. Ernst Werner, *Die Geburt einer Grossmacht—Die Osmanen (1300-1481): Ein Beitrag zur Genesis des türkischen Feudalismus, Forschungen zur mittelalterlichen Geschichte* (Berlin, 1966). Halil Inalcik, *The Ottoman Empire: The Classical Age 1300-1600* (London, 1973).

4. J. Gilissen, "La notion d'empire dans l'histoire universelle: Les grands empires," *Recueils de la Société Jean Bodin pour l'histoire comparative des institutions*, vol. 31 (Brussels, 1973), p. 793. This weighty volume contains the studies announced at the meeting of the Société Jean Bodin in Rennes between 11 and 15 October 1966. Of particular interest for the subjects discussed in the present article are the contributions on the empire of Alexander the Great (by Claire Préaux), on the Roman Empire (by Roger Rémondon), on the Byzantine Empire (by Hélène Ahrweiler), and on the Ottoman Empire (by T. Gökbilgin).

5. Cf. the classic work by Franz Cumont, *Les réligions orientales dans le paganisme romain*, 4th ed. (Paris, 1929).

6. M. B. Chatzopoulos, *The Hellenism of Sicily during the Roman Period (264-44 B.C.)* (in Greek) (Athens, 1976).

7. Henri-Irénée Marrou, *Histoire de l'éducation dans l'antiquité*, 4th ed. (Paris, 1958) pp. 329 ff. Aymard, *Rome*, pp. 175 ff. K. N. Iliopoulos, *Roman Policy in Latin Writers and Their National Consciousness* (in Greek) (Athens, 1974). Idem, *Philhellene and Anti-Hellene Trends in Ancient Rome and Roman Humanism* (in Greek) (Athens, 1975).

8. Marrou, *Histoire de l'éducation*, pp. 329 ff.

9. S. Lambros, "Greek as the Official Language of the Sultans," *Neos Hellenomnemon* 5 (1908):40-78; idem, "Greek Public Letters of the Sultan Bayezid II," ibid., pp. 155-189 (both in Greek). F. Babinger and F. Dölger, "Mehmed II frühester Staatsvertrag (1446)," in *Byzantinische Diplomatik*, ed. F. Dölger (Ettal, 1956), pp. 262-291. A. Bombaci, "Due clausole del trattato in greco fra Mahometto II e Venezia, del 1446," *BZ* 43 (1950):267-271. Idem, "Nuovi firmani greci di Mahometto II," *BZ* 47 (1954): pp. 298-319. Hélène Ahrweiler, "Une lettre en grec du sultan Bayezid II (1481-1512)," *Turcica: Revue des études turques* 1 (1969): pp. 150-160. Elisabeth A. Zachariadou, "Early Ottoman Documents of the Prodromos Monastery (Serres)," *Südost Forschungen* 28 (1969):1-12.

10. G. Georgiades Arnakis, *The First Ottomans: A Contribution to the Problem of the Collapse of Hellenism in Asia Minor (1282-1337)* (in Greek) (Athens, 1947), pp. 70 ff. Speros Vryonis, "The Byzantine Legacy and Ottoman Forms," *Dumbarton Oaks Papers* 23/24 (1969-1970):251-308. Idem, *The Decline of Medieval Hellenism in Asia Minor and the Process of Islamization from the Eleventh through the Fifteenth Century* (Berkeley and Los Angeles, 1971).

11. Cf. D. A. Zakythinos, *Introduction to the History of Civilisation* (in Greek) (Athens, 1955), pp. 54 ff.

12. Ibid., pp. 38 ff.

13. André Aymard, "L'Orient et la Grèce antique," *Histoire générale des civilisations*, vol. 1 (Paris, 1953), pp. 287 ff. Cf. the truly pioneering remarks of Spyridon Zambelios with respect to Hellenism and on the "fusion of Greece and the East": *Folk Songs of Greece* (in Greek) (Corfu, 1852), pp. 37 ff.

14. J. G. Droysen, *Geschichte des Hellenismus* (1833-1843; 2d ed. 1877-1878).

15. E. Will, C. Mossé and P. Goukowsky, *Le monde grec et l'Orient*, vol. 2; *Le IVe siècle et l'époque hellénistique: Peuples et civilisations* (Paris, 1975) pp. 337 ff, with bibliography.

16. Ibid., p. 567.

17. Aymard, "L'Orient et la Grèce antique," p. 499.

18. Ibid., pp. 470 ff., 499 ff. Will, Mossé, and Goukowsky, *Le monde grec*, pp. 567 ff., 583 ff., 608 ff.

19. Cf. Antoine Meillet, *Aperçu d'une histoire de la langue grecque*, 7th ed. (Paris, 1965), a work of fundamental importance. J. O. Hoffman, A. Dobrunner, and A. Scherer, *Geschichte der griechischen Sprache*, 2 vols. (Berlin, 1969). J. Humbert, *Histoire de la langue grecque* (Paris, 1972).

20. "Art et société à Byzance sous les Paléologues" (actes du colloque organisé par l'Association international des études byzantines à Venise en septembre 1968), in *Bibliothèque de l'Institut Hellénique d'études byzantines et post-byzantines de Venise*, no. 4 (Venice, 1971). Steven Runciman, *The Last Byzantine Renaissance* (Cambridge, 1970).

21. D. A. Zakythinos, *Byzantium: State and Society: A Historical Survey* (in Greek) (Athens, 1951) pp. 143 ff.

22. D. A. Zakythinos, "États-sociétés-cultures: En guise d'introduction," in "Art et société à Byzance sous les Paléologues," p. 12 = *Byzance: État-société-economie*, Variorum Reprints, no. 12 (London, 1973), p. 12.

23. Lynn White, Jr., ed., *The Transformation of the Roman World: Gibbon's Problem after Two Centuries, Medieval and Renaissance Studies, Contributions,* 3 (Berkeley and Los Angeles, 1966). Karl Christ, *Von Gibbon zu Rostovtzeff: Leben und Werk führender Althistoriker der Neuzeit* (Darmstadt, 1972). Michel Baridon, *Edward Gibbon et le mythe de Rome: Histoire et idéologie au siècle des lumières* (Paris, 1977).

24. D. A. Zakythinos, "Post-Byzantine and Modern Greek Historiography," *Praktika tis Akadimias Athinon* 49 (1974):97*-103*; idem, "Spyridon Zambelios: The Historian of Byzantine Hellenism," ibid., pp. 303*-328*; (both in Greek).

25. Oswald Spengler, *Le déclin de l'Occident: Esquisse d'une morphologie de l'histoire universelle, traduit de l'allemand par M. Tazerout*, vol. 2 (Paris, 1948), p. 89.

26. A. H. M. Jones, *The Later Roman Empire 284-602: A Social, Economic and Administrative Survey*, vol. 2 (Oxford, 1964) p. 712.

27. A. H. M. Jones "The Greeks under the Roman Empire," *Dumbarton Oaks Papers* 17 (1963):1-19.

28. N. K. Petrokheilos, *Roman Attitudes to the Greeks* (Athens, 1974).

29. Gilbert Dagron, "L'Empire romain d'Orient au IVe siècle et les traditions politiques de l'Hellénisme: Le témoinage de Thémistios," in *Travaux et Mémoires, Centre de Recherche d'Histoire et de Civilisation Byzantines*, vol. 3 (Paris, 1968), pp. 1–203. Idem, "Aux origines de la civilisation Byzantine: Langue de culture et langue d'état," *Revue historique* 241 (January–March 1969):23–56. Cf. D. A. Zakythinos, "The *Tabula Imperii Romani* and Research into the History of Hellenism under the Roman Empire" (in Greek), *Praktika tis Akadimias Athinon* 47 (1972):316* ff.

30. L. Lafoscade, "Influence du latin sur le grec," in Jean Pischari, ed. *Études de philologie néo-grecque*, Bibliothèque de l'Ecole des Hautes Études: Sciences Philologiques et Historiques, vol. 92 (Paris, 1892), pp. 117 ff. Cf. Marrou, *Histoire de l'éducation*, pp. 345 ff., 542 ff. Jones, *Later Roman Empire*, vol. 2, pp. 986 ff.; vol. 3, pp. 330 ff.

31. Jacques Pirenne, "Les Empires du Proche-Orient et de la Méditerranée: Rapport de synthèse," in *Les grands empires*.

32. Will and Mossé, *Le monde grec*, p. 343.

33. F. E. Peters, *The Harvest of Hellenism: A History of the Near East from Alexander the Great to the Triumph of Christianity* (London, 1972), p. 22.

34. D. A. Zakythinos, *The Making of Modern Greece: From Byzantium to Independence* (Oxford, 1976).

35. Cf. the works referred to in n. 10.

36. Zakythinos, *The Making of Modern Greece*, pp. 140 ff.

37. A. Siegfried, *L'âme des peuples* (Paris, 1950), p. 5.